Creating Orthographies for Enda

Creating an orthography is often seen as a key component of language revitalization. Encoding an endangered variety can enhance its status and prestige. In speech communities that are fragmented dialectally or geographically, a common writing system may help create a sense of unified identity or help keep a language alive by facilitating teaching and learning. Despite clear advantages, creating an orthography for an endangered language can also bring challenges, and this volume debates critical questions arising from these. Whose task should this be – that of the linguist or the speech community? Should an orthography be maximally distanciated from that of the language of wider communication for ideological reasons, or should its main principles coincide for reasons of learnability? Which local variety should be selected as the basis of a common script? Is a multilectal script preferable to a standardized orthography? Can creating an orthography create problems for existing native speakers?

DR MARI C. JONES has published extensively on language death theory and dialectology, principally in relation to Welsh and to Insular and Mainland Norman. Major research monographs include *Language Obsolescence and Revitalization* (1998), *Jersey Norman French: A Linguistic Study of an Obsolescent Dialect* (2001), *The Guernsey Norman French Translations of Thomas Martin: A Linguistic Study of an Unpublished Archive* (2008), and *Variation and Change in Mainland and Insular Norman: A Study of Superstrate Influence* (2015). Her co-authored textbook, *Exploring Language Change* (2005), also engages with a number of aspects of language variation and change. Dr Jones has edited many volumes on language change and on endangered languages, including *Language Change: The Interplay of Internal, External and Extra-Linguistic Factors* (2002), *The French Language and Questions of Identity* (2007), *Sociolinguistique de la Langue Normande: Pluralité, Normes, Représentations* (2009), *Language and Social Structure in Urban France* (2013), *Keeping Languages Alive* (Cambridge University Press, 2013), *Endangered Languages and New Technologies* (Cambridge University Press, 2014) and *Policy and Planning for Endangered Languages* (Cambridge University Press, 2015).

DR DAMIEN MOONEY'S research focuses on contact-induced transfer in bilingual speech, language death theory, and the role of language and dialect contact in the loss or retention of pronunciation and grammatical features in regional varieties of French and the regional languages of France. Major publications include his monograph *Southern Regional French: A Linguistic Analysis of Language and Dialect Contact* (2016).

Creating Orthographies
for Endangered Languages

Edited by

Mari C. Jones and Damien Mooney

CAMBRIDGE
UNIVERSITY PRESS

University Printing House, Cambridge CB2 8BS, United Kingdom

One Liberty Plaza, 20th Floor, New York, NY 10006, USA

477 Williamstown Road, Port Melbourne, VIC 3207, Australia

314-321, 3rd Floor, Plot 3, Splendor Forum, Jasola District Centre, New Delhi - 110025, India

79 Anson Road, #06-04/06, Singapore 079906

Cambridge University Press is part of the University of Cambridge.

It furthers the University's mission by disseminating knowledge in the pursuit of education, learning and research at the highest international levels of excellence.

www.cambridge.org
Information on this title: www.cambridge.org/9781316602584

© Cambridge University Press 2017

This publication is in copyright. Subject to statutory exception and to the provisions of relevant collective licensing agreements, no reproduction of any part may take place without the written permission of Cambridge University Press.

First published 2017
First paperback edition 2020

A catalogue record for this publication is available from the British Library

ISBN 978-1-107-14835-2 Hardback
ISBN 978-1-316-60258-4 Paperback

Cambridge University Press has no responsibility for the persistence or accuracy of URLs for external or third-party internet websites referred to in this publication, and does not guarantee that any content on such websites is, or will remain, accurate or appropriate.

Philip Griffith Jones (1937–2015)

This volume is dedicated to the memory of Mari's beloved father, Philip Griffith Jones, who encouraged her, inspired her and gave her a sense of wonder. He taught her how precious a gift it is to speak an endangered language, and how important it is to ensure that these languages are kept alive.

Contents

List of Contributors		*page* ix
1	Creating Orthographies for Endangered Languages MARI C. JONES AND DAMIEN MOONEY	1
2	Who Owns Vernacular Literacy? Assessing the Sustainability of Written Vernaculars CHRISTOPHER MOSELEY	36
3	Hearing Local Voices, Creating Local Content: Participatory Approaches in Orthography Development for Non-Dominant Language Communities MANSUETO CASQUITE AND CATHERINE YOUNG	54
4	Orthographies 'In the Making': The Dynamic Construction of Community-Based Writing Systems among the Náayeri of North-Western Mexico MARGARITA VALDOVINOS	69
5	Community-Driven, Goal-Centred Orthography Development: A Tsakhur Case Study KATHLEEN D. SACKETT	88
6	Writing for Speaking: The N|uu Orthography SHEENA SHAH AND MATTHIAS BRENZINGER	109
7	Reflections on the Kala Biŋatuwã, a Three-Year-Old Alphabet from Papua New Guinea CHRISTINE SCHREYER	126
8	When Letters Represent More Than Sounds: Ideology versus Practicality in the Development of a Standard Orthography for Ch'orti' Mayan KERRY HULL	142

9 The Difficult Task of Finding a Standard Writing System
   for the Sioux Languages   155
   AVELINO CORRAL ESTEBAN

10 Orthography Development in Sardinia: The Case of *Limba Sarda
   Comuna*   176
   ROSANGELA LAI

11 Breton Orthographies: An Increasingly Awkward Fit   190
   STEVE HEWITT

12 Spelling Trouble: Ideologies and Practices in Giernesiei/
   Dgernesiais/Guernesiais/Guernésiais/Djernezié ...   235
   JULIA SALLABANK AND YAN MARQUIS

13 Orthography Development on the Internet: Romani on YouTube   254
   D. VIKTOR LEGGIO AND YARON MATRAS

14 Orthography Creation for Postvernacular Languages: Case
   Studies of Rama and Francoprovençal Revitalization   276
   BÉNÉDICTE PIVOT AND MICHEL BERT

15 Changing Script in a Threatened Language: Reactions
   to Romanization at Bantia in the First Century BC   291
   KATHERINE MCDONALD AND NICHOLAS ZAIR

Bibliography   305
Index   331

Contributors

MICHEL BERT, Université Lyon 2, France

MATTHIAS BRENZINGER, Centre for African Language Diversity (CALDi), University of Cape Town, South Africa

MANSUETO CASQUITE, independent literacy and education consultant, the Philippines

AVELINO CORRAL ESTEBAN, Universidad Autónoma de Madrid, Spain

STEVE HEWITT, former Editor of Records, UNESCO

KERRY HULL, Brigham Young University, Provo, Utah, USA

MARI C. JONES, Department of French, University of Cambridge and Peterhouse, Cambridge, England, UK

ROSANGELA LAI, Università degli Studi di Firenze, Italy

D. VIKTOR LEGGIO, University of Manchester, England, UK

YAN MARQUIS, freelance researcher and language teacher, Guernsey, Channel Islands

YARON MATRAS, University of Manchester, England, UK

KATHERINE MCDONALD, Department of Classics and Ancient History, University of Exeter, England, UK

DAMIEN MOONEY, Department of French, University of Bristol, England, UK

CHRISTOPHER MOSELEY, School of Slavonic and East European Studies, University College London, England, UK

BÉNÉDICTE PIVOT, Université Lyon 2, France

KATHLEEN D. SACKETT, SIL International, USA

JULIA SALLABANK, School of African and Oriental Studies, University of London, England, UK

CHRISTINE SCHREYER, University of British Columbia, Canada

SHEENA SHAH, Centre for African Language Diversity (CALDi), University of Cape Town, South Africa

MARGARITA VALDOVINOS, Instituto de Investigaciones Filológicas, Universidad Nacional Autónoma de México, Mexico

CATHERINE YOUNG, SIL International

NICHOLAS ZAIR, Faculty of Classics, University of Cambridge and Peterhouse, Cambridge, England, UK

1 Creating Orthographies for Endangered Languages

Mari C. Jones and Damien Mooney

1 Introduction

The creation of new orthographical systems is often considered a key component of language revitalization efforts. The ability to encode an endangered language can facilitate the implementation of literacy programmes, which aim to reverse language shift by facilitating teaching and learning. Due to the fact that many endangered languages are unwritten, language planning involving orthography development (or graphization) is seen as 'an essential prerequisite for many activities in favour of their maintenance and revitalization, such as dictionary writing, curriculum development and the design of language-teaching courses' (Lüpke 2011:312). Additionally, in speech communities that are fragmented dialectally or geographically, a common writing system may enhance the status and prestige of an endangered language and may help create a sense of unified identity. Graphization can, in a sense, legitimize an endangered language owing to the widespread belief that a language must be written in order to be considered a language: 'the existence of a written form almost lends mythical qualities to a language' (Lüpke 2011:320; cf. 'graphocentrism', Blommaert 2004).

Despite these apparent advantages, when a language is endangered, creating an orthography can bring with it a great number of challenges. The act of creating a new writing system requires the orthographer to consider a complex array of linguistic and, crucially, extra-linguistic factors. The trained linguist will at first be concerned with the type of script to adopt and with the level of linguistic structure that the orthography should represent, as well as with other issues such as establishing word boundaries and marking suprasegmental features. Secondly, they will also be required to take into account a wide variety of socio-political, psychological, and practical issues: the role of the native speaker in graphization, ideological distance from surrounding languages, knowledge of a dominant language's orthographical conventions, cognitive and pedagogical issues involving reading, the existence of legacy orthographies, and technological reproduction. Many of these linguistic and extra-linguistic factors differ in scope in situations involving endangered languages when compared with unwritten languages more generally (cf. Cahill and Rice 2014), and this volume will debate critical questions in this regard, with specific reference to obsolescent and revitalizing varieties.

In this introduction, we discuss the linguistics, sociolinguistics, and ideology of orthography development for endangered languages. We begin by discussing one of the central aims of orthography development, the creation of a literacy programme (Section 2), before broaching the issues involved in the standardization of endangered languages (Section 3), a process often considered to be a prerequisite for graphization. The discussion of linguistic (Section 5) and extra-linguistic (Section 6) factors involved in the development of new orthographies provides a detailed overview of the primary frameworks and issues involved. These issues are subsequently debated by the contributors to this volume (Section 7), focusing on a wide variety of case studies from around the world.

2 Literacy for Endangered Languages

Local literacy is often considered to be a 'powerful tool' for promoting and validating the use of endangered languages undergoing language shift (Grenoble and Whaley 2006:186), and therefore it can be seen to alleviate the pressure to speak and use the language of wider communication. Language revitalization efforts are commonly focused on the development of literacy programmes for endangered languages, as such programmes are seen to raise the status of the language involved, to modernize the language for use in a variety of social domains, and to facilitate school-based revitalization efforts (Grenoble and Whaley 2006:102). Literacy programmes for obsolescent languages are dependent on the existence of a developed orthography, and for that reason orthographies are essential for language revitalization models, which emphasize the effectiveness of literacy in reversing language shift. There are, of course, many other essential components of effective literacy programmes, in addition to orthography development: 'other aspects include developing primers, teaching reading and writing, facilitating a variety of reading materials, training teachers, holding writer's workshops, and a host of other activities' (Rice and Cahill 2014:3). Therefore, the process of graphization does not in and of itself facilitate literacy or language revitalization – it must be integrated carefully into the larger process of corpus planning for endangered languages (Lüpke 2011:312–313).

Endangered languages are, by definition, subordinate and dominated by languages of wider communication, the majority of which have their own well-established orthographies. When literacy in the language of wider communication is highly valued, the development of literacy programs for the endangered language can raise its status and prestige, encouraging and validating its use in a wider variety of domains. It is also possible, in situations where the speakers of an endangered language are not literate in the dominant language, that the acquisition of literacy can facilitate the acquisition of the dominant language, thus accelerating language shift, contrary to the central aims of language revitalization efforts (Grenoble and Whaley 2006:102). In the context of language revitalization, however, speakers of endangered languages are frequently at least partially literate in the language of wider communication. In this scenario, the development of a local literacy programme will bring the endangered language into direct competition with the dominant language and with its domains of use. This competition is absent for languages that are not threatened with extinction, and endangered language situations 'differ fundamentally from those where there is no encroaching or dominant language of wider communication' (Grenoble and Whaley 2006:126). Despite these possible drawbacks, Grenoble and Whaley (2006:102) argue for multiple literacies in language revitalization situations – that is, literacy in the endangered language and in the language of wider communication. The promotion of multiple literacies must, however, reduce competition between the dominant language and the endangered language by creating specific literacy contexts and domains of use for the latter.

The potential role of literacy in the endangered language speech community must be fully evaluated before orthography development and the creation of literacy programmes (Lüpke 2011:312), because existing domains of use and contexts for writing are often occupied by the language of wider communication. It is therefore necessary to identify an 'ecological niche' (Lüpke 2011:313) for writing or to create a context for written forms of endangered languages so that these can compete with the languages of wider communication: 'this claim is supported by the work in local literacies which shows that literacy programs succeed when they are perceived as needed by the community and when the acquisition of literacy has some direct application to life in the community' (Grenoble and Whaley 2006:127). Literacy materials in endangered languages ('endographic traditions') that replicate materials already available in the dominant language ('exographic traditions') are often viewed positively by the speech community in the first instance because they place both languages on equal footing, but Lüpke warns that such materials 'have little or no practical use because established exographic traditions pre-empt the introduction of endographic ones for the same functions' (2011:319). Only when a niche can be identified or a context can be created for endographic writing systems should orthography development and literacy programming begin. If such contexts cannot be identified or created, we must question the necessity of local literacy. Often, the obvious contexts for use of the endangered language in its written form are those pertaining to local traditions or local culture, but Grenoble and Whaley (2006:129) advise that, for literacy efforts to be successful, they must extend beyond traditional cultural domains. They suggest encouraging, for example, writing for personal needs (e.g., writing diaries, writing notes, making lists), as this practice requires a personal investment and commitment on the part of the writer (and of any potential recipients) to use the local language in these contexts.

Several types of literacy programme have been proposed and should be considered before pursuing such a programme, and before an orthography can be developed. The concept of 'traditional literacy', which has as its central goal the teaching of reading and writing, is associated with literacy in languages of wider communication and with 'formal, Western-style' education (Grenoble and Whaley 2006:103); it is thus too restrictive and inapplicable to endangered language and revitalization contexts. We must consider understandings of literacy more relevant to the context of language revitalization (adapted from Grenoble and Whaley 2006:103–111):

(i) *Autonomous literacy:* Autonomous literacy posits reading and writing as technical skills, independent of the social context and culture in which they are used (see Goody and Watt 1963). Within this model, a binary distinction is drawn between preliterate societies and literate societies, and literacy is viewed as a vehicle for social and cognitive change. Preliterate societies are considered underdeveloped (socially and cognitively), whereas literate societies are considered developed and modern: 'on a cognitive level, it is argued that literacy is necessary for the cognitive development of certain skills, such as scientific reasoning, logic, abstract thinking, and the ability to distinguish between literal and metaphorical meanings' (Grenoble and Whaley 2006:105). The view that, in order to become socially and cognitively equal, preliterate societies must become literate has since been discredited (see Goody 1987), but the situation remains that illiteracy is frequently stigmatized, underlining the potential importance of literacy programmes to status planning for endangered languages.

(ii) *Vai literacy:* The concept of Vai literacy was developed by Scriber and Cole (1981) during five years of research with the Vai people in Liberia. They argued that it is formal education that influences cognitive development rather than literacy in absolute terms. Scribner and Cole's (1981) study demonstrated empirically that literacy is not a purely technical skill, refuting the claims of autonomous literacy models and showing literacy to be a social construct, or a social practice, which can be revised and re-examined within its social context. For them, literacy is not simply about learning to read and write; it also involves the acquisition of knowledge about how to apply these skills in specific contexts and for specific purposes.

(iii) *New Literacy Studies:* New Literacy Studies (Street 1984; Barton 2006) emphasize the social and cultural context of literacy, focusing on literacy as a 'collection of things people do rather than a cognitive condition or skill' (Sebba 2011:36). Literacy is viewed here as a social practice that will necessarily vary depending on the social context in which it finds itself. These studies require extensive ethnographic research into endangered language speech communities, to establish the individual needs of such communities before establishing a literacy programme; the development of an orthography and teaching materials is not seen as sufficient to promote and maintain literacy. New Literacy Studies highlight the potential impact of literacy on cultural practice, such as oral performance, and the researcher is reminded that the introduction of literacy will undoubtedly face the challenge of altering social practice (Grenoble and Whaley 2006:110).

(iv) *Functional literacy:* The concept of functional literacy is commonly associated with adult education programmes and with UNESCO's worldwide literacy campaign: 'though the UNESCO plan asserts that each individual literacy program must develop its own operational definition of literacy, it is clear that, for UNESCO, literacy involves both reading and writing' (Grenoble and Whaley 2006:111). UNESCO's campaign emphasizes the links between literacy and socio-economic advantage and views literacy as providing access to specific opportunities for development and growth.

Community involvement and the consultation of native speakers are essential elements of any successful literacy programme, including the development of new orthographies (see Section 6). Modern literacy models insist on a conception of literacy that is firmly embedded in the social context of a given endangered language; literacy must respond explicitly to the needs of the specific speech community involved. The most efficient way of ascertaining these needs is to involve members of the speech community in the development of literacy programmes, or, ideally, 'literacy will be the product of a grassroots kind of movement, coming from within the community itself and involving community participation in all phases of development' (Grenoble and Whaley 2006:103). An idealized 'bottom-up' literacy campaign may prove difficult, particularly in preliterate societies, leading to a need for outside intervention by trained linguists. The speech community should, however, always be afforded ownership of the literacy programme if it is to succeed; community support is the key component of language revitalization, including orthography development and the creation of literacy. The trained linguist should avoid at all costs the implementation of a literacy programme (including associated orthographies and pedagogical materials) that has not received community approval. Grenoble and Whaley (2006:126) summarize the core criteria for assessing community support before the introduction of local literacy: (i) the usefulness of a literacy programme must be recognized and approved by traditional community members (e.g., elders, politicians, religious leaders); (ii) local contexts for literacy must be identified and approved by community members; (iii) there must be continued widespread use of the endangered language as a spoken language; (iv) there must be support for the maintenance of local literacy by (local) educational systems. Criterion (iii) reminds the language planner that the development of orthographies and of literacy programmes must not be pursued independently of larger status and corpus planning goals as part of language revitalization efforts. Widespread spoken use of a language reinforces and supports the development and implementation of literacy campaigns for unwritten languages, but in the context of revitalization, endangered languages are by definition undergoing a rapid reduction in speaker numbers. Literacy programmes must therefore be implemented as part of a larger revitalization programme, because 'creating literacy will not, in and of itself, revitalize a language' (Grenoble and Whaley 2006:126).

3 Standardization for Endangered Languages

Linguistic standardization is often viewed as a prerequisite for orthography development, and indeed, standard ideologies are frequently centred on the highly codified written form of language (Bradley 2005:1; Seifart 2006:285; Lüpke 2011:313; Sebba 2012b:59). For Fishman, 'in the modern world, standard dialects are written languages and they have definite written conventions, as far as writing system, orthography and grammatical structure are concerned' (1991:346). Standardization is deemed necessary before orthography development, for a variety of reasons: writing may become idiosyncratic without linguistic standardization, rendering it inaccessible to a critical mass of speakers (Grenoble and Whaley 2006:130); a standard writing system is often seen as necessary for language promotion and for the development of formal teaching materials (Sallabank 2013:170); a standardized orthography encourages language use in a wider variety of domains, potentially raising the language's status at the community level (Sallabank 2013:172; Grenoble and Whaley 2006:154); standardization and a standard orthography may help create a sense of a unified identity for the speech community. These advantages, particularly those relating to the status and community perception of the language involved in standardization, are said to be even more crucial within the context of revitalization (Fishman 1991:347). Successful corpus planning, including orthography development, constitutes a 'powerful tool' towards achieving the goal of reversing language shift if the standardized orthography can be read and understood by a large number of speakers (Grenoble and

Whaley 2006:130). Despite these clear advantages, the process of developing orthographies for endangered languages is often controversial and fraught with various linguistic and ideological issues, particularly when the language involved is spoken over a large geographical area and exhibits high levels of dialectal variation.

Dialectal variation is frequently viewed negatively by lay speakers, because it may give the impression that the speech community is fragmented both linguistically and in terms of its identity. While standardization is often considered a solution to this problem, the selection of linguistic forms to serve as the basis of a standard language can emerge as a contentious and divisive issue, particularly in the context of language endangerment and revitalization; the standard language may be seen to privilege speakers of one dialect over others (Grenoble and Whaley 2006:102). When endangered languages exhibit high levels of diatopic variation, or when multiple dialects are seen to be in competition, several options are available during the process of linguistic and orthographical standardization: (i) the unilectal approach, or selecting one particular dialect for standardization; (ii) the dialectal approach, or creating multiple standards; (iii) the multilectal approach, or creating a standard that contains linguistic features from a number of dialects; (iv) the common core approach, or creating a standard that emphasizes linguistic features common to all dialects.

The selection of one particular dialect to form the basis of the standard language and orthography is known as the unilectal, or 'reference dialect', approach to standardization: a single dialectal variety is promoted as the form of language to be used in formal and written domains, and speakers of other dialects are required to '[work] out the equivalences with their own dialects or [to learn] the standard as a new variety' (Sebba 2012b:110). The selection process is influenced by both geographical and social factors: '(a) the relative location (a central location may have fostered a widespread regional comprehension due to bidialectalism); (b) the number of speakers; and/or (c) an elevated level of prestige' (Karan 2014:115). It is commonly the most prestigious dialect that is selected for standardization in the unilectal approach, and problems may arise when there is no 'generally agreed-upon prestige dialect' (Cahill 2014:12). The unilectal approach should not, in theory, create problems for orthography development, because systematic differences – those exhibiting a one-to-one isomorphic correspondence – between the standard and non-standard dialects can accurately be represented by a single orthography (Venezky 1970:264). Fishman notes that it is necessary, particularly in the context of language revitalization, to avoid selecting a 'highly divergent dialect' for the role of standard (1991:343). From a linguistic perspective, problems may arise when, for example, a single phoneme in the standard dialect has two reflexes in another dialect, but problems associated with the unilectal approach are normally social in nature. It is of utmost importance that the dialect selected for standardization be accepted by speakers of all dialects, if it is to succeed. If not, speakers of dialects that closely resemble the standard may be viewed as having an unfair advantage (Fishman 1991:343); resistance to the standard may occur if the written form is seen to depart too much from spoken varieties (Grenoble and Whaley 2006:130).

When linguistic differences between dialects impede mutual comprehension, or for ideological reasons, a 'dialectal' approach may be adopted: multiple standard dialects and corresponding orthographies are created during the standardization process. There are several drawbacks to this approach, however. The dialectal approach is not encouraged in revitalization contexts because it 'emphasizes' linguistic differences and socio-cultural distance between groups, resulting in linguistic and social fragmentation' (Karan 2014:115). Indeed, Marcellesi (1983:216) notes explicitly that polynomia is easier to implement in situations of language maintenance than when attempting to reverse language shift. This is because revitalization efforts commonly attempt to elevate speaker numbers by encouraging second-language learning, and while native speakers may have no problems using and interpreting multiple dialectal orthographies, 'second language learners need a model to aim at' (Sallabank 2013:173). By contrast, when the aim is to promote literacy among fluent speakers, the development of a 'teaching orthography', which may be modified to reflect the linguistic forms of various dialects, may provide additional support from a pedagogical perspective (see the 'differential' approach, Karan 2014:116–117). In practice, the dialectal approach is uncommon; it is rare to find dialects that are so different from each other that no common orthography can be created, because 'dialects, by nature, are characterized by systematic phonological differences' (Venezky 1970:264).

It is necessary to distinguish between a dialectal approach, where individual standard orthographies are created for different dialects, and a multilectal approach, where the orthography created contains linguistic features from several different dialects. From a linguistic perspective, the development of a multilectal orthography involves representing 'the phonologies of many dialects of a language [which] are compared and accounted for in designing the orthography' (Simons 1977:325). Allerton (1982) recommends that all potential phonemic contrasts should be represented in the composite orthography: if two contrastive phonemes of one dialect, for example, correspond to only one phoneme in another dialect, the multilectal orthography will require speakers of the latter to 'represent in writing a distinction which they do not make in speech' (Sebba 2012b:110). Thus, a multilectal orthography does not represent any one spoken variety of the language (Cahill 2014:13; Grenoble and Whaley 2006:152), but the integration of linguistic features from a range of spoken varieties can serve to foster a common identity for the speech community at large. The creation of a composite orthography is therefore commonly motivated by socio-political or sociolinguistic factors (Berry 1968:741; Karan 2014:117). Indeed, decisions regarding the linguistic features to include in the composite orthography will often depend heavily on the relative prestige of and socio-political relations among the contributory dialect groups (Seifart 2006:285). Simons (1994) presents a multilectal orthography as preferable to a unilectal one because the latter requires a large number of speakers to rote-learn various aspects of the unilectal system. Grenoble and Whaley (2006:153) argue, however, that this recommendation may not always be practical in situations of language revitalization – such as, for example, when dialects exhibit different levels of vitality and the decision to use the 'healthiest' variety as the basis of a unilectal standard may be more effective. Additionally, the development of a multilectal orthography may instigate socio-political tensions relating to the over- or under-representation of features from the contributing dialects: 'the apparently "neutral" question of how best to accommodate different varieties within a single orthography leads directly to issues of power and authority' (Sebba 2012b:112).

A final option is the development of an 'artificial' or common-core orthography which involves developing a writing system that emphasizes structural features that are common to all dialects. This frequently involves a certain degree of historical reconstruction, using prior forms of the language in which dialectal differences were less pronounced. The development of a common-core orthography, also known as a 'unilectal approach based on an artificial dialect' (Karan 2014:117), is more often motivated by socio-political rather than linguistic factors (Venezky 1970:264). Common-core orthographies have had limited success, and many linguists do not recommend them in situations of language revitalization (Karan 2014:117; Bradley 2005:4; Venezky 1970:264): the perception of the new standardized system as artificial and inauthentic may cause speakers to reject the newly developed orthography.

It is worth emphasizing at this point that status planning for newly developed orthographies and newly standardized dialects of all kinds must convey clearly to the speech community that the standard dialect is an additional variety and that it does not aim to replace spoken dialects: 'all dialects should remain valid in speech within their own traditional speech networks and communities' (Fishman 1991:342). The domains of use for the new standard must be clearly communicated to all members of the speech community, and spoken dialects of the language must be presented as equally valid. This is often difficult, particularly when the standard dialect and orthography are propagated by, and associated with, the education system, implicitly raising the prestige of the standard dialect. The success of standardization will be dependent on a common consensus that it is not an attempt to regulate speech or spoken dialects. In theory, creating separate domains for the written standard and for spoken dialects is possible with careful language planning that encourages bidialectal competence. Indeed the celebration of local speech forms goes hand in hand with the postmodern Zeitgeist, which has led to an 'increasingly positive attitude to local, non-standard varieties [...] particularly in areas where bi-dialectalism is defined clearly' (Melchers 1987:187). Promoting bidialectalism can alleviate concerns during the standardization process about the loss of linguistic diversity.

Standardization can have both positive and negative outcomes for endangered languages. As indicated above, encouraging the development of standard dialects in an effort to reverse language shift can paradoxically result in the loss of local language varieties. Local varieties may adopt non-local or standardized forms via the process of de-dialectalization or dialect death due to the elevated prestige attached to standard forms (Sallabank 2013:172). When a unilectal or skewed multilectal approach is adopted, the attribution of prestigious social values to one dialect at the expense of others can lead to social stratification because speakers will have unequal access to the standard form of language (Grenoble and Whaley 2006:155). In turn, this social stratification can cause problems for revitalization efforts: the standard language may only 'appeal to those whose life-style is modern/urban, a life-style in which written, formal and extra-local communication are all crucial aspects of the total repertoire' (Fishman 1991:349), leading to social inequality. Grenoble and Whaley (2006:155–156) note, however, that situations of language shift emerge originally from social and sociolinguistic inequality between dominant and endangered speech communities and that, while standardization can create inequality within the endangered speech community, this may be the price to pay for minimizing inequality at a macro level between members of the endangered language speech community and speakers of the language of wider communication.

We have already noted that the existences of a prescriptive standard can raise the status of an endangered language due to the commonplace ideology that 'real' languages are written, standard languages. Jaffe insists that 'orthography is one of the key symbols of language unity and status itself' and that 'it is not only important to "have" an orthography, but it is crucial for that orthography to have prescriptive power – to be standardized and authoritative, like the orthographies of dominant languages' (2000:505–506). On the basis that authority and prescriptivism go hand in hand, Sebba (2011:44) argues that there is socio-political and socio-cultural agreement that spelling should be invariant – that is, that the introduction of writing entails the introduction of ideologies about correctness and about what is 'right' and what it 'wrong' in terms of language use (Karan 2014:109). Indeed, Grenoble and Whaley (2006:154) note that native speakers place less emphasis on correct language use before a language is given a written form.

In contrast, there are situations in which standardization may not be appropriate for endangered languages or where optionality in spelling may prove more useful than invariance: 'an orthography for a particular language may be standardized, but it does not have to be, and even if there is a standard orthography for a language, variation may be present, either officially legitimated or not' (Sebba 2011:36). For Fishman, standardization and a standardized orthography may not be necessary at all in situations where no written standard can be agreed upon because such uniformization would cause interdialectal tensions or because of the existence of large dialectal differences (1991:344–345). In particular, the creation of an orthography for endangered languages will not be necessary until stage 5 on Fishman's GIDS is reached, after intergenerational transmission is well established within the speech community. Potential socio-political and cultural tensions during standardization and orthography development may require language planners to resist the temptation to intervene: 'when people do not see eye to eye on orthography issues, when the process gets messy and factions seem to be having a tug-of-war, it may be wise to take standardization off the agenda for a while' (Karan 2014:118).

Alternatively, language planners may wish to develop an orthography that permits varying degrees of optionality in spelling. Allowing for variability in spelling may encourage speakers to write more freely than if a single invariant standard is imposed (Karan 2014:107), but Sebba argues that invariance is often viewed as essential by orthography users and that they expect a 'set of rules' for writing correctly: 'complaints from the public and pedagogies always seem to be about deviation from the prescribed norm, rather than taking the forms of appeals for more diversity' (2012b:107). Even if optionality is permitted by the orthography, Sebba notes that social values may attach to competing forms: even when they are both 'officially' acceptable, they may not be afforded equal status in terms of prestige (2012b:109). It is true that many dominant languages, such as English and Norwegian, permit a degree of optionality within their orthographies, but Fishman argues that this only 'seems to be acceptable if at least they are socio-politically self-regulating and not undergoing language shift' (1991:345). While it seems that this optionality may not be appropriate for endangered languages, primarily because of the status and prestige afforded to invariant orthographies, Fishman warns that it may be seriously detrimental to revitalization efforts to impose a written standard on 'an adamantly unwilling or seriously ailing speech community' (1991:345). Nevertheless, Grenoble and Whaley (2006:156) argue that in the modern era, endangered language communities cannot afford to be complacent about the development of a written language, and the standardization that this often entails, if they are to resist language shift in favour of increasingly dominant languages of wider communication.

4   Orthography Development for Endangered Languages

The creation of a (standardized) orthography is commonly viewed as a necessary step in the development of documentation and literacy programmes for endangered languages (Seifart 2006:275; Grenoble and Whaley 2006:137). The creation of a written norm is often viewed as an integral part of modern language (Sgall 1987:22) and an indispensable tool in the reversal of language shift. While an orthographical system may be defined simply as 'a system for representing a language in written form' (Rice and Cahill 2014b:2), the process of developing an orthography is influenced by, and dependent upon, a wide variety of linguistic and extra-linguistic factors: 'beyond purely linguistic considerations, there are a range of social, psychological, economic, political, and historical issues involved in making decisions about how to write a language' (Grenoble and Whaley 2006:137). It is important to take account of all relevant factors to ensure that the resultant orthography is '(i) mechanically suited for the language it is to reflect, (ii) compatible with, or at a minimum, not alien to its social-cultural setting, and (iii) psychologically and pedagogically appropriate for its speakers' (Venezky 1970:256). This section provides general information on the different types of script and on different orthographic systems available to the orthography developer, before discussing in detail the various linguistic (Section 5) and extra-linguistic (Section 6) factors involved in orthography development. The following conventions are used: /a/ – phonemic representation; [a] – phonetic representation; <a> – orthographic representation (following Seifart 2006:276 and Rice and Cahill 2014:6).

It is first necessary to distinguish between a script, a graphic system, and an orthography. The visual shape of the letters, or graphemes, used by a writing system is known as its script (Seifart 2006:277) – e.g., Arabic script, Latin script, Cyrillic script, Devangari script. A graphic system is the abstract underlying type of writing system used and may be alphabetic, syllabic, logographic, etc. (Lüpke 2011:313). An orthography, by contrast, is a specific application of a given script, and graphic system, to a particular language: 'for the orthography of a particular language, a script must be chosen (or devised, or developed) and then applied to the writing of that language by determining a set of conventional correspondences between the characters provided by the script and the words, sounds or syllables of the language' (Sebba 2011:35–36). The correlation between script and religion can be very strong, highlighting the importance of considering socio-cultural factors when making choices about the type of script to be used (Lüpke 2011:323). Additionally, a single language may be written using two, or multiple, different scripts, graphic systems, or orthographies; this is known as 'digraphia' (Lüpke 2011:316; Grenoble and Whaley 2006:144) – e.g., use of the Roman alphabet for Croatian and the Cyrillic alphabet for Serbian.

Four main types of graphic system can be distinguished (Grenoble and Whaley 2006:139): (i) alphabetic, (ii) consonantal, (iii) semi-syllabic, and (iv) logographic. Graphic systems (i)–(iii) are collectively referred to as 'phonographic' systems because the basic units of these systems correspond to elements of the language's sound system (Seifart 2006:277). First, alphabetic systems use single symbols, or graphemes, that represent (more or less directly) the language's phonemes (Seifart 2006:277; Grenoble and Whaley 2006:139). The Greek, Latin, and Cyrillic alphabets are the most commonly used alphabetic systems. Many linguists prefer to use the Latin alphabetic system for documentation purposes because it displays a close relationship to the transcription system employed by the International Phonetic Alphabet (Lüpke 2011:313). Second, consonantal systems use individual symbols to represent consonant phonemes, marking vowels only optionally, usually using diacritics (Grenoble and Whaley 2006:139). Consonantal graphic systems may be considered a sub-type of alphabetic systems, of which Arabic is an example. Third, semi-syllabic systems, or syllabaries, use graphic symbols that correspond to a language's individual syllables – e.g., Japanese. Cross-linguistically, syllabaries tend to contain a higher number of symbols than do alphabets, and they can therefore take longer to learn. For this reason, syllabaries are better suited to languages that have a small number of distinct syllables and when there is a 'high correspondence between a syllable and a morpheme – that is, where syllable and morpheme boundaries tend to coincide' (Grenoble and Whaley 2006:139).

Finally, logographic systems use graphic signs, or 'logograms' to represent morphemes. These systems do not link symbols to elements of the language's sound structure and are often referred to as 'morphographic' (Seifert 2006:277), as opposed to the phonographic systems described above: 'even if two morphemes are pronounced identically, they will be represented by distinct symbols' (Grenoble and Whaley 2006:139) – e.g., Chinese. Seifart (2006:298) argues that the term 'logographic' is inappropriate for these systems because graphemes or characters used in these systems always correspond to morphemes and not to words – as 'logographic' implies – noting, however, that in languages such as Chinese, words tend to be monomorphemic. Morphographic systems have the advantage of permitting the same characters to be pronounced differently by speakers of different dialects (Bradley 2005:7) but have numerous drawbacks: many more characters must be learnt, because morphological systems are more extensive than phonological inventories; existing morphographic systems are difficult to adapt to other unwritten languages because there are no sound–spelling correspondences; and these systems can become extremely large for languages with extensive morphology (Grenoble and Whaley 2006:139–140).

Overall, it is argued that morphographic systems are inferior to phonographic ones (Sebba 2011:37; Grenoble and Whaley 2006:139; Bradley

2005:1), with alphabetic systems recommended for endangered language orthographies owing to their relative simplicity (Bradley 2005:1) and on the basis that they more accurately represent spoken language (Sebba 2011:37; Goody and Watt 1968:37–38). Alphabetic systems also contain fewer symbols than other systems do, and they tend to be used by languages of wider communication (Grenoble and Whaley 2006:139). It may be argued that morphographic systems have the long-term advantage of not requiring reform due to sound change (which may be necessary for phonographic systems that are based on a strict phonemic principle; see Section 5) in addition to the fact that they do not require a single spoken standard (Bradley 2005:2). In spite of this, Grenoble and Whaley argue that, owing to the particular nature of language revitalization, alphabetic systems should be used when creating orthographies for endangered languages, 'barring an overriding symbolic value that may be derived from the use of a syllabary or logographic writing system' (2006:158): it is critical that the sounds of an endangered language be identifiable from its orthography because, in the context of language shift and revitalization, many semi- and second-language speakers will be targeted by literacy programmes.

5 Creating Orthographies: Linguistic Factors

Orthography development requires a variety of 'conventional relationships' (Sebba 2011:37), between the language and the writing system, to be established. Successful orthography development must clearly establish the following linguistic conventions (adapted from Sebba 2011:38): (i) the script and graphic system to be used, including the specification of a closed set of graphemes (Lüpke 2011:321–322; Seifart 2006:276); (ii) the nature of sound–spelling correspondences or how graphemes, or sequences of graphemes, map onto phones/phonemes, or sequences of phones/phonemes; (iii) the representation of sounds in specific positions (e.g., medially, finally); (iv) the manner in which homonyms are to be distinguished orthographically; (v) the means by which features such as tone or vowel length are marked; (vi) the use of diacritics and similar marks (accent, diaeresis, tilde, caron); and (vii) the rules for marking word boundaries and for punctuation (Rice and Cahill 2014:2; Lüpke 2011:321–322; Seifart 2006:276–277; Coulmas 2003:35). The establishment of these conventional relationships typically requires trained linguists or those with 'high level of metalinguistic awareness' (Grenoble and Whaley 2006:130) to participate in orthography development.

5.1 The Phonemic Principle

The choice of orthographic forms, according to Sgall (1987:2), follows one of three principles: (i) phonetic, reflecting the pronunciation of words (phonographic); (ii) etymological, reflecting the origin of words or their morphemic structure (morphographic); or (iii) historical, reflecting traditional practices in cases where the spelling of a word cannot be justified by the other two principles. Traditionally, there has been a general consensus that orthographies should reflect, as far as possible, the structure of the language it aims to represent (Sgall 1987:4; Venezky 1970:259). Smalley (1964), for example, presents five maximums, or essential criteria, which are required for the development of a successful orthography, the second of which is that an orthography must possess 'maximum representation of speech' and that it must represent 'all and only the distinctive sounds of the language being written' (Hinton 2014:144).

Principle (i), the 'phonetic' principle referred to in the previous paragraph, is more commonly referred to as the 'phonemic principle' in the context of orthography development, and, since Pike's (1947) discussion and promotion of the concept, 'it has become... customary to regard orthographies as "optimal" if they adhere to the often invoked "phonemic principle" according to which a one-to-one relationship between phonemes and graphemes is ideal' (Lüpke 2011:329). Pike proposed that orthographies should exhibit an isomorphic relationship between sounds and symbols: 'a practical orthography should be phonemic. There should be a one-to-one correspondence between each phoneme and the symbolization of that phoneme' (Pike 1947:208). Luelsdorff (1987:ix) conceptualises this phonemic principle in terms of two 'uniqueness' criteria, the uniqueness of pronunciation of a grapheme and the uniqueness of spelling of a phoneme; each letter should have a unique sound value, and each phoneme should be represented by a single letter (see Sgall 1987:10–11). It is worth noting that Pike's recommendation requires individual symbols to represent phonemes and not phones: the orthography should represent the phonemic, and not the phonetic, system of the language. Grenoble and Whaley (2006:141) argue that this is because surface phonetic realizations are subject to higher levels of change over time than is the case in the more abstract phonemic system, and thus phonemic alphabets are seen to be more stable. Additionally, while phonetic realizations may differ between closely related dialects, the phonemic system tends to be similar (Grenoble and Whaley 2006:141), and so a phonemic orthography may accurately correspond to all dialects.

5.2   The Functional Load

If a newly developed orthography is to obey the phonemic principle, it is necessary to establish the sounds of the language in question that are contrastive. From a strict structural perspective, the existence of a single minimal pair is sufficient to establish a sound as a distinct phoneme, and, by the phonemic principle, this sound unit should then be represented by a single, unique grapheme. However, it is not always necessary to represent all such phonemic contrasts in the orthography; the 'functional load' of each phoneme must be taken into account. Hockett (1955) defines formally 'functional load' thus: 'assuming that two phonemes, x and y, can contrast at all, then the functional load carried by the contrast will be greater if both x and y have relatively high text frequencies than if one has a high frequency and the other has a low frequency, and greater under those second conditions than if both x and y have low frequencies' (cited in Grenoble and Whaley 2006:147). The functional load of a phoneme, therefore, is related to its frequency and to the absolute number of contrasts in which it is involved (Seifart 2006:280; Lüpke 2011:333) as well as, crucially, to 'the extent to which users of the orthography rely on that feature in reading and writing the language' (Bird 2001:14; see Grenoble and Whaley 2006:147 for the factors that determine functional load). It is important to represent orthographically those phonemes with high functional loads, because meaningful distinctions are dependent on these sounds units; phonemes with low functional loads, in comparison, may not need to be distinguished orthographically.

If a phoneme has a low functional load, the principle of 'under-representation', or 'under-differentiation', may apply: 'while it is true that orthographies should reduce potential ambiguity of a written message, they should also be simple. And in order to achieve this simplicity, it may be justified not to represent features that do not have a high functional load, even if they are contrastive from a strictly structural point of view' (Seifart 2006:281). Under-representation provides a means of simplifying the orthography when the phonemic system of a given language is relatively large, making the written form easier to learn (Grenoble and Whaley 2006:148), but deviating from the phonemic principle (using one symbol for more than one sound) can also lead to ambiguity in the form of homographs (words that are pronounced differently but which have the same orthographic form). This ambiguity can be offset, however, by syntactic, semantic, or contextual cues from the surrounding discourse (Lüpke 2011:332; Seifart 2006:281). Under-specifying phonemes with a low functional load can also facilitate the development of pandialectal orthographies in the case of languages that display relatively minor differences in their phonological inventories (Lüpke 2011:332). In comparison, the principle of 'over-representation', or using more than one grapheme for a given phoneme, may be applied when it is deemed necessary to mark allophonic contrasts (Cahill 2014:17; Grenoble and Whaley 2006:148) or to mark phonemic distinctions that occur in one dialect but not in others (cf. Allerton 1982).

Within phonographic writing systems, then, it is often necessary to depart from the phonemic principle for a variety of reasons, such as, for example, distinguishing homophones (Jones 1950:232; Venezky 1970:259; Lüpke 2011:329). Chief among the arguments for diverging from an isomorphic sound–spelling relationship is the retention of morpheme identity in orthographical representations, to which we will now turn.

5.3 Morphophonemic Spelling

The primary argument against a strict one-to-one sound–spelling correspondence in any writing system is that orthography should aim to reflect all levels of language structure, not just its phonology (Venezky 1970:263; Grenoble and Whaley 2006:141). Morpheme and word-identity recognition have been shown to be important in the reading process (see Section 6), and distinguishing morphemes orthographically may avoid the ambiguity associated with homograms representing distinct, but homophonic, morphemes in phonographic systems (Sgall 1987:21). In this way, morphophonemic spelling can prove useful in languages with a high degree of homophony (Grenoble and Whaley 2006:141). Morphophonemic systems use individual symbols, or combinations of symbols, to represent phonemes, but these symbols do not exhibit an isomorphic relationship with phonemes; symbols chosen prioritize the representation of distinct grammatical morphemes, often in their underlying form, to indicate morpheme identity and promote consistency of morpheme shape. For example, the vowel /a:/ in the German words *Stahl*, *Staat*, and *Rabe* is represented by <ah>, <aa>, and <a> on the basis that the /a:/ vowel is present in three different morphemes (Sgall 1987:12). There is a link between 'etymological', or 'historical', spelling and morphographic writing systems, in that spelling based on etymology often, but not always, facilitates the identification of distinct morphemes that have come to be pronounced in the same way in modern usage (Sgall 1987:21). These morphemes would be represented identically in a strictly phonographic orthography. In contrast, the spelling of morphemes can be 'constant in different contexts despite pronunciation differences because the spelling represents an older stage of the language, when these forms were in fact pronounced in the same way' (Seifart 2006:298). Morphographic orthographies have the advantage of being relatively transparent phonemically while also minimizing ambiguity; Grenoble and Whaley (2006:142) argue that an ideal orthography would have as its basis both phonemic and morphemic principles. In the context of language revitalization, however, the phonemic principle should be given priority due, once again, to the role of second-language learners and semi-speakers in reversing language shift. Such speakers have been shown to benefit from more phonographic systems in the earlier stages of literacy (see Section 6).

5.4 Orthographic 'Depth'

The concept of orthographic 'depth' is central to the distinction between phonographic and morphographic writing systems, where 'the metaphor of "depth" [...] refers to the level of linguistic structure at which the forms are orthographically represented' (Seifart 2006:279). 'Shallow' orthographies are largely transparent from a phonological perspective, with clear phoneme-to-grapheme correspondences – e.g., Finnish (Lüpke 2011:331); graphemes often correspond closely to the surface realization of linguistic forms, often marking allophonic variation, and therefore the phonemic principle is privileged by shallow orthographies. 'Deep' orthographies, in contrast, are relatively opaque from a surface phonological perspective and exhibit a strong correspondence between orthographic representations and underlying linguistic forms; each distinct morpheme is frequently represented by one, invariable written form which does not indicate morphophonological changes that the morphemes undergo in context (Seifart 2006:279). Deep orthographies are often used for languages with quite distinct morphophonological and phonetic representations – e.g., English (Seifart 2006:279). Preserving the visual image, or shape, of morphemes can, however, result in a high frequency of irregular sound–spelling correspondences (Lüpke 2011:331). Equally, a strict phonographic orthography will render opaque the relationships between the written form and the language's underlying morphological structure. A strict distinction between shallow (phonographic) and deep (morphophonemic) is rarely possible in practice; we have seen that phonographic orthographies may deviate from the phonemic principle in order to avoid ambiguity or to facilitate the transition from spelling to meaning. For example, in English, the plural morpheme is consistently represented as <-s> in *clumps, monsters,* and *horses* even though the phonetic realization is distinct in each case: [s], [z], and [əz], respectively (Venezky 1970:261). While phonographic orthographies are better suited to endangered languages, primarily because they are more easily learnable for non-fluent speakers, it is often not practical for any given orthography to occur in a pure phonographic or morphographic form; most successful orthographies will combine elements of both systems. Phonographic orthographies often replace strictly phonemic forms with the underlying form of morphemes 'when the morphological distinctions which are important in the language are obscured by limitations on the distribution of phonemes – leading to the neutralization of contrasts' (Snider 2014:28; Gudschinsky 1972:22). The traditional binary distinction between shallow and deep orthographies may not, in fact, be as appropriate to orthography development as previously thought, given that the distinction itself is 'locked into phonological theories that predate the 1970s' (Snider 2014:27; cf. Chomsky and Halle 1968), or dependent on the somewhat-dated theoretical distinction between surface and underlying forms.

5.5 The Lexical Orthographical Hypothesis

Snider (2014) argues that insights from Stratal Optimality Theory (Kiparsky 1998, 2000) and the theory of lexical phonology (Mohanan 1982, 1986) may provide a more apt framework within which to consider the level of linguistic structure to represent orthographically: 'whether the preferred orthographic representation is phonemic or morphophonemic, the level that works best from a practical viewpoint is consistently the output of the lexical phonology' (Snider 2014:27). We must note, however, that the primary argument for a lexical phonological approach to orthography development is that native speakers are more aware of the output of lexical phonology than of any other phonological level, which may be inappropriate in situations of language revitalization given the dwindling numbers of fluent speakers involved. Nonetheless, Snider argues that the Lexical Orthography Hypothesis (hereafter, LOH) provides a more welcome framework for orthography development than does the phoneme (structuralism) or the morphophoneme (generative phonology) (2014:30). The LOH makes a distinction between lexical processes and postlexical processes (Kutsch Lojenga 2014b:85): lexical processes involve phonological rules which apply within polymorphemic words; postlexical processes result in surface realizations that can take place across word boundaries. Snider (2014:38) illustrates the lexical-postlexical distinction with an example from Polish: the Polish word for 'ice', /lod/, is pronounced as [lut], and the translation from the underlying form to the surface form involves both types of process. First, the /o/ vowel is raised to [u] by a lexical process when followed by a word-final non-nasal consonant that is [+voice]. Because this process occurs regularly, and /o/ never surfaces as [o] in this context, Snider argues that this type of rule is 'lexicalized' in the minds of native speakers (2014:30–31). Second, word-final voiced consonants in Polish are devoiced by a postlexical process, and thus /d/ surfaces as [t] in the word for 'ice'. We may note that the postlexical rule here obscures the conditioning environment for the lexical rule (i.e., voiced consonants). The LOH posits that native speakers are 'relatively unaware of the output of post-lexical processes, they are much more aware of the output of lexical ones, and this explains why native speakers often prefer to write words as they are realized after they have undergone lexical processes and before they have undergone post-lexical ones' (Snider 2014:31). Because of this, it is recommended that morphophonological processes taking place at the lexical level (lexical processes) be represented in the orthography, while those taking place postlexically should not be marked, instead opting for the (underlying) morphophonemic form (Snider 2014:36; Kutsch Lojenga 2014b:85). The Polish orthography follows these basic principles, with [lut] represented orthographically as *lód*: the <ó> grapheme distinguishes [u] from [o] (represented orthographically as <o>), a lexical process;

the <d> grapheme corresponds to [t] but indexes the underlying morphophonemic form /d/, a postlexical process. A further argument for not representing the output of postlexical processes orthographically is that surface forms may have phonemic status, leading to the creation of homograms in phonographic systems – e.g., English *prince* [pɹɪ̥nts] and *prints* [pɹɪ̥nts] would both be represented identically in the orthography. In sum, the LOH is a principled alternative to the perhaps dated and impractical distinction between shallow and deep orthographies, providing a clear dichotomy on the basis of which decisions can be made about the orthographic representation of surface forms: 'outputs [...] that result from lexical processes should be represented, and those that result from post-lexical processes should not' (Snider 2014:44).

5.6   Establishing Word Boundaries

For languages that have no written tradition, codification in the form of an orthography must segment natural speech into individual words in the written form. In many cases, this will be relatively straightforward, but in others it will require extensive research and detailed 'analysis in the domains of morphology (including, of course, morphophonology) and clause syntax' (Kutsch Lojenga 2014b:77). During orthography development, the establishment of word boundaries will involve either (i) conjunctive writing (joining morphemes), (ii) disjunctive writing (separating morphemes), or (iii) intermediate solutions using hyphens or apostrophes (Kutsch Lojenga 2014b:78). Word-boundary decisions can be made on purely linguistic grounds by analysing the morphological and syntactic structure of the language, but this must be supplemented with information from native speaker intuitions and may need to take into account the conventions used by languages with similar morphosyntactic structures. From a linguistic perspective, the establishment of word boundaries involves, first, the identification of the language's permissible syllable structures and its grammatical morphemes (Kutsch Lojenga 2014b:80–81): word boundaries should not leave orthographic words with impossible syllable structures; the grammatical distinction between affixes, clitics, and independent (or free) morphemes is extremely important for the establishment of boundaries between words. Kutsch Lojenga argues that it is necessary to organize grammatical morphemes into these three categories before investigating morphophonological processes and their surface forms and that 'for each category, one needs to know the underlying form and, in the case of affixes and clitics, the allomorphs, and the rules by which these are produced' (2014b:85). It is recommended that affixes be written conjunctively – i.e., joined to the lexical morpheme to which they grammatically and phonologically are bound (Kutsch Lojenga 2014b:82). Free morphemes, in contrast, are independent and are neither grammatically nor phonologically bound; they should therefore be represented disjunctively in the orthography – i.e., separated from adjacent morphemes. Clitics, in comparison, are grammatically independent, but often phonologically bound, and may be written conjunctively or disjunctively. Clitics will often be written conjunctively, or using hyphenation, if they influence adjacent lexical morphemes, or vice versa, by phonological processes, and disjunctively if they do not. In addition to these basic grammatical distinctions, a range of grammatical, phonological, and semantic criteria govern the placement of word boundaries orthographically (for further discussion, see Kutsch Lojenga 2014b and Van Dyken and Kutsch Lojenga 1993).

5.7   Marking Tone

In certain parts of the world, the development of orthographies for tonal (endangered) languages – which use variations in pitch to distinguish lexical and grammatical categories – involves, crucially, the establishment of conventional relationships orthographically for the representation of tonal distinctions. Tonal systems may use lexical tone to distinguish units at the word or syllable level (Grenoble and Whaley 2006:149), or grammatical tone to mark morphological distinctions within the verb system and in other areas of the grammar, such as plurality, gender, and case marking (Kutsch Lojenga 2014a:52). The orthography developer will need to decide the phonological level on which to mark tone (Cahill 2014:17) or, indeed, whether it is necessary to represent tones at all (Seifart 2006:293). These decisions will rely heavily on an assessment of the language's tonal system (Kutsch Lojenga 2014a:53), including its contrastive tones, distinctive rising and/or falling tones, and tonal melodies. Additionally, the orthographer must take account of the presence or absence of tonal processes and the functional load of tone.

Determining the functional load of tonal distinctions is essential to orthography development decisions. It seems logical that, as with phonemic distinctions, tone should be marked orthographically in line with Pike's phonemic principle. However, as with phonemes, tonemes that carry a low functional load may be under-differentiated in the orthography in interest of simplicity. Kutsch Lojenga distinguishes two main types of tonal languages: those with 'stable' tone and those with 'moveable' tone (2014a:49). In languages with stable tone, the functional load of lexical and grammatical tonemes is more often high; in languages with 'moveable' tone, the functional load of tonemes is heavier for grammatical than for lexical tones. It is recommended, therefore, that tone be marked consistently in the lexicon and the grammar for languages with stable tone, but only in the grammar for languages with moveable tone. Marking tone distinctions in languages with stable tone, or marking tone on every syllable, will promote consistent word images; this has been shown to facilitate reading for fluent speakers (see Section 6). In languages of the second type, moveable tones must be marked on the basis of their surface realization, 'because this is the point where the grammatical contrast becomes evident' (Kutsch Lojenga 2014a:63); phonemic tones cannot be written consistently on each word, as the realization of tones varies according to context. It is therefore recommended that tonemes with a heavy functional load be represented orthographically because a lack of tonal marking may lead to ambiguity during the reading process – though, arguably, fluent speakers may be able to determine tonal distinctions on the basis of the surrounding linguistic context. New or semi-speakers, by comparison, may benefit from a more transparent representation of tonemes to facilitate ongoing learning of the endangered languages.

In addition to considering the functional load of tonemes, the orthographer must also take account of the conventions used in surrounding languages and languages of wider communication with which the endangered language finds itself in contact. If the language of wider communication is not a tone language, or if it is a tone language for which tone is not marked in the orthographical representation, local attitudes may require the system of the dominant language to be replicated in the new orthography (Grenoble and Whaley 2006:149). For example, in many African tone languages, tone is not represented at all orthographically, even where it has a heavy functional load, because the colonial national languages, such as French, are not tonal and thus do not mark tone in their orthographies.

If the decision is taken to mark tone, or to partially mark tone, orthographically, the orthographer must then decide on the graphemes or orthographic symbols used to do so. Tone may be marked orthographically by using diacritic accents, punctuation marks, numbers, or consonant letters that are not currently used in the orthography (Lüpke 2011:332; Kutsch Lojenga 2014a:54). If diacritic accents are used to distinguish different types of tone, Kutsch Lojenga suggests using an acute accent for high tones, a grave accent for low tones, a wedge for rising tones, and a circumflex accent for falling tones (2014a:55). One problem associated with the use of diacritic accents to mark tone is that speakers will often omit them (Bradley 2005:6), but Kutsch Lojenga notes that speakers may actually suggest the use of accents when they are aware of a toneme's contrastive function in situations where the language of wider communication uses accents, even if these diacritics are used with a different function in the dominant language (2014a:57). Additionally, native speakers may perceive an orthography which employs diacritics to 'look' or 'seem' difficult to read, and so newly developed orthographies should avoid 'diacritic overload' (Grenoble and Whaley 2006:146; Kutsch Lojenga 2014a:51). These problems associated with the use of diacritics are also relevant when using diacritic accents to mark other suprasegmental features such as stress or when marking features such as gemination, vowel length, or vowel quality (Lüpke 2011:333). For example, the standardized Occitan orthography uses <o> to represent /u/ and <ò> to represent /ɔ/; this often poses problems for non-fluent speakers, who are usually first-language French speakers, since the use of <o> for /u/ is not transparent from a French orthographical perspective, where the sequence <ou> represents /u/ (Mooney 2015). If punctuation, in contrast, is used to mark tone, level tones may be marked by punctuation marks preceding the syllable, and a combination of punctuation marks may be used on both sides of monosyllabic words to mark contour tones and rising and falling tones (Kutsch Lojenga 2014a:57); one drawback involved in the use of punctuation to mark tones is that other devices must be found for punctuation marking (Bradley 2005:6).

6   Creating Orthographies: Extra-Linguistic Factors

In addition to the range of linguistic factors, and to the problem of areal appropriateness, considered above, the process of orthography development must, crucially, take into account a range of non-linguistic issues: the sociolinguistics of writing systems; the role of the native speaker in orthography development; ideological distanciation from dominant-language speech communities; the transfer of literacy to or from the dominant language in a contact situation; cognitive and pedagogical issues relating to reading and writing; the existence of heritage or traditional orthographies; and practical issues concerning technology use. In fact, it is these extra-linguistic factors that are paramount, because a linguistically elegant orthography will only be deemed a success if it is accepted by the speech community for which it is intended: 'an effective orthography is not only (a) linguistically sound, but is also crucially (b) acceptable to all stakeholders [native speaker input], and (c) usable' (Cahill 2014:10). Indeed, it is often on the basis of social, cultural, or psychological factors that deviation takes place from widely assumed best practice, from a linguistic perspective, in orthography development (Venezky 1970:258; Sebba 2012b:7; Hinton 2014:140). Of Smalley's (1964) five maximums for developing an adequate new writing system, four are extra-linguistic: (i) maximum motivation for the learner (speaker input); (ii) maximum representation of speech (linguistic considerations); (iii) maximum ease of learning (cognitive factors); (iv) maximum transfer (of literacy); and (v) maximum ease of reproduction (practicality) (adapted from Hinton, 2014:144). Thus, as Fishman notes, it is necessary to go beyond the linguist's professional skills and to 'go outside the code and to confront the real world if writing systems were not only to be devised but employed' (Fishman, 1977:xi). Mark Sebba's (2011, 2012a, 2012b) work on the sociolinguistics of writing systems emphasizes that orthography is primarily a socio-cultural matter because linguistic signs used to represent language index, or can come to index, social meaning; matters of social identity, national identity, cultural politics, representation, and voice must therefore be integrated in the orthography creation process (Sebba 2012b:6; Rice and Cahill 2014:3).

6.1 Native-Speaker Input

Smalley's (1964) first maximum – maximum motivation for the speaker – is presented as the most important factor for successful orthography development. This maximum refers to the acceptability of the orthography to the speech community: 'if the people for whom the system is designed are not motivated to use it, the orthography is a failure no matter how perfect its internal design' (Hinton 2014:144). Creating an acceptable orthography is invariably achieved by integrating native speakers into the decision-making process. When choosing a reference dialect, a script, individual symbols, and defining conventions, members of the speech community must be given an opportunity to give their opinion about how their language should be put down on paper (Karan 2014:132). Grenoble and Whaley (2006:156) suggest that the best way to achieve this is to form committees composed of representative speakers from all dialects in order to make standardization decisions in consultation with trained linguists. The integration of native-speaker evaluations into the orthography creation process may lead, however, to tensions between the linguist and the speech community. If speakers identify a problem in the developing orthography, the linguist must take this into account even if the negative evaluation is subjective and/or has no purely linguistic basis (Cahill 2014:20). Additionally, in situations where the speech community is not previously literate in the language of wider communication or has had little exposure to formal education, it may be difficult to fully integrate speakers into the orthography development process (Cahill 2014:22). Nonetheless, strong efforts must be made to seek the opinions of local leaders and native speakers, regardless of the feeble linguistic awareness they may be assumed to have (Grenoble and Whaley 2006:137–138). It must be emphasized that establishing the speech community's attitudes towards and acceptance of a new orthography must be achieved before literacy programmes are created, before pedagogical materials are created, and before official endorsement is sought, since 'official endorsement does not necessarily promote popular acceptance' (Karan 2014:113). While some linguists have successfully imposed standard orthographies in the past, in the area of language obsolescence, it appears that this approach is no longer practical (Sebba 2012b:73; Rice and Cahill 2014:3). Metalinguistic analysis and thorough linguistic analysis without consulting native speakers is 'no prophylactic against language endangerment, shift or death' (Sebba 2012b:79); it is conscientious status planning, and not corpus planning, that is paramount.

6.2 Ideological Distanciation

Orthographies often come to be powerful symbols of the languages they represent: the script and orthographic symbols (characters and diacritics) chosen may be strong 'identity markers' which can result in positive or negative ideological reactions from within and outside the speech community (Sebba 2011:39). This is at odds with the linguist's assessment of orthographic conventions where character choice is often made on the basis of practicality or to promote maximum representation of speech. For speakers, in comparison, the visual appearance of orthographies may be a means of establishing symbolic distance from or symbolic closeness to speakers of other languages or varieties (Cahill 2014:14; Sebba 2011:42, 2012b:112; Grenoble and Whaley 2006:143). The linguist, therefore, must be aware of the conventional relationships used in the orthographies of neighbouring or related languages, and of the symbolic value possessed by these relationships, because 'local opinion might call for either conformity with, or divergence from, such conventions' (Grenoble and Whaley 2006:138).

The establishment of symbolic distance from neighbouring languages is particularly pertinent in situations of language endangerment where threatened varieties struggle to gain status and legitimacy. Since language shift frequently emerges as a result of colonization, endangered speech communities may seek to create ideological independence from former colonial powers by using orthographical conventions that are maximally distinct from those of the language of wider communication (Sebba 2012a:3; Seifart 2006:284). In other situations, however, the prestige associated with former colonial languages may cause speakers of the endangered language to seek closeness to and association with this prestige. For example, Sjoberg (1966:268) notes that, in the African context, native speakers of local languages are often reluctant to have their language 'look' overly different from English or French in their respective former colonies. Modelling the orthography of an endangered language on that of a language of wider communication is, indeed, common: the Manx orthography is modelled on English, Sranan on Dutch, and Haitian Creole on French (Sebba 2012b:114). Grenoble and Whaley recommend, in fact, that, in most situations, an orthography that is based on that of the language of wider communication is desirable because 'speakers of endangered languages are commonly literate, or semiliterate, in the language of wider communication, and so adapting its orthography can spread the process of learning to read and write a local language' (2006:145).

The question of whether a newly developed orthography should resemble or be maximally distinct from the language of wider communication is particularly important in situations where the endangered language is typologically or 'genetically' very close to the language with which it is in contact (Fishman 1991:350). Visual similarity to the dominant language may foster the (perhaps undesirable) idea that the endangered language is a sub-par, deformed, or debased variety of the language of wider communication, thus posing a problem for status planning. The practice of 'distanciation' involves 'changing the spelling and rules and calling the final product a "language"' (Sebba 2012b:78; see Paksoy 1989:7). Thus, corpus planning efforts may seek to minimize what may be interpreted as negative structural similarities between the endangered language and the language of wider communication by '(a) stressing and (b) increasing differences between Xish and stronger rivals' (Fishman, 1991:350). Such distanciation is often referred to as *abstand* (literally, 'distance'; Kloss 1967, 1978), which is facilitated by the process of *ausbau* (literally, 'building away' or 'development') and involves making the threatened variety appear to be less like the dominant language than it actually is from a strictly linguistic perspective. Whereas *abstand* refers to the linguistic distance between a given language and other, similar languages, *ausbau* is related to the process of elaboration of function whereby the newly developed orthography aims to raise the status of the endangered language and to promote its use in 'high' domains by underlining its distinctiveness from the language(s) of wider communication.

Sebba (2011:40) discusses the cases of Haitian Creole (in contact with French) and of Galician (in contact with Spanish and Portuguese) to illustrate the *abstand-ausbau* paradox: in Haiti, the use of orthographic conventions that resemble French appear to indicate that Haitian Creole is a variety of French, in ideological terms; in Galicia, the use of Spanish orthographic conventions may help to distinguish Galician from Portuguese, to which it is linguistically more similar (though Spanish is the language of wider communication in this context). Thus, the process of *ausbau*, and the creation of *abstand*, involves establishing linguistic autonomy from related languages by 'reshaping' the visual representation of the language while the linguistic structure of the language(s) remains, in principle, unchanged (Kloss 1967:29) – e.g., Scottish and Irish Gaelic, Galician and Portuguese, Danish and Swedish, Czech and Slovak, Afrikaans and Dutch (Sebba 2012b:113, 117). Once again, it is social, cultural, and ideological factors, such as the creation of *abstand*, and not linguistic factors, which appear to be paramount in making orthographical choices, particularly in situations of language endangerment. These ideological constructs may find themselves in conflict with the linguist's attempts to represent linguistic structure accurately or to integrate elements from neighbouring languages in order to facilitate the transfer of literacy skills (Lüpke 2011:330–331).

6.3 The Transfer of Literacy

It is rare for orthography development to take place in a vacuum: the creation of literacy is commonly 'introduced through contact with another culture which already has a written tradition' (Fishman 1977:xiv). If the endangered speech community is already literate, or partially literate, in the language of wider communication, it may be advisable that the newly developed local orthography follow at least some of the conventional relationships of the dominant language's orthography in order to promote maximum ease of learning or, in Smalley's (1964) terms, to promote 'maximum transfer' (Cahill 2014:18; Seifart 2006:284; Venezky 1970:265): 'it is important to be able to transfer reading knowledge from one well-learned language to the new system' (Hinton 2014:145). Alternatively, if the speech community is not literate, it may be advantageous for the new orthography to resemble that of the language(s) of wider communication in order to facilitate multiple literacies, as advised by Grenoble and Whaley (2006) – that is, literacy in the minority language and in the dominant language:

> An orthography that resembles the orthography of the dominant language may be advantageous in order to facilitate acquisition of the orthography of the endangered language for those who are already acquainted with the one of the dominant language, and to facilitate the acquisition of the orthography of the dominant language for those who acquire the one of the endangered language first. (Seifart 2006:284)

Therefore, if literacy in the language of wider communication is already established, or if it is desirable in the future, orthography development for endangered languages should aim to integrate elements borrowed from the dominant language. For example, Manx is closely related to both Irish and Scottish Gaelic, but its orthography is markedly distinct from both of these languages, as it incorporates a large number of English spelling conventions (Sebba 2012b:61). Kutsch Lojenga suggests that this is particularly important for symbols chosen to represent the vocalic system of the language to facilitate a smooth transfer or literacy, because 'the psycholinguistic intuition of the speakers of a particular language is normally very much influenced by the sound values that were attached to the vowel symbols when they learned to read in an official language or a language of wider communication' (2014b:76).

Problems arise, however, when certain phonemes, for example, are represented inconsistently in the dominant language's orthography, usually for historical reasons; e.g., the Spanish /k/ is represented by <k>, <c>, and <qu> in different contexts. In such cases, it is not recommended that the idiosyncratic pseudo-historical distribution be replicated in the newly developed orthography (Seifart 2006:287). Additionally, the spelling conventions of the dominant language should not be followed slavishly, particularly if this involves marking phonemic contrasts found in the dominant language that are not present in the language for which the new orthography is being developed (Venezky 1970:264). Alternatively, the endangered language may contain phonemes which have no equivalent in the language of wider communication, and thus no obvious orthographic symbol will be available. In these cases, Grenoble and Whaley (2006) suggest the following options: 'creating an entirely new symbol; borrowing one from another orthographic system; creating a new symbol through combining existing symbols into digraphs or trigraphs as needed; using a diacritic; or reassigning a symbol used for a sound in the language of wider communication which is not found in the local language, i.e. reassigning unused symbols of an alphabet to different phonemic values' (2006:146). The Manx orthography developed by John Phillips, however, chose in these cases to represent phonemic contrasts only when the English spelling conventions provide a means of doing so but to ignore Manx contrasts that are not present in English, which is not advisable (Sebba 2012b:62; see Thomson 1969:181).

Borrowing elements from the orthography of the language of wider communication during orthography development for endangered languages continues to be a contentious issue. The facilitation of transfer to and from dominant or neighbouring languages is often considered to facilitate language shift rather than to counteract language obsolescence (Sebba 2012b:77). This is because literacy in the indigenous language is often seen as transitional in that it will eventually lead to 'full' literacy in the language of wider communication (Sebba 2012b:75). Of course, the maximum of 'maximum transfer' may also find itself in direct conflict with efforts to achieve *abstand* when the indigenous language community wishes to distance itself from an oppressed past (Sebba 2012b:76). Nonetheless, Grenoble and Whaley suggest that it is 'typically best not to inhibit the learnability of an orthography for culturally symbolic purposes' (2006:159), placing relative simplicity, or learnability, above other extra-linguistic and linguistic factors that may be considered during orthography development.

6.4   Cognition and Pedagogy

It has been argued previously that learning to read and write has cognitive and psychological advantages for the individual speaker and for the speech community, with mother tongue, or indigenous, literacy being preferable to literacy in a foreign language (Lüpke 2011:319). Many cognitive factors must be taken into account when developing a new orthography for an endangered language, including, crucially, the learnability of the linguistic system represented by the orthography and the differential reading abilities of fluent speakers and second-language learners.

Smalley's (1964) third maximum for orthography development is 'maximum ease of learning' for the speaker in terms of the relative simplicity of the orthography. Grenoble and Whaley (2006:158) note that the orthographer must strike a balance between purely linguistic principles, such as one-symbol-to-one-sound isomorphism, and overall learnability, particularly for languages with large phonemic inventories; it is of utmost importance that newly developed orthographies be easily learned in order to increase the likelihood that they will be used (Sgall 1987:15), given the lack of institutional support in situations of language revitalization. The use of digraphs and diacritics should be carefully considered during orthography development, because these symbols may increase the system's complexity and thus reduce its learnability. Venezky (1970:260) notes that the use of digraphs both increases average word length and introduces ambiguities where the symbols used in a digraph have a single sound value in one word (e.g., go<u>ph</u>er, [f]) but introduces independent values in another (e.g., ha<u>ph</u>azard, [ph]). Sgall (1987: 17–18) offers two useful scales relating to the learnability of an orthography: the scale of complexity, or 'complexness', which provides a hierarchy of learnable graphemic forms; the scale of univocality which classifies graphemes according to their functional distribution.

Sebba (2012b:8) notes that increasing research on the relationship between spelling, phonology, and cognitive processes has led to concern amongst teachers about using the same pedagogical methods for different types of student. Pike's (1947) phonemic principle appears to be incompatible with more recent research on the reading process, because it relies on the following assumptions: '(1) that the reading process involves little more than producing sounds from symbolic stimuli, (2) that human language processing is isomorphic to the descriptions of language which structural linguists produce, that is, proceeds from one discrete level to the next in the order of phonology, morphology, syntax, and semantics, and (3) there is a psychological reality to the phonemic system which [the] linguist derives' (Venezky 1970:264). It seems that following the phonemic principle in orthography development is only advantageous for beginners, who benefit from a close correspondence between graphemes and phonemes. In the context of language revitalization, second-language learners will most likely learn the language alongside its orthography, and in such cases, the orthography should provide them with information on how to pronounce the language they are learning. For fluent speakers, in comparison, conveying phonological information orthographically is less important, because they identify meanings, not sounds, during the reading process (Venezky 1970:260). These meanings are frequently most easily derived by identifying morphemes rather than phonemes or by providing access to still-deeper levels of linguistic structure, such as syntactic information (Sgall 1987:15):

Traditionally, writing has been viewed as a representation of a language's sound sound system. Current research on reading, in contrast, suggests that writing is better viewed as embodying the *entire* linguistic system, meaning that it connects with and represents other parts of the language – such as morphology, syntax, or semantics – and not just the phonology. (Grenoble and Whaley 2006:141, their emphasis)

Thus, second-language learners benefit from shallow orthographies, while fluent speakers are better served by deep ones (cf. Seifart 2006:287). The phonemic or morphophonemic principles may again find themselves in conflict, because, from a practical standpoint, it is much more likely that a single orthography will be developed for use by both fluent speakers and new speakers. For example, Seifart (2006:276) notes that an orthography that represents graphically word-final devoicing would be easier to learn for beginners, indicating pronunciation in the orthography; advanced or fluent readers, in contrast, benefit from a constant word image where morphemes are written consistently, ignoring postlexical morphophonological processes. Fluent or advanced readers rely on what is known as 'sight vocabulary' during the reading process, with written words recognized and processed as entire units, and thus the preservation of morphemic graphic identity is extremely important for these readers (Seifart 2006:282; see Dawson 1989:1). It is not clear, however, how orthographies that facilitate 'sight vocabulary' contribute to the writing (rather than the reading) process for fluent speakers (Seifart 2006:283). The 'lack of exclusiveness' (Sgall 1987:16), with no one-to-one correspondence between graphemes and phonemes, can pose difficulties, even for fluent speakers, when spelling words for which the orthographical word image is not known. Nonetheless, Seifart (2006:283) argues that, since reading is more frequent than writing, the needs of readers are more important than those of writers. In the context of language revitalization, however, second-language learners and partially fluent speakers may make up a substantial part of the speech community, and so their needs must also be taken into account during orthography development.

6.5   Pre-Existing Orthographies

When developing orthographies for endangered languages, the linguist must take account of pre-existing legacy, or traditional, orthographies that have been used to write the language in the past and of the spontaneous writings of the speech community before any literacy training has been provided (Karan 2014:113). In both cases, it will be necessary to establish the socio-cultural and linguistic history of these orthographies, the support that currently exists for such writing systems, and the members of the speech community who make use of these systems (Cahill 2014:15). When legacy orthographies exist, Karan (2014:113) argues that they should be accommodated and that the integration of their conventions, and in particular of highly symbolic graphemes (Lüpke 2011:323), should be considered in the context of new orthography development: 'it may be better to live with an inconsistent orthography – even if inappropriate from a linguistic or psycholinguistic perspective' (Seifart 2006:284). Such integration will help to avoid di- or multi-graphia or the use of multiple orthographies to represent the same language variety, as well as the divisive effects of these situations from an ideological perspective (Lüpke 2011:318). At the very least, transliteration principles should be elaborated to facilitate transfer from any existing knowledge of pre-existing orthographies to the newly developed orthography (Lüpke 2011:323). The development of a new orthography in a context where previous orthographies exist is, in essence, a type of orthographic reform and entails all of the sociopolitical issues involved in such reform. Because of this, Bradley (2005:7) advises that speech communities should never be forced to reform or replace an existing orthography when no consensus to do so has been achieved.

6.6   Practical Concerns

Smalley's (1964) fifth and final maximum requires an orthography to have 'maximum ease of reproduction' in terms of its suitability for use with currently available technological and printing tools (Hinton 2014:146). For this reason, it may be necessary to make concessions on purely linguistic grounds in order for the resultant orthography to be reproduced easily – using, for example, existing keyboards which may be better suited to the language of wider communication (Grenoble and Whaley 2006:138; Seifart 2006:287). The larger the grapheme inventory of a newly developed orthography, the less suitable it is likely to be for use with writing technologies (Lüpke 2011:326). It is essential that non-Unicode characters not be used in newly developed orthographies, given the ever-present and growing use of word processing in writing. Additionally, given the traditional use of endangered languages in informal domains, text messaging is often found to be a predominant context for writing, and so only characters that are replicable on mobile telephones should be used in these contexts (Lüpke 2011:329).

7   Overview of the Volume

This volume considers the various linguistic and extra-linguistic factors involved in the creation of orthographies for endangered languages, debating a variety of themes and issues involved in orthography development: the use of newly developed orthographies in the creation of literacy programmes; the choice of a reference dialect for standardized orthographies; the extent to which newly developed orthographies can alter linguistic behaviour; the attachment of social and/or ideological values to the orthography created, or to elements thereof; the roles of linguists and native speakers in the development of orthographic conventions; the conformity of script and grapheme choices to the will of the speech community; distanciation strategies employed to distinguish an endangered language from the language of wider communication; the transfer of literacy to and from languages of wider communication; the establishment of orthographies as identity markers; the importance of an officially recognized orthography to status planning efforts; the learnability and ease of use of new orthographic conventions; and orthography development in the age of technological advancement.

This volume comprises fifteen chapters, which identify the linguistic and extra-linguistic factors relevant to orthography design in a wide variety of different languages around the world, discussing the application of these factors with particular reference to a rich diversity of contexts and situations of language endangerment. The case studies discussed emphasize the importance of extra-linguistic and socio-cultural factors in the creation of orthographies for endangered languages; no step-by-step guide to orthography development can be offered in purely linguistic terms, due to the (linguistic and social) diversity presented by the contact situations examined.

Chapter 2, by Christopher Moseley, editor of the *UNESCO Atlas of the World's Languages in Danger*, draws on responses to a survey conducted among linguists and missionaries engaged in creating Roman-based orthographies for thirty previously unwritten languages. The survey examines, critically, the dissemination of literacy materials, the transfer of literacy to and from languages of wider communication, the influence of educational traditions inherited from colonial administrations, the role of native-speaker informants, the choice of a reference dialect, ideological distanciation (*ausbau*), and the use of diacritic accents in developing orthographies. This chapter examines the factors that affect the suitability of a language to be used for reading and writing and focuses on the potential use of mobile telephones and handheld tablet devices for 'bridging the gap' between literacy in vernacular languages and those of wider communication.

Chapters 3 to 8 discuss participatory approaches to orthography development whereby native speakers are integrated fully into the decision-making process. These chapters examine tensions between the linguist's mission to achieve maximum representation of speech, maximum ease of use in the newly developed orthography, and the (changing) will of native speakers and community members – whose motivations are often identity based and ideological in nature – with a firm historical and cultural basis. In Chapter 3, Mansueto Casquite and Catherine Young exemplify the numerous advantages of mother-tongue-based, multilingual education (MTB-MLE) in the endangered languages of the southern Philippines, highlighting the ways in which participatory approaches empower and integrate 'local voices' into the decision-making process, ensuring effective orthography development by promoting acceptability and ownership within the speech community. Margarita Valdovinos examines the role of 'mediating actors' in the development of orthographies and the implementation of related language policies in Chapter 4. She reports on the results of community-based orthography workshops for the variety of Náayeri spoken in Jesús María (Mexico) and demonstrates the advantages of providing basic linguistic training to community members to enable them to make informed decisions, based on both linguistic and extra-linguistic factors, during the creation of a new orthography. In Chapter 5, Kathleen Sackett maintains that orthographic decisions are ultimately the community's to make. She discusses in detail the case of the Tsakhur language spoken in Azerbaijan for which the development of a Roman alphabet, similar to that of Azerbaijani, began in 2011 in an effort to facilitate mother-tongue literacy efforts, previously complicated by the use of a Cyrillic script for Tsakhur in the Russian Federation. Sackett underlines the importance of ascertaining community goals in the process of orthography development – such as, for example, promoting linguistic competence among the youngest generation – and advocates deviation from the phonemic principle for reasons of learnability, for ease of reproduction, and to reflect community needs and wishes. In Chapter 6, Sheena Shah and Matthias Brenzinger present the results of an ongoing project which aims to promote effective orthography development for the extremely endangered non-Bantu click language, N|uu, in South Africa. The CALDi project emphasizes the links between scholars and speakers, as well as the effectiveness of these links in reducing this highly complex language to writing; the discussion focuses on issues such as the transfer of literacy to and from Afrikaans and emphasizes the importance of speaker participation during orthography creation, facilitated by community-based workshops. In Chapter 7, Christine Schreyer discusses the reflections of the Kala language community, in Papua New Guinea, on their three-year-old alphabet in order to address the problems and benefits of orthography development for Kala speakers. Schreyer emphasizes the dynamic nature of the orthography development process as well as the need, for the community, to reflect on their orthography and change it when it does not fully meet their needs; focused group discussions, centred around key assessment criteria, are shown to facilitate community ownership and further engagement with the newly developed orthography. Drawing on original data, Kerry Hull examines in Chapter 8 the challenges faced by the Ch'orti' community in Guatemala in adopting and promulgating a newly developed orthography. Hull illustrates the tensions that may arise when a linguist outsider is tasked with aiding the community in their orthography development efforts, concluding that perceived phonetic and linguistic accuracy are secondary to issues of community control, authority, and ownership; ideological distanciation, facilitated by *ausbau*, is shown to be more important than linguistic accuracy.

Chapters 9 to 12 provide cases studies from the United States, Italy, France, and the Channel Islands. The focus in these chapters is on the adequacy of previous attempts to create orthographical conventions for endangered languages spoken in these countries, highlighting the advantages and drawbacks of pre-existing and legacy orthographies from both a linguistic and social perspective. In each of the four chapters, the authors provide recommendations for the future of orthography development in these communities as well as for the contribution of any such development to revitalization efforts; the complex situation presented to the linguist and to the community when a variety of orthographic systems are already in existence can, indeed, hamper current and future revitalization efforts. In Chapter 9, Avelino Corral Esteban reviews the merits of and problems associated with multiple competing orthographies created to represent two related dialects of the Sioux language spoken in the United States. The choice of one of these dialects as the reference dialect for orthography development (a unilectal approach) has caused both linguistic and ideological tensions within the Sioux speech community. This chapter assesses the extent to which each orthography achieves a 'maximum representation of speech' for both dialects considered, discussing in detail salient linguistic issues such as the phonemic principle, functional load, under-representation, and the representation of allophones, before considering non-linguistic factors including the transfer of literacy (to and from English), ideological distanciation, and ease of reproduction. Rosangela Lai considers previous attempts to standardize Sardinian in orthographic form in Chapter 10, focusing explicitly on the recently elaborated *Limba Sarda Comuna* (hereafter, LSC) orthography, which was developed from a top-down perspective without native-speaker participation. Lai provides a detailed examination of the often-conflicting principles employed in the development of LSC and bemoans the inapplicability of a (somewhat covert) unilectal approach to the Sardinian context; the transfer of literacy to and from Italian appears, despite *ausbau* efforts, to be encouraging language shift, at least for some dialectal speakers. In Chapter 11, Steve Hewitt provides a detailed linguistic analysis of the multiple competing orthographies available to write the Breton language, focusing on issues such as the representation of dialectal variation and the social and ideological divide between native and new speakers, before proposing a supradialectal orthography, developed by the author, which lacks many of the inconsistencies present in pre-existing Breton orthographies. Julia Sallabank and Yan Marquis discuss in Chapter 12 the wide range of (unofficial) orthographic conventions available to write Guernsey Norman French, highlighting the inconsistencies between rhetoric and practice; the transfer of literacy to and from both French and English is shown to be bound up in a variety of ideological constructs. Sallabank and Marquis consider the future of Guernsey Norman French to be in the hands of new speakers and learners and thus propose a new, shallow orthography which best fits the needs of these groups while at the same time integrating symbolic and emblematic graphemes from pre-existing writing systems for extra-linguistic reasons.

In Chapter 13, Daniele Viktor Leggio and Yaron Matras consider the merits of a polycentric, speaker-focused, bottom-up codification process facilitated by online social networks in the standardization of orthographic conventions for the Romani diaspora. The dialectal and geographical fragmentation of the Romani speech community has traditionally impeded interdialectal communication, but the language is increasingly being written in various computer-mediated environments. Leggio and Matras demonstrate the way in which Romani speaker interactions create online networks, each characterized by the adoption of the spoken variety of the users, with resultant orthographical conventions which exhibit minimal distanciation from a variety of languages of wider communication that make use of the Roman alphabet.

Bénédicte Pivot and Michel Bert examine in Chapter 14 the role of orthography development and literacy when the goal of reversing language shift is absent. The authors argue that, for so-called 'postvernacular' languages, language revitalization is secondary to the preservation and ideological celebration of the endangered language. For such languages, orthography development and the creation of literacy may raise the status of the postvernacular language by imbuing it with strong symbolic or emblematic values, but tensions between official attempts to revitalize these languages and the community's ideological goals lead the authors to question the need for a standardized orthography in the postvernacular context.

In the final chapter, Chapter 15, Katherine McDonald and Nicolas Zair provide the volume with a novel historical sociolinguistic dimension by examining the way in which the script of Oscan, a language that ceased to be spoken some two thousand years ago, was influenced by pressure from dominant political powers and by language shift at the hands of Latin. This chapter comprises a detailed linguistic analysis of the creation of a new orthography for Oscan using the Roman alphabet and considers a variety of pertinent linguistic and extra-linguistic factors, which are also relevant to orthography creation in the modern day.

This volume emphasizes the importance of integrating linguistic, extra-linguistic, and contextual factors into the process of orthography development for endangered languages in order to provide ailing speech communities with effective writing systems that best fit their needs – writing systems that may act as powerful tools in combatting impending language death.

2 Who Owns Vernacular Literacy? Assessing the Sustainability of Written Vernaculars

Christopher Moseley

1 Introduction

This chapter considers the sustainability of written vernaculars and draws on responses to a survey I conducted among linguists and missionaries engaged in creating Roman-based orthographies for thirty previously unwritten languages. Much has been written about the value of literacy, vernacular or not, for indigenous peoples, but comparatively little has been concerned with the propagation of the written vernacular to a critical mass of self-sustainability. A sustainable vernacular is not necessarily the same as a language emerging from endangerment. A purely oral language is transmissible without being codified, but in the interdependent world of the twenty-first century, only written codification of a language enables it to be sustained to a critical point of viability that can ensure its intergenerational propagation. A prerequisite to literacy is an agreed orthography. This chapter, therefore, asks whether – in the new democratization of literacy that digital technology makes possible – it is necessary to use an orthography that was already agreed in the predigital era or whether spelling can be made up on the spot as required by the individual user. It also surveys the latest developments in making literacy available in more ephemeral digital media through commercial and charitable distribution of handheld devices.

Of the world's endangered languages, many are classified as 'unwritten', as a glance through the compendia – such as *Ethnologue: Languages of the World* (the endangered languages catalogue) or the *UNESCO Atlas of the World's Languages in Danger* – will quickly show. As the general editor of the latter volume, I have been curious since its publication to know whether there is a relationship between being an unwritten language and being an endangered one.

It might be assumed that in the twenty-first century world there cannot be any unwritten, purely spoken languages that are not endangered. Depending on the definition of *endangerment*, that may indeed be true: the printed media are the instruments of power – political, economic, and social – which reach into even the remotest corners of the earth, and a language that is only spoken has only restricted local use. There are definitely still 'uncontacted' languages in the world that must exist as purely spoken media, but even if in a state of equilibrium, these certainly are not in a state of expansion. They are bound to be encroached on. This sense of inevitable encroachment on a pristine linguistic environment is part of what fuels the movement to save threatened languages.

Reversing the coin, can there be languages with a written tradition that are endangered? Of course there can, and there are many examples. Writing is not a guarantee of a language's survival. But it is a guarantee of a language's potential perpetuation: that is, even if it were to die out of use as a spoken medium, there is always the chance that it can be revived on the basis of its written record.

Whether endangered and unwritten or endangered and written, the vast majority of these languages exist in a state of multilingualism. That is, their speakers and writers cannot expect to communicate in the vernacular in all domains of life, and they must therefore expect to use another language in at least some situations.

Before taking over the editorship of the UNESCO atlas, I conducted research into the expectations of speakers of minority languages from their newly created orthographies. I chose a sample of languages, about thirty in all, that could be said to be in transition from unwritten to written, through the agency of outside orthography creators – mostly missionaries working for the Summer Institute of Linguistics, now SIL International (cf. among other chapters, Hull, Schreyer, this volume), but some secular scholars as well. The initial focus of my research was on the factors motivating the choice of graphemes to represent the phonemes of a language. I sent out a questionnaire to the volunteer linguists and got detailed responses from most of them. This chapter presents a selection of the questions and the answers from just one (typical) respondent. A full list of respondents is given in the Appendix.

However, before considering the principles of good orthography development, it is worthwhile considering the factors that affect the viability of a language as a written and read medium.

2 The Theoretical Background: Critical Factors for the Viability of a Written Language

Just because a language has a writing system does not guarantee its future use. There is a substantial literature on the sociolinguistic factors involved in the choice of script (see, for example, Unseth 2008). The prominence of the various factors differs from culture to culture, but as a theoretical starting point, one may expect the following factors to come into play in ascertaining the critical point of viability:

(i) The ratio of numbers of native speakers to those of impinging languages
(ii) The present status of other measurable factors, such as those on Fishman's (1991) Expanded Graded Intergenerational Disruption Scale (hereafter, EGIDS; Lewis and Simons 2010)
(iii) The present status of the orthography in the eyes of the speakers (cf. Casquite and Young, this volume)
(iv) The incorporation of the vernacular into the local education system (cf. Shah and Brenzinger, this volume)

One finding which was repeated strikingly often in the responses to my survey of new written languages was the sense of frustration that written materials in these languages were scanty. In one sense, this was inevitably to be expected: the orthographic systems were mostly new, and there had been little time to develop written materials in them. Yet the frustration was more concerned with the prospects for the future dissemination of the language. Opportunities to test and further develop the orthography with the speakers may or may not have continued, either autonomously or under the guidance of the original orthographer, but in my follow-up questions to the respondents in 2010, four years after the original questionnaire, it became clear that in only a few cases had further dissemination of the written vernacular proceeded.

The responses quoted here are from a pair of linguists – in this case missionaries – working on the Tanna language of Vanuatu. The extent of the answers and the nature of the problems expressed were fairly typical of the responses received. Not all questions are relevant to the topic at issue here, so some of them have been omitted.

First I asked for details about the linguists and their work:

Language(s) on which you are working, its/their location and genetic affiliation:
NWI – SW Tanna, Vanuatu

Reasons for your interest in/commitment to the project:
We want people to know the Lord.

Length of time spent so far with the speech community:
Four years

Nature of your training/academic qualification:
Two years @ SIL school, M.Div.

These responses were typical in that the linguists were missionaries trained in both divinity and linguistics, with some few years' placement in the community already behind them. Their missionary aims are reflected in the later responses in this questionnaire concerning the role of vernacular literacy and the future of the language.

The next section concerned details about the orthography project.

Are you devising a script from scratch, or developing an existing orthography?
There was no existing orthography before we came.

Were the letter values assigned on the basis of nearby languages of literacy with similar phoneme inventories, or on that of a metropolitan or colonial language? (cf. Casquite and Young, this volume)
Both. The metropolitan language uses the English alphabet. We've modified it, and nearby languages use a modified English alphabet.

In each case, I asked the linguists to append a table of the phonemes/distinctive segments of the language they were working on and the letter values assigned to them, as well as those of the language which served as a model for their choices, if there was one.

Were native speakers consulted in devising the script and making the choices? (cf. Casquite and Young, Valdovinos, and Shah and Brenzinger, this volume)
Yes

If so, in what language were they/you already literate?
Some native speakers are literate in Bislama.

Was a range of dialects considered in devising the standard orthography? (cf. Leggio and Matras, Lai, and Hewitt, this volume).
Three dialects within the SW Tanna language, 90% lexical similarity

If so, was one dialect taken as the standard, or is the standard orthography based on a compromise between several varieties?
Based on the dialect of the village in which we live/work

Is a particular variety of the language considered (more) prestigious by both literate and illiterate speakers? On what grounds?
No

In assigning graphemes to phonemes, was transfer to literacy in the majority orthography a major consideration? (cf. Hewitt, this volume)
Yes

In what way did the orthography of any neighbouring or related indigenous language affect your choice of script?
Very much so. Not so much because people in related indigenous language groups will be reading our orthography – that won't be happening very much – but because the four linguists on the island think it's good to have one island-wide orthography.

If the choices of graphemes were made by the speakers or their representatives, can you explain and discuss their motives (especially with regard to sounds/features that are not shared with neighbouring languages)?
  (i) Speakers do not want diacritics (e.g., don't want voiceless nasals represented). (cf. Shah and Brenzinger, Leggio and Matras, Esteban, and Sallabank and Marquis, this volume)
  (ii) They wanted to use some graphemes that were introduced in neighbouring languages by missionaries a hundred years ago. (cf. Shah and Brenzinger, this volume)
  (iii) They do not want double articulation (velarized/palatalized consonants) represented, because they don't particularly hear the sound as /pw/ /mw/ /kw/.

Which phonemes (or distinctions between them) have caused the greatest trouble for you and your native-speaker informants?
The rounded, voiced, palatalized semi-vowel represented as /v/

Is tone a contrastive feature of the language? If so, how is it shown in writing?
No

Is length of consonants/vowels contrastive in the language? If so, how is it shown?
No

Is nasalization or any other suprasegmental feature contrastive in the language? If so, how is it shown?
No

The nature of the responses was very uniform in some respects. The Roman alphabet was universally used as the basis of the script (cf. Sackett, this volume). Native speakers were generally consulted as to choice of graphemes, and the influences on their choices came primarily from adjacent languages (multilingualism being the norm), secondarily from metropolitan languages used in the education system. Graduation to majority-language literacy from the vernacular seemed almost axiomatic.

The questionnaire went on to elicit details about the speakers of the language:

How many speakers of the language are there?
3,001

Is the number of speakers in decline, stable, or growing?
Growing

How are the speakers distributed? Rural/urban?
100% rural

What other languages are used by the speakers?
Bislama, Whitesands (Tanna)

In what settings?
When talking to foreigners, people from other islands, or people from other languages on the island

What is the political situation in the speakers' territory?
More or less stable parliamentary democracy

How does it affect your own work?
Having a stable democracy is a contributing factor to the overall feeling of peace and happiness in our setting.

List the contact languages with other communities and their status as perceived by these speakers.
Bislama is the trade language; it is not a high-status language. English would be a high-status language. The vernacular is seen as 'the most difficult language', and as a 'bush' language, but does not have a low status by the speakers.

Is the language publicly devalued or actively discouraged by national/local authorities?
It is encouraged at the national/local level. But virtually all educational materials are in English. The government encourages development of vernacular educational materials – but the whole education system is based on knowing English.

If so, in contrast to what language(s) of greater prestige?
English

What was typical about these responses was that the population was rural, multilingual, and reliant on a metropolitan language for dealings with the wider world. Absolute numbers of speakers varied greatly across the questionnaire responses.

The next set of questions elicited details about the speech community and its attitudes:

What value do the native speakers see in literacy?
Little. Being able to read the Bible.

What value do the speakers see in their language itself, and in vernacular literacy?
Great value – most people over 40 only speak the vernacular. They are aware that maintaining their language will maintain their culture.

Is there an organized literacy campaign for both adults and children?
Yes

If so, is it initially conducted in the majority language?
No

How do children learn to read, and in what language?
In English, at school

Does regular, organized formal education exist for the speakers? For what age range?
There are two primary schools in our language group. Grade 1–6 [6–11 years of age].

Who runs the local schools?
Government. There is another primary school run by the Assemblies of God.

How are the teachers of vernacular/majority literacy qualified? Are they native speakers?
Some are native speakers. Some are trained at a teachers college. Some are not.

What is the initial language of literacy acquisition?
One school is Francophone, one is Anglophone.

What is the language of instruction?
Vernacular

How far is the language expected to carry them through formal schooling?
Vernacular literacy can only take a person through second grade. After that, English literacy is expected through high school.

How do adults learn to read, and in what language?
They don't.

Who runs adult literacy classes?
Nobody

Once literate, what reading opportunities exist for children, and for adults?
School. Bislama Bible. Vernacular materials printed by us. Scripture portions in the vernacular, and primers.

How long has literacy training existed for this community?
In the vernacular: three years. In English/French: seventy-five years.

Vernacular literacy was seen as being of limited value – unsurprising considering the response that literacy training in the vernacular had existed for three years, compared with seventy-five years of metropolitan literacy experience. In view of the fact that the vernacular was a thriving spoken medium, the skill of reading seemed to be held in quite low esteem. The missionaries may well have affected the speakers' attitude to vernacular literacy – that it is a means of reading Scripture – but they are not the first missionaries to this community, and the speakers may already have restricted literacy to this limited function in their lives. While it might be expected that an orthography might alter linguistic behaviour in some speech communities, in this one the scope for its use was seen as limited by both the orthographer and the community of users.

The questionnaire then elicited details about dissemination of the language:

Through what media would you, and the speakers, expect to see their writing done? (Handwriting, typing, computers?)
In the vernacular – by the Bible translation project, on the computer. In Bislama – the local speakers hand-write an occasional piece.

What printing facilities exist for the language?
My printer

What distribution facilities exist for reading material in the language?
Bible portion dedication ceremonies, workshops

Have reading materials already been prepared in the language? If so, what kind, and how are they distributed?
Yes. Primers, New Testament portions, shell books.

What recommendations would you make for fostering literacy in the orthography on which you have worked?
Primers, workshops, materials for the primary schools.

What is your own view of the future for this speech community and its language?
Language maintenance for at least 50 years. Low literacy in the vernacular.

What value do you yourself place on the speakers' literacy?
High

These answers reveal the limited scope for printing and dissemination, and also the limited domains of literate activity expected of this language, now and in the future. Literacy as a secular activity – reading and writing over a wider range of domains – is not considered a realistic possibility. This is not merely a reflection of the missionaries' attitude, however; this speech community was multilingual and already assuming that the function of the written language is largely religious.

Summarizing the responses more generally, it can be noted that missionaries and lay orthographers, in making their choices of graphemes, were restricted in the range of options by a number of factors, including:
(i) The (colonial or ex-colonial) language of primary school instruction and previous literacy (cf. Shah and Brenzinger, this volume)
(ii) Government prescriptions and proscriptions in the country in question

(iii) Some transcontinental or regional recommended standards for orthography creation which are cited in the responses – such as the 'Cameroon national alphabet' in that country, for example
(iv) The speech community's overt desire to be different from its neighbours (cf. Hull, Leggio and Matras, and Lai, this volume)
(v) The individual linguist's own preferences
(vi) The availability of writing materials, printing equipment, and computer keyboards (cf. Sackett, this volume)

3   Literacy in a Changing Reading Environment

Much has been written about the value of literacy for indigenous peoples, vernacular or not, in the work of Brian Street (Street 1984) and Barton (1994), but comparatively little of this has been concerned with the propagation of the written vernacular to a point of a critical mass of self-sustainability. The ownership of a sustainable vernacular is not necessarily the same as a language emerging from endangerment, for reasons which I hope will become clear in the following discussion; the two concepts are related but not identical. A purely oral language is perfectly transmissible without being codified in writing – thousands of generations of human linguistic history are proof enough of this. But under the political and economic pressure of the increasingly interdependent world of the twenty-first century, only the written codification of a language to enable it to be sustained to a critical point of viability can ensure its intergenerational propagation. Recall from earlier discussion that the following factors come into play in ascertaining just what this critical point of viability is:

(i) The ratio of numbers of native speakers to those of impinging languages, both indigenous and imported/national/official
(ii) The present status of other measurable factors on an objective scale of measurement, such as Fishman's EGIDS
(iii) The present status of the orthography in the eyes of the speakers (which is qualitatively different from its efficiency as a linguistic tool, and is more concerned with its perceived status as distinct from, or similar to, that of other languages of literacy)
(iv) The incorporation of the vernacular into the local education system

All this assumes that the unwritten language needs to be codified in writing at all. Among languages of North America and Australia which are at a critically endangered stage, there may be resistance by the owners of the language to perceived interference by outsiders attempting to standardize and codify the language by committing it to writing and using it in the education system. Boynton (2014) has argued persuasively for caution in assuming the need to create a writing system, on the basis of her work among Wangkatha speakers in Western Australia.[1]

Recently it has become clearer than ever that literacy does not involve mere book-reading and letter-writing; there are new and ephemeral written media to consider. The spread of electronic media and the widespread availability of cheap mobile telephones means that instant, ephemeral written or typed communication is no longer the sole prerogative of the First World or the Second World but even of the small communities in multilingual societies with weak local infrastructure, a restriction from which they can break free. And this has implications which have not been fully understood yet for literacy in small languages.

The presence of small or recently written languages in digital social media communications is at the moment dispiritingly small, from the point of view of diversity. Just how small that presence currently is becomes clear from the publicity for Worldreader services reported in May 2014:

> A new report by UNESCO says that mobile devices can boost literacy rates in developing countries, potentially reaching almost all of the world's population. Furthermore, an expensive tablet or smartphone is not necessary. In fact, many e-book readers use featurephones.
> The report surveyed 5,000 people in Ethiopia, Ghana, India, Kenya, Nigeria, Pakistan, and Zimbabwe. 'In places where physical books are scarce, mobile phones are plentiful' [...] But there is still a lack of interesting content available and 60% of respondents said they consider that a barrier to reading on mobile devices. Popular genres, based on clicks per menu item on Worldreader[2] Mobile, are romance, followed by books about religion. The most popular search terms were 'Harry Potter', 'Romeo and Juliet', 'Animal Farm', and 'Twilight'.

The astonishing thing about this Worldreader/UNESCO project is that the announcement does not mention 'language' at all. The implication from the results of the survey is that the reading on mobile devices is being done either in the original metropolitan language or a translation into another majority language from that metropolitan language, thus further enhancing the lopsided split between literacy in majority languages and true vernacular literacy. Since UNESCO was cited as the source of the report, its multilingual credentials would surely be unimpeachable. Yet, sources that were originally written in English were cited as the most popular. I inquired further and got a reply from Tanja Commike of the Worldreader project:

> To answer your questions, I would say that our library is representative not only of what local publishers offer us but of what our schools (teachers and project managers) request – most of our schools teach primarily in English. That said, we understand and really believe in the importance of literacy efforts delivered in mother tongue and so, when we had trouble acquiring high quality content in mother tongue, we proactively went out and translated a series of 30 leveled readers into 11 languages and sought

out – through a considerable amount of investigation – a couple hundred existing leveled readers. In fact, a great deal of our efforts last year were dedicated to ensuring we had content across many languages, particularly early reading content.

We're also working hard on making our mobile application accessible to non-English speakers. Right now there's a section that allows users to read in other languages and all the writing under our icons can be auto translated into other languages. However, the cost of fully optimizing our app for all languages (auto translation can be tricky – we've optimized for Swahili only so far as I know) has proved quite costly and labor intensive, as we also need to acquire a critical mass of books across genres in one language before doing this. It's something we're pursuing, really want to deliver on but can't immediately fulfill, so please bear with us.

According to the report, the five thousand people surveyed all lived in multilingual countries: Ethiopia, Ghana, India, Kenya, Nigeria, Pakistan, and Zimbabwe. All except the first of these are or have been members of the Commonwealth and thus carry an Anglophone educational heritage. This Worldreader venture, then, at least in its initial phase, serves to drive a further wedge between the metropolitan and the vernacular, in terms of literacy.

The difference between the telephone as a speaking/listening device and as a reading/writing device, if it were made explicit here, might reveal some interesting dichotomies. The Worldreader project is of course concerned with reading and literacy. But even transferred into a digital medium, these are still books, and literacy involves much more than book-reading. Can there be other interests at work that wish to encourage vernacular literacy through electronic media? Recently, I became aware of the work of one particular charity, Feed the Minds, which is a charitable organization based in London and dedicated to literacy in its more basic sense: training people to protect their interests through being able to read and write. It makes no overt mention of language on its website, www.feedtheminds.org (last accessed 3 November 2015).

Social media and the use of electronic texting appear to be eradicating the stigma attached to the written use of endangered or 'shame-ridden' languages. Maybe that is because their use in this medium is ephemeral and private, directed at an audience that shares the language, and therefore not seeking any official sanction. But it will imply an agreed orthography. A distinguishing feature of literacy is an ability to handle an agreed spelling system, even if in texting one might deviate from it.

I mention this issue as an illustration of the control of the paths to literacy. If the manufacturers of software and of mobile devices, at the top end of the consumption chain, cannot perceive the linguistic needs of the consumers who speak small vernaculars at the bottom end, then what hope is there for those small vernaculars? On the other hand, in a market-driven economy, who should question the demands of the consumer? Doesn't it behove the linguist to concentrate on the bottom end and try to find out where the communications consumers demand come from?

Literacy learning is inevitably part of an educational process – either for children or for adults, either in a metropolitan or a regional language or in the home vernacular. It is the common experience in multilingual societies for children to accept, early in life, that there is a hierarchy of languages in their lives and a set of domains for each. If vernacular literacy training is to be a part of a national education system, this is a major headache for the authorities in a multilingual state. The more languages have to be provided for within a single state, the thinner will be the spread of available resources – and the fewer the materials available in each individual language. Lack of variety in materials is in itself a factor in a language's chances of survival.

To take an example of a multilingual state which tries to provide for its written vernaculars, let us consider Mexico. Norbert Francis and John Reyhner (2002) dealt with this issue in a study they called 'Biliteracy: Teaching and Writing in the Indigenous Language'. Before any materials could be prepared in any language (and – particularly important in the case of Mexico – the chain of dialects and varieties), two important principles had to be established, and I quote:

(i) Alphabets and other word-processing technologies correspond to the practical, classroom settings where children, who actually speak the language, will be learning how to read and write. Practical alphabets are to be designed that avoid unnecessary graphic complexity.
(ii) Every attempt should be made to unify criteria among different dialects of each language to arrive at common spelling patterns.

The authors go on to describe the contents of a typical first-grade primer in any indigenous Mexican language, with the visual prompts of illustrations of familiar items from the reader's life to enhance learning of spelling conventions and morphological detail. Such an approach on a national scale is rare in today's world.

What kind of approach can be applied in Australia, where nearly all surviving indigenous languages are in a moribund state? In their paper 'Literature for the Semi-Literate: Issues for Emerging Literacies in the Kimberley Region of North-Western Australia', Joseph Blythe and Frances Kofod point out that:

The primary issue for emerging literacies of the Kimberley region of North-western Australia is that the would-be speech community consist of largely illiterate older language speakers and younger (semi-) literature groups who only partially know the languages in question. The challenge in producing literature and literacy materials lies in deciding who should be the target audience and how to target them. Ultimately the perception of the target audience dictates the format of most emerging language materials.

Among the semi-speakers of some Australian vernaculars, including the Kimberley languages, 'ownership' of a language is a very real issue. When work to produce a dictionary in collaboration between linguists and speakers had been going on for a long time:

Regular meetings discussing the publication had taken place but members of the community council in the area only realized close to completion of the project that publication would mean that anyone anywhere would be able to access the information. There was concern that people might use it without referring to the speakers and language owners. There was also concern that white people, because of their superior skills in reading and writing (a 'whitefella technology') would be able to learn the language more quickly than descendants of the speakers, the true language owners and that local businesses might pick out a few words to use in their business names and paying lip service to the original country owners without consulting them, thus continuing the marginalization of the people whose land and livelihood has been stolen. They are correct in feeling dispossessed and marginalized but in this region of the Kimberley very little tourist information even mentions the original Aboriginal inhabitants so any acknowledgment is probably better than none. Publication of the dictionary was banned. There is one print out which is only referred to in very limited contexts. The linguist involved feels that until the policy changes the work of many years is wasted.

For users of endangered and minority languages in an age of mass communications, the results of either an educational tradition inherited from a colonial administration or feudalism in a multilingual state where one ethnic group has the ascendancy can be very similar. Take the apparently contrasting cases of Nepal and Mozambique, two outwardly very different countries. In the case of Nepal:

It was not until 1950 that the country was opened to outside influence and the beginning of the breakdown of the feudal system. At the beginning of this era, the language of the Bahun elite, Khas or Nepali, was standardized with dictionaries, grammars published. School materials were created in Nepali. In 1951, the literacy rate was less than two percent and there was no means nor tradition for any form of political participation. It was felt for four decades that Nepali was needed to unify the country. (Morgan and Gurung 2002)

The need for one language to unify the nation was the educational philosophy of the times. For example, in Mozambique, Portuguese was chosen to unify the country even though it was the colonial language and was not spoken by the majority of the people. In 1978, it was still believed that rapid economic and social development would be possible, and for this it was essential to teach literacy rapidly and massively. Portuguese seemed to be the rapid and economic solution. Apart from this, twenty years ago the paradigm of 'One Language, One Nation' – from the days of the French Revolution – held sway. The Mozambique Liberation Front, the liberation movement that succeeded in uniting the people in the struggle for national independence and then set itself up as the Frelimo Party, had, as one of its priorities, the consolidation of national unity and believed that to achieve this the promotion of a common language was indispensable. The same story broadly applies to English in neighbouring Zimbabwe. Linguistic colonialism is too big an issue to go into here, except insofar as it impinges on vernacular literacy. It goes a long way to explaining the kind of reading material that is now available in postcolonial nations. National unity takes precedence over the presence of the vernacular in countries whose boundaries were drawn up by outsiders.

An expatriate trained linguist who is working with an indigenous community to create literacy is usually there for a fixed amount of time, and when that time is over, if there is no established momentum of independent life, then the vernacular is a fragile plant that might disappear back among the linguistic undergrowth. Mary Raymond, who worked with adults and children among the Arop and Karnai peoples of Papua New Guinea, was aware of this when she wrote, in 2007:

An expatriate linguist's commitment to working on a particular language, and to literacy work in that language, usually has an endpoint, whether in the long or short term. As in the Karnai case, a follow-up programme to a literacy event is not always possible. I do not believe that this negates the value of running short term literacy initiatives, where these can be self-contained and produce a concrete end result in and of themselves. Teaching basic literacy skills to children probably does not fall into this category, but working with already literate adults on transfer of literacy skills to the indigenous language is a more achievable short term project, particularly with the concrete goal of producing texts both for documentary purposes and for community use. The ultimate goal of any literacy programme instituted by an expatriate linguist, however, is that the programme will eventually gain sufficient momentum in the hands of the community that it can continue long term without outside assistance; whether this is achievable depends very much on the community itself, and on how successfully the community and the linguist have been able to work together to prepare for this outcome.

Indigenous literacy movements can sometimes be emblems of the difference, the distinctiveness, of one speech community from another. The exclusivity can be enhanced by the creation of a unique script. One example of this is N'ko, in West Africa, created by the self-taught Guinean trader Souleymane Kante in 1949 to transcribe the Maninka language, but which has spread to other Niger-Congo languages.

The N'ko script was developed during the French colonial period in West Africa. French rule resulted not only in the spread of French political control but also in what Phillipson (1992) calls 'linguistic imperialism'. This ideology was integral to the colonial order, which vaunted French language and civilization while marginalizing indigenous languages and cultures. As Suret-Canale (1971:382) noted, 'under the French system, there was no serious and systematic study of African linguistics, nor was there any printed literature in the local languages nor was there any system of transcription [...] this system was to favour political awakening of the African peoples, and finally boomerang upon its initiators'. French language learning became the cornerstone of French colonial primary education and its *mission civilisatrice* (or 'mission to civilize') African subjects. The French colonial government's 'Report of Education' at the 1944 French Africa Conference in Brazzaville forbade the use of local vernaculars in both private and public schools in French African colonies. Manning (1988) notes that colonial language policy had dramatic effects on local language literacy. In West African language communities split by colonial boundaries, residents in British colonies learned to transcribe their languages, while neighbouring French subjects remained illiterate in their native languages. The small segment of the population selected to attend French colonial schools learned literacy skills necessary for colonial administration and communication with Paris. The vast majority of the population was left on its own to develop literacy skills adapted to indigenous languages and cultures.

The Spanish colonial legacy to education and literacy was similar to that of the French. Thus one finds situations throughout Hispanic America in which Spanish is the only medium of instruction until recent decades or even to the present, and 'grassroots' literacy movements are slow to take root. Take the Shipibo people of Peru, for example. Fifty years ago, although the language had been recently written, there were no reasonable opportunities for monolingual Shipibo speakers to learn to read. The few schools in existence in the region were monolingual in Spanish, a language understood by only a handful of Shipibo people (Tacelosky 2000). According to data from the Peruvian ministry of education in 2013, however, the situation had changed: there were 56 bilingual intercultural Shipibo schools, including secondary, and only 27 per cent of the population was illiterate.

Economic factors have to be considered too. Literacy material for small languages can be expensive to print and uneconomic to distribute to small populations. Consider the case of Rotuman, an outlier language of Fiji. As Vamarasi (2008) writes:

Rotuman is an Eastern Oceanic language of Rotuma, an outlier island of the Fiji Islands. The Rotuman language has approximately 9,000 speakers, only 2,500 of whom live on Rotuma. The history of literacy in the language is an interesting one. At one time Methodists and Roman Catholics wrote all lexical words differently, the former writing them only in the 'long' form, the latter writing them only in the 'short' form. Maxwell Churchward brought an end to that chaos in 1928 with his orthography, in which words are written as they are spoken, long or short. All education on the island after grade 3 [8 to 9 years' old] is in English, though Rotuman is the exclusive language of the home and church. The literacy rate is high, perhaps near 85%. One of the main threats to the language is the fact that, apart from a recently completed Rotuman Bible, there is virtually no written material in Rotuman.

In spite of its long written tradition, then, Rotuman remains an oral language.

But what happens to a politically powerless, non-metropolitan, but widely spoken language where a colonial administration imposed from Europe is overlaid on a regional cultural and religious tradition which is much older but also ethnically alien? Such a situation exists in North Africa with the Berber languages generally, and with the Tuareg language specifically. Tuareg is one of the Berber languages that run across North Africa. It has remained, however, the most pure of these Berber languages, containing relatively few French and Arabic loan words. The three main dialects are Tamahaq, Tamasheq, and Tamajeq, which correspond roughly to the three political divisions – Algeria, Mali, and Niger. First, there is the influence of the French. Algeria, Mali, and Niger were all French colonies from the late nineteenth century up until independence in 1960. The French culture and civilization brought the French language, written in Roman script, as the language of official power. The French culture and period of colonization had, and still exert, an important influence on the people. Second, there is the influence of the Arab culture, which is largely limited to Algeria but is also found to a lesser extent in the north of Mali and Niger. Islam brought its own script, and Arab culture and the Arabic script are inseparably linked. As Suleiman (2003:33) observed, 'the Arabic script still functions... to create a community out of signs not sounds [...] with respect to the Islamic culture.' Third, there is the traditional Tuareg culture itself, closely tied to a script. For more than one thousand years, the Tuareg have had their own script, called Tifinagh (or Shifinagh in the Niger dialects). The Tuareg culture and language are intrinsically linked with Tifinagh. It can be written left to right, right to left, top to bottom, or bottom to top, with corresponding changes of orientation to the letter shapes. It is a script whose origin traces back to the Phoenician script (O'Connor 1996:113). Interestingly enough, even though the Tuaregs have long had this script, it has traditionally been used very little – documented for 'love letters, family notes, and domestic ornamentation' (O'Connor 1996:115), as well as for branding camel, decorating leather objects, and inscribing 'incantational phrases' on tent posts and ridgepoles (Prussin 1995:92, 97). It functions, therefore, as a writing system in a very limited sense. This has given rise to the Tuareg people being labelled as the only oral culture in the world possessing its own script. Savage (2008) comments:

By virtue of association with the language of the Koran, the Arabic script has strong symbolic religious and sacred value, and the Roman script has high prestige associated with its 'utility' in the outside world. The Tuareg language, however, is relegated to the lower status of domestic usage, and the Tifinagh script, for writing personal letters and owners' names on objects. This explains why some Tuaregs (in particular the youth) see little point in exerting themselves to learn to read and write their own language – they see no practical application, whereas the promise associated with mastering literacy in French (for the sub-Saharans) and Arabic (for the Algerians) is very attractive. These youth represent a growing minority who are willing to forego their attachment to the past, identifying themselves with other cultures and languages (and scripts) for the promise of a better future, and are a source of tension with the majority of Tuareg people who do maintain a strong sense of identity.

4 Conclusion

Nation-states which are multilingual face the dual challenge of forging national unity through a single-language policy and addressing the pressure from minorities for the recognition of their languages. Despite national policies – which may be the result of colonial policies or reactions against them – and however liberal these may be towards endangered languages, new technologies for the acquisition of literacy pose a challenge to the future of small vernaculars that is still little understood.

Appendix

Following is the list of respondents to the questionnaire and the languages concerned.

    Ken and Mendy Nehrbass (Tanna, Vanuatu)
    Kevin L. Walters (Dazaga, Niger)
    Elizabeth and Thomas Willett (Southern Tepehuán, Mexico)
    Hope Hurlbut (Labuk-Kinabatangan Kadazan, Sabah, Malaysia)
    Valerie and Nicasio Martínez (San Pedro Quiatoni Zapotec, Oaxaca, Mexico)
    Martin Paviour-Smith (Aulua, Malakula, Vanuatu)
    Leila Schroeder (Tharaka and other Bantu languages, Lake Victoria, Tanzania)
    Phil and Chris Carr (Bamu, Papua New Guinea)
    Mark Miller (West Coast Bajau, Sabah, Malaysia)
    René van den Berg (Muna, Sulawesi, Indonesia)
    Mary Pearce (Kera, southern Chad)
    David Foris (Sochiapan Chinantec, Mexico)
    Naomi Nagy (Faetar, Apulia, Italy)
    Richard Nzogi (Lugwere, Uganda)
    Michael Cahill (Konni, northern Ghana)
    Robert Papen (Michif, Western Canada and North Dakota, French/Cree mixed language)

Mark Van de Velde (Eton, Cameroon)
Steve Parker (Chamicuro, formerly spoken in Peru, and Panobo, Peru)
Charles A. Mortensen (Northern Emberá, Panama/Colombia)
Ken Decker (Belize Kriol)
Paul and Barbara Thomas (Komo, Bantu, Democratic Republic of the Congo)
Soini and Kaija Olkkonen [Somba Siawari (Burum-Mindik), Borong (Kosorong), Mabe (Mape), Papua New Guinea]
Ginger Boyd [Central Yambassa, comprising Nulibie, Numaala, Nuasue (Yangben), and Bantu, Central Cameroon]
Terry Schram (Mazatec of Jalapa de Díaz, Oaxaca, Mexico)
David Riggs (Zapotec Amatlán, Oaxaca, Mexico)
Steve Quakenbush (Agutaynen, Palawan, Philippines)
Doug Trick (Sama Southern, Tawi-Tawi Province, Philippines)
David Mead (Mori Bawah, Celebes, Indonesia)
Grace Tan, Marilina Vega, and Willy Vega (five languages of Sarawak)
Thomas Saunders (five languages of the Kimberley region, Western Australia)

Notes

1. Press release by Worldreader, May 2014 (www.worldreader.org; last accessed 19 June 2015).
2. Worldreader was founded in 2010 by David Risher, a former executive at Microsoft and Amazon, and Colin McElwee, a former marketing director at Barcelona's ESADE Business School. A major goal was to provide more than one million mobile users with access to free e-books by the end of 2015.

3 Hearing Local Voices, Creating Local Content: Participatory Approaches in Orthography Development for Non-Dominant Language Communities

Mansueto Casquite and Catherine Young

1   Introduction

Progress towards the Millennium Development Goals (hereafter, MDGs) advanced unequally, with even the most low-level development goals failing to impact minority ethnolinguistic communities – as evidenced by the number of out-of-school children and those who attend schools where instruction is delivered in a language that the learners do not speak (Pinnock 2009a:26; Heugh and Skutnabb-Kangas 2010:3).

The Sustainable Development Goals (2016) continue to attempt to address inequities in education design and delivery, particularly through the indicators listed in the targets associated with Goal 4. However, language and culture continue to be critical issues around access and delivery of quality education, issues that are increasingly part of the educational discourse but, unfortunately, have not adequately impacted classroom practice (UNESCO 2000:17; Pinnock 2009a:26; Heugh and Skutnabb-Kangas 2010:6; Pinnock et al. 2011:7). The inclusion of local languages in the design of the school curriculum can be transformational, empowering learners from ethnolinguistic communities, which are often excluded from access to quality basic education.

2   Endangered Languages and Local Language Education

Fishman (1991:87–111) describes an eight-stage Graded Intergenerational Disruption Scale (hereafter, GIDS) that depicts language use and a minority language's 'private and public functions' (May 2001:2; Baker 2011:5; cf. Moseley, this volume). Communities and other agencies can use information elicited from the criteria of this scale to assess the linguistic vitality of a particular endangered language where the higher the number on the scale, the greater the degree of threat to the language continuing to the next generation.

Stage 8	Social isolation of the few remaining speakers of the minority language. Need to record the language for later possible reconstruction.
Stage 7	Minority language used by older and not younger generation. Need to multiply the language in the younger generation.
Stage 6	Minority language is passed on from generation to generation and is used in the community. Need to support the family in intergenerational continuity (e.g., provision of minority language nursery schools).
Stage 5	Literacy in the minority language. Need to support literacy movements in the minority language, particularly when there is no government support.
Stage 4	Formal, compulsory education available in the minority language. May need to be financially supported by the minority language community.
Stage 3	Use of the minority language in less-specialized work areas involving interaction with majority language speakers.
Stage 2	Lower government services and mass media available in the minority language.
Stage 1	Some use of the minority language available in higher education, central government and the national media.

Figure 3.1 Fishman's Graded Intergenerational Disruption Scale for threatened languages (1991:87–111).

Information within the scale indicates the conditions that need to be in place in order for a language to be passed on from one generation to the next; Fishman gives helpful direction in planning appropriate educational interventions for endangered language communities that may contribute to re-establishing a dying language. The key indicators in this scale (summarized in Figure 3.1, adapted from Baker 2011:60) determine whether languages are being passed on intergenerationally. Suggestions for actions and activities that would contribute to the reversal of language shift are given in stages 4 to 8 of the scale.

Fishman's GIDS has provided theoretical underpinning for the actions of most practitioners of language revitalization. Lewis and Simons (2010) reviewed such evaluative systems and attempted to align them to form an elaborated evaluative scale of thirteen levels, a system which is also used by the *Ethnologue: Languages of the World* (Lewis, Simons, and Fennig 2015) to categorize language vitality. Using this expanded system, a language can be evaluated by answering five questions regarding 'the identity function, vehicularity, state of intergenerational language transmission, literacy acquisition status, and a societal profile of generational language use' (Lewis and Simons 2010:120). These frameworks and evaluative systems provide an analytical approach to describe language vitality and aid the identification of the actions that may be helpful in order for a language to move to greater vitality; in each, educational provision in the language of the child is a key indicator of linguistic vigour. Minority ethnolinguistic communities that are potentially endangered may not realize that access to education in their mother tongue is a human right that is within statutes that many countries have enacted. It is then important to assess ways in which teachers and other educators can be effective advocates for learners from ethnic minority communities and support them in the development of education, beginning in their mother tongue.

Crystal (2000:127–166) suggests several steps to be taken to protect languages from extinction and to raise the prestige and use of language among those who are speakers of the language. These steps include developing ways through which mother-tongue speakers of minority languages can increasingly become aware of their legitimate power in the eyes of the dominant language community, including gaining an awareness of international legislation. Through application of effective strategies for multilingual education, education can become a celebration of ethnolinguistic richness and diversity, providing participants with the skills, knowledge, and values for participation in the global international community and retention of their own languages and culture. This can produce an integration and inclusion of individuals and communities that previously have been isolated and marginalized. Formal and non-formal education perform a powerful social role in the lives of children, and thus education systems and policy formulation impact language maintenance and revitalization.

3   Orthography Development for Literacy and Education

In multilingual contexts, fully developed, dominant languages can be a means of oppression of local and non-dominant languages when national and official languages take the centre stage, at the expense of smaller or more-localized languages. Schaeffer notes that 'Ethno-linguistic minorities or even majorities are kept out of the mainstream of their nation's social, economic, and political life and institutions, and how these excluded people are let into that mainstream life – if at all – only once they leave behind their ethnic and linguistic identity and take on the language and culture of the dominant society, a society usually larger in numbers, richer, and more politically powerful' (cited in Kosonen and Benson 2013:ix). Despite the prevalence of multilingualism in most nation-states of the world, the languages that are used in education are most often national and international languages, based on the 'long-standing fallacy' (Benson and Kosonen 2013:2) that unity is built around a single language. Kosonen and Benson continue: 'Using one language and excluding many others actually creates divisions, inequalities and inequities, because it means that hundreds of millions of people worldwide are forced to learn – or teach – through a language in which they are not proficient.'

However, research demonstrates that literacy and education programmes – both formal and non-formal – that have significant and sustained results are those that have a thorough and thoughtful incorporation of the languages with which the learner is familiar, building on a foundation of the learner's home language and culture (Alidou et al. 2006; Benson 2004; Heugh 2002, 2005a, 2005b; Pinnock 2009a, 2009b; Ramírez et al. 1991; Thomas and Collier 2002; UNESCO 2006, 2007a; Walter and Dekker 2008; Walter and Chuo 2012). Case studies documenting evidence of such approaches in Asia have been produced, demonstrating that 'Minority language students enjoy more success in school if they develop literacy skills in their mother tongue early in their education' (UNESCO 2007b; see also UNESCO 2007c).

When content instruction (for example, science, environmental studies, or mathematics) is provided in a language that students understand, learning is not dependent on mastery of a second language. Similarly, when the language of the classroom is the language of the learner, teachers and students can communicate naturally and teachers can easily adapt content to the needs and competence level of the learners. A pedagogical advantage of mother-tongue-based multilingual education is the use of the learner's first language to teach beginning reading and writing, building both greater awareness of phonic components of the text and comprehension. Thus, research also demonstrates the effectiveness of cross-linguistic transfer of reading and writing skills, particularly when it takes place from the first language to a second language (Zaretsky and Schwarz 2014; Hipfner-Boucher, Lam, and Chen 2014).

A basic component in such educational design and delivery is a wide variety of appropriate instructional materials written in the local languages of learners and reflecting their cultural context and life experiences – validating learners' cultural identity and valuing their linguistic heritage – ideally alongside systematic corpus planning to integrate the uses of the local language into the community to support lifelong learning.

Grinevald (1998:139) emphasizes the necessity of considering corpus and status planning as mutually contributing to language revitalization, particularly in the context of endangered languages:

Corpus planning (standardization of orthography, lexicon and grammar, production of pedagogical materials) without status planning (creation of opportunities for public and official use of the language in all spheres of political and economic life) will not ensure the maintenance of a language. The decline in the vitality of a language is linked to the pervasive negative socioeconomic incentives and the rampant social discrimination that speakers of indigenous languages have to endure.

Thus, a thoughtful and careful choice of writing system is needed to support effective delivery of local language education for both children and adults, where the orthography is appreciated and accepted, primarily, by the speakers of the language and, ideally, by civil society and government institutions responsible for educational delivery (cf. Moseley, this volume).

Such acceptance, as described by Crystal, is most often promoted when speakers of the language are key participants in a decision-making process (cf. Valdovinos, this volume). In fact, Rice and Cahill (2014:3) note that 'the days when an outside linguist unilaterally establishes an orthography are fading, at least in many areas of the world' (cf. Shah and Brenzinger, and Valdovinos, this volume). Karan (2014) describes two case studies – including one from the Tagakaulu Kalagan community of the Philippines – which illustrate that 'The ideas of a linguist, a consultant, a committee or a government do not necessarily line up with the desires of the people and that sometimes bad decisions are made'. Thus, language communities and other stakeholders embarking on mother-tongue-based multilingual education initiatives must collaborate to establish a writing system that accurately represents the phonological components of the language, support education in the local language and, often, also support the transfer of literacy skills from the first language to the second language (UNESCO 2007a:187) and then to additional languages (cf. Moseley, this volume). Undoubtedly, developing an orthography is a complex process, involving an understanding of:

(i) The social context
(ii) What the community wants
(iii) How the community makes decisions
(iv) How different dialects are perceived
(v) How other languages used by the community are written
(vi) Political factors (e.g., government requirements) (cf. Sackett, this volume)

With consideration to each of these factors, Smalley (1964) has suggested five central principles for designing an effective orthography that have become known as 'Smalley's maximums' (cf. also Sackett, and Esteban, this volume). These include:

(i) Maximum acceptability – through the involvement of a representative group of community participants in decision making, promoting ownership (cf. Shah and Brenzinger, and Schreyer, this volume)
(ii) Maximum ease of learning – a writing system that will be easy to read, both for new readers and those who can already read in another language (cf. Shah and Brenzinger, Schreyer, and Lai, this volume)
(iii) Maximum representation – an orthography that accurately represents the linguistic components of a language (cf. Shah and Brenzinger, and Hewitt, this volume)
(iv) Maximum ease of reproduction – symbols that can be easily represented with the technologies available to the community (cf. Sackett, this volume)
(v) Maximum ease of transfer – consideration given to other languages that speakers may want to read and write; for example, and if appropriate, the choice of script and decisions about spelling rules for local language

orthography development may take into account the script and spelling rules of national and official languages (cf. Shah and Brenzinger, and Sackett, this volume)

As Sebba (2012b:167) notes:

> Orthographies are not simply remarkable technological achievements, though they are that. They are also complex social and cultural achievements, best viewed as sets of practices – some highly conventionalized and others relatively unconstrained. They are 'not socially neutral exteriors of written language, but integrated parts of language itself, where the issues of history, identity, ethnicity, culture and politics which pervade language are also prominent.

Such an ideological approach and the principles described earlier are crucial in order that the orthography developed becomes an effective element of a strong and sustained mother-tongue-based programme. However, this happens best when there is collaborative effort between stakeholders. Siefart (2006:275) echoes Sebba and writes (cf. Moseley, and Sackett, this volume):

> The idea persists that a good orthography is simply one that represents all phonological contrasts. However, orthography development is, in fact, a highly complex issue, which involves not only phonological, prosodic, grammatical and semantic aspects of the language written but also a wide variety of non-linguistic issues, among them pedagogical and psycholinguistic aspects of reading and writing and the sociolinguistic situation.

Thus, academics and members of speech communities need to work well together, through productive discussions, respectful debates, mutual agreement and positive decisions for the benefit of the language community and the learners, countering traditional approaches where power is held by the outside 'expert' linguist (cf. Shah and Brenzinger, and Sackett, this volume).

4   Innovations in Orthography Development: Participatory Approaches

Linguistic analysis is crucial, and, as mentioned previously (Cahill and Rice 2014), traditional approaches to orthography development have tended to focus primarily on phonetic and phonemic data analysed by a descriptive linguist, in order to design a writing system – with a primary emphasis on linguistic accuracy. Hinton (2014), in her paper describing orthography development among Native American communities, writes about the challenges of 'code-external' considerations (of the community) and 'code-internal' design factors that concern linguists and describes approaches focused on building trust between communities and linguists.

In recent years, however, innovations in orthography development have tended to highlight the importance of the process of orthography development and building consensus among the speech community. Page (2013:2) emphasizes that the identification of an appropriate writing system that will be adopted and used by the community is not an 'event but a process' and notes (2013:6) that 'The participatory model contrasts with the idea of orthography development as a largely scientific process where an outsider, often a linguist, would analyse the sound system of the language, and propose an orthography for the community to use.'

Approaches such as the Alphabet Design Workshop (ADW) (Easton and Wroge 2002; Easton 2003), were introduced by SIL International in Papua New Guinea between 1999 and 2002, when SIL International held an orthography development subcontract with the Elementary Teacher Education Support Project (ETESP) of Papua New Guinea's National Department of Education (NDOE) and the Australian Agency for International Development (AusAID). During this time, SIL assisted elementary teachers and communities from 103 languages or dialects to make decisions on how to write their own language and what symbols to use for its sounds. Easton (2003:1) describes the approach: 'The ADW relies on speakers' perceptions of their language rather than phonological analysis, and consequently reflects the "sound system" in its cultural context as viewed by the speakers of the language.' This innovation empowers the ethnolinguistic community to own the orthography development process, giving them the ability to appreciate, accept and eventually use the orthography they have developed, as they make decisions about ways in which to use their language and culture for education and development.

5   Participatory Orthography Development in the Philippines

The history of education planning in the Philippines has reflected continuing shifts between policies dependent on the national administration of the time and their socio-economic and nationalistic allegiances. However, empirical research in the Philippines has demonstrated that the use of the first language of the learner has the greatest impact in delivering effective learning outcomes (Castillo 2000:43; Dekker 2003:145; Nolasco 2008:6; Walter and Dekker et al. 2008:6; Walter and Dekker 2008:13). Through intensive advocacy and growing awareness of the role of language in education, on 14 July 2009, a Department of Education Order (Department of Education 2009) was signed, institutionalizing mother-tongue-based multilingual education in all public and private schools from pre-school to high school and prescribing the use of mother tongue as the language of learning and instruction. Subsequently, through Republic Act 10533 (Republic of the Philippines Congress 2013), known as the Enhanced Basic Education Act of 2013, the Department of Education mandated the implementation of mother-tongue-based multilingual education (MTB-MLE) across the country, with institutional support provided for

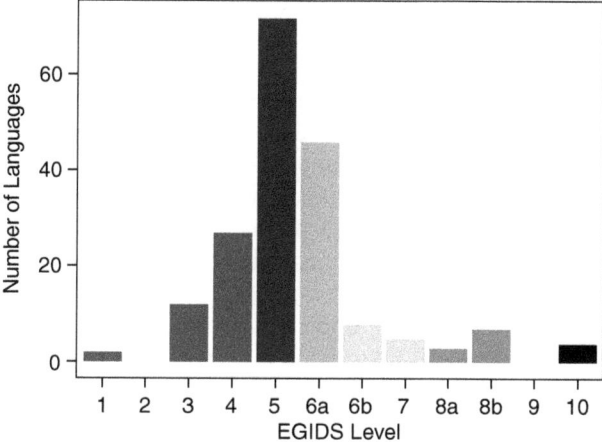

Figure 3.2 EGIDS chart.

nineteen languages (Department of Education 2013). In this way, MTB-MLE in the Philippines has become a component of the Department of Education's K(indergarten)+12 programme, an educational reform adding two additional years to the basic education provision and supporting the use of local languages from kindergarten to grade 6 (11-year-olds).

Multilingualism is an expectation and norm within the Philippines. To have more than one language in one's linguistic repertoire is common, and those languages are usually used in differing social or functional domains (Rappa and Wee 2006:65). The *Ethnologue* (Lewis, Simons, and Fennig 2016) lists 183 living languages for the Philippines. English is the statutory national working language, and Filipino, the statutory national language – as of 1987, Constitution, Article 14(6). The Expanded Graded Intergenerational Disruption Scale (EGIDS) status of languages of the Philippines (see Figure 3.2) reflects a significant proportion of languages at levels 3–6a, indicating that many languages are in vigorous use among all generations (*Ethnologue* 2015).[1] The EGIDS level of a language is taken as a predictor of its likely longevity (cf. Leggio and Matras, Sackett, Schreyer, and McDonald and Zair, this volume). Among the complex dynamics of relationships between national and international social, economic, and educational systems and the consequent pressures to adopt national and international languages, there is an increase in the potential for intergenerational transmission of languages to be interrupted, along with a decrease in their use and impact.

Thus, the implementation of MTB-MLE responds both to the need to institute quality approaches to educational delivery for learners from non-dominant language communities (with the goal of increasing learning outcomes) and also to language and culture maintenance and revitalization (cf. Shah and Brenzinger, this volume).

The development of instructional and reading materials for the implementation of mother-tongue-based multilingual education was identified as a specific challenge to effective and systematic implementation of the Enhanced Basic Education Act. Writing system development was seen as a specific technical issue that presented a barrier to materials production, particularly in languages in which language development activities – including orthography development – had been limited.

SIL International's office in the Philippines received requests from regional offices of the Department of Education, the Department of Education – Autonomous Region of Muslim Mindanao (hereafter, ARMM) (DepEd ARMM 2012), international NGOs, and community organizations to help support the development of appropriate writing systems in order to assist the development of effective materials. Language communities participating in these activities at various venues included the Central Sama (sml, EGIDS level 4), Yakan (yka, EGIDS level 4), and Sama Bangingih (sse, EGIDS level 5), all from the Sulu Archipelago; and the Mapun (sjm, EGIDS level 5) from Tawi-Tawi and Cagayan de Sulu (Mapun) Island, the Sangil (snl, EGIDS level 5), and the Iranun (ill, EGIDS level 6a) from Maguindanao Province, all in the southern Philippines.

Through dialogue with those requesting technical assistance, a decision was taken to adopt a participatory approach using aspects of the Alphabet Design Workshop approach (Easton and Wroge 2002) (cf. Hewitt, this volume). Preparation also involved identifying descriptive linguistic data and written materials available from national and international researchers which could contribute to the information set that local language speakers could use in decision making.

Coordination and planning are key factors in the facilitation of a participatory orthography development event. It was important that participants be identified to represent the breadth of the language areas in focus, based on preliminary studies prepared by SIL International and the Department of Education. In practical terms, eight days for a workshop – including a weekend when participants could, if possible, return to the home area in which their languages are spoken, or at least interact with other speakers – was a helpful timeframe.

In order to address language variants of pronunciation and lexicon, different geographic locations where the language is spoken should be represented in such a process in order that contrasting issues can be addressed and analysed (cf. Hewitt, this volume). In the case of the Philippines under discussion, this often meant ensuring representation from upland mountain areas as well as coastal regions or representation from different island communities where a language is spoken. This was particularly significant when supporting the development of languages in the Sulu Archipelago in the south-west of the Philippines. Thus, an initial activity of the writing system development events involved building appreciation of language varieties among participants by mapping home location and discussing known language variants and influences. It also has been important to ensure diversity in the multidisciplinary teams of participants and facilitators in terms of age, role, and status in order to support the widest possible participation in, appreciation for, and acceptability of the writing system that is developed. While working with the Department of Education in the Philippines, participants have included community elders – such as datus and, in one case, a sultan – and both political and social leaders, mother-tongue teachers, government schoolteachers, journalists, artists, and representatives from the youth sector.

5.1   Tools, Trade, and Techniques

Collaboration and the right tools are essential in designing an effective orthography, and the voice of the speech community is the primary tool. Community consultation and participation are the principal methods. The key decision makers are the speech community, whereas the role of outsiders can be to ensure that the speech community is empowered and given the necessary help to make its orthography systematic, effective, and efficient. In this way, communities can, potentially, become equipped to help other speech communities move ahead in orthography development. When the participants have been identified and informed, the role of the facilitators is to structure activities that will promote interaction, negotiation, and informed decision making. To do this, a cyclical process was adapted from Easton and Wroge (2002:14) in order to create a systematic, participatory approach (see Figure 3.3).

During the Philippines experience, through guided activities, participants were asked to write a story in their language using a writing system that they know, and they were given time to read those stories aloud. Together with linguistic consultants, the participants made an inventory of symbols and phonemic segments. Data were analysed by identifying the problems and through discussion of possible solutions to these problems; the stories were then rewritten using the agreed solutions and systems. Enough time was given for more discussion of ambiguous segments. Next steps included preliminary decision making, technical validation, and field testing (cf. Schreyer, this volume). Participants' edited stories were recorded at a natural pace using the SIL software Speech Analyzer 3.1 (SIL International 2012), after which the vowel segments were plotted using the freeware JPlotFormants to provide acoustic characterization of the vowels. Comparative analysis of the phonetic

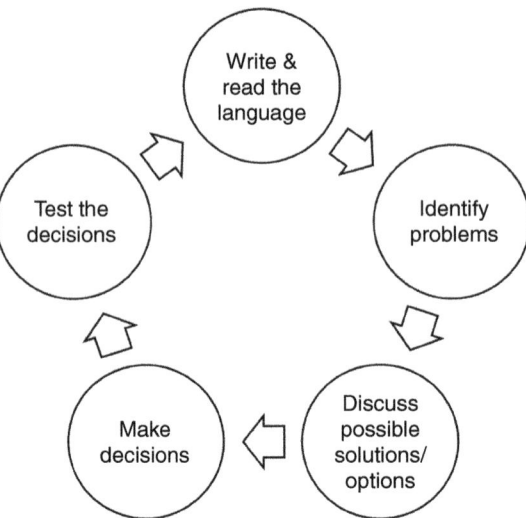

Figure 3.3 Process diagram.

segments of the different varieties of the languages in focus during different events was made with JPlotFormants (Billerey-Mosier 2002). After a thorough investigation and analysis of the ambivalent vowel segments, participants based their choices on options revealed through analysis. Stories were then rewritten with more accurate orthographic representations before field testing.

Each participant was able to return home taking two edited stories that used the preliminary orthography decisions. They were also provided with a matrix for testing the preliminary orthography, to be completed with responses from both adult readers and schoolchildren. The field testing focused on the choices of symbols and spelling rules. The participants returned to the workshop after two days for a more thorough discussion of the field testing results, employing the cyclical process as described previously.

5.2 Dialogue and Dissent

During these participatory activities, it was evident that there were differing opinions on the rationale for decision making. Some related to geographical differences in pronunciation and lexicon, while other opinions related to the degree to which orthographic choices should be influenced by the orthographic conventions of the national language (cf. Sackett, and Lai, this volume). Participants and facilitators need to develop a safe space in which opinions can be expressed in order to pursue consensus in decision making.

Communication within the group can be spoken, unspoken, verbal, non-verbal, explicit, or implied, and facilitators who are not cultural insiders need to recognize that there may be hierarchical issues among participants of which they are unaware or situations in which participants are deferring to social or institutional authorities in the group. It will also be important to differentiate between true and false consensus within the group. True consensus can occur when the discussion has explored all angles of an issue and considered a range of possibilities and everyone is in full agreement. However, this is not always possible: the interim goal in orthography development processes is to ensure that everyone feels that they have had the opportunity to put forth their views and influence a decision and are prepared to promote the decisions taken.

5.3 Outputs

During the activities in the Philippines, specific outputs included a spelling guide, aimed at teachers of grade 1 (6-year-olds), that outlined the features of the orthographic choices, included the symbols chosen, presented preliminary spelling rules and incorporated an alphabet chart that could be used by teachers in the classroom (cf. Shah and Brenzinger, this volume). It also included word lists of vocabulary items used in elementary education and stories produced in the workshop that may be used by the teachers. The goal of this output was to provide schoolteachers with a reference guide to support ongoing production of teaching/learning materials to be used in the implementation of mother-tongue-based multilingual education as well as to systematize the decisions made.

6 Issues and Implications

Orthography development, including linguistic investigation, analysis and description, even when done by members of speech communities, requires time – particularly the field testing of the suggested writing system, including the chosen symbols, representation of grammatical features and spelling rule definition. It may take some years until a system is standardized and well accepted. For example, Karan (2014:131) notes that modifications were being made to the Shona writing system throughout much of the twentieth century. However, if education is to be delivered in the local language, a working orthography needs to be established through which learners can develop literacy skills and teaching/learning materials can be developed.

It is important to emphasize that throughout this process an initial orthography can be modified if use indicates that changes would be helpful and are necessary. Thus, Karan (2014:132) notes that:

Testing an orthography is essential. It will reveal effectiveness, acceptability, degree of potential extendability across dialects and, possibly, needs for revision. Time should not be seen as expenditure but rather as an investment which will yield good returns [...] Publishing need not be halted when there is variation in writing. During the early experimental and testing stages, it may be prudent to print in smaller numbers.

The democratization of Internet-based technologies, through smartphone applications and mobile phone networks, is one such innovation that could encourage greater equity in access to and participation in decision-making processes associated with writing system development (cf. Sallabank and Marquis, this volume). It could also provide spaces that support stakeholders as they learn about the rationale for choices surrounding orthographic conventions. Social networking sites such as Facebook and Twitter are being used by communities to discuss issues relating to writing system development, and such collaborative sites can also support the development of appropriate teaching/learning materials that can lead towards agreement on writing systems. One immediate action by a language community in the southern Philippines after an orthography development event was to launch a Facebook page, encouraging participants to post using the local language.

6.1 Limitations of the Approach

A participatory approach can be an excellent tool to support the design and development of a writing system, but there also are limitations that need to be considered.

Accurate representation can be missed if phonological analysis is not given careful attention. Traditional tools like recording, acoustic analysis/plotting and wordlist gathering have proven to be effective and can be helpful to promote increased accuracy of representation. Thus, participants – either outsiders or members of the speech community – who have knowledge of the phonology of the language in focus (or at least the phonology of that language family) are helpful for the purpose of giving technical assistance in identification of ambivalent segments.

In an area where the phonology of the local language contrasts significantly with the phonology of the national language, an approach that emphasizes maximum involvement of members of the speech community in foundational phonological research may be necessary before embarking on the process described here. The work of Kutsch Lojenga (1996) describes participatory approaches in linguistic analysis and complements the philosophical approach to orthography development advocated in this chapter.

Additional challenges exist when scaling such an approach to engage with large language communities or highly stratified societies, particularly when identifying the range of participants to engage in the process. Within a large ethnolinguistic community embarking on orthography development, there may be insufficient healthy interaction between actors from specific geographical areas, socio-economic sectors, religious sub-groups, or other competing interests among those 'homogenously classified as the community' (Keene 2007), leading to a lack of understanding and, potentially, a growing hostility between groups. In many cases this makes 'productive engagement across the cultural interface very difficult, with distrust and power dynamics being major challenges' (Smith and Wisbey 2013:15).

Significant follow-up is needed after such an approach to orthography development, and orthography development should be seen as a process rather than the development of a product. Field testing is an ongoing process (cf. Schreyer, and Lai, this volume) and therefore need not, and should not, be rushed. A continuing dialogue and post-workshop monitoring and evaluation can support a strong intellectualization of the language. A working orthography will become more effective if, through time, ambiguity is addressed through continuing community engagement and stakeholder collaboration.

6.2   The Role of the Facilitator

There are prerequisites required for an effective participatory approach to orthography development that honours the voices of community members whilst respecting the need for a writing system that represents the component parts of the language and supports learning to read and write for both first-time learners and those transferring their literacy skills from another language. It is important that facilitators are well trained and understand both the facilitation techniques they will be using and the goals of using an approach that promotes local decision making. Facilitators will possibly need to mediate disagreement when participants – or groups of participants – express varying opinions or, potentially, form sub-groups around preferred choices within the writing system. Careful choices of participatory tools and strategies that foster discussion, dialogue, and decisions are critical to support the speech community towards consensus.

If facilitators of such a participatory approach are outsiders – either from the majority speech community of the nation or foreigners – the need to act as reflective practitioners intensifies. Development agencies can either intentionally or unconsciously introduce 'concepts, value systems, administrative structures and power dynamics directly counter to the communities' own cultural understanding' (Smith and Wisbey 2013:18). Development in this context puts the responsibility on practitioners to adequately address power differentials and narratives of inferiority in their interactions with minority groups (Smith 2010).

A major criticism (Colom 2013) of participatory orthography development approaches hinges upon the relationship between the outsider and insider in such a process. Colom notes that the validity and integrity of participatory approaches have been questioned, saying, 'Development practitioners and organizations are not passive facilitators. They own the tools, choose the topics and ultimately "shape and direct the processes". So rather than a shift in power relations, participatory development was seen as a mask that perpetuates the dominance of mainly western actors over the recipients of aid.' Thus, those involved in designing orthography development approaches must realize that using participatory tools is neither evidence nor assurance that local voices are being heard. Facilitation methods must consciously pay attention to the impact of coercive power relations and social relationships in enabling community agency in decision making.

7   Conclusion

As decisions are made, the speech community is empowered, and through these events, a growing appreciation of the endangered language and its culture is observed. Sustainable participation and community involvement are happening, enabling local voices to echo through the fabrics of endangered language communities. When orthographies are established and used by these communities, education programmes that allow the use of the mother tongue are implemented strongly in all schools, enabling learners to continue to develop their cognitive skills using the language that they know best (cf. Sackett, this volume).

It is evident from our experience that technical capacity for design and implementation of mother-tongue-based education is not the primary element constraining the effectiveness and sustainability of such programmes. Rather, sustainability will be realized when those with national and regional institutional responsibility for education and local community groups are equipped to function interdependently, using their skills and knowledge to create systems and approaches that are responsive to the needs of learners from endangered ethnolinguistic communities. The inclusion of local voices in the development of appropriate writing systems is a step towards such sustainable provision.

Note

1. www.ethnologue.com/profile/PH (last accessed 19 June 2015).

4 Orthographies 'In the Making': The Dynamic Construction of Community-Based Writing Systems among the Náayeri of North-Western Mexico

Margarita Valdovinos

1 Introduction

This chapter's starting point lies in a previous paper dedicated to the study of the different interactions associated with the public education system in a Mexican indigenous community (Valdovinos 2014). In this earlier publication, I stated that, like any other public policy, literacy processes could not be fully understood by taking into account only their political dimensions (a 'top-down' perspective – cf. Lai, this volume) or else only their community-based point of view (a 'bottom-up' perspective). What I call 'mediating actors' – local institutions and the social actors related to them – must also be considered, since they are the participants directly involved in the actual adoption and institutionalization of policies.

This chapter presents a case study in which mediating actors occupy a central position in the materialization of a particular linguistic policy – namely the adoption of an orthographic system for the Chwíse'etaana Náayeri (Cora Mariteco), an indigenous language spoken by approximately five thousand people in the state of Nayarit, in north-western Mexico.[1]

In 2012, organizing a workshop on orthography in the Náayeri community of Jesús María, I realized that this event represented an ideal opportunity for the study of the social dynamics of orthography development. Different questions arose from that experience and now serve as guidelines for the current discussion. These questions include: why were all previous attempts at creating an orthographic system for the benefit of the Mariteco set aside if the people of the community seemed so eager in such an endeavour? To what extent did the people of the community participate in previous attempts to develop an orthography? Was the lack of representation of the community in those former projects related to the rejection of the resulting orthographic systems? Was the nature of the linguistic analysis considered more important than any social involvement? Can the community truly play an active role in the development of an orthographic system? (For further consideration of these points, cf. Sackett, and Shah and Brenzinger, this volume.)

My experience in organizing this workshop has led me to consider orthography development as a social process that must be conceived in its diachronic dynamism. The development of an orthography should not be reduced to a linguistic analysis that is imposed by an external group. Rather, it must be seen as a series of interactions between all the mediating actors involved: teachers, local intellectuals, political leaders, and external non-governmental agents such as researchers. It is through their joint discussions and practices that ideas about language, language use, and standardization are identified, analysed, and sometimes adopted as official policies.[2]

The development of an orthography is a long and complex process that involves not just present interactions, but also what has been done before and expectations for the future (cf. Casquite and Young, this volume). Ideas about orthography may change due to the influence of previous events related to orthography-making processes even before the community has adopted any actual system. Opinions and perspectives may change throughout the entire process of the development of an orthographic system (cf. Sackett, this volume), even after its official adoption. Because of this, it seems more convenient to speak about orthographies 'in the making' rather than defining rigidly what 'the' orthography should look like before community members consciously adopt it.

This chapter considers the development of orthographies among the Náayeri from this dynamic perspective. It starts by exploring the national political context in which literacy policies are promoted and applied to indigenous communities in general and, in particular, to the Náayeri case. It then explores literacy acquisition processes that have taken place among the Náayeri of Jesús María and analyses the dynamics of the community-based project I organized there in 2012 in order to promote the development of an orthographic system. The chapter concludes with a series of observations on the logistics of orthography development and its dynamic aspects.

2 Literacy Policies in Mexico and in the Náayeri Context

Since the colonial period, Mexican society has been strongly influenced by Spanish culture. One of the most important and salient aspects of Mexican culture to date is language: Spanish has been considered the official language since the establishment of the Mexican state. Nonetheless, many Native American languages were spoken throughout the Mexican territory before the Spanish conquest and are even now in use.

Today, around 6.6 per cent of the Mexican population speaks one of the remaining indigenous languages originally spoken in the territories that now constitute modern-day Mexico (INEGI 2010).[3] Historically, the speakers of these languages have been discriminated against and undermined, and even openly oppressed and marginalized, through different kinds of linguistic attitudes. Only recently has the Mexican government engaged in an effort to determine how many indigenous languages are still spoken in the territory, to classify them and promote their recognition and use.

In 1957, the International Labour Organization (hereafter, ILO) established a first international agreement consecrated to the existence of indigenous communities within recognized states around the world. In 1989, a revision of this document led to the establishment of the Indigenous and Tribal Peoples Convention, commonly known as C169 (Comisión Nacional de los Derechos Indígenas en México 2012). Mexico ratified this convention one year after its issue, and, in 1992, the *Official Bulletin of the Federation* (*Diario Oficial de la Federación*) published an important amendment to Article 4 of the National Constitution. This modification recognizes for the first time in Mexican history the multicultural constitution of the country based on the existence of indigenous peoples (González Galván 1994:105).

The Neo-Zapatista uprising in 1994 accelerated the official recognition of the indigenous peoples, and the Mexican government was eventually compelled to sign the San Andrés Larrainzar Agreements (Tratados de San Andrés Larrainzar) on the rights and culture of the indigenous people. But it was not until 2001 that the *Official Bulletin of the Federation* published the so-called Indigenous Law (*Ley Indígena*), which explicitly lays down the rights of the indigenous peoples of Mexico (Gamboa Montejano 2008:13).

Article 2 of the Constitution has been amended in a particularly significant way. In it, the law declares that the Mexican nation has a multicultural composition based originally on its indigenous peoples – namely, those who are descended from the populations that settled in modern-day Mexico at the beginning of the colonial period and who still preserve their own social, economic, cultural, and political institutions (or part of them) (CPEUM 2011).

One of the most important consequences of this amendment consists in the ratification of the General Law of Linguistic Rights of Indigenous Peoples (Ley General de Derechos Lingüísticos de los Pueblos Indígenas) of 2003, which recognizes all indigenous languages as national languages. Another important consequence was the establishment of the National Institute of Indigenous Languages (INALI, Instituto Nacional de Lenguas Indígenas) in 2005, an institution given the responsibility of preserving, developing, and studying the indigenous languages spoken in the areas that constitute modern-day Mexico. Today, 68 indigenous languages have been officially recognized as national languages alongside Spanish. These languages are classified into eleven families and consist of 364 linguistic varieties (INALI 2008:31–112).

During the 1970s, the Mexican government created the Bilingual Education General Office (Dirección General de Educación Bilingüe) with the express purpose of advancing the use of national languages other than Spanish in the educational system, specifically in the classroom. In other words, this programme introduced the use of native languages into the official educational system and promoted the elaboration of teaching materials in these languages. Nevertheless, most of these efforts have failed, as the introduction of indigenous languages in official public education was usually carried out without any particular understanding of the native cultures and without sufficient studies of the indigenous languages and their phonological systems, both of which are necessary for the establishment of adequate orthographic systems.

The implementation of bilingual programmes in schools demanded the adoption of orthographies for all native languages spoken throughout Mexico in order to print appropriate teaching materials in those languages. This process, however, has been developed with different degrees of success in each region, and only the most recognized languages (such as Nahuatl, Yucatec Maya, Mixtec, and Zapotec) have been the object of enough attention to establish coherent orthographic systems in accordance with their dialectal varieties.

Náayeri (Cora) is one of the 68 indigenous languages spoken in Mexico. It belongs to the southern branch of the Uto-Aztecan family usually known as Sonoran and, along with Wixarrika (Huichol), forms the Corachol sub-family. According to official Mexican sources, there are about 20,000 Náayeri speakers (INEGI 2010) who use one of the eight dialects of this language that have been identified so far – namely Corapeño, Presideño, Mariteco, Sanfrancisqueño, Tereseño, and Meseño as well as the Rosarito and Dolores varieties. There is still no full description of the Náayeri dialects, and only a few works give consistent linguistic descriptions of some of the most spoken dialectal varieties.[4] The inconsistency with which Náayeri has been studied is apparent in the *Ethnologue*, which only mentions the two dialects studied by two members of the SIL.[5]

In order to study Mariteco, the dialectal variety spoken in Jesús María, it is important first to distinguish it from the other varieties identified in the El Nayar dialectal group proposed by the *Ethnologue*. The speakers of Mariteco use a particular set of laminal consonants (/ty/, /ny/, /ky/, and /ly/) that are contrastive phonological elements of this dialect but seem to be absent in other varieties.

When working with any of the Náayeri dialectal varieties, it is necessary to go beyond official numbers. Mexican censuses do not describe the use of any particular dialectal variety, but Mariteco speakers can be estimated at around

Orthographies 'In the Making' 73

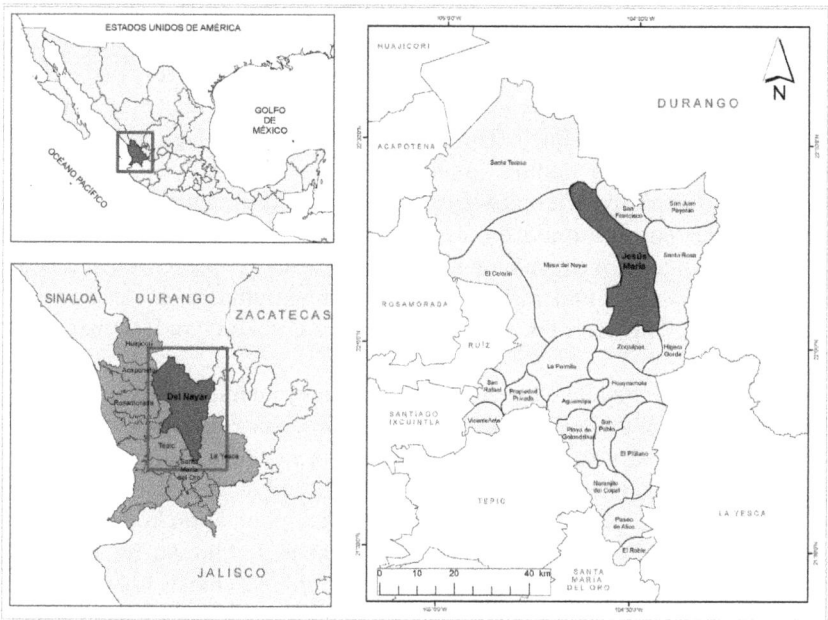

Figure 4.1 The location of Jesús María.

4,000. This variety is one of the most well known and well studied, but, because of recent social change, it has become one of the most endangered dialects of the region during the past five years. Jesús María, the capital of this community, became the political and economic centre of the region and has been dramatically increasing, both in terms of size and number of inhabitants, by embracing numerous non-indigenous Mexican citizens from the region. This fact alone is responsible for broadening the adoption of Spanish as a lingua franca, a situation that has increased over the past ten years with the introduction of electricity, television, and, more recently, highways. This has led most of the people living in the town of Jesús María (Nayarit) to abandon their native language, which in turn has led to a severe decline in the number of speakers of this dialectal variety: only about two out of every ten children still use it.

As mentioned earlier, the Náayeri people are organized in agrarian communities. These social units not only share a common territory but also a set of ritual and political institutions and the use of a common dialectal variety (see Figure 4.1). Different communities surround the locality of Jesús María. The populations of each of these communities speak different dialects. From this geo-political setting emerges a particular linguistic reality, as the population of each of the communities bordering the Jesús María territory displays in their way of speaking a certain lexical influence from the neighbouring dialect and, at the same time, the presence of a strong phonological reaffirmation of those features of Mariteco that contrast it from those neighbouring dialects.

Above and beyond the interaction attested between dialects, Náayeri is in contact with regional Spanish. The influence of this language, related with the dominant national culture, must also be understood as a complex process that affects in different ways the centralized towns and the smaller hamlets dispersed all around the Mariteco territory (see Figures 4.2a and 4.2b). The influence of Spanish is stronger in the larger settlements, where most of the governmental institutions are concentrated, whereas Spanish is barely spoken in hamlets that only contain a school and, sometimes, a medical post.

In order to understand the logistics of orthography adoption, it is imperative to take into account these sociolinguistic dynamics, as writing appears both as the means and the purpose of the only institution present in all social contexts – namely, the school. The school is one of the most influential institutions with regard to linguistic practices among the Náayeri population for two main reasons: first, because it is in this social context that children, for the very first time, gain awareness of the implicit confrontation that exists between their language and Spanish; second, because it is in school where children and young adults are confronted with writing practices.

3   Contexts of Literacy in Jesús María

In the social dynamics of Jesús María, Náayeri is the language used at home and in any public situation other than the commercial domain and the administration of political matters related to non-traditional institutions. These dynamics imply that the use of Spanish is related to any social transaction linked with national, federal, or municipal institutions – such as hospitals, the police force, law courts, social services, and even the schools. In this context, it is not surprising that, in the larger towns, young parents educated in Spanish through formal education choose to use this language at home in order to provide their children with more opportunities to deal with those official institutions, considered an important part of modern life.

This situation may be clarified by analysing how the Náayeri relate to educational institutions during their lifetimes. For the past ten years, their first experience related to school has begun before the age of three, when the mothers of young children are invited to take part in a set of workshops organized to teach them how to stimulate the learning process of their toddlers. The mothers are invited to learn songs and riddles in Spanish so they can use them later with their children. This set of activities, considered by the government as one of the most innovative programmes in indigenous education, has

Figures 4.2a and 4.2b Town and hamlet in Jesús María community.

important consequences for the native languages, as it promotes the use of Spanish among young mothers as the linguistic channel of their children's learning process. This new dynamic breaks with the traditional, monolingual interactive context that has preserved the use of Náayeri as the centre of the intimate relationship between mothers and their young children.

The second formal educational experience takes place among children between the ages of 3 and 4. At this stage, children are admitted to preschool, where they become part of a group in which social interactions are based on the leadership of a teacher. Teachers prepare their class in Spanish and formally start teaching children their first words in the language. In this context, children will construct a parallel between reading, writing, formal learning, and the teacher-student relationship through the medium of Spanish (Valdovinos 2014: 80–92).

When the children reach 6 and 7 years of age, they are admitted to elementary school. Parents are now faced with a choice with regard to their children's education, as there are two schooling systems: federal schools in which all education is taught in Spanish and bilingual schools, which provide education for indigenous populations in their native language. Bilingual schools are supposed to provide a remedy to the national linguistic complexities of Mexico. They are expected to offer a basic elementary school education in the native language, which will increasingly provide tools facilitating the acquisition of Spanish. Children are expected to transit progressively from completely Náayeri-medium instruction in the first year to fully Spanish-medium instruction by the sixth grade (12-year-olds). This programme assigns to the native language the most significant role in the literacy process undergone by the children.

Despite the fact that Náayeri is the first and main language used for literacy in the bilingual schools, it is clear from the outset that literacy activities are planned and organized based on those that are related to Spanish teaching, as Náayeri is conceived as inadequate for reading and writing activities. This particular conception is not just a myth, as it is based on concrete facts related to different situations. Just to mention the most important, it is sufficient to analyse the basic facts regarding Náayeri education.

Bilingual teachers – as people commonly call teachers working in bilingual schools who are supposed to teach in Náayeri – are provided only a very basic training in reading and writing in their own language, making it very difficult to use this language to prepare teaching materials for their class. The situation becomes even more complicated by the way in which the Mexican government organizes the distribution of bilingual teachers in the indigenous communities: teachers are usually assigned to schools in communities that are not their own. This strategy, originally conceived as a means of preventing the formation of power groups (*cacicazgos*), has resulted in a complicated scenario whereby bilingual teachers are assigned to communities in which children speak different dialectal varieties of the language from their own. Thus, in order to communicate easily with their students, teachers end up teaching their classes in Spanish. Teachers are not directly responsible for this complex situation; on the contrary, it should be attributed more directly to the government's lack of knowledge regarding the internal characteristics of indigenous languages and their dialectal varieties.

Recently, the Mexican government, through the National Institute of Indigenous Languages, has begun a process of identifying all the native languages and dialects that are spoken in the country; there is already a first attempt at cataloguing them (INALI 2008). Nevertheless, more efforts are needed to analyse the internal structures of these languages and to propose for each of them specific writing systems that take into account their dialectal varieties. In the meantime, linguists, anthropologists and teachers, as well as people from different spheres and organizations, have undertaken private initiatives in order to propose a preliminary linguistic analysis capable of supporting basic orthographies for some of the languages spoken by the different indigenous communities of Mexico. There have been different attempts at establishing an orthographic system for Náayeri. This chapter analyses the three cases that I consider to be the most influential – namely, the public education chart, the SIL charts, and the Náayeri-as-a-second-language chart.

In the 1990s, the Bilingual Education System in Mexico elaborated an orthographic chart for Náayeri and established its use in order to produce teaching materials (see Figure 4.3). This chart uses the Roman writing system but attempts to mark the difference between the way these graphic symbols are used in Spanish and the way they are proposed for Náayeri: for instance, the adoption of <k> instead of <c> in order to avoid the /s/ pronunciation triggered by the presence of /e/ or /i/ after the <c>. It also includes the use of an apostrophe to mark the laryngealized vowels as well as the <ɨ> to represent the close central unrounded vowel.

Although this orthography is based on a description of the language, it lacks a careful analysis of its phonological structure. This is made clear by the absence of laminal consonants (/ty/, /ny/, /ky/, and /ly/) and of labialized consonants (/pw/, /mw/, /tw/, /chw/, /rw/, and /kw/). The main problem with this orthographic system may be related to the fact that it seems to be founded on a mixed version that draws on all of the Náayeri dialectal varieties.

The books that were produced using this chart are confusing since they mix texts from all the dialectal varieties of Náayeri without specifying their origin and because they omit the graphic representation of the particular phonetic properties of each dialectal variety. The resulting effect is, in all cases, a sort of universal Náayeri that can barely be understood and that does not allow any of the communities of speakers to identify with any of the texts.

Upper case	Lower case
A	a
B	b
CH	ch
E	e
G	g
I	i
Ɨ	ɨ
J	j
K	k
L	l
M	m
N	n
O	o
P	p
R	r
S	s
T	t
TS	ts
U	u
X	x
Y	y
'	'

Figure 4.3 Bilingual education orthographic chart (based on Departamento de Educación Indígena n.d.).

Eugene Casad, a linguist from the SIL, started studying the Mariteco dialect in the 1970s and proposed an orthographic system for it (Casad 1884). A second study by Donald Roth, also from the SIL, was inspired by this first proposition and resulted in a similar orthographic chart, although in this case for the Tereseño dialect (see Figure 4.4).

The orthographies elaborated by the SIL have the advantage of having been created from a phonological analysis of particular dialectal varieties and also of including some of the laminal consonants (/ty/ and /ny/). They both display difficulties, as they simply adopt the same characters used in Spanish to write down Náayeri sounds. For example, <c> represents /k/ regardless of the ambiguity created by its use in Spanish, and <hu> is used to indicate the semivowel /w/. Another problematic aspect of these writing systems is related to the misinterpretation of stress as tone and the inconsistent use of the laryngealized vowels marked with a <'> – sometimes between two vowels (<V'V>) and sometimes only after a single vowel (<V'>). At the same time, these works have been inspired by the orthography used for classical Nahuatl, as they use the <tz> to represent the voiceless alveolar affricate /ts/.

a	p
c	qu
ch	r
e	s
hu	t
i	ty
ɨ	tz
j	u
l	v
m	x
n	y
ny	'
o	

Figure 4.4 Orthographic chart for Tereseño Náayeri (based on Roth 2008).

In this orthographic system, some features of the Náayeri language are not considered, and pitch accent is analysed as a phonological tone, causing some confusion in the way that prosodic stress is represented. These aspects, drawn from the aforementioned orthographies, make it somewhat unstable and unable to follow the rules of Spanish orthography.

In 2014, a group of scholars prepared a book for learning Náayeri as a second language: *Wa'mwatye Náayeri nyúuka* (Santos, Parra, Muñiz, and Zeferino 2014). This included an orthography chart (see Figure 4.5). The phonological analysis they use seems to go beyond the previous descriptions – although it does not go far enough, as some aspects of the language remain inconsistently represented. This is particularly clear in the use of <'> and <h> for the graphic representation of laryngealized and aspirated vowels.

The following chart (Figure 4.6) displays a comparative analysis of the three different orthographic systems considered here. As has been demonstrated in Valdovinos and Kim (2014), any writing system elaborated for Náayeri needs to take into account the suprasegmental phenomena related to the presence of, for example, stress patterns, laryngealization, tonality, and vowel length.

4 A Community-Oriented Orthography Workshop

This chapter began by providing an account of the socio-cultural situation of the Náayeri people and the way in which they adopt their practices regarding the acquisition of reading and writing skills in the community. The information presented hitherto shows that the elaboration of any orthography for the Náayeri language is inevitably the result of different processes that are

Phoneme	Sign	Ex.	Meaning
/b/	b	básta'	'elder person'
/tʃ/	ch	chi'	'house'
/k/	k	ka'akái	'sandal'
/l/	l	liméeta	'glass bottle'
/m/	m	míistyu	'cat'
/j/	y	yáuhka	'avocado'
/w/	w	wíinyi	'sugar cane'
/kʷ/	kw	kwaxpwá	'plum'
/mʷ/	mw	mwaarí	'turtle'
/nʸ/	ny	nyúukari	'word'
/pʷ/	pw	pwáasi	'belt'
/n/	n	náayeri	'Cora'
/p/	p	pínyin	'watermelon'
/s/	s	síikuri	'shirt'
/t/	t	tá'u	'egg'
/tʸ/	ty	tyeetyé	'rock'
/ts/	ts	tsímuuri	'broom'
/ʂ/	x	xúuxu'	'flower'
/h/	h	ha'	'water'
/ʔ/	'	ka'nyí	'bag'
/ɽ/	r	re'rí	'gourd'

Phoneme	Sign	Ex.	Meaning
/a/	a	anáh	'feather'
/e/	e	einyí paná'	'How are you?'
/i/	i	íchui	'lizard'
/u/	u	úuka	'women'
/a:/	aa	náayeri	'Cora'
/e:/	ee	néerime	'face'
/i:/	ii	íinari	'spindle'
/u:/	uu	túuturu	'flute'
/ɨ:/	ɨɨ	tɨɨtsikai	'hummingbird'

Figure 4.5 Chart of Náayeri as a second language (after Santos, Parra, Muñiz, and Zeferino 2014:47–49).

indirectly related to the members of the community (for further discussion of these, see for example Casquite and Young, and Sackett, this volume).

However, by analysing the previous orthographic systems created for Náayeri, I realized that none of them was created with the direct participation of the members of the community. Despite the fact that all the authors of the systems have had the help of native speakers as assistants, not one of these efforts incorporated a socialization phase into their proposals before the

	Bilingual education chart	SIL charts	Náayeri as a second language
Previous linguistic analysis	Yes	Yes	Yes
Based on one dialectal variant	No	Yes	Yes
Dialectal variant	—	*Mariteco* and *Tereseño*	*Mariteco*
Present Cora features	• Laryngealized vowels • ɨ	• Laryngealized vowels • Some laminal consonants • Long vowels • ɨ	• Laryngealized vowels • Laminal consonants • Labialized consonants • Long vowels • Some aspirated vowels • Stress • ɨ
Absent Cora features	• Laminal consonants • Labialized consonants • Long vowels • Aspirated vowels • Nasalization • Stress • Tones	• Labialized consonants • Some laminal consonants missing • Labialized consonants • Aspirated vowels • Nasalization • Stress • Tones	• Nasalization • Some aspirated vowels missing • Tones

Figure 4.6 A comparative chart of previous orthographic systems used for Náayeri.

finalization of the orthographic system (on this point, cf. Casquite and Young, Brenzinger and Shah, and Sackett, this volume). This means that all these orthographic conventions were presented to the community only once they had already been applied to the elaboration of printed materials. This also means that it was only through these printed documents that the orthographies were presented to the community.

In addition, I noticed that none of the previous orthographic systems were based on a careful phonological study of the language. This situation brought me face to face with a larger problem, since I was also unable to provide any study of that kind previous to a workshop I organized for the purposes of elaborating a new orthographic system. At that point, my phonological analysis of the Mariteco variety was still a work in progress. My approach implied, above all, viewing orthography development as a social process. This perspective brought me to consider as a sine qua non the idea of making the community participate in the analysis that preceded the orthographic chart. Participants understood from the very outset what kinds of studies were important in defining a useful set of orthographic symbols to represent the sounds of a language. Thus, although at that point the phonological analysis of Mariteco was still incomplete, the community could then be involved in the process.

I therefore convened the First Community-Based Workshop for the Study of Mariteco. The workshop was organized in Jesús María in October 2012 and sponsored by the National Autonomous University of Mexico (hereafter, UNAM) and the National Institute of Indigenous Languages (hereafter, INALI). It was conceived as an open event so that anyone in Jesús María interested in the process of writing and reading in Náayeri could join. The meeting was preceded by an open assembly that attracted the attention of local political and cultural leaders.

One of our most salient observations was no doubt the fact that many of the twenty-five participants made several references to previous writing systems. Their questions made me realize that all of them had a previous experience of orthographies and that these experiences triggered different kinds of responses to what was taught at the workshop (emotional, logical, political, and so forth). In order to deal with these unexpected reactions, the participants were invited to keep their focus within the bounds of linguistic analysis.

The week-long workshop served as a point of departure to invite the participants to understand the dynamics of linguistic analysis. Three types of people attended: self-educated adult men, young CONAFE teachers who were there to learn more about the written use of their mother language,[6] and more experienced teachers who considered themselves as having a good enough knowledge of their language to use it to read and write. The first two groups were clearly open to learn all they could, whereas the members of the latter group felt that they already had enough knowledge of the Náayeri writing system to question what was being presented in class. This situation compelled me to begin by showing the entire class that, most of the time, Cora orthographic systems were based on the linguistic principles of Spanish and that this fact could cause problems in the way particular aspects of Náayeri were represented graphically. For this reason, I started working with the group on minimal pairs whose contrastive elements were absent in Spanish, such as laryngealized vowels, long vowels, and aspirated vowels. With the aid of different types of exercises, all participants realized that the writing practices they had previously acquired all contained some problematic aspects.

From these first observations, my team and I taught a series of lessons in linguistics in order to introduce participants to different aspects of linguistic

Consonants		Bilabial	Alveolar	Alveo-palatal	Retroflex	Palatal	Velar	Glottal
Occlusive	vl	p pʷ	t tʸ tʷ				k kʷ	
							kʸ	
	vd							
Aricates	vl		ts	tʃ tʃʷ				
Fricatives	vl		s	ʃ				h
	vd	β						
Nasals	vd	m mʷ	n nʸ				ŋ	
Laterals	vd				l lʸ			
Retrofex flap	vd				ɾ ɾʷ			
Approximant	vd	w				y		

Vowels		Front	Central	Back
		unrounded		rounded
Close	[– ATR]	i iː i̱		u uː u̱
	[+ ATR]		i iː i̱	
Open–mid		ɛ ɛː ɛ̱		
Open		a aː a̱		

Figure 4.7 The Náayeri phonetic chart produced during the workshop.

analysis. We began by giving a brief presentation of the phonetic symbols and discarded those that were not present in Náayeri. We then used the remaining symbols to create a general analysis of Náayeri phonology. Next, we taught some elements of morphology and syntax. The idea of teaching each of these aspects was to show the logistics of linguistic analysis while at the same time defining the graphic signs with which the language was going to be written. The different exercises and discussions helped us convey to the participants the importance of using Náayeri as the point of departure for the analysis, for we realized that metalinguistic conversations tended to be oriented towards the structure of Spanish, the language learnt at school.

Once the group was aware of the importance of distinguishing certain aspects of the language through the use of particular symbols, participants were helped to construct a phonetic chart for Mariteco using the elements they had learned during the workshop (see Figure 4.7). In this exercise, particular attention was given in determining what those aspects of Cora were that could not be explained using the Spanish alphabet.

The system proposed by the group was then analysed to see if it was consistent. Thereafter, it was used to propose an orthographic system (see Figure 4.8).

Consonants		Bilabial	Alveolar	Alveo-palatal	Retroflex	Palatal	Velar	Glottal
Occlusive	vl	p pw	t ty tw				k kw ky	
	vd							
Aricates	vl		ts	ch chw				
Fricatives	vl		s	x				h
	vd	b						
Nasals	vd	m mw	n ny				n	
Laterals	vd				l ly			
Retroflex flap	vd				r rw			
Approximant	vd	w				y		

Vowels		Front	Central	Back
		Unrounded		Rounded
Close	[– ATR]	i ii i'i		u uu u'u
	[+ ATR]		ɨ ɨɨ ɨ'ɨ	
Open–mid		e ee e'e		
Open		a aa a'a		

Figure 4.8 The Náayeri orthographic system as proposed during the workshop.

The group was invited to analyse the principles of other orthographic systems through their history and dynamics. The comparison made the participants realize how arbitrary the selection of some characters could be and how, in different languages, a single orthographic symbol could represent different sounds.

Three main objectives guided the workshop, each of them with the aim of encouraging participants to relativize the way in which they saw their own literacy practices. First, the idea was to motivate a social context in which there was a place for metalinguistic discussion and where a particular vocabulary and ideas could be introduced to participants. This objective was accomplished by presenting different aspects of linguistic analysis. The second goal consisted in using minimal pairs to demonstrate that single aspects of the way a language is represented graphically may vary by establishing a distinction of meaning. This was conceived as a way of explaining the importance of using graphic representations for any aspect of the language considered to be a contrastive element. The third goal was to show how arbitrary orthographic representations may be. To this purpose, we worked on comparing the way in which different languages produced their own orthographic systems and how these systems have changed over time.

The workshop's last session was devoted to the distinctive features of Mariteco. Participants were invited to compare the orthographic chart created during the workshop to the systems used in the extant materials. This activity demonstrated that different symbols could be related to the same sound independently of their use in other languages. The group decided to adopt temporarily a system in which <w>, the symbol used in the workshop to represent the rounded consonants, was changed to <u>, the symbol commonly used in previous orthographies. People considered the use of <u> to be closer to Náayeri and therefore useful in distinguishing it from the language of their Huichol neighbours (cf. Hull, Lai, this volume).[7]

The workshop ended with a discussion of certain phonetic elements related to tone (Valdovinos and Kim 2014) and the importance of considering them in future studies. At first, participants seemed confused, but this confusion served to begin a discussion about elements that they could identify without knowing how to represent them in writing. The participants and the organizers agreed that there is still much to do but that some goals had been achieved. One of the important issues that remained for future debate was the adoption of certain Spanish sounds already used in Mariteco, such as [o] or [g]. No definitive answers were proposed, but this and other questions were put on the agenda for future workshops. All accepted a provisional orthographic model that took into account all the aspects analysed during the workshop.

5 Conclusions

The community-based workshop for the creation of an orthographic system among the Náayeri of Jesús María was a rich experience that provided several elements to reflect upon concerning the dynamics of adopting a writing system for unwritten and endangered languages. First, it showed that the initial rejection of an orthography should not be interpreted as a lack of interest on the part of the community. Reading and writing are often considered to be impositions from a different cultural background, and orthographies tend to be viewed in the same way.

The influence of modernity is encouraging indigenous communities to feel closer to writing practices. In this context, the existence of an orthographic system to express themselves in their own language appears to be increasingly appreciated. Nonetheless, it is important to understand how an orthography can best be introduced to a community of speakers. At this stage, participation on the part of the community seems to be an essential variable governing the success of such a venture and should be seen as a point of departure rather than a mere possibility.

Bringing people closer to a written version of their own language is a long process that implies the convergence of two ways of thinking and acting: the logistics of literacy and the cultural ideas of the community of speakers. Because of this, trying to understand first the internal dynamics of the community is essential for the eventual implementation of an orthographic system. The creation of an orthographic system cannot be reduced to a mere linguistic analysis and must take into account the desires and expectations of the speakers, as well as their previous experience of such systems. It is also important to fully understand the link between language and identity, and to seriously consider the existence of dialectal varieties as markers of this relationship. Therefore, it is sometimes more convenient to include the aspects that make the speakers recognize the written language as their own rather than set those items apart, in order to obtain a more 'inclusive' written version of a language. Interaction with a speaker's previous knowledge will also be a constant factor. All potential readers will have some idea of previous orthographies and will be using their experience to contrast it to the new proposals. This also applies to the influence of national or official languages spoken within the same territory. In the case of Náayeri, Spanish is in a constant dialogue with any situation related to the field of literacy.

All aspects considered thus far lead us to consider orthography development as an ongoing social process (on this point, see also Casquite and Young, and Schreyer, this volume). In any social situation concerning orthography planning, the outcome is always 'in the making'. When I adopted a dynamic perspective with respect to the results we could achieve after the workshop, participants were concerned at first, but they soon realized that their views on orthography were already changing and that it was only normal that, with the inclusion of more elements, these would continue to evolve. The idea of orthographies 'in the making' motivated the participants of the workshops to continue finding their way towards a more adequate writing system and to see what they knew so far as a huge step forward. As far as the INALI was concerned, the workshop was a 'first', to be replicated in order to continue working with the people of the community. At least three more meetings to discuss a Náayeri orthographic system have now taken place in the region. Only time will tell if the INALI will continue working with the community, identifying its needs, and constructing culturally accepted versions of the language in a written form, or whether it will demand the 'unification' of as many dialects as possible under a common orthography, leading to the creation of a system that may very well be considered as shared by all Náayeri speakers but that would certainly lack cultural recognition on the part of the actual speakers of the individual dialectal varieties of this endangered language.

Notes

1. The Náayeri are commonly known as *Cora* in Spanish. Both terms (Náayeri and Cora) are used with reference to the culture, the group, and the language. This

language is used by 20,793 speakers (INEGI 2010) organized in smaller territorial units called agrarian communities (*comunidades agrarias*). Each community possesses a particular political system, follows a set of religious practices and uses a dialectal variety of the Náayeri language. This research was conducted in the agrarian community of Jesús María, where people are called Chwíse'etaaka in Náayeri and Mariteco in Spanish. Both terms are also used to refer to the dialectal variety. The research was funded by financial support from PAPIIT Project No. IA400415 (UNAM).

2. Other research has emphasized the necessity of privileging the social aspects over and above the linguistic facts in the context of orthography development (cf. Cahill 2014:9–25; Seifart 2006:275–299) (cf. also, for example, Moseley, Casquite and Young, Hull, and Sackett, this volume).

3. On 14 January 2014, the Mexican Presidential Office reported 11,132,562 indigenous people, which is close to 10 per cent of the total Mexican population (www.presidencia.gob.mx/5-datos-sobre-los-pueblosindigenas-en-mexico/; last accessed 7 May 2015). The variance between these data and that which is reported by the National Census is due to the fact that National Census considers only the speakers of an indigenous language, whereas the Presidential Office also takes into account the members of indigenous communities who do not speak an indigenous language.

4. See Casad (1984) for Mariteco, Vázquez (2002) for Meseño and Corapeño, and Roth (2008) for Tereseño.

5. The *Ethnologue* groups eight different dialectal varieties in the El Nayar group (crn), stating that there exist 9,480 speakers and that it is considered a level 5 (developing) language: Corapan, Dolores, Rosarito, Jesús María, La Mesa del Nayar, Presidio de los Reyes, San Francisco, and Los Gavilanes (www.ethnologue.com/language/crn; last accessed 28 April 2015). This is not accurate, as it includes varieties whose phonological structure has been proven to be different in consistent ways. This classification proves once again the implementation of a 'top-down' policy for the identification of languages and dialects and also confirms the lack of information concerning these dialects' phonological structure. The assignment of level 5 assumes the use of a standardized form of literature. This is clearly not the case for any of the Náayeri communities, which may be more compatible with the 6b level (threatened), described in the *Ethnologue*'s webpage as 'used for face-to-face communication within all generations, but it is losing users'.

6. The National Council of Educational Motivation (CONAFE, Consejo Nacional de Fomento Educativo) was created in order to provide teachers for the smallest and more isolated hamlets in the Mexican countryside. CONAFE recruits young students and provides them a brief training before sending them to teach groups of students between 7 and 12 years of age. After two years of service, the young teaching assistants receive a full scholarship, which allows them to continue their high school education.

7. This decision was later changed again, when the community decided to use <w> once more for street signs, as I witnessed during my field trip in May 2015.

5 Community-Driven, Goal-Centred Orthography Development: A Tsakhur Case Study

Kathleen D. Sackett

1 Introduction

Orthography development for vulnerable languages can encourage and enhance language maintenance and revitalization efforts. A new orthography, however, may also hinder such efforts if the process of development is not handled well (Grenoble and Whaley 2006:159). Recent discussions have debated whether orthography development is the linguist's or the community's task. Since orthography development is much more than an academic exercise, it often evokes strong emotions in all stakeholders. For example, community members might desire to express their unique identity in their orthography (cf. Leggio and Matras, Hull, and Lai, this volume), even at the expense of pedagogy, or strong internal and external pressures might exist for the orthography to be patterned after majority or national languages (cf. Shah and Brenzinger, and Leggio and Matras, this volume). Therefore, it is important that the linguist work together with the wider community to aid them in decision making so that they can make informed decisions which enhance the creation of a sustainable orthography. One way linguists can assist in orthography development is to help the community develop goals and principles to follow during the development process (on this point, cf. Casquite and Young, Valdovinos, and Shah and Brenzinger, this volume).

This chapter examines how goals and principles were applied to develop a new Roman-based orthography for the Tsakhur in Azerbaijan. First, I briefly discuss the Tsakhur sociolinguistic situation. Next, I look at orthography development basics and the Tsakhur orthography problem. Further, I discuss how a series of community discussions was used to set goals and guiding principles for establishing the Roman-based orthography. Then, I show examples illustrating how the Tsakhur orthography committee used the principles in decision making. Finally, I consider the potential impact the orthography might have on future language development.

2   The Tsakhur

Tsakhur (ISO 639–3:tkr) is a Nakh-Dagestani/north-east Caucasian language in the Lezgic sub-family of languages. It is spoken by approximately 50,000 people in north-west Azerbaijan and south-west Dagestan.[1] Approximately half of the Tsakhur live in 22 villages in the Zaqatala and Qax regions of Azerbaijan. Tsakhur language vitality varies by region. In Dagestan and the Qax region of Azerbaijan, it is a 6b on the EGIDS scale (used for face-to-face communication within all generations, but it is losing users) and in the Zaqatala region of Azerbaijan a 6a (used for face-to-face communication by all generations, and the situation is sustainable). The Tsakhur call themselves 'Yiqbı', and their language 'Yedna Miz' or 'Ts`əxna Miz'.

Throughout their history, the Tsakhur have had various attempts at orthography development that have been abandoned or had little effectiveness. In the fifteenth century following the introduction of Islam, the Tsakhur adopted an Arabic script. All that remains of this script are a few stones with inscriptions. In 1934, a Roman script was developed by Anatolii Genko as a part of Lenin's plan to introduce Roman orthographies throughout the Soviet Union (Ibragimov 1990:4).[2] A few publications, including a primer written by Genko, were produced using this orthography. However, in 1938, according to a new Stalinist policy, all languages in the Soviet Union were required to adopt a Cyrillic orthography (Schulze 1997:5). Nothing of note was produced using the Tsakhur Cyrillic orthography until after the collapse of the Soviet Union. Since that time, a newspaper, a children's magazine, and several books have been published using the Cyrillic script (Schulze 1997:10). Ibragimov (1992) claims that the Cyrillic alphabets used in Dagestan are inexpedient, which makes them less desirable outside Russia. Following independence in 1991, Azerbaijan began the process of adopting a Roman script to replace the Cyrillic script for Azerbaijani. The country adopted the new Azerbaijani Roman orthography in December of 1991 (Hatcher 2008:111). In 1997, a Tsakhur orthography using Roman and Cyrillic graphemes (see Appendix 1) and a primer were introduced in Azerbaijan. This orthography, however, was ineffective. With minimal classroom hours to teach mother tongue, it never gained popularity. In 2010, the Tsakhur community living in Azerbaijan requested my assistance to develop a Roman-based orthography. In the spring of 2011, the Tsakhur community formed an orthography committee for this purpose.

3   Orthography Development

3.1   *A Few Basic Concepts*

As communities begin language development activities, they often use national languages as a pattern for their development activities (cf. Casquite and Young, and Leggio and Matras, this volume). This, however, can lead to unrealistic planning, as national languages generally have had writing and educational systems for long periods of time. Similarly, national languages are used in domains such as higher education and government where an endangered language is less likely to be used. Djité (2009) suggests that promoting a language in domains where it would hold back a community adds to the oppression of minority peoples. Therefore, language development should be undertaken after considering both linguistic and non-linguistic factors.

Orthography development, as a language development activity, must also consider linguistic and non-linguistic factors. Cahill (2014) includes the following non-linguistic considerations: governmental policies and restrictions, sociolinguistic factors, educational and psycholinguistic factors, and practical production factors such as fonts (cf. Casquite and Young, and Valdovinos, this volume). Seifart (2006) adds existing orthographies and dialect variations to the list of non-linguistic factors to be considered when developing an orthography (cf. Hewitt, this volume). Thus, one role a linguist can play in orthography development is to help the community consider and evaluate the sociolinguistic, socio-economic, socio-political, educational, and production factors relating to language development in their community and incorporate this into orthography development and language planning.

There are differing opinions as to the role of linguistic research and analysis in orthography development. As discussed by Casquite and Young, and Esteban (this volume), Smalley (1964) holds that a good orthography is phonemic. He also claims that the following five criteria need to be met when establishing a new writing system: maximum motivation for the learner, maximum representation of speech, maximum ease of learning, maximum transfer, and maximum ease of reproduction. While agreeing that an orthography should be phonemic based, Bauernschmidt (1977) adds that it should provide for accurate and efficient communication as well as consider sociolinguistic issues. According to Sebba (2007), a linguistically based orthography is not always particularly helpful, because orthography development is a social practice. Like many of the chapters in the present volume, Bow (2012) states that mother-tongue speakers should be included in orthography development and that ultimately the power to make decisions should be given to them. I propose that orthography decisions already lie in the hands of the community and that the role of the linguist is to help the community make linguistically informed decisions so as to avoid developing an orthography that could lead a language that is already at risk down the road to endangerment. Once a community understands the role that an orthography can play in their language development activities, then they are better equipped to make decisions. The result is a more sustainable orthography and language development programme.

3.2 The Tsakhur Problem

As the linguist asked to assist the Tsakhur community in orthography development, it was important that I not overlook the full extent of the sociolinguistic, socio-political, and socio-economic situation of the Tsakhur in Azerbaijan. Rice and Cahill (2014) recognize the importance of phonological analysis in assisting with early-stage orthography development, but they add that social and political factors need to be considered to promote acceptability and usability. Sebba (2007) includes Priestly's warning that linguists who do not consider psychological, sociological, and political factors in orthography development may have a difficult time. Thus, I gave linguistic input to the committee when it was needed, but my greater contribution in the process was helping the community think through a series of questions related to their sociolinguistic, socio-political, and socio-economic situation in order to help them make well-informed decisions.

The Tsakhur, a minority community trying to establish their ethnic identity, express a desire to have an orthography with unique graphemes that would be immediately identifiable as iconic Tsakhur. Yet they also recognize that the vitality of their language is dependent upon the youth using it and passing it down to the next generation. They desire an orthography that would be easy for the youth to learn and use with various forms of technology and with limited formal literacy training. However, the desire to express their ethnic identity through their orthography and that of developing a youth-focused orthography are at cross-purposes. As a linguist, I could help them identify their primary goal for developing a new orthography as well as examine and place Tsakhur language use in the greater context of their complex linguistic situation.[3]

4 Community Goals

In order to facilitate the work of orthography development, the community decided to form a committee to oversee the process. The committee consisted of several Tsakhur school teachers; a Tsakhur scholar; and myself (in a consultant role), a non-Tsakhur, non-Azerbaijani linguist working with a non-profit language development organization.

4.1 Setting a Goal

The first step in helping the community make linguistically informed orthography decisions was helping them identify and articulate their primary goal for orthography development. Through a series of discussions, they articulated that their goals included the following:

(i) An orthography that was a dynamic part of their society
(ii) An orthography that provided a means of written communication for today's youth
(iii) An orthography that would inspire future generations to use their language in domains where it is not currently being used
(iv) A sustainable orthography that would not require outside help for its use as technologies change
(v) An orthography that did not alienate the Tsakhur community living in the Russian Federation

Ultimately, they were motivated to establish a Roman-based orthography to facilitate and encourage Tsakhur literacy among the youth living in Azerbaijan (cf. Shah and Brenzinger, this volume).

4.2 Evaluating the Sociolinguistic and Socio-Political Situation of the Tsakhur

Even with defined goals, the committee struggled to understand how to begin developing an orthography. Since most Tsakhur are literate in Azerbaijani and/ or Russian, they believed that their orthography had to work and function in a manner similar to either or both of these languages. It was clear that, while they could clearly articulate their goals, they were struggling to relate those goals to their sociolinguistic and socio-political situation. As a result, I asked the committee to organize a community discussion that would allow them to put their situation in context. The committee needed to understand the community's goals for their language and culture, the language contact and use, the necessary components for success in their context, the available mother-tongue literacy opportunities, and the use of technology in their community (see Appendix 2). Once they evaluated these areas, community members and committee members were better equipped to make sustainable orthography decisions.

4.2.1 Goals for Language and Culture The Tsakhur express that their strongest desire is for their language to be passed down to the next generation. They also desire its continued use in all domains where it is currently being used as well as an increase in domains of use in the local context. In order to enjoy basic written communication and literature, they would like to have access to adequate literacy materials. Since the Tsakhur communities living in Azerbaijan and Dagestan have maintained a strong connection (they have, for centuries, been sheep herders who grazed their sheep in scattered mountain pastures in the summer while sharing common lowland pastures in the winter) and shared a dialect, those in Azerbaijan expressed a desire to do all they could to encourage communication with Dagestani communities.[4] They also realize that they have lost much of their oral literature and would like to see efforts made to preserve these stories in whatever medium possible.

The Tsakhur living in Azerbaijan acknowledge that much of their cultural knowledge is in danger of being lost as the older generation dies. They would like to see efforts made to preserve this knowledge before that happens. They would like to be able to present cultural knowledge to the younger generation in a way that would be appreciated. As urbanization and modernization takes place, the Tsakhur would like to have formats in which they could celebrate and enjoy their culture. Those living in Azerbaijan are keenly aware that they are separated from their kinspeople by an international border and that this is a threat to maintaining a singular cultural identity. Hence, they want to do everything they can to maintain a singular cultural identity (cf. Leggio and Matras, this volume).

4.2.2 Language Contact Given their geographic locality and history, the Tsakhur in Azerbaijan are exposed to Azerbaijani, Russian, and Turkish languages on a daily basis. While many individuals may only have passive exposure to Russian and Turkish through television, technology, or the Internet, a large number of them regularly use Azerbaijani in both written and spoken forms. Most business is conducted in Azerbaijani; however, there is still use of Russian in some business sectors. Secondary schools are predominately taught in Azerbaijani. A few schools in the region have sections in which instruction is conducted in Russian, and in the regional centre of Zaqatala there is a secondary school where all instruction is conducted in Russian. Depending on the higher educational institution, the language of instruction could be Azerbaijani, Russian, or English.

4.2.3 Success When asked what was necessary for their children to be successful, those involved in the discussion unequivocally answered that higher education was an important step towards success. In order to accomplish this, they would need to be literate in the national language and an international language. The Tsakhur desire financial stability for their children and equate this with higher education. Finally, they said that to be successful, people must understand the world around them, including their cultural roots and language.

4.2.4 Mother-Tongue Literacy At present, the Tsakhur have limited access to literacy materials and formal mother-tongue language classes. Azerbaijani educational policy allows for classes in the endangered minority languages for two hours a week in grades 1–4 (6–10 years of age).[5] Very few schools are taking advantage of these hours, as they lack materials and trained teachers and are concerned about it taking away from other courses, thereby putting their children at a perceived disadvantage to Azerbaijani children.

4.2.5 Technology Mobile phones and texting are widely used by the Tsakhur in Azerbaijan. A growing number of the younger generation have smartphones. Community members shared during the discussions that they text in Azerbaijani, Russian, or Tsakhur. They expressed that they found the Tsakhur Cyrillic script difficult to use, making it hard to text with Tsakhur friends and relatives in Dagestan. The younger generation reported that they would like to text one another in Tsakhur using a Roman-based script. Personal computers are gaining popularity, although many young people have access to them only at Internet clubs/cafés. In general, the computers in use are equipped with Azerbaijani, Russian, and English keyboards. Most of the people have only basic computer skills. Computers are most often used for e-mailing, instant messaging, social media, and playing games.

5 Principle-Based Decisions

After the community discussion, the Tsakhur orthography committee felt that they needed to establish guiding principles which they would use to develop a Roman-based orthography. This would help them evaluate proposals that were potentially at cross-purposes with the community's stated goals. This section discusses the guiding principles and gives examples of how they were applied to orthographic decision making.

5.1 Principle One: The Principle of Cyrillic Correspondence

> The Roman-based orthography would as much as possible correspond to the Cyrillic-based orthography used in Dagestan.

Initially, some community members wanted to develop a Roman-based orthography with a one-to-one correspondence between the Roman-based and Cyrillic-based graphemes. However, this would provide a transliteration of the Cyrillic script, which would not result in a new sustainable orthography. This approach would lead to an orthography that was also more difficult to read and write and would not support transfer from Azerbaijani. Thus, what was needed was a well-thought-out Roman-based orthography that took into consideration the Cyrillic-based graphemes (for an analogous situation see, for example, Moseley, and Shah and Brenzinger, this volume).

5.1.1 Semivowel-Vowel Sequences The Cyrillic orthography in Dagestan includes four vowels that represent a word-initial semivowel-vowel sequence as shown in (1).

(1)   /ye/ <е> /yo/ <ё> /yu/ <ю> /ya/ <я>

Some of the committee members thought that it would be good to have equivalent graphemes in the Roman-based orthography. Upon closer examination and linguistic input, the committee realized that there was a much more elegant solution. In Tsakhur there are seven /yV/ sequences, as in (2).

(2)
			Cyrillic	Roman
/ye/	/yed/	'mother'	<ед>	<yed>
/yo/	/yoq'uble/	'three'	<ёлкьубле>	<yoq`uble>
/yu/	/yuv/	'tree'	<юв>	<yuv>
/ya/	/yaba/	'fork'	<яба>	<yaba>
/yɨ/	/yɨq'/	'soup'	<йыкь>	<yıq`>
/yɨˤ/	/yɨˤχ/	'lard'	<йыIх>	<yı`x>
/yi/	/yitʃi/	'sister'	<йичи>	<yiçi>

For the three sequences that do not have Cyrillic equivalents (/yɨ/, /yɨˤ/, /yi/), the Cyrillic-based orthography represents them with the sequences <йы>, <йыI>, and <йи>, respectively, as in (2). The Roman-based orthography could employ a similar strategy for all semivowel-vowel sequences using <yV>, as shown in the last column of (2). The committee feels that this is the most elegant solution for representing these sequences and that it allows for the use of characters found only on the standard Azerbaijani keyboard even though it does not represent a one-to-one correspondence to the Cyrillic-based orthography.

5.1.2 Representation of the Glottal Stop

Since Azerbaijani has no glottal stop, community and linguistic input was needed to determine an appropriate representation for it. In the official Cyrillic-based orthography used in Dagestan, the glottal stop is represented by the hard sign <ъ>, a diacritic. Based upon the limitations of the Azerbaijani keyboard, the orthography committee felt that <`> would be the best grapheme choice to represent glottal stop. As illustrated in (3)–(5), the glottal stop occurs word initially, medially, and finally in Tsakhur.

(3)
			Cyrillic	Roman
	[ʔulʲ]	'eye'	<ул'>	<ul>
	[ʔosbɨ]	'logs'	<осбы>	<osbı>
	[ʔasta]	'halva'	<аста>	<asta>

(4)
	[haʔu]	'1cl.did'	<гьаъу>	<ha`a>
	[hawʔu]	'3cl.did'	<гьавъу>	<hav`u>
	[hoʔo]	'yes'	<гьоъо>	<ho`o>

(5)
	[maʔ]	'sheep fat'	<маъ>	<ma`>
	[tsʲeʔ]	'goat'	<цIеъ>	<ts`e`>
	[t'uˤʔ]	'rope'	<тIуIъ>	<t`ü`>

Since Tsakhur has no initial vowels, the Cyrillic script does not mark initial glottal stops preceding a vowel, as in (3). Likewise there is no motivation for marking them in the Roman-based orthography, also shown in (3). In the Cyrillic-based orthography, final glottal stops are marked as in (5), since it is an attested phoneme with near minimal pairs, as illustrated in (6).

(6) /maʔ/   'sheep fat'   /ts'eʔ/   'goat'
     /dama/ 'river'   /ats'e/   'full'

Thus, the committee decided to also mark final glottal stops in the Roman-based orthography, as in (5).

Since there are no phonemic vowel sequences in Tsakhur, the committee was uncertain whether or not glottal stops occurring word medially between two vowels or following a semivowel and preceding a vowel should be marked as in (4). Through informal observation, the committee noted that teenagers inconsistently marked glottal stops between vowels and following a semivowel (more formal testing may produce a different result). Based upon these observations and the principle of Cyrillic correspondence, the committee determined that glottal stops occurring between vowels and following a semivowel should be marked in the Roman-based orthography as it is in the Cyrillic-based one, as illustrated in (4).

With this decision, the orthography committee needed to examine whether <`>, the only available diacritic, was being overused in the proposed orthography. Table 5.1 demonstrates the uses of <`> in the proposed Roman-based orthography, including the marking of ejectives, voiced uvular plosives, high–mid pharyngealized vowels, and glottal stops. While it is not an ideal solution to use one diacritic to mark four different types of phonemes, the environments where they occur do not overlap, which avoids confusion.

Table 5.1 *The use of <`> in the proposed Tsakhur Roman-based orthography (after Sackett 2013:58).*

Orthographic representation	Phonemic representation	English gloss	Feature represented
<ç`ər>	/tʃʕaʕr/	'hair'	Ejective
<k`uk`>	/k'uk'/	'spoon'	Ejective
<vəq`ə>	/vaʕq'aʕ/	'sheep'	Ejective
<p`əp`əl>	/p'aʕp'aʕl/	'ash'	Ejective
<g`arg>	/ɢarg/	'mountain goat'	Uvular plosive
<mı`q>	/mıʕq/	'ice'	Pharyngealized vowel
<ts`e`>	/ts̪ʲeʔ/	'goat'	Glottal stop

Munro (2014) states that one rule of good orthography development is that every symbol or combination of symbols represents the same phoneme (cf. also McDonald and Zair, this volume). She adds, however, that if this rule is violated because it makes the orthography less intimidating and does not impede communication, there should be no problem. The use of <`> in Tsakhur enables the community to have an orthography with minimal digraphs that do not hinder communication.

5.2   Principle Two: The Principle of Youth Focus

> The main purpose for establishing a Roman-based orthography is to facilitate and encourage Tsakhur literacy among the youth living in Azerbaijan.

From the beginning, the Tsakhur community has been insistent that the main goal for developing a new orthography is to help encourage literacy among the young people (cf. Casquite and Young, this volume). One way to accomplish this is to provide an orthography that is easily accessible. In the Cyrillic-based orthography, palatalized consonants are marked by the four iotated vowels <я, е, ё, ю>, <ь>, or <`> (from an English keyboard).[6] As discussed previously, in Section 5.1.2, the diacritic <`> is already used to represent several features in the Roman-based orthography. Since the Cyrillic-based orthography uses a variety of strategies for marking palatalization and the Azerbaijani Roman keyboard only has one diacritic, in order to determine how to represent palatalization, the committee members needed to understand the phonological analysis and usage of palatalization in Tsakhur.

Tsakhur has phonologically conditioned palatalization, as illustrated in (7), and phonemic palatalization, as in (8) and (10).

(7)   /χiw/   [χʲiw]   <xiv>   'village'
       /ʃit'ʲ/   [ʃit'ʲ]   <şit`>   'bird'
       /lit/   [lʲit]   <lit>   'shepherd's wool cape'
       /gade/   [gadʲe]   <gade>   'boy'
       /nibeluχ/   [nʲibʲeluχ]   <nibelux>   'newborn'

Following lengthy discussions, the committee initially decided that, in the Roman-based orthography, palatalization would be marked with <Cy>. However, they did not feel that this was an elegant solution and that it would be easier for the youth if phonologically conditioned palatalization were not marked, as in (7).

(8)   /dutʲak/   [dutʲak]   <dutyak>   'recorder/flute'
       /dʲak:uj/   [dʲak:uj]   <dyakkuy>   'cuckoo bird'
       /gʲo:ʁij/   [gʲo:ʁij]   <gyooğiy>   'rain'
       /sʲo/   [sʲo]   <syo>   'bear'

/xʲan/   [xʲan]   <xhyan>   'water'
/nʲak/   [nʲak]   <nyak>   'milk'
/lʲule/   [lʲulʲe]   <lyule>   'barrel of a gun'

The committee feels that marking initial and medial phonemic palatalized consonants with <Cy>, as in (8), would not present a problem for the youth. Azerbaijani marks borrowed words with palatalized consonants using <Cy>, as in (9).

(9)   /manʲak/   <manyak>   'maniac'
        /konʲak/   <konyak>   'cognac'
        /katʲa/   <Katya>   'Katya'

In summary, the committee members did not feel that using <Cy> was a good solution, especially for word final palatalization. Some proposed using the English apostrophe as in the Cyrillic-based orthography. However, that went against the principle of technological accessibility, since it requires switching between keyboards when typing. One member proposed not marking word final palatalization at all. Initially, this solution was met with scepticism but gained popularity when the committee examined how the youth pronounced word final palatalization. They found that the majority of today's youth do not palatalize word final consonants. They then examined the few known minimal pairs differing in word final palatalization, as illustrated in (10).

(10)   /zal/   [zal]   'room' RUS   /zalʲ/   [zalʲ]   '1sg.DAT'
        /val/   [val]   'record' AZ   /valʲ/   [valʲ]   '2sg.DAT'
        /ɢul/   [ɢul]   'slave' AZ   /ɢulʲ/   [ɢulʲ]   'window'

Seifart (2006) states that when there are few examples in a large corpus of a given feature that distinguishes between utterances, the need to represent that feature in an orthography is minimal. Further, in Tsakhur, one member of each of these pairs is a borrowed word. The sematic domains of the words in each pair differ enough to cause no confusion in context – as illustrated in (10). Thus the committee proposed that word final palatalization not be marked, as in (11), since the absence of marking represents Tsakhur as it is spoken in Azerbaijan by the youth and causes no confusion in reading for the older generation.

(11)   <zal>   'room' RUS   <zal>   *<zaly>   '1sg.DAT'
        <val>   'record' AZ   <val>   *<valy>   '2sg.DAT'
        <g`ul>   'slave' AZ    <g`ul>   *<g`uly>   'window'

Munro's (2014) second rule of orthography development states that every phoneme of the language must always be represented the same way. However, she concludes that this rule needs to be broken if doing so better serves the language and community needs. This is precisely why the Tsakhur orthography committee chose to mark palatalization in two different manners.

5.3 Principle Three: The Principle of Technical Accessibility

All graphemes must be from a standard Azerbaijani Roman keyboard.

Seifart (2006) proposes that where there is no access to the necessary software and computer skills, the usability and archiving of digital files will be better ensured if the graphemes chosen can be produced on a mechanical typewriter – as this ensures easy language production on a standard keyboard. Wise (2014) recounts how the Yanesha' alphabet was recently revised in order to enable the Yanesha' to produce their own literacy materials using any computer with a Spanish keyboard. The Tsakhur orthography committee knew that in this electronic age choosing to use a standard Azerbaijani keyboard would allow for maximal language production by community members (cf. Esteban, this volume). They understand that this will make it possible for them to produce their own language materials and communicate electronically without outside help. They hope this decision will encourage more members of the community to use the language, especially in those domains that have traditionally been oral and are now being communicated digitally.

Tsakhur has 34 basic consonant phonemes (see Table 5.2), while Azerbaijani has 24 represented by 23 consonant graphemes (see Table 5.3). This presents an obstacle to creating an orthography that only uses the characters on a standard Azerbaijani keyboard while maintaining direct correspondence between the Azerbaijani and Tsakhur graphemes.

Table 5.4 shows the dorsal plosive phonemes and graphemes in Tsakhur and Azerbaijani. It is important to note that Azerbaijani has a separate grapheme <g> to represent the voiced alveo-palatal but not for the voiceless plosive.

Table 5.2 *Basic Tsakhur consonant phonemes.*

	Labial	Dental	Alveolar	Alveo-palatal	Velar	Uvular	Glottal
Plosives	p	t			k	q	
	p'	t'			k'	q'	ʔ
	b	d			g	ɢ	
Affricates			t͡s	t͡ʃ			
			t͡s'	t͡ʃ'			
				d͡ʒ			
Fricatives	f[7]		s	ʃ	x	χ	h
			z	ʒ[8]	ɣ	ʁ	
Nasals	m	n					
Laterals		l					
Flap		ɾ					
Semivowels	w			j			

Table 5.3 *Basic Azerbaijani consonant phonemes.*

	Labial	Dental	Alveolar	Alveo-palatal	Velar	Glottal
Plosives	p	t		c	k^9	
	b	d		ɟ	g	
Affricates				t͡ʃ		
				d͡ʒ		
Fricatives	f		s	ʃ	x	h
	v		z	ʒ	ɣ	
Nasals	m	n				
Laterals		l				
Flap		ɾ				
Semivowels				j		

Table 5.4 *Tsakhur and Azerbaijani dorsal plosive phonemes and graphemes.*

Azerbaijani				Tsakhur			
Alveo-palatal		Velar		Velar		Uvular	
/c/	<k>	/k/	<k>	/k/	<k>	/q/	<q>
/ɟ/	<g>	/g/	<q>	/g/	<g>	/ɢ/	<g`>

Some committee members felt that this grapheme should be used to represent /gʲ/ in the Tsakhur Roman-based orthography. This presented a problem since Tsakhur has uvular as well as velar voiced and voiceless plosives. In order to use only those graphemes found on a standard Azerbaijani keyboard, the committee determined that in this instance a near one-to one-correspondence was the best solution and would cause minimal if any problems with transfer.

Similarly, a variety of representations for the Tsakhur uvular voiceless plosive /q/ were proposed. The two most viable were <q> or <qh>. In order to determine the best solution, the committee looked at examples such as (12) and (13).

(12) /qow/   <qov> or *<qhov>   'nose'
     /jiqij/   <Yiqiy> or *<Yiqhiy>   'Tsakhur'
     /mɨq/   <mıq> or *<mıqh>   'oak'

(13) /aˤ.raˤq.q'ar/ 'hazelnut.pl'
                    <ərəqq`ar> or *<ərəqhqh`ar> or *<ərəqqh`ar>
     /qeq.qʷas/   'dry.POT'
                    <qeqqvas> or *<qheqhqhvas> or *<qheqqhvas>

The examples in (12) led the committee to believe that /q/ could potentially be represented by <qh>. However, the examples in (13) proved to be unacceptable to the committee, as they believe that using <qh> would over-complicate reading and writing. Thus, they determined that as long as this was the only consonant grapheme without a near one-to-one correspondence, <q> would be an acceptable representation of /q/, believing that, in this case, accessibility and readability were more important than ease of transfer.

5.4 Principle Four: The Principle of Easy Transfer

> Tsakhur graphemes should as much as possible correspond to Azerbaijani graphemes promoting easy transfer from Azerbaijani to Tsakhur.

Hinton (2014) states that in multilingual situations with little or no minority language education, maximal transfer is related to ease of learning. Seifart (2006) claims that when the orthography of an endangered language resembles the orthography of the dominant language, that of the endangered language is more easily acquired. Therefore, given the sociolinguistic situation of the Tsakhur in Azerbaijan, it was important to the committee that the Tsakhur Roman-based orthography be maximally transferrable from Azerbaijani, as this would provide the Tsakhur with the best opportunity for increased literacy in mother tongue, while simultaneously supporting literacy in Azerbaijani (Tsakhur children tend to lag behind their Azerbaijani counterparts in learning to read and write in Azerbaijani) (cf. Shah and Brenzinger, Hull, and Esteban, this volume).

Previously, in Section 5.3, I discuss why the committee chose to use <q> to represent a different phoneme in Tsakhur than in Azerbaijani. With this exception, Azerbaijani consonant graphemes maintain a similar phoneme representation in Tsakhur (see Appendix 1).

Tables 5.5 and 5.6 represent the vowel phonemes in Tsakhur and Azerbaijani, respectively. Since they share the vowels /i, e, ɨ, a, u, o/, the committee decided to keep the same graphemes for Tsakhur as are used in Azerbaijani, namely <i, e, ı, a, u, o>.

Table 5.5 *Tsakhur vowel phonemes*.

	Front	Central	Back
High	i, iː		u, uˤ
		ɨ,[10] ɨˤ	
Mid	e, eː		o, oˤ
Low		a, aˤ	

102 *Kathleen D. Sackett*

Table 5.6 *Azerbaijani vowel phonemes.*

	Front	Central	Back
High	i, y		u
		ɨ	
Mid	e, ø		o
	æ		
Low		a	

The graphemes in (14) had yet to be used in the Roman-based Tsakhur orthography.

(14)   Other Azerbaijani vowel graphemes
       /y/ <ü>   /ø/ <ö>   /æ/ <ə>

The Tsakhur pharyngealized vowel phonemes /uˤ, oˤ, aˤ, ɨˤ/ also needed grapheme representation. One committee member, considering the principle of Cyrillic correspondence, wanted to find a diacritic to use to mark all pharyngealized vowel graphemes in the same manner as in the Cyrillic-based orthography, as illustrated in (15).

(15)   Tsakhur Cyrillic pharyngealized vowel graphemes
       /uˤ/ <уI>   /oˤ/ <оI>   /aˤ/ <аI>   /ɨˤ/ <ыI>

With only one diacritic, <`>, available on a standard Azerbaijani keyboard, this was not possible, as the fact that this diacritic already marks a number of phonological features could complicate reading and writing. Therefore, the committee analysed how the three remaining Azerbaijani vowel phonemes – whose graphemes had not been used – are pronounced when Azerbaijani words are borrowed by Tsakhur (see Tables 5.7 and 5.8).

Since Azerbaijani front rounded and low front vowels are realized as pharyngealized vowels in Tsakhur, the committee determined that using the Azerbaijani vowel graphemes, as illustrated in (16), was not likely to cause problems for reading and writing.

(16)   /uˤ/ <ü>   /oˤ/ <ö>   /aˤ/ <ə>

The committee believes that these representations are close equivalents and therefore remain true to the principle of easy transfer. Preliminary observations have shown this to be the case.

The pharyngealized vowel /ɨˤ/ remained without representation. Since no equivalent phoneme exists in Azerbaijani and no Azerbaijani vowel graphemes remained unused, an alternative solution was needed. The two proposed

Table 5.7 *Azerbaijani borrowed words with front rounded vowels (after Sackett 2013:74).*

Azerbaijani	Tsakhur	Gloss	Tsakhur Roman
/yzyr/	[uˤzuˤr]	'forgiveness'	<üzür>
/yty/	[uˤtuˤ]	'iron'	<ütü>
/øzæk/	[oˤzʲek]	'cell'	<özek>
/ølym/	[oˤlyˤm]	'death'	<ölüm>

Table 5.8 *Azerbaijani borrowed words with low front vowels (after Sackett 2013:75).*

Azerbaijani	Tsakhur	Gloss	Tsakhur Roman
/ædat/	[aˤdat]	'tradition'	<ədat>
/æzab/	[aˤzab]	'suffering'	<əzab>
/æmæl/	[aˤmaˤl]	'deed'	<əməl>

graphemes that the committee considered were <ı`> and <ıə>, illustrated in (17) and (18).

(17)   <ı`>
       /sɨˤvaˤ/   <sı`və>   'fox'
       /qɨˤrqɨˤmɨˤt'/   <qı`rqı`mı`t'>   'frog'

(18)   *<ıə>
       /sɨˤvaˤ/   *<sıəvə>   'fox'
       /qɨˤrqɨˤmɨˤt'/   *<qıərqıəmıət'>   'frog'

Since Tsakhur has no vowel or /iʔaˤ/ sequences, using <ıə> to represent /ɨˤ/ should cause no problem with reading or writing. However, the committee believes that in order to remain close to the Azerbaijani orthography, digraphs should be avoided, as they only occur in a few borrowed words in Azerbaijani. The committee had already proposed three consonant digraphs, as illustrated in (19), and wanted to avoid using any others.

(19)   /ɣ/ <gh>   /x/ <xh>   /t͡s/ <ts>

Thus, it was determined that <ı`> would be the best representation of /ɨˤ/, even though the diacritic <`> was already being used to represent several other phonemes (see Section 5.1.2, Table 5.1; cf. Shah and Brenzinger, this volume).

5.5 Principle Five: The Principle of Acceptability

The orthography would be based on the Tsakhur dialect as spoken in Zaqatala.

Unlike many other Nakh-Dagestani languages, Tsakhur has minimal dialectal variation. Broadly speaking, the main dialect, Tsakhur, is spoken in Dagestan and Azerbaijan. The Gelmets dialect is spoken in the village of Gelmets in Dagestan. In Azerbaijan, minimal variations occur from village to village.[11] Even with minimal variations, the committee felt that the orthography should be based on one standard that would be accepted by all Tsakhur communities. They determined that the language as spoken in Zaqatala was the most centralized and widely accepted; thus, the committee decided that the orthography would be based upon Tsakhur as spoken in Zaqatala. As literacy develops among the Tsakhur in Azerbaijan, it may be seen that orthographic decisions and writing conventions organically develop based upon another variant. Neither languages nor orthographies are stagnant, so this should not be a problem as long as it does not hinder language development.

6 Results

Since being introduced in 2012, several short books and a picture dictionary have been published using the proposed Tsakhur Roman-based orthography. Community members report that the publications are in demand. Whether this is motivated by a desire to read or a desire to possess the publication has not been reported. I have witnessed people of various ages reading the materials. One individual requested that all of the materials available in the proposed Tsakhur Roman-based orthography be brought to him while in hospital, as he was bored and wanted something to read. A schoolteacher reported that the picture dictionary was the most frequently checked-out book in his school's library. A more formal survey is needed to determine to what extent individuals in Tsakhur communities are reading and writing using the new Roman-based orthography and what impact that might have on the overall use of the language.

At present, several local educators are developing a primer using the proposed Roman-based orthography. They hope to obtain government approval for this orthography as well as permission to publish the primers. Once primers have been published, the orthography can be used in formal Tsakhur classes at the local schools. Whenever that takes place, more data will be available to understand how, if at all, the introduction of a Roman-based orthography in Azerbaijan has altered linguistic behaviour.

7 Conclusion

In summary, orthography development needs to be looked at as an interdisciplinary activity that includes linguistics, sociolinguistics, sociology, and anthropology (cf. Casquite and Young, this volume). Orthography development evokes strong emotions in all stakeholders, from the linguist to community members. Ultimately, orthography development is successful only when the orthography produced is accepted and used in the local community. Therefore, it is important that linguists and community members work together to develop an orthography that meets the goals of the local community (cf. Moseley, Casquite and Young, Shah and Brenzinger, and Schreyer, this volume). In order to do this, they must understand the sociolinguistic and sociopolitical situation. Similarly, community members need to be informed of the potential consequences of orthography decisions. By developing a set of guiding principles, the community and linguist can refer to them as they make orthography decisions. This will enable an orthography to be developed that meets the developed goals and addresses any emotional considerations or sociolinguistic concerns.

Appendix 1

Table 5.9 *The Tsakhur alphabet.*

	Tsakhur phonemes	Azerbaijani	Proposed Tsakhur Roman (2012)	Tsakhur Cyrillic	1997 Tsakhur alphabet
1.	/a/	A a	A a	A a	A a
2.	/aˤ/		Ә ә[12]	АI аI	АI аI
3.	/b/	B b	B b	Б б	B b
4.	/dʒ/	C c	C c	Дж дж	C c
5.	/tʃ/	Ç ç	Ç ç	Ч ч	Ç ç
6.	/tʃʼ/		Ç` ç`	ЧI чI	ÇI çI
7.	/d/	D d	D d	Д д	D d
8.	/e/	E e	E e	E e, Э э	E e
9.	/f/	F f	F f	Ф ф	F f
10.	/g/	G g[13], Q q	G g	Г г	G g[14], Q q
11.	/ɢ/		G` g`	Къ къ	Къ къ
12.	/ɣ/	Ğ ğ	Gh gh	ГI гI	QI qI
13.	/ʁ/		Ğ ğ	Гъ гъ	Qъ qъ
14.	/h/	H h	H h	Гь гь	H h
15.	/χ/		X x	X x	X x
16.	/x/	X x	Xh xh	Хь Хь	Хь Хь
17.	/ɨ/	I ı	I ı	Ы ы	I ı
18.	/ɨˤ/		I` ı`	ЫI ыI	II ıI
19.	/i/	İ i	İ i	И и	İ i

Table 5.9 (cont.)

	Tsakhur phonemes	Azerbaijani	Proposed Tsakhur Roman (2012)	Tsakhur Cyrillic	1997 Tsakhur alphabet
20.	/ʒ/	J j	J j	Ж ж	J j
21.	/k/	K k[15]	K k	К к	K k
22.	/k'/		K` k`	КI кI	КI кI
23.	/q/		Q q	Хъ хъ	Хъ хъ
24.	/q'/		Q` q`	Кь кь	Кь кь
25.	/l/	L l	L l	Л л	L l
26.	/m/	M m	M m	М м	M m
27.	/n/	N n	N n	Н н	N n
28.	/o/	O o	O o	О о	O o
29.	/oˤ/		Ö ö[16]	ОI оI	ОI оI
30.	/p/	P p	P p	П п	P p
31.	/p'/		P` p`	ПI пI	PI pI
32.	/r/	R r	R r	Р р	R r
33.	/s/	S s	S s	С с	S s
34.	/ʃ/	Ş ş	Ş ş	Ш ш	Ş ş
35.	/t/	T t	T t	Т т	T t
36.	/t'/		T` t`	ТI тI	TI tI
37.	/ts/		Ts ts	Ц ц	Ƶ ƶ
38.	/ts'/		Ts` ts`	ЦI цI	ƵI ƶI
39.	/u/	U u	U u	У у	U u
40.	/uˤ/		Ü ü[17]	УI уI	UI uI
41.	/w/	V v	V v	В в	V v
42.	/j/	Y y	Y y	Й й	Y y
43.	/z/	Z z	Z z	З з	Z z
44.	/ʔ/		`	ъ	ъ

Appendix 2

1. What is/are your goal(s)...?
   - For your language
     - For your children
     - For future generations
     - In which modes (oral, written, etc.)?
     - In what contexts?
     - For recording, documenting, and analysing
   - For your culture
     - Relating to cultural practices
     - Relating to cultural identity
     - Relating to what your children and future generations know and practice
     - Relating to documentation

2. With what majority languages do you have contact, and how do you use those languages?
   - How many languages are used in your community on a daily basis?
     - What are they?
     - What contexts?
   - What language(s) is/are used for instruction in the local school(s)?
   - What language(s) is/are used for instruction at institutions of higher learning?
3. What does your community consider necessary for success?
   - Relating to education
   - Relating to community
   - Relating to job or position
   - Relating to personal life
4. What does mother-tongue literacy look like in your community?
   - What materials are available?
   - What courses are available?
   - What is the community interest/support for it?
   - What is official interest/support for it?
5. How is technology used in your community?
   - Do community members text?
     - What languages and scripts do they use for texting (or would they *like* to use for texting)?
     - What types of mobile phones do they use?
     - What ages of people text?
     - Whom do they text?
   - Do community members use computers?
     - Do they own them or use them at an Internet club/café?
     - What are the primary functions for which computers are used in your community?
     - What ages of people use computers?
     - What standard keyboards are readily available for use in your community?

Notes

1. Ibragimov's estimation (1990:1). According to the 2010 Russian census, 12,769 individuals identified their nationality as Tsakhur. In the 2009 Azerbaijani census, 12,300 individuals self-identified as Tsakhur, with 95.3% reporting Tsakhur as their mother tongue.
2. Anatolii Nestorovich Genko (1896–1941) was a Soviet scholar from Leningrad who died in prison during the German occupation. Following his death, several of his works were published, including an Abaz grammar (1955) and a Tabassaran dictionary (2005).

3. Since the Tsakhur live both in Russia and Azerbaijan and have only been separated by an international border since the fall of the Soviet Union, they continue to use Azerbaijani and Russian in daily life. They have access to Azerbaijani, Turkish, and Russian television and radio. The Tsakhur also desire to be a part of the greater world; thus there is a felt need to learn English.
4. Tsakhur has one main dialect with minor local variations. A separate dialect is spoken in the village of Gelmets in Dagestan. Further linguistic research needs to be conducted in the village of Sunbunchi in Azerbaijan to determine if it is a separate dialect or a sub-dialect.
5. This is what the minority communities understand. I could find no formal documentation of this policy.
6. Iotation is the appearance of the palatal approximant /j/ before a vowel at the beginning of a word or between two vowels in the middle of a word, creating a diphthongoid (a partial diphthong).
7. This phoneme is found only in borrowed words.
8. This phoneme is found only in borrowed words.
9. This phoneme is found only in borrowed words and is represented by <k>.
10. Schulze (1997) represents this phoneme as /ə/, and Kibrik and Testelec (1999) represent it as /ɨ/.
11. Further research is needed to determine to what extent the Tsakhur spoken in the village of Subunchi varies from that of the other villages in Azerbaijan.
12. Represents /æ/ in the Azerbaijani alphabet.
13. Represents /ɟ/ in the Azerbaijani alphabet. Tsakhur does not have this phoneme.
14. Represents /gʲ/.
15. This grapheme also represents /c/ in the Azerbaijani alphabet.
16. Represents /ø/ in the Azerbaijani alphabet.
17. Represents /y/ in the Azerbaijani alphabet.

6 Writing for Speaking: The Nǀuu Orthography

Sheena Shah and Matthias Brenzinger

1 Introduction

With only three known remaining fluent speakers, all in their eighties, Nǀuu features prominently as the most endangered, still-spoken language of Southern Africa (Moseley 2010). Among linguists, Nǀuu (ISO 639 code: ngh) was thought to be extinct for several decades (cf. Traill 1999:27). In the late 1990s, through an initiative of Nigel Crawhall, Nǀuu speaker Elsie Vaalbooi made a radio announcement in which she asked other speakers to make themselves known. Some twenty elderly speakers, scattered throughout the Northern Cape province of South Africa, revealed their competence in the language (Chamberlin and Namaseb 2001). Since then, most of these speakers have passed away. Today, Nǀuu is spoken by three sisters only, all residing in the vicinity of Upington. Hanna Koper is the oldest, followed by Griet Seekoei; Katrina Esau (also known as Ouma Geelmeid), aged 84, is the youngest. Their younger brother, Simon Sauls, only remembers some Nǀuu words and phrases and therefore could be referred to as a semi-speaker at best. The sisters are not in regular contact with one another, mainly due to restrictions in mobility as a result of old age and poor infrastructure. Nǀuu, for that reason, is no longer used in natural conversations on a daily basis. This chapter describes the 'Writing for Speaking' project,[1] which aims to establish a shallow orthography that allows students who are non-native speakers of Nǀuu to read and pronounce new Nǀuu words, even those that they have never heard before.

Nǀuu is one of the 'non-Bantu click languages', a term suggested by Westphal (1971). Together with other languages spoken by former hunter-gatherers and pastoralists in Southern and Eastern Africa, Nǀuu was grouped as a member of the 'Khoisan' language family. This language family, however, proved not to exist as more language data became available and as the methods for analysing them advanced (Güldemann 2014a; Güldemann and Vossen 2000). While some scholars continue to use this rather problematic term, we adopt Westphal's label in order to also avoid confusion with the various kinds of discourse in Southern Africa in which 'Khoisan' is employed with different meanings (Brenzinger 2013, 2014).

While more than one hundred non-Bantu click languages might still have been spoken a century ago, only about a dozen of them are currently in use as community languages (Brenzinger 2013). |Xam, ǂUngkue, ǁXegwi, and N|uu – all languages belonging to the !Ui language family – were once spoken by former hunter-gatherer communities in most parts of present-day South Africa. |Xam, documented by Wilhelm Bleek and Lucy Lloyd in the 1870s, became extinct in the 1920s (Bleek 1929a). In post-apartheid South Africa, this language features prominently in the South African coat of arms and appears on all notes and coins of the South African currency. Although |Xam is the most visible !Ui language, N|uu is the only language of this family which is still spoken.

The rapid physical and cultural decline of hunter-gatherers who spoke non-Bantu click languages began with the arrival of the European settlers more than two centuries ago (Penn 2005). The colonizers, together with their Nama- or Afrikaans-speaking clients, murdered them in large numbers (De Prada-Samper 2012). Surviving members of the hunter-gatherer communities were marginalized and linguistically assimilated (Traill 1996). !Ui languages were abandoned by their speakers in favour of South East Bantu languages, such as siSwati and isiZulu (cf. Ziervogel 1955:36), as well as isiXhosa. In Lesotho, speakers of !Ui languages shifted to siPhuthi (Orpen 1874:3), while in the Northern Cape of South Africa, former hunter-gatherers predominantly speak Afrikaans as their mother tongue and Nama in some cases. 'Bushman' languages have left an impact on the languages they shifted to; for example, some of the *Karretjie Mense* ('donkey-cart people') of the Upper Karoo 'perceive their spoken version of Afrikaans to be a Bushman language' (Prins 1999:48). However, as far as we know, the three elderly women in Upington are the last remaining speakers of a !Ui language, namely N|uu.

2 The N|uu Speakers of the ǂKhomani Community and Their Language

The three N|uu-speaking sisters identify themselves as belonging to the ǂKhomani community. Members of this community, which may comprise up to four hundred people, all claim to be descendants of N|uu speakers. ǂKhomani, a xenonym, gained considerable currency during the San land claim and became more widely used only in the late 1990s (Crawhall 1999). ǂKhomani San, 'rather than meaning an ethnic unit, refers to a specific collective that was formed during the land claim process' (Ellis 2012:21). Nevertheless, ǂKhomani has been adopted by the N|uu speakers and their relatives as their ethnonym (Brenzinger forthcoming), and they emphatically sing their 'ǂKhomani San anthem' (Shah and Brenzinger 2016). N|uu has not been regularly used in everyday communication for several decades.

The remaining speakers, for that reason, underwent a process of rediscovering the language they were exposed to as children, and in discussions among themselves, meanings and structural aspects of the language returned to their memories.

By far, most ǂKhomani speak Afrikaans, the prevailing language in the Northern Cape province of South Africa, as their mother tongue. Fewer than thirty ǂKhomani in Witdraai and Welkom use Nama as their first language, but even among these few Nama-speaking families, the younger generation has shifted to Afrikaans. Members of the ǂKhomani community continue to be among the most marginalized and disadvantaged people of South Africa, both economically and socially.

Various names exist for the language, which the speakers themselves call Nǀuu. Nǀusa/Nǀuusaa (Krönlein 1861), Nǀusa (Pabst 1895), ǀNu (Pöch 1910), ɴǀfiuki/Nǀhuki (Westphal 1971), and ǀŋuʰːci/ǀŋuʰci (Traill 1974) appear in publications, but they do not all refer to the language known as Nǀuu today. For example, Güldemann (2006; 2014b) identifies Krönlein's Nǀusa/Nǀuusaa as a 'misclassified ǀXam variety'. The only grammar of the language which has so far been published uses Nǀuuki, a nominalized form of Nǀuu, the latter meaning literally 'to speak Nǀuu' (Collins and Namaseb 2011:7).

Between 1910 and 1920, Dorothea Bleek introduced the term ǀɴ to refer to a dialect or language cluster to which Nǀuu belongs (Bleek 2000:7). Güldemann adopts this name in the spelling of Nǁng for a language which comprises several dialects, with Nǀuu being one of them. Güldemann (2014b) suggested Nǁng as a cover term to include an eastern variety, ǀ'Au, and a western variety, Nǀuu. His name ǀ'Au for the eastern speech variety was never accepted by the community. Doke (1936) and Maingard (1937) refer to the Nǀuu language as ǂKhomani. While the community adopted ǂKhomani as the name of their community, the language is referred to by most scholars and all present speakers as Nǀuu or Nǀuuki only.

Nǀuu is characterized by one of the largest phoneme inventories in the world. In the Nǀuu practical orthography, 114 speech sounds are represented: 45 click phonemes, 30 non-click consonants, and 39 vowels. The most striking phonemic feature of Nǀuu is its set of bilabial clicks. Nǀuu is one of the three still-spoken languages in the world which employ this click type as phonemes. The other two languages are Taa and ǂHoan-Sasi (or ǂ'Amkoe). Taa is spoken in Botswana and Namibia and is claimed to be genetically related to Nǀuu (Güldemann 2014a). ǂHoan-Sasi is spoken in Botswana, and Heine and Honken (2010) convincingly established a genealogical ǂHoan-!Xun unit that they named Kx'a.

The documentation of Nǀuu started in the late 1920s. The early researchers include Dorothea Bleek (1929b, 1956), Clement Martyn Doke (1936), Louis

Fernand Maingard (1937), and Ernst Westphal (1953–1971). Since the 'rediscovery' of Nǀuu in the late 1990s, three major documentation projects produced modern descriptions of the language with the assistance of the last speakers:
  (i) A research project funded by the National Science Foundation (USA; hereafter, NSF), referred to here as the 'American group'[2]
  (ii) A research project funded by the Endangered Languages Documentation Programme (UK; hereafter, ELDP), referred to here as the 'German group'[3]
  (iii) A PhD project funded by the University of Cologne and the German Academic Exchange Service (DAAD)

While scholars of the first group conducted research mainly on the phonetic and syntactic structures (see Exter 2008:5 for a detailed list of publications), those of the second group worked on a discourse-based description and analysis of the language. In collaboration with members of the first group, Mats Exter wrote a PhD dissertation on the phonetics and phonology of Nǀuu. The two groups, as well as Exter, compiled extensive wordlists (Sands et al. 2006; Güldemann et al. 2007–2014; Exter 2013), and Collins and Namaseb (2011) published a modern grammar of the language.

An Andrew W. Mellon–funded project led by the authors of this chapter, Matthias Brenzinger and Sheena Shah, started in 2012. This project hosted at the Centre for African Language Diversity (CALDi) at the University of Cape Town lays the main emphasis on bridging the gap between scholars and speakers. In close collaboration with community members, a practical community orthography was established and language teaching materials produced (Shah et al. 2014a, 2014b; Shah and Brenzinger 2016).

3 Regionally Dominant Orthographies: IPA versus Roman Letters

In establishing a Nǀuu community orthography, some widely accepted principles were reviewed. It is generally accepted that an orthography should be linguistically sound (i.e., adequately represent the phoneme inventory) and should be acceptable to the community (i.e., embedded in the political and social environment). (See, for example, Cahill and Rice 2014; Grenoble and Whaley 2006; Hinton 2001; Seifert 2006; Casquite and Young, Schreyer, and Lai, this volume.) Furthermore, the applicability of the orthography in community teaching efforts as well as technical considerations with regard to the reproduction of reading, teaching and learning materials are factors that need to be taken into consideration.

In developing an orthography, it was assumed that it should not diverge from dominant national standards. Orthographies for African languages in the southern part of the continent were, not surprisingly, first developed for the major languages – namely isiZulu, isiXhosa, Sesotho, and other Bantu languages.

Orthographies for isiZulu and isiXhosa, two of the Nguni languages, were already in place in the 1820s (Bleek 1858).[4]

One of the questions to be addressed in orthography development for non-Bantu click languages is how click phonemes should be represented. Not only these languages, but also eleven of the Southern Bantu languages have clicks in their phoneme inventories. In all Bantu languages, clicks are written with Roman letters. The relatively small number of distinctive clicks in these Bantu languages allows for this choice. The advantages of employing Roman letters for clicks are that they are well established and widely used in the orthographies in the region (cf. Moseley, and Sackett, this volume). This led the government of Botswana to enforce the use of Roman letters for clicks in all languages spoken in the country. The orthography of Naro, a non-Bantu click language of Botswana, was developed according to this directive. However, it continues to be the only non-Bantu click language in Southern Africa which uses Roman letters to represent clicks.[5]

The visual familiarity with Roman letters is, however, misleading when such letters are used for representing click sounds. Knowing the letters <c>, <q>, and <x> does not help those who are not literate in Nguni languages and who do not know how to produce the dental, alveolar, and lateral clicks, respectively. The dominant Bantu languages spoken in Botswana do not have clicks, and for that reason, click-containing place names in this country are often spelt incorrectly, as are personal names on IDs. For example, *Xade* is the official spelling of a former settlement in the Central Kalahari Game Reserve, and the Roman letter <x>, following the Nguni writing convention, should represent the lateral click – i.e., [ǁade]. The name of this settlement, however, is pronounced as [ǀade], with a dental click. The correct spelling using Roman letters for clicks should therefore be *Cade*.

While clicks stand out when using IPA symbols, they are less visible when Roman letters are used. The IPA click symbols are prominent and easy to read even in trigraphs, whereas Roman letters for clicks, together with their accompaniments, may appear as cumbersome consonant clusters. For example, in Naro, [ǂx'] is written as <tcg'>, and *tcg'ari* 'careless, clumsy' is therefore pronounced as [ǂx'ari] (Visser 2001).

In addition to the use of Roman letters for clicks, further complications arise in the Naro orthography, which adopts writing conventions from different languages. The use of <g> – following the Setswana orthography – for the voiceless velar fricative [x] sets off a domino effect in which the phonetic value of [g] can no longer be represented by <g>. Naro opted for the Setswana spelling of [g], namely <gh>. Furthermore, the voicing of clicks, indicated by <g> in other orthographies, required an additional modification in Naro. The letter <d> represents the voicing of clicks in this orthography. Thus, <g> is equivalent to [x], for example in *gàm* [xàm] 'lion'; <gh> is equivalent to [g], for example in *ghãa* [gã:] 'duck'; and <dc> is equivalent to [gǀ], for example in *dcàà* [gǀà:] 'shelter' (Visser 2001).

While the first choice for representing clicks, based on extra-linguistic factors, would be the conventions of the Nguni languages, all community orthographies for non-Bantu click languages, with the exception of Naro and Sandawe, use the IPA click symbols. Clicks are complex sounds that occur in large numbers and high frequencies in non-Bantu click languages. The number of distinct click phonemes in the eleven Southern Bantu languages that borrowed clicks from non-Bantu click languages is relatively low and ranges from 2 clicks in Mbukushu to 29 in Yeyi. The non-Bantu click languages, by contrast, use large numbers of click phonemes – i.e., 83 in Taa (!Xõó), 55 in ǂHoan (ǂ'Amkoe), 47 in Jul'hoan, 45 in Nǀuu, and 32 in Khwe (Miller 2011:424). For the reasons outlined in this section, the Nǀuu community orthography follows the practice of most orthographies for non-Bantu click languages – such as Khwe, Ts'ixa, and Khoekhoegowab – in using the IPA click symbols.

4 Nǀuu Orthographies and Materials Developed

Levi Namaseb began supporting community language teaching efforts in the late 1990s and wrote Nǀuu by consulting existing orthographies for non-Bantu click languages. From mid-May 2000 onwards, he ran Nǀuu language workshops for the ǂKhomani youth which took place in Upington, Andriesvale, Rietfontein, Welkom, and Olifantshoek (Levi Namaseb, personal communication 2015). By directly involving the Nǀuu speakers in these places, Namaseb taught Nǀuu to interested community members in the form of 'very informal classes' (Namaseb n.d.:1). He focused in particular on 'sounds and example words with those sounds, speech acts and useful phrases in everyday occasions, songs, prayers, stories told or dramatized' (Namaseb n.d.:1). Many of his songs, stories, and prayers are still used today.

Namaseb's initial attempts to write the language were based on the spelling system of Khoekhoegowab, his mother tongue. This meant that, for example, voicing was not distinguished, as is the case in Khoekhoegowab, and therefore the Nǀuu terms for 'springbok' and 'gemsbok' were spelt the same – i.e., *!ae* (Namaseb 2003). The present Nǀuu orthography accounts for this distinction: 'springbok' is spelt as *g!ae*, and 'gemsbok' as *!ae*.

Other linguists then began working on the language and supported community teaching efforts. Based on his analysis of the Nǀuu sound inventory, Exter provided orthographic and phonemic recommendations in 2003 (Crawhall 2004:272). The 'American group' began their work on Nǀuu in 2004 and studied in particular its sound system and morphosyntax. In 2005, a Nǀuu primer was produced for teaching purposes (Namaseb et al. 2005). The primer lists 94 orthographic conventions for 41 click consonants, 19 non-click consonants, and 34 vowels, and provides example words accompanied by drawings from community members for about half of them. In addition to the primer, Collins and Namaseb's (2011) grammar contains stories which employ this orthography.

From 2007 onwards, the 'German group' conducted linguistic fieldwork on Nǀuu and proposed a revised orthography. This new orthography was used in a collection of various types of Nǀuu texts, including traditional tales, personal stories, recipes, prayers, and phrases (Siegmund et al. 2008). The hitherto only printed and illustrated storybook written in Nǀuu involved Ouma Geelmeid and Claudia du Plessis, and its development and production were supported by Martina Ernszt and Alena Witzlack-Makarevich (SASI 2012). The orthography used in this storybook is a blend of the orthographies developed by both groups. In addition, posters illustrating basic body part terms and animal names were produced by the German group but used the orthography conventions of the American group.

Based on the previous spelling conventions of their group, Collins and Namaseb further elaborated on the Nǀuu orthography (Collins and Namaseb 2011:109). The basic orthographic principles listed by them were followed as much as possible in the Nǀuu orthography established for the teaching efforts of Ouma Geelmeid. However, this was not possible in all respects, as outlined in the following discussion.

4.1 The Present Nǀuu Community Orthography

In January 2012, the only written materials used in the Nǀuu classes were the three posters designed by the German group. CALDi members were asked for support in the production of further teaching materials. Based on the previous attempts to develop a Nǀuu orthography, one of the main activities of the CALDi project was the production of Nǀuu alphabet charts (cf. Casquite and Young, and Valdovinos, this volume). Nǀuu orthography conventions, such as the representation of the Nǀuu sound inventory and the spelling of Afrikaans and Nama loanwords, were thoroughly discussed with the community members. While the scholars tried to divert as little as possible in these writing conventions from the previous attempts mentioned in the introduction to this section, this was not always possible, since conflicting conventions had been in place. In consultation with Claudia du Plessis and one of the former Nǀuu students, Mary-Ann Prins, adjustments in the Nǀuu orthography were suggested. With Ouma Geelmeid being the only speaker actively teaching the language, her pronunciation and knowledge of the language were the sole base in the development of the alphabet charts and teaching materials. For the Nǀuu alphabet charts, all symbols and letters used by Claudia in writing Nǀuu in the classes were included, thus also letters which only occur in loanwords.

The alphabet charts were officially launched at a community workshop on 24 March 2014 and have been in use at Ouma Geelmeid's school since then.

4.2   Materials Produced in the Nǀuu Orthography

Along with the three alphabet charts, an illustrated quadrilingual animal poster was designed by the CALDi group members. Each Nǀuu animal name is accompanied by a photo and by translations in English, Afrikaans, and the local variety of Nama, spoken by a few members of the ǂKhomani community. An illustrated trilingual (Nǀuu, Afrikaans, English) reader[6] using the Nǀuu community orthography has also been produced (Shah and Brenzinger 2016). The contents of the reader and also the format are tailored towards the community needs in their Nǀuu teaching and learning efforts. The reader comprises twelve semantic fields, and all words, phrases, and sentences included derive from natural conversational contexts. In addition to the semantically ordered sections, games, prayers, and songs are supplementary teaching tools. The Nǀuu terms used by Ouma Geelmeid in her language classes have been compiled in Nǀuu-Afrikaans-English and Afrikaans-Nǀuu-English glossaries.

4.3   Practical Considerations

As mentioned in Section 2, an eastern and a western variety of the language are distinguished by scholars and speakers. The eastern variety ceased to be spoken when Hannie Koerant passed away in Olifantshoek on 8 March 2015. The present community orthography is based on the western variety – more specifically on the idiolect spoken and taught by Ouma Geelmeid. The Nǀuu orthography was designed to be used by the literate co-teacher and students who acquire Nǀuu from the non-literate speaker. As the orthography and teaching materials serve as primary language learning devices for students, it is intended that they represent as much as possible the actual spoken language and pronunciation. For pedagogical reasons, we decided to adopt a shallow orthography with a close sound–symbol representation.[7] Even though an over-representation of the sound inventory results in a larger number of graphemes, the community members found it easier to read and write Nǀuu by representing the actual sounds of the spoken terms. At present, only two community members – namely Claudia du Plessis and Mary-Ann Prins – are able to confidently read and write the language.

4.4   Technical Considerations

In discussions on technical aspects of the Nǀuu orthography, the involved community members wished to avoid diacritics altogether (cf. Esteban, and Leggio and Matras, this volume). This proved not to be feasible. The use of the circumflex to represent the nasalization of vowels was introduced by Namaseb in the earliest attempts to write Nǀuu. Thus, [ã] is written as <â>, etc., as in most other community orthographies of non-Bantu click languages. The German group decided to use <n> instead of the circumflex. Since <n> also occurs as a consonant, <nn> was chosen by them to represent [n]. In their orthography, [ã] is written as <an>, and [an] is spelt as <ann>. For example, the Nǀuu term for 'to work' is *sîisen* [sĩ:sən] in the community orthography,[8] but it is spelt by the German group as *siinsinn* or *siinsnn*. The use of <nn> for [n] was considered cumbersome by the community members, who preferred to maintain the circumflex.

In the Nǀuu orthography, apostrophes are employed to represent glottalization (i.e., glottal stops and glottalized clicks) as well as ejectivization (i.e., ejective consonants). Apostrophes, and not IPA [ʔ] and [ʼ], are used to represent glottal stops and glottalized clicks in orthographies of most non-Bantu click languages.[9] Glottalized clicks [ʘˀ], [ǀˀ], [ǃˀ], [ǂˀ], and [ǁˀ] are therefore represented as <ʘ'>, <ǀ'>, <ǃ'>, <ǂ'>, and <ǁ'>. The Nǀuu word for 'to be sick, in pain', for example, is spelt *ʘ'ui'i*, where the first apostrophe represents a glottalized bilabial click [ʘˀ] and the second apostrophe a glottal stop [ʔ]. Delayed aspiration is spelled as <'h> – for example, as <ǀ'h> in the word *ǀ'hoba* 'grave'. Following the practices of scholars working on non-Bantu click languages, apostrophes in Nǀuu, in addition, indicate ejective affricates – namely <ts'> [t͡sʼ], as in *ts'axam* 'eye', and <kx'> [k͡χʼ], as in *kx'a* 'to drink' – and fricated ejected clicks such as <ǀx'> [ǀχʼ], as in *ǀx'a* 'hand'. This double assignment for apostrophes is a common practice in orthographies of African languages and does not pose any problems in the actual reading of Nǀuu texts.

First suggested by Patrick Dickens (1991:101) for Juǀ'hoan and also adopted by both the American and German groups, the use of the Roman letter <q> to mark vowels as pharyngealized (or 'pressed', see Dickens 1991:101) has also been employed in the Nǀuu orthography. This writing convention leads to a double representation in which the letter <q> is realized either as [ʕ] or as the voiceless uvular stop [q], as seen in the Nǀuu term *quaqî* [quaʕĩ] 'to be very hungry'.

Vowel length is a distinctive feature and is represented in the Nǀuu orthography by a doubling of vowels. Minimal pairs are, for example, *le* [le] 'heart' versus *lee* [leː] 'blue wildebeest'; *ǂqhi* [ǂqʰi] 'fast' versus *ǂqhii* [ǂqʰiː] 'hat'; *kx'a* [k͡χʼa] 'to drink' versus *kx'aa* [k͡χʼaː] 'to cry'; *kyu* [kʲu] 'mouth' versus *kyuu* [kʲuː] 'to hear, understand'; and *nǀa* [ŋǀa] 'and, with' versus *nǀaa* [ŋǀaː] 'head'. The doubling of vowels to indicate a long vowel rather than the IPA [ː] is common practice in community orthographies.

Tone is not marked in the Nǀuu orthography, even though there is evidence that lexical tone is in fact a distinctive feature in Nǀuu (Exter 2008). Exter (2015) provides minimal pairs for this – for example, /ŋǁŋ̀ŋ́/ 'blanket' versus /ŋǀŋ̩̀ŋ̩̀/ 'house'. Since Ouma Geelmeid does not consistently produce such tonal differences, tone is not marked in the Nǀuu orthography.

4.5 The Treatment of Afrikaans Loanwords

Even though the ǂKhomani speak a regional variety of Afrikaans, also referred to as *Oranjerivier-Afrikaans* (Roberge 2002), the spelling of Afrikaans loanwords in Nǀuu follows the orthography of Standard Afrikaans. The reason for choosing this convention is that children learn to read and write in Standard Afrikaans at school (cf. Casquite and Young, this volume).

As observed by Sands et al. (2007:59), Afrikaans loans do not usually replace existing Nǀuu terms but are limited to borrowed cultural concepts and new objects. These loans are often incorporated into Nǀuu – for example, by adding Nǀuu suffixes. Thus, the term for 'ring' (Afr. *ring*) is spelt *ringsi* (-*si* is the singular suffix in Nǀuu), and the term for 'tea' (Afr. *tee*) is spelt *teesi*.

The terms for 'donkey' (Afr. *donkie*), by applying the Standard Afrikaans spelling, are written as *donkiesi* (singular) and *donkieke* (plural) (-*ke* is the plural suffix in Nǀuu). Since they are pronounced as [doŋkisi] and [doŋkike], respectively, they would otherwise have been spelt as *dongkisi* and *dongkike*.

In Afrikaans, <tj> in word-initial position is pronounced as [t͡ʃ]; for example, *tjap* 'stamp' is pronounced as [t͡ʃɑp]. The pronunciation of <tj> differs with the diminutive suffix -*tjie* (-*jie*). In this case, it is no longer pronounced as [t͡ʃi] but as [ki]. For example, the term for 'small leg' in Afrikaans, *beentjie*, is pronounced as [beːɲki] or [biːɲki]. In words that end in <d>, the diminutive is -*djie* (suffix -*jie*), but it is still pronounced as [ki]. For example, 'little bed' in Afrikaans is spelt *bedjie* and pronounced [bɛːki]. One such Afrikaans word which has been borrowed into Nǀuu is *baadjiesi* [baikisi] 'jacket' (Afr. *baadjie* [baiki]).

The Nǀuu speakers sometimes modify Afrikaans words when speaking Nǀuu, and the Afrikaans spelling was not always applied in these cases. Examples that fall into this category include *fotusi* (Afr. *foto*) 'photograph', *vadoekusi* (Afr. *vadoek*) 'dishcloth', *karkisi* (Afr. *kar*) 'car', and *laasi* (Afr. *lap*) 'cloth'.

5 The Nǀuu Alphabet Charts

As requested by the community members, alphabet charts for teaching purposes were developed in the CALDi project. The decision on the actual choice of sounds which are represented in the Nǀuu alphabet was based on research conducted by linguists in the past few decades. The different phoneme inventories established by scholars for Nǀuu and their wordlists made it possible to

Writing for Speaking: The Nǀuu Orthography 119

discuss minimal pairs in great detail with community members. Speech sounds which only occur in loanwords were also included in the alphabet.

The Nǀuu alphabet charts are not intended to challenge the phoneme inventories proposed by other scholars. In order to accommodate the non-Nǀuu-speaking users, allophones are represented in the charts. Differences might also be caused by the fact that Ouma Geelmeid's pronunciation of the Nǀuu terms has been the sole reference for the charts, which aim to capture her idiolect as much as possible. In the charts, all speech sounds are assigned graphemes, which are accompanied by Nǀuu terms and photos. Three alphabet charts were developed featuring click consonants, non-click consonants, and vowels.

5.1   The Click Chart

Both the German group and the American group agreed on the same 45 distinct clicks. Additional clicks postulated by Exter (2008:28) could not be verified with Ouma Geelmeid, and for that reason, the Nǀuu click chart also features 45 clicks (see Table 6.1). The basic click types are represented with the current IPA symbols for clicks – i.e., <ʘ> for the bilabial clicks, <ǀ> for the dental clicks, <!> for the alveolar clicks, <ǂ> for the palatal clicks, and <ǁ> for the lateral clicks.

The order of clicks in the chart follows that found in the IPA chart. This canonical order of clicks is in accordance with the places of their articulation and has also been suggested for practical use by Fehn et al. (2014). With the exception of the uvular fricated ejected clicks,[10] scholars generally use the same conventions for representing click accompaniments. The community orthography follows them in this respect. It places <g> (voicing) and <n>/<m>[11] (nasalization) before the respective click and thus adopts the most common practice among the writing conventions.

While Ouma Geelmeid was consistent in the pronunciation of words with regard to the basic click types, there was variation with regard to click accompaniments in some respects. She was not always consistent in the nasalization and voicing of clicks. The uvular aspirated stop series of clicks were at times realized simply as aspirated clicks.

5.2   The Consonant Chart

The Nǀuu consonant chart displays 30 non-click consonants alphabetically (see Table 6.2). Most consonants are written according to IPA conventions. Several consonants occur exclusively in Afrikaans loanwords. These are (1) the alveolar stops <t> and <d> – for example, *teesi* (Afr. *tee*) 'tea' and *dromsi* (Afr. *drom*) 'drum'; and (2) the labiodental fricatives <f> and

Table 6.1 Nǀuu click graphemes.

	Voiceless	Voiced	Glottal	Nasalized	Aspirated	Aspirated nasal	Uvular fricated	Uvular stop	Uvular aspirated stop	Uvular fricated ejected
Bilabial	ʘ	gʘ	ʘ'	mʘ			ʘx	ʘq		
Dental	ǀ	gǀ	ǀ'	nǀ	ǀh	ǀ'h	ǀx	ǀq	ǀqh	ǀx'
Alveolar	ǃ	gǃ	ǃ'	nǃ	ǃh	ǃ'h	ǃx	ǃq	ǃqh	ǃx'
Palatal	ǂ	gǂ	ǂ'	nǂ	ǂh	ǂ'h	ǂx	ǂq	ǂqh	ǂx'
Lateral	ǁ	gǁ	ǁ'	nǁ	ǁh	ǁ'h	ǁx	ǁq	ǁqh	ǁx'

Writing for Speaking: The Nǀuu Orthography

Table 6.2 *Nǀuu consonant graphemes.*

	b	d	dy [ʝ]	f	g	h		
j [d͡ʒ]	jh [d͡ʒʰ]	k	kh [kʰ]	kx' [k͡χ']	ky [kʲ]	l	m	
n	ng [ŋ]	ny [ɲ]	p	q	r	s	t	
ty [c]	tyh [cʰ]	tyx [c͡χ]	ts [t͡s]	ts' [t͡s']	v	x	z	

Table 6.3 *The orthographical representation of [ʝ], [kʲ], and [c].*

IPA[12]	Nǀuu community orthography	German group	American group	English
[ʝ]	dy	dy	j	'to walk'
[ʝaˤn]	dyaqn	dyaqn	jaqn	
[kʲ]	ky	ty	c	'navel'
[nǂõˤekʲu]	nǂôqekyu	nǂoqentyuu	nǂôqecu	
[c]	ty	ty	c	'to be naked'
[cʰoe]	tyhoe	tyhoe	choe	

<v> – for example, *fotusi* (Afr. *foto*) 'photo' and *vadoekusi* (Afr. *vadoek*) 'dishcloth'.

The Nǀuu orthography differs from the IPA conventions with respect to the palatal nasal [ɲ] and velar nasal [ŋ], which are represented by <ny> and <ng>, respectively, in the community orthography.

The chart represents [ʝ], [kʲ], and [c] as <dy>, <ky>, and <ty>. In Ouma Geelmeid's pronunciation, these sounds occur, for example, in *dyaqn* [ʝaˤn] 'to walk', *nǂôqekyu* [nǂõˤekʲu] 'navel', and *tyhoe* [cʰoe] 'to be naked'. The previous attempts to spell these terms differ, and the American group and German group apply different graphemes for the respective sounds (see Table 6.3). The community orthography aligns more closely to the graphemes proposed by the German group. The orthography differs with that of both groups in that it represents the actual pronunciations of the sounds – for example, <ky> and <ty>. While Ouma Geelmeid was consistent in the pronunciation of the three aforementioned words, this was not always the case with other terms containing these sounds. For example, *tyuuke* 'men' was mostly pronounced as [cu:ke], but sometimes also as [kʲu:ke]. This latter pronunciation would be spelt as *kyuuke*.

Table 6.4 *Nǀuu vowel graphemes.*

a	â	aa	âa		ae	ai	ao	au	âe	âi	âu	aq	âq
e		ee		ea								eq	
i	î	ii	îi	ia									
o		oo	ôo	oa	oe				ôa	ôe		oq	ôq
u		uu	ûu	ua	ue	ui					ûi	uq	

5.3 The Vowel Chart

Thirty-nine vowels are orthographically represented in the Nǀuu vowel chart (see Table 6.4). These include 16 plain vowels and 23 (21)[13] diphthongs. There are 5 short and 5 long vowels, as well as 6 nasalized vowels (2 short and 4 long).[14] In addition, there are 11 (9) plain and 6 nasalized diphthongs. While 4 plain pressed (pharyngealized) vowel diphthongs exist, only 2 also occur as nasalized pressed vowel diphthongs. Their orthographic representation has been discussed previously, in Section 4.4.

Pharyngealized vowels and vowel length were consistently produced by Ouma Geelmeid. There was, however, some variation in the nasalization of vowels. One example which looks especially suspicious is the Nǀuu terms *ǁhaike* 'milk' and *ǁhâi* 'breasts'. 'Breasts' and 'milk' in Nǀuu might be polysemous, as in other languages, such as *pîi* in Khwe (Kilian-Hatz 2003:104). However, nasalization and the *-ke* plural suffix distinguish the terms 'milk' and 'breasts' in Nǀuu. Even more surprising may be that *ǁhâi* in Nǀuu means 'breasts' as well as 'teeth'; Nǀuu homophones may be the result of the recent collapse of the tonal categories in the language (Bonny Sands, personal communication 2015).

6 Writing Conventions in the Nǀuu Reader

Several writing conventions were already in place and contribute to the current writing practice. As is common in other orthographies of non-Bantu click languages, such as for Khoekhoegowab and Khwe, clicks at the beginning of a sentence, as well as in personal and place names, are capitalized. Depending on the position of the click accompaniment, the capital letter may precede or follow the click:

MƟôa ke ǃqhûia. 'The cat is fat.'
ǀ'Hoba ke harua. 'The grave is far away.'

Other writing conventions include the following:

(i) Lexemes are written as one word, and morpheme boundaries are not marked.
(ii) The linker *ke*, the preceding plural marker *ka*, the negative markers *ǁu* and *ǁam*, and the irrealis marker *si* are written as separate words.
(iii) Subject and object pronouns are written separately: for example, <u>Na</u> si ǀ'ai <u>a</u>. '<u>I</u> will call <u>you</u>.'
(iv) Nominal compounds are written separately: for example, ǀurisi ǀqhuisi 'aeroplane' (lit. 'iron bird').
(v) Serial verbs are written separately: for example, ǀAu ke <u>ǂhuu kyîi</u>. 'The springhare <u>hops around</u>.'
(vi) Re-duplications are written as two words: for example, Gǃae ke <u>ǂhuu ǃhûu</u>. 'The springbok <u>runs away</u>.'
(vii) Nominal stems and suffixes, such as the singular and plural suffixes, -*si* and -*ke*, are written as one word.
(viii) *Wh* words and the obligatory *xe* are written conjunctively: for example, <u>Kyuuxe</u> nǃaria nǀa karkisi? '<u>Who</u> is driving the car?'
This does not work, however, for <u>Kyui gao xe</u>? '<u>What</u> is this?' where *gao* 'thing' is inserted between *kyui* 'what' and *xe*.

Kanǁaa 'to stay' consists of the prefix *ka-*, indicating a repetitive action, and the verb *nǁaa* 'to be' (Collins and Namaseb 2011:20). As with other verbs with this prefix, *kanǁaa* is written as one word. In this case, an unavoidable ambiguity in the pronunciation of this word arises, as it could be pronounced as either [kan ǁa:] or [ka nǁa:]. In some other words, where clicks appear in word-medial positions, the disjunctive spelling was frequently used by the community members, such as with *siǃuxu* 'zebra', which was often written as *si ǃu xu* in order 'to make it easier to read' (Claudia du Plessis, personal communication 2014).

7 Conclusions

The establishment of a Nǀuu orthography, as well as the development of teaching and learning materials, was a joint effort between community members and linguists (cf. Sackett, and Valdovinos, this volume). Both groups contributed to the decision-making processes, and in order to enable informed choices, previous orthography development efforts were consulted and discussed in great detail.

The fact that Afrikaans is the dominant language among the ǂKhomani community and is also the mother tongue of the last Nǀuu speakers was the baseline for the development of Nǀuu teaching materials (cf. Lai, this volume). Compromises made on technical aspects seemed unavoidable, such as the problematic double assignment of sounds to one symbol or letter (cf. Sackett, this volume). A more serious weakness of the orthography might, however, be the ambiguity in the pronunciation of certain graphemes caused by accepting the use of another orthography, namely Standard Afrikaans, for the spelling of Afrikaans loanwords.

The community orthography was officially established through the launch of the printed alphabet charts on 24 March 2014. One month later, Ouma Geelmeid received the Order of the Baobab in silver from Jacob Zuma, the president of South Africa: 'For her excellent contribution in the preservation of a language that is facing a threat of extinction. Her determination to make the project successful has inspired young generations to learn.'[15]

There is a strong desire among ǂKhomani members to reclaim documents about their past – such as those on Nǀuu archived at the University of Cape Town and other institutions – in order to be able to reconstruct and understand their history. The symbolic use of Nǀuu is increasing among them without necessarily equating to increased competence in the language. Nǀuu audio recordings and written documents which enshrine important aspects of their cultural heritage can, however, only be accessed by ǂKhomani community members who are literate and at least proficient to some extent in Nǀuu.

In order to produce teaching and learning materials which can efficiently be employed in a situation in which the speakers are non-literate and the literate are non-speakers, a shallow orthography as close as possible to the actual speech is of eminent importance. We therefore accepted an over-representation of the sound inventory for pedagogical reasons. Since only one Nǀuu speaker is involved in these community language teaching efforts, the orthography and the materials were tailored to her specific teaching environment. It is hoped that Nǀuu students will not only be able to read Nǀuu texts from the archives, but also continue to learn to speak the language even when they will no longer be taught by Nǀuu speakers. For these reasons, the Nǀuu orthography was established with the aim of developing materials which allow 'writing for speaking'.

Notes

1. This chapter is based on fieldwork conducted by the authors in the Northern Cape between 2012 and 2014. We wish to express our gratitude to the Andrew W. Mellon Foundation, the University of Cape Town, the Endangered Language Fund, and the University of Kiel for funding our fieldtrips. We also wish to thank Bonny Sands and Alena Witzlack-Makarevich for valuable and highly constructive comments and corrections on an earlier version of this chapter. Spelling conventions proposed here are based on Ouma Geelmeid's pronunciation and have been agreed upon by the community in consultation with the authors. The community orthography project was driven by the enthusiasm, dedication, and expertise of Ouma Geelmeid, Claudia du Plessis, and Mary-Ann Prins, and we thank them for their support of this project and their friendship.

2. Members of this research group include Bonny Sands, Chris Collins, Amanda Miller, Johanna Brugman, and Levi Namaseb. Except for Levi Namaseb, who is Namibian, all are American.
3. Members of this research group include Tom Güldemann, Alena Witzlack-Makarevich, Martina Ernszt, and Sven Siegmund.
4. Other major Nguni languages are siSwati and isiNdebele.
5. The only other non-Bantu click language which uses Roman letters to represent clicks is Sandawe, spoken in Tanzania (East Africa).
6. The development of the reader was supported by the Endangered Language Fund.
7. For a thorough discussion on the advantages and disadvantages of deep versus shallow orthographies, see Cahill and Karan (2008).
8. Nasalization of long vowels is marked with a circumflex on the first vowel only.
9. Khoekhoegowab is a prominent exception, as a simple click symbol does not represent a plain click, but instead a click followed by a glottal stop – e.g., <|> represents [|ʔ] (Brenzinger 2003).
10. For [|χ'], the German group writes <|qx'> and the American group writes <|x'>. The latter spelling was chosen in the community orthography.
11. Following common practice, nasalization of bilabial clicks is written with <m>.
12. The IPA transcriptions do not always follow those of the German and American groups, but instead reflect the idiolect of Ouma Geelmeid.
13. <Ea> and <ia> might not, as pointed out by Bonny Sands, represent actual diphthongs but occur as a root-final vowel (either <e> or <i>) followed by an -a morpheme.
14. The community spelling convention represents four of the five nasalized vowels postulated by Exter (2008:51). In Ouma Geelmeid's pronunciation, we were not able to auditorily differentiate between the nasalized <i> and <e>. In consultation with the community, we decided to use the nasalized <i> as a default. The American group treats [õ] as a predictable variant of [ũ], since nasalization has the effect of perceptually lowering vowel height, so a lowered variant is phonetically explainable but a raised variant would not be (Bonny Sands, personal communication 2015). Together with the community, we decided to distinguish [õ] and [ũ] in the spelling, as we established a rather shallow orthography which represents allophonic variation. We also spell, for example, 'leg' as *jhîi*, while all others transcribe this term as [kʰǐː]. They treat this consonant as a predictable allophone of /kʰ/. Before front vowels, the pitch is rising and gives the perception of the consonant being voiced, while it is phonetically not voiced. We, however, accept an over-representation in the practical orthography to accommodate a spelling which captures the words as they actually sound.
15. www.thepresidency.gov.za/pebble.asp?relid=17217&t=79 (last accessed 20 June 2015).

7 Reflections on the Kala Biŋatuwã, a Three-Year-Old Alphabet from Papua New Guinea

Christine Schreyer

1 Introduction

Many academic articles in the field of orthography development describe best practices, including the increasing trend to involve community members in orthography development (Cahill and Rice 2014; Seifart 2006), yet few academic studies provide community reflections on the new writing system as it continues to stabilize. Why might this be? In her article 'Standardization: What's the hurry?' Karan writes, 'What might seem like a novel idea to some is that writing systems need to be tested and that the expectation should be that they are not fixed once and for all (Baker 1997) but are subject to change' (Karan 2014:109). Not only do writing systems require testing, which often occurs during the development process (cf. Sallabank and Marquis, and Lai, this volume), but they also require community reflection after the development stage, in order to determine if the orthography has met the needs of its intended users (cf. Sackett, this volume). This is particularly important in endangered language communities where disagreement on appropriate writing systems might cause confusion and lead to 'orthography wars' (Hinton 2014; cf. Hull, this volume) rather than language revitalization. This chapter describes the 2010 development of the Kala biŋatuwã (or Kala alphabet), including how this orthographic system was developed as part of a community-based research project both to document the Kala language and to raise the level of use of the Kala language. The chapter describes Kala community members' reflections on the Kala biŋatuwã, as well as my own observations of the orthography in use during our trip to the Kala villages in the summer of 2013, in order to illustrate the types of issues that might be important to consider in developing a wider reflective process for orthography development in other endangered language communities. First, I provide background on the Kala language – an Austronesian language spoken in six coastal villages in the Morobe province of Papua New Guinea – including the level of endangerment and the development of the Kala Language Committee. Next, I describe the parallel dialectal approach to orthography development that the Kala community engaged in to develop their new alphabet and how this approach is tied to the best practices of orthography development. In examining community members' reflections on their new alphabet, I include, whenever possible, community members voices, since I argue, as do many others, that the most successful writing systems are those that community members feel ownership over (Bow 2012; Rice et al 2012; cf. Shah and Brenzinger, this volume). Finally, I discuss the benefits and challenges of incorporating community members' reflections into evolving orthographies rather than rushing into standardization.

2 Background on the Kala Language

Kala is an Austronesian language spoken by approximately two thousand individuals in six coastal villages in the Morobe province of Papua New Guinea (Wagner 2002). The Kala names of the villages, from north to south, are Manindala[1] (also known as Kela); Lambu (also known as Laugui); Apoze (also known as Lokanu); Kamiali (also known as Lababia); Alẽso (also known as Buso); and Kui. The northern villages (Manindala, Lambu, and Apoze) each have their own distinct dialect, with phonological and lexical differences, while the three southern villages (Kamiali, Alẽso, and Kui) share a dialect. Language shift to Tok Pisin (the national lingua franca) and English (the official language of education) is common across Papua New Guinea (Dobrin 2008; Foley 2004; Kulick 1992) and is occurring in varying degrees throughout the Kala villages (see Table 7.1). The *Ethnologue* (Lewis, Simons, and Fennig 2015) states that Kala's language status is 6a – vigorous in the EGIDS, meaning that 'The language is used for face-to-face communication by all generations and the situation is sustainable' (2015). However, this information is incorrect.[2] Tok Pisin is becoming the language of main communication and the language of intergenerational transmission in some of the Kala villages, including Manindala, Kui, and Lambu.

Prior to the research that my team and I conducted in May and June of 2010, very little linguistic research had previously been conducted with Kala speakers (Collier and Collier 1975; Johnson 1994). My involvement with the Kala speakers grew out of my colleague John Wagner's doctoral research on

Table 7.1 *Language shift in Kala villages.*

High language shift	High-to-medium language shift	Medium language shift
Manindala	Kui and Lambu	Apoze, Alẽso, Kamiali

resource management practices in two Kala-speaking communities – Kamiali and Kui (2002). During his doctoral research, Wagner realized that the village of Kui was experiencing greater language shift to Tok Pisin than the village of Kamiali. He also realized how fundamental the Kala language was for transmitting environmental knowledge, and this, as well as his desire to continue his relationship with the communities, became the impetus for our joint research project on Kala language education and local ecological knowledge (discussed later).

Before discussing this project, however, I return to the topic of Kala's language endangerment. As Foley writes about the state of language endangerment in Papua New Guinea:

While language endangerment is not as advanced as in some other areas of the world such as Australia and the Americas, most of the languages of New Guinea are spoken by very small speech communities, under a couple of thousand speakers and in many cases much less, and the inexorable advance of economic development, modernization and globalization threaten their viability as elsewhere, so that the current linguistic richness will certainly be greatly depleted by the turn of the next century. (2004:28)

Though the historically small speech communities in Papua New Guinea could easily be threatened due to economic development, modernization, and globalization, it is important to recognize that 'no single factor alone can be used to assess a language's vitality or its need for documentation' (UNESCO 2003a:7). As a result, the UNESCO Ad Hoc Group on Endangered Languages has developed six factors to analyse a language's vitality, including: '1) Intergenerational Language Transmission; 2) Absolute Number of Speakers; 3) Proportion of Speakers within the Total Population; 4) Shifts in Domains of Language Use; 5) Response to New Domains and Media; and 6) Availability of Materials for Language Education and Literacy' (UNESCO 2003a:7). Using Wagner's earlier research, as well as my own experiences working with Kala speakers, I use the UNESCO criteria to assess the vitality of the Kala language overall, rather than for each village (see Table 7.2).

Using these six factors of vitality (UNESCO 2003a), it becomes clear that the Kala language is 'definitively endangered' (level 3 on the UNESCO scale) due to the small community size, the lack of Kala language use in new domains, and the limited number of written materials, despite the multilingual tendencies of the community members and the strong intergenerational transmission (which is, in fact, not occurring in all of the Kala villages). Moreover, Kala community members themselves are concerned about language shift, and, in association with John Wagner, they formed the Kala Language Committee (comprised of two men and one woman from each village) in 2006. The goals of the Kala Language Committee are to raise awareness about Kala language shift and to develop more Kala usage in their communities, specifically within

Table 7.2 *Kala vitality factors.*

Language vitality factors	Kala language
1. Intergenerational language transmission	'Stable yet threatened (5–): The language is spoken in most contexts by all generations with unbroken intergenerational transmission, yet multilingualism in the native language and one or more dominant language(s) has usurped certain important communication contexts. Note that multilingualism alone is not necessarily a threat to languages' (UNESCO 2003a:7)
2. Absolute number of speakers	'It is impossible to establish a hard and fast rule for interpreting absolute numbers, but a small speech community is always at risk' (UNESCO 2003a:8)
3. Proportion of speakers within the total population	'Definitively endangered. . . . A majority speak the language' (UNESCO 2003a:9)
4. Shifts in domains of language use	'Multilingual parity (4): One or more dominant languages, rather than the language of the ethnolinguistic group, is/are the primary language(s) in most official domains: government, public offices and educational institutions. The language in question, however, may well continue to be integral to a number of public domains, especially in traditional religious institutions, local stores and those places where members of the community socialize' (UNESCO 2003a:9)
5. Response to new domains and media	'Minimal. . . . The language is used in only a few new domains' (UNESCO 2003a:11)
6. Availability of materials for language education and literacy	'Written materials exist and children may be exposed to the written form at school. Literacy is not promoted through print media' (UNESCO 2003a:12). Total grade: 18 (divided by 6 factors of vitality) = 3 – *Definitively endangered*

Kala language elementary schools, but also to document ecological knowledge, which often is more easily described in the Kala language since the language of Tok Pisin lacks specificity.

3 The Kala Language Education and Local Ecological Knowledge Project

The development of an orthography was one of the first goals of the Kala Language Committee, and this task was tackled in the summer of 2010 when Wagner, myself, and our research assistant, Chara DeVolder, began our work with the Kala Language Committee. Using language documentation interviews that Wagner had collected in 2006, I began a preliminary phonological analysis of the Kala language in 2009. Then, during May and June of 2010, we conducted further language elicitation interviews with two expert Kala speakers (one male and one female) in each of the six Kala-speaking villages. Following review and discussion, we held an Orthography Decision Workshop in the Kala village of Kamiali with all of the Kala Language Committee members. At this meeting, the committee members decided on the symbols that should be included in their new alphabet (for further details, see Schreyer 2015a). Ultimately, the symbols chosen are capable of representing all the separate dialects of Kala (a parallel dialectal approach to orthography development, which will be discussed later). Following the committee's decision, we held literacy training workshops for all interested Kala speakers, and community researchers and Kala language teachers from all six villages joined in this process. During the time period between this workshop in June 2010 and our return to the Kala-speaking villages in May of 2013, we worked with the Kala Language Committee, our community researchers, and the Kala language teachers to document more Kala language (including stories, songs, and environmental knowledge) and to publish the first Kala dictionary in 2012 – *Kala Kaŋa Bi Ɖa Kapia – Diksineri bilong Tok Ples Kala – Kala Dictionary* (DeVolder et al. 2012). This short trilingual dictionary includes all four of the Kala dialects and is organized into different semantic domains.

Wagner and I returned to the Kala language communities to continue our work on this project with community members in May 2013. During our first committee meeting, it became evident that many community members had not had the opportunity to learn the new Kala orthography, with the exception of our main partners in this project, including the teachers in the Kala language schools. The priority for our time in the Kala villages then was to hold local workshops in each of the six Kala villages so that more community members, and in particular parents, could also learn how to use the Kala orthography. After each local workshop, we held focus group discussions with our Kala Language Committee partners in order to capture their reflections on the orthography and its use. Before discussing these reflections, I turn first to a discussion of the 2010 development of the Kala orthography in relation to best practices within orthography development.

4   Kala Biŋatuwã – a Parallel Dialectal Approach

Early orthographies for previously unwritten or endangered languages often focused on the linguists' desires rather than the communities', but, as Rice and Cahill write, 'In these times, local people are often intimately involved in orthographic choices. The days when an outside linguist unilaterally establishes an orthography are fading, at least in many parts of the world' (2014:3). More and more scholars are also realizing that 'orthographic systems cannot be conceptualized simply as reducing speech to writing, but rather they are symbols that carry historical, cultural and political meanings' (Woolard and Schieffelin 1994:65). As Sebba writes in his book *Spelling and Society*, 'Orthographies are microcosms of language itself, where the issues of history, identity, ethnicity, culture, and politics, which pervade language, are also prominent' (2007:167; cf. Sackett, Hull, and Leggio and Matras, this volume).

The new Kala orthography was a community-based project that developed out of a partnership with Wagner and me as academic research partners who assisted the Kala Language community in their orthographic choices (cf. Casquite and Young, this volume). The Orthography Design Workshop we held with the Kala Language Committee was similar to those in Easton's (2003) discussion of Alphabet Design Workshops in other areas of Papua New Guinea, which allowed for 'the process to be controlled by, and belong to, the community itself' (Easton 2003:2; cf. Valdovinos, this volume). Following a basic phonological analysis of Kala from the recordings Wagner conducted in 2006 and then our interviews with Kala speakers in 2010, I provided suggestions to the Kala Language Committee on potential symbols to use in their alphabet.[3] The Kala Language Committee then debated the suggestions I made and came to an agreement on the symbols to use via a consensus process (Schreyer 2015a). The topics that we discussed in our orthography workshop prior to the decision-making process in 2010 included both linguistic factors, such as orthographic depth and functional load (Seifart 2006), and non-linguistic factors, such as pedagogical challenges, other existing orthographies, dialectal variation, and technical production (Seifart 2006; cf. also Sackett, this volume). One of the most important ideological aspects of the Kala orthography development process is the unity the Kala Language Committee has maintained throughout our continuing projects on Kala language documentation.

As Kala is a language that has four different dialects, there was the potential for discrepancy in representing the language (Bow 2012; Seifart 2006; Terrill and Dunn 2003; cf. Hewitt, this volume). However, since the development of the Kala Language Committee in 2006, the villages have stressed the importance of working together. In fact, the Kala name for the project has become *Kala Walo Nua*, which literally means the 'Kala One Mouth' project – but *walo*, or 'mouth', is also the Kala word for 'way of speaking'. This motto appears on Kala language project T-shirts (see Figure 7.1). One large conch shell horn (known as a *dau* in Kala) appears in the middle of the design, with 'UBC' written on it to illustrate the partnership between University of British Columbia researchers and the Kala Language Committee. Around this larger shell are six smaller conch shells, which represent the six different Kala villages. Therefore, the words and imagery indicate that, even though there are six villages with different dialects, they are all Kala speakers who wished to share an orthography due to their shared identity (cf. Leggio and Matras, this volume).

Figure 7.1 Selep and Thomas from Alēso village wearing Kala Walo Nua T-shirts. May 2013, Alēso village.
(Photo: C. Schreyer)

In fact, previous research on the Kala language conducted by SIL researchers occurred in only two of the Kala villages and at different time periods (Apoze in 1975 and Kui in 1994). It is my opinion that this isolation of dialects was one of the reasons that previous attempts at orthography development by SIL linguists were not successful and community members did not use the proposed SIL orthographies to write Kala (Collier and Collier 1975; Johnson 1994). In contrast, the more recent process was community based. The name of the Kala orthography in the Kala language is the *Kala biŋatuwã*. The word *ŋatuwã* means 'bones' (as can be seen in Figure 7.2 under the symbol <ŋ>). *Kala biŋatuwã*, therefore, literally means that the orthography forms 'the bones of Kala words', which indicates the in-depth Kala community involvement in this process.

This desire for all of the villages and different dialects to work together led to Kala speakers using what I call the parallel dialectal approach to orthography development. As Cahill writes, 'For efficiency's sake, it is often felt desirable to devise an orthography that will serve all of language group, even one with fairly divergent dialects' (2014:12). The two common approaches to a unified

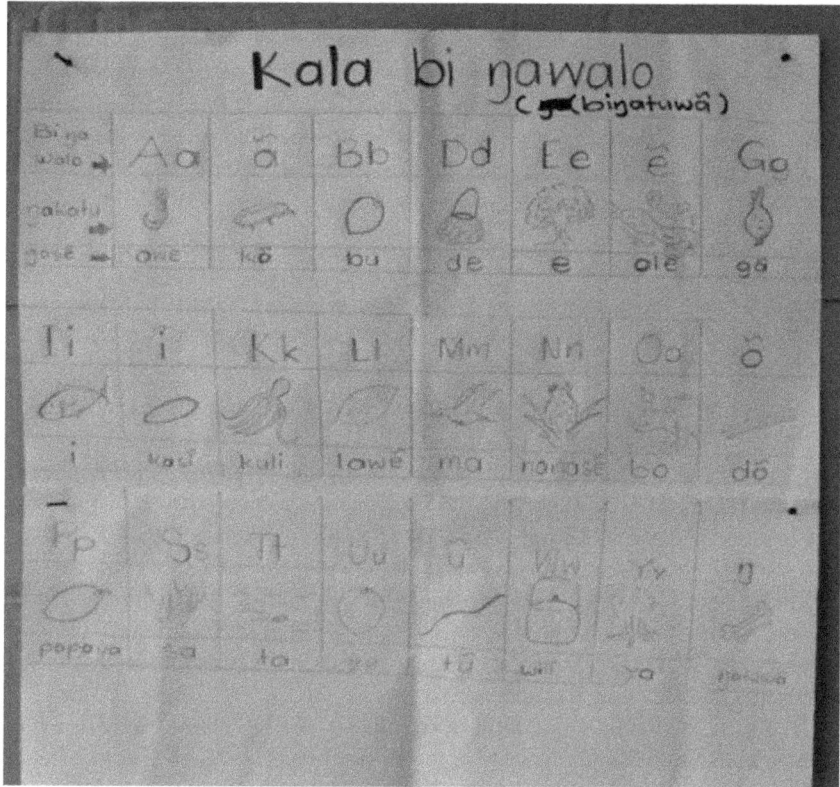

Figure 7.2 Kala alphabet chart from Alēso village, May 2013.
(Photo: C. Schreyer)

orthography where multiple dialects exist are known as the unilectal and multilectal approaches. In the unilectal approach, 'the most prestigious dialect is chosen as the standard for orthography, and the other dialects adapt to it' (Cahill 2014:12). In the Kala case, if this method had been adopted, it is quite possible that the southern dialect (spoken in Kamiali, Alēso, and Kui) would have been chosen as the prestige dialect, since it is spoken by a majority of people. This approach was not considered by the Kala speakers, however, who stressed the importance of unity in diversity, as seen in the aforementioned *Kala Walo Nua* motto. Interestingly, upon independence in 1975, Papua New Guinea enshrined the principles of diversity within their constitution, and the phrase 'unity in diversity' is the country's national motto. As Malone and Paraide write, 'Since independence, the government of P[apua] N[ew] G[uinea] has considered linguistic diversity a resource rather than a problem and the desire to maintain traditional languages and cultures remains strong in most parts of the country' (2011:707, my insertions). The Kala Language Committee is enacting a similar perspective in their choices. Members also emphasized that a shared orthography allowed individuals from each village to understand more thoroughly each other's ways of speaking. As Nero Kaposing, our Kala Language Committee chairperson, stated in one of our focus group discussions:

> I think that Apoze's way of speaking is theirs, our way of speaking is ours, Alẽso's is theirs, Kui's is theirs, Lambu's is theirs, but all of the ways of speaking must be in one book. So, if I don't understand Manindala's way of speaking, but I have the book, I can understand Manindala's dialect. And, if they don't understand my way of speaking, from Kamiali, if they have this book, they can understand too.[4]

The ability to have shared resources and wider communication will help support Kala language revitalization as well.

In the multilectal approach, 'the orthography has elements of several dialects, not just one. This means that the orthography does not fully represent anyone's actual speech' (Cahill 2014:13; cf. Lai, this volume). Karan further expands on these different approaches in her chapter as well and writes that the multilectal approach, 'by taking the linguistic realities of all the varieties into consideration, it would, hopefully, avoid the stigmatizing of some' (2014:117). However, yet another approach, which also avoids stigmatization, is possible – namely the parallel dialectal approach.[5]

For the Kala biŋatuwã, symbols were chosen for the sounds in all of the dialects, and then individuals write in their own dialect, using the standardized set of symbols. The phonology of all of the Kala dialects is fairly consistent, although two dialects (Apoze and Lambu) have an extra phoneme /z/. However, despite the fact that not all of the dialects use or even know this sound, it does appear in the written depictions of the alphabet in all of the villages. For example, the Kamiali Kala language chalkboard includes the letter <z> (see Figure 7.3), since the Kala Language Committee wanted everyone to know all of the letters of the Kala alphabet so that wider communication is possible between the dialects, thus encouraging language revitalization. The parallel dialectal approach, which builds on the cultural and social identity of Kala speakers as united in their diversity, works easily for the language's linguistic structures, but languages with more complex differences between dialects or different ideological stances may find this approach challenging.

In sum, the development of the Kala orthography was one in which I was able to bring my linguistic knowledge to the speakers as a tool for them to use to help them decide which symbols to include in their alphabet (cf. Giffen 2015). This approach is also similar to the 'midwife' approach to orthography development (Rice et al 2012:11), which is 'based on exchange and integration of

Figure 7.3 Kala biŋatuwā in the Kamiali Kala language classroom, May 2013.
(Photo: C. Schreyer)

knowledge and experience of linguist and language community'. The midwife approach also emphasizes reflection, since it sees orthography development as a process (cf. Casquite and Young, this volume), but the reflection seems to still occur during initial development rather than after an extended period of use. In the next section, I argue for the importance of reflection as an extended and engaged process.

5 Reflections on the Kala Biŋatuwā

As stated earlier, very little literature on orthography development addresses the necessity of actively reflecting on new orthographic use over an extended period of time. However, as Casquite and Young (this volume) note, Karan stresses the importance of not rushing into standardization and writes that 'Testing an orthography is essential. It will reveal effectiveness, acceptability, degree of potential extendibility across dialects, and possibly, need for revision' (2014:132). Yet, there do not seem to be any case studies available that describe an extended development process, despite the fact that all orthographies need time to settle and standardize. More research on this topic – such as this discussion of the Kala biŋatuwã – is essential since it is evident that orthographies do change as people use them (Stebbins 2001; Hinton 2014). Ottenheimer's article on the numerous Shinzwani writing systems discusses the shifting views the speakers had about the orthography she helped develop over the course of her fieldwork career in the Comoro Islands (2001), but even this article does not describe checking in on speakers after the 'final' decisions were made.

Karan also writes that 'If an orthography is presented as a work in progress rather than a finished work, introducing necessary changes will likely be easier' (2014:132). In this vein, although the Kala Language Committee had chosen symbols for the sounds of their language in 2010 and we had published the first Kala dictionary with this alphabet (2012), we still wanted people to have the opportunity to provide feedback on any pieces of the alphabet that they thought were confusing. As I have explained elsewhere (Schreyer 2015b), continually evolving language materials are important for prestige planning (Haarmann 1990), since this creates active and updated products. Moreover, community members need to be involved in the evolution of these materials, from the beginning edits to new editions of books, so that any changes are more easily accepted and embraced (cf. Sackett, this volume). In relation to orthography, I noticed that the publication of the dictionary, which included Kala words in printed, professional form, both raised the prestige of the orthography and also gave people the opportunity to see the writing in another way (not just hand-written) so that they could decide if something was spelt correctly. Therefore, as Karan writes, 'Publication need not come to a halt if an agreement is not reached' (2014:118) or if an orthography is still in flux.

It is also worth considering that some communities may not see books as permanent records in the same way as Western society does; for these communities, books might represent new cultural materials. Paper does not last long in the tropical, coastal Papua New Guinea environment, where it gets wet and easily worn through – and eaten by rats and cockroaches. Therefore, if paper is not permanent, this gives community members and academics the opportunity to develop a range of language materials, including orthographies.

With this conception of process and reflection in mind, we specifically asked our Kala language community partners questions in focus group discussions about their thoughts and impressions of their orthography three years after its development, including:

(i) Where did you learn the Kala alphabet?
(ii) Is it easy to learn? Why?
(iii) What types of things have you written in the Kala alphabet?
(iv) What do you think about the 'titi' [nasalization] mark?
(v) Are there any letters you want to change?

(vi) What do you think about the <l> symbol? Are you confused about the [l] and [ɹ] sounds?

Many of these questions focus on issues that are discussed in the best practices literature for orthography development, including readability and representation (Cahill 2014; Seifart 2006). We were particularly curious about what we had been calling the 'titi' mark – namely the tilde symbol used over the vowels to mark nasalization – since this was the symbol that had caused the most debate in our original orthography workshop in 2010. Letters that were marked for nasalization using a tilde were originally known as, for example, 'letter <a> titi', because *titi* is the Kala word for 'waves' of the ocean in the southern dialect of Kala. The reference to waves was important to Kala speakers as a coastal people. However, during our 2013 local workshops in each of the six Kala villages, we realized that *titi* is a word from the southern dialects and that each of the northern villages had their own name for 'wave', including *taŋaoti* (Apoze), *gũsa* (Lambu), and *gũgũ* (Manindala).

Beyond the more formal focus group discussions, we also had informal conversations with Kala community members about their thoughts on the orthography and made note of any uses of the orthography in the villages during our time in Papua New Guinea in 2013, such as the Kala biŋatuwã in the Kamiali Kala language classroom (see Figure 7.3).

From these discussions and observations, it was clear that both general community members and the Kala Language Committee members thought that the letter <l> was potentially problematic. This letter was a source of confusion for people because they felt that although there were /l/ sounds in Kala, there were /ɹ/ sounds also and that the letter <r> should therefore be included as well. The phrase that was often pointed out as needing an <r> was *tulula anda* ('good afternoon'), which is often pronounced as [tɹuɾa ænda]. In informal Kala speech, the first vowel is often dropped, and a consonant cluster develops with a more pronounced [ɹ] sound. This can also be seen in the word for 'moon', which would be written as *galawe* in the southern dialects of Kala but is often pronounced [gɹawe]. Therefore, since [l], [ɾ], and [ɹ] are all allophones of the phoneme /r/, the Kala Language Committee originally decided to use the letter <l> to represent this sound; but due to the influence of the English and Tok Pisin alphabets, many people thought that the letter <r> should also be included (cf. Sackett, and Leggio and Matras, this volume). However, many of the Kala Language Committee thought that the sound [ɹ] was also borrowed into Kala from English. For instance, as James Gasu, a committee member from Apoze village, stated, 'In our language, [l] is the true sound. [ɹ] is something that came from the influence of the Whiteman. If we were to bring <r> into our language [alphabet], we wouldn't be speaking real Kala.' Kokie Dei, a community researcher from Manindala village, agreed with James, saying, 'In Manindala, in our natural tongue, our mother tongue, we don't have an *r* sound, we have an *l* sound' (my translation). As a result, throughout our time in the Kala villages in 2013, we had many discussions about the letter <l>, including whether to add the letter <r> or perhaps to develop a new symbol to represent the fact that the sound changes in different contexts and words. Nero Kaposing, Kala Language Committee chairman from Kamiali village, commented, 'I don't think we should change the <l> because this letter is already in 'typing machines', so it's easy to type. It's there. But, when I'm talking, I need to understand, I'm Kala, my language is special, I have this [ɾ] inside.' During the final workshop in 2013, the Kala Language Committee made the decision to keep the alphabet the same as was decided in 2010, using an <l> to represent the allophones of [l], [ɾ], and [ɹ], but emphasized the necessity of Kala language teachers to be well trained in describing the linguistic manner and placement of this sound so that students do not confuse it with the English letters <l> and <r>.

We were also concerned with readability and ease of use of the Kala orthography (cf. Casquite and Young, and Shah and Brenzinger, this volume). Geam Nero, a community researcher from Kui village, commented on the ease of use of the orthography when she said, 'Yes, it's easy. It's easy, but if we taught all the elementary students and all of the parents, if they all knew, it would be even easier.' Therefore, issues of access to orthography and developing literacy are also important to reflect on, including orthography promotion. Mark Yakam, the Kala language teacher from Alêso, also had this to say about the ease of learning the Kala biŋatuwã: 'This alphabet is the same, everybody understands it. The new parts are the vowels, right? The <ã> and <ẽ>, and this <ĩ> and <õ>and <ũ>. These letters all of the children need to learn, and their parents too. The alphabet doesn't have any differences, it's the vowels that are different – that's all.' Mark is focusing here on the ease with which people will be able to learn the Kala language system if they know how to read and write in English or Tok Pisin (for an analogous point, see Sackett, and Hull, this volume), which shows that language shift is occurring in the Kala communities. However, he feels that the orthography will help people – specifically children in the Kala language schools – learn the Kala alphabet first and then shift to the English alphabet. Many individuals were happy with the use of the nasalization symbols, such as Kamiali Kala language teacher Takwa Nadap, who said, 'I think, the titi mark makes all of the letters, all of the sounds, come very clear.'

However, others did have concerns about knowing both when to use the symbol and how to use it. For example, when asked if he is ever confused about the titi mark, Kibra Abu, Kala language teacher in Kui village, replied, 'Yes, if I am writing some words quickly and the sounds don't come clearly, then I'm confused about where the titi goes. Sometimes I forget about the titi mark.' We also saw this as an orthographic challenge

Reflections on the Kala Biŋatuwã, a Three-Year-Old Alphabet   139

in our workshops teaching the Kala biŋatuwã in the Kala villages in 2013. We noticed that people would often add the velar nasal symbol <ŋ> after the nasal vowel instead of using the nasalization mark, since the related language of Jabêm, which does not have phonemic nasal sounds, often has the word-final <ŋ>. Many older individuals were educated in Jabêm before English became the language of education (Paris 2012; Ross 1996), and they had a difficult time separating their knowledge of the Jabêm writing system from what they knew about the Kala language. This relationship to Jabêm also impacted some of the choices that the Kala Language Committee made in 2010 (see Schreyer 2015a).

A different concern existed in Manindala village, where there is the highest level of language shift amongst Kala speakers. In this village, Tok Pisin and English have also impacted ease of learning of the Kala biŋatuwã. As Claude Ellisha, Kala Language Committee member from Manindala, commented, 'The top of the alphabet, the gũgũ [also known as 'titi' or nasalization mark], the people who've been in town, they don't understand this mark well. When they come back, they confuse everyone. They use <ng> [instead of the gũgũ mark; my insertions].' However, despite these concerns, individuals were still in favour of using the wave symbol to mark these nasalized sounds. There was discussion at our final Kala Language Committee meeting in 2013 about whether or not we should keep the name 'titi' for these letters. In the end, the suggestion was made that everyone should understand what the other dialects use for this symbol but that each community should continue to use their own word for 'wave' (titi, taŋaoti, gũsa, and gũgũ) when teaching the orthography. This aligns well with the parallel dialectal approach for orthography creation that the Kala community has implemented throughout their orthography development. It also indicates that reflection is needed not only for the symbols chosen, but also for what the names of the symbols will be, since many languages use symbols that are modified from Roman characters.

6 Conclusions

During our reflection process from 2013 and the following 2013 Kala Language Committee meeting, no changes were deemed necessary for the Kala biŋatuwã. The Kala Language Committee also agreed that the last meeting in 2013 was the final chance to alter the writing system, since they felt that altering anything in the future would confuse people, especially as more and more books are published. While ample time for reflection and for the standardization of orthographies is necessary, and more in-depth scholarship is needed on the extended period of this process, it is important to remember that 'Once a writing system is in use, changing it becomes less and less desirable, as written materials proliferate in the system, the commitment to it is strengthened, and the bias of familiarity sets in' (Hinton 2014:165). In the case of the Kala orthography, our Kala Language Education and Local Ecological Knowledge project has been aided by the efforts of our biology colleagues from the Bishop Museum, including Ken Longenecker, who has worked to publish both his own scholarly work in Kala as well as materials to help support the community's interest in marine conservation (Longenecker et al. 2012, 2015). As Budd and Raymond note, since 'Melanesia is characterized by small homogenous language communities occupying a small geographical area [...] communication of ideas and coordination of language initiatives is easier than in larger, more dispersed communities' (2007:57). This seems to be true for the Kala orthography initiative, including the active reflection about the Kala biŋatuwã.

The items that the Kala Language Committee and other Kala speakers reflected on in regards to their new orthography were tied to issues that are often discussed during orthography creation but needed more engagement now that people had begun writing more and writing diverse items. First is the issue of representation: did the <l> symbol fully represent the realities of the Kala language? Second is readability: was the nasalization symbol clear, and, in terms of teaching others about the orthography, was the name appropriate? Third is ease of use: was the orthography easy to learn and to teach others? Was information easily shared across the Kala dialects? In the end, it seemed that the Kala biŋatuwã was adequately meeting the needs of the Kala speakers for those who had learned the orthography. The remaining challenge for the Kala speakers, in 2013, was teaching more people how to use the orthography and encouraging more writing across the villages. Nasingom Alinga, the vice-chair of the Kala Language Committee from Lambu village, was enthusiastic about sharing the Kala orthography. He commented this to me in the focus group discussion in Lambu village: 'You are a linguist, someone who studies languages, and why some languages die or people forget them. If we [the committee] didn't learn the alphabet, we couldn't teach it to the big men, and all of the students, and all the children. It's a good time to learn this alphabet, and it will be good when everyone knows this alphabet' (my insertion).

There are both benefits and challenges to conducting a similar engaged reflection of orthographic evolution with other new writing systems. For instance, while participation in the initial orthographic development process develops community engagement and ownership over their orthographies, involving community members in a lengthy evaluation process serves to further the ownership and level of engagement that community members feel towards their orthography. Moreover, since many orthographic decisions are made quickly in language documentation projects, an evolving and extended evaluation of the orthography (cf. Valdovinos, this volume) allows for more time to document the linguistic structure of the language, including what the exceptions to the spelling rules might be. Similarly, while more scholars are recognizing the significance of cultural, social, historical, and political ideologies on orthographic development (cf. Hull, Sackett, and Leggio and Matras, this volume), these can be even harder to predict than anomalies in the linguistic structures. Giving speakers time to use their orthography in different domains enables more on the ground use, which may need to be adjusted at a later date.

The challenges of a lengthy and engaged reflective process include a desire to rely too much on your own instincts as the linguistics expert rather than on the expertise and desires of the speakers. Furthermore, if not enough people have been using the orthography, or if they have not been using it in diverse domains, there is the challenge of not having enough information for reflection. Another issue might be having feedback that is too diverse, causing division within the community at this later date of reflection and possibly a large amount of change in the orthography. Often, this diverse feedback might be connected to other ideological impacts, and it is important to recognize this in order to develop solutions to these issues. As orthographies and the ability to express oneself in writing are key aspects of UNESCO's language vitality scale, it is imperative that scholars continue to develop ways to assist communities in developing orthographies that will be embraced and utilized. As this discussion of the Kala biŋatuwã has shown, an engaged and extended reflection period may be a missing piece in the development of successful orthographies for languages that are both endangered and unwritten.

Notes

1. Unless otherwise noted, all Kala words are written in the newly approved Kala writing system. This writing system marks nasal vowels using the same diacritics as in the IPA, and the <ŋ> symbol is also used to mark the velar nasal sound. Phonemes will be marked between sideways slashes, such as /j/, while allophones will be marked with square brackets, such as [ɛ], and graphemes will be marked with angle brackets, such as <a>.
2. The *Ethnologue* also states that Kala is spoken in ten villages. This is also incorrect. Moreover, literacy rates in the native and second language are listed as 15–25% for both, and there is no source for this information. It does not match my own experiences in the Kala village, where the majority of individuals are literate in Tok Pisin.
3. The phonological analysis was basic, since, as Bird writes, 'Phonological studies that support a new orthography are often superficial – in terms of empirical coverage, level of analysis, and attention to morphology; thus their findings must necessarily be regarded as tentative' (2001:153).
4. All focus group discussions were originally conducted in Tok Pisin, and quotations presented here in English were translated by the author.
5. Rudes (2000) has described a similar approach, known as the 'flexible spelling system', where words are spelt in each dialect according to how they are pronounced.

8 When Letters Represent More Than Sounds: Ideology versus Practicality in the Development of a Standard Orthography for Ch'orti' Mayan

Kerry Hull

1 Introduction

With the Pan-Maya Movement in the 1980s, there was a need to standardize the bewildering number of orthographies that had been used to write Mayan languages from the sixteenth century onwards. This move anticipated the revitalization efforts that would require publishing resources in the native languages. In the 1970s, the Proyecto Lingüístico Francisco Marroquín (hereafter, PLFM) made initial progress by introducing an alphabet that was appropriate for the types of sounds found in Mayan languages. In 1986, the Academia de Lenguas Mayas de Guatemala (hereafter, ALMG) made further strides in formalizing a single orthography for the twenty-one Mayan languages of Guatemala (England 1998). This chapter, based on my fieldwork experience of working with the Ch'orti' Maya over the past sixteen years, discusses the challenges encountered by the Ch'orti' in adopting the ALMG alphabet and promulgating their own versions of this orthography. Two main issues will be considered: first, the two competing orthographies that were developed by SIL and, later, Ch'orti' language revitalization groups; second, the ideologically driven changes in orthographic conventions among the Ch'orti' by some in language revitalization groups. I show that, while accepting in principle the agreed-upon orthography of the ALMG, some Ch'orti' revitalization groups sought further changes, driven not by idiosyncratic phonological concerns of correctness relevant to Ch'orti', but rather by ideology: they wanted to distance their orthography as much as possible from that of Spanish (cf. Moseley, Sackett, Lai, and Leggio and Matras, this volume). As I will argue, their changes were towards less phonologically transparent, less correct, and less effective in terms of learnability.

2   The Ch'orti' Language

Ch'orti' is part of the eastern branch of the Ch'olan family of Mayan languages and is one of its three remaining members since the extinction of Ch'olti' around the seventeenth century. Ch'orti' is one of thirty-one Mayan languages, over twenty-one of which are still spoken in Guatemala today. Ch'orti' is used in a limited region in the departments of Chiquimula and Zacapa and the *municipio* of Olopa in southern Guatemala. A handful of elderly speakers are still to be found in northern Honduras. Native speakers of Ch'orti' have been steadily declining, and, whereas estimates on the extreme end place the possible number of speakers at about 52,000 (Cojti 1992), based on my own fieldwork with the Ch'orti', fluent native speakers of the language today number much closer to 12,000. The SIL lists 30,000 total ethnic Ch'orti' as recently as 2000, but it does not provide more specific information on the number of actual speakers. The *Ethnologue* classifies Ch'orti' as a 'developing' language, but UNESCO has declared Ch'orti' in Guatemala to be 'definitely endangered', with only 11,734 speakers and, in Honduras, 'critically endangered', with only 10 remaining speakers. Based on my observations during more than thirty months of fieldwork throughout the Ch'orti' region, I can report that there are numerous ethnically Ch'orti' communities where Ch'orti' is hardly used or is completely absent. Ch'orti' demographics are also decreasing in some areas. For example, Wisdom (1940:1) lists the town of La Unión as one of the areas where the 'majority' of indigenous Ch'orti' lived in the 1940s. In 1964, the *Diccionario Geográfico* lists a Ch'orti' population of La Unión at 64 per cent, but by 1994, a government census showed only 94 indigenous residents (Dary et al. 1998:31, note 6) in a population of over 25,000. Fortunately, there are several remaining hamlets where Ch'orti' is indeed thriving and is the dominant language in daily interactions.

The influence of Spanish on Ch'orti' since the Conquest has penetrated most facets of the language. For example, while most Mayan languages are VOS, Ch'orti' has adopted Spanish syntax, and today it is primarily (though not exclusively) SVO. Lexical borrowings are common, and neologisms introduced by modern language revitalization groups are meeting with little success. Due to this level of Spanish integration in the language, since the early 1990s there has been an effort by some in the Ch'orti' community, as one of the leaders of this movement explained to me, to 'purge' the Ch'orti' language of many linguistic and orthographic features related to Spanish in order to 'take control' once again of their language. The intention is not only to eradicate Spanish terms, but also to 'cleanse' the language of any imposed system, including orthography (cf. Valdovinos and Esteban, this volume).

3 Language Revitalization and Orthographic Conventions

Within Guatemala, the first attempt by the government to assist and promote indigenous languages and issues came with the formation of the Instituto Indigenista Nacional (hereafter, INN) in the 1940s. This led to the first formal discussion of Mayan orthographies in the First Linguistic Congress (1949). Attending were 48 individuals: 23 Maya, 12 ladinos (non-indigenous Guatemalans), and 12 North Americans. A Ch'orti' speaker was among the 23 Maya groups represented. The resulting proposal of this conference was that the new alphabet would be as close to that of Spanish as possible 'so as to make the transition from Mayan literacy to Spanish literacy (and vice versa) as easy as possible' (Lewis 1993:4; cf. Sackett, and Shah and Brenzinger, this volume). The benefit of using a Spanish-based orthography was that it was either familiar or already known by some and would therefore facilitate reading in Ch'orti'. The drawbacks of this system, however, were that it was not phonologically accurate in some cases (as the later PLFM and ALMG's orthographies would be) and that it came with the baggage of colonialism in the eyes of some. Nevertheless, by adhering closely to the conventions of Spanish orthography, the INN did pave the way for the promulgation of essentially this same alphabet by the SIL.

The SIL was the first outside organization to have a direct influence on Mayan orthographies in Guatemala. DeChicchis (n.d.:176) has summarized this early process as follows:

It is important to mention that the official orthographic system of 1962 was formulated in consultation with the Summer Institute of Linguistics (SIL). Also, SIL received special permission from the Guatemalan government to establish its original compound in Zone 2 of Guatemala City. The compound comprised a library, a print shop and bindery, a chapel, offices, meeting rooms, and living quarters. As part of the quid pro quo for certain sweetheart concessions involving land use and taxes, SIL agreed to use orthographies for the Mayan languages which conformed to the Spanish tradition (rather than to an international linguistic tradition, e.g., Americanist, IPA) in its publications, and SIL agreed to promote such orthographies through its literacy education of the Maya.

The reach of the SIL was profound, as it quickly established itself as the authoritative voice regarding Mayan orthography. Its virtual monopoly over issues regarding Mayan orthographies was not seriously challenged until the formation of the PLFM.

Thanks to the efforts of Terrence Kaufman, the 1970s saw the rise of the first indigenous and North American collaborative effort towards accurate language description and documentation by the PLFM in parts of Guatemala. Under Kaufman's direction came a new proposal to do away with the SIL alphabet because of phonetic inaccuracies and ethnocentric origins in the Spanish alphabet (Kaufman 1970). Efforts to replace the SIL alphabet were met with considerable resistance from the SIL organization, which even went so far as to ask their members to pray that the proposal to change alphabets would 'either be dropped or turned down' (Fischer 2010:124; see also Stoll 1982:268). The SIL has sought to keep control of orthographic determination out of the hands of the indigenous Maya by opposing the ALMG's alphabet (England 1996:184–186:185; see also Woolard 1998:23). In the 1980s, however, the tides began to shift towards language revitalization – a move that would forever help to lessen the influence of the SIL-supported alphabet in Guatemala.

In the 1980s and 1990s, a grass-roots movement began in Guatemala, supported by numerous intellectuals within various Maya communities. Until this point, only sporadic efforts had been made towards the development of any type of pan-Mayan identity by the INN and by the aforementioned initial linguistic efforts in the 1970s on the part of the PLFM. However, in the 1980s, leaders hailing from disparate Maya groups sought to unite (to some extent) the many distinct Maya communities under a single banner – that of 'Maya'. This lofty and arguably over-ambitious goal was criticized by some for the assumption that these groups of intellectuals and leaders could and did speak for their respective language communities (Brown 1998).

The aims of these groups centred on political, educational, and economic reform. As Warren has noted, 'Maya culture represents the meaningful selective mix of practice and knowledge, drawn on and resynthesized at this historic junction by groups who see indigenous identity as highly salient to self-representation and as a vehicle for political change' (1998:12). In addition, language and cultural revitalization were key components of efforts to re-establish and connect to their 'Maya' identity. Enter orthography. With the new interest in preserving and promoting their native languages came the need to formalize an official or standard orthography for this nascent 'Maya' conglomerate.

The effort towards a unified political voice facilitated the organization of the ALMG, a group whose influence on the orthographic process has been considerable. Indeed, since its foundation in the late 1980s, the ALMG's impact on language revitalization has grown incrementally until the present day. The challenge to create a single alphabet that accurately represented all the possible phonemes in Mayan languages and that satisfied each of the individual groups was somewhat daunting. Since Mayan languages have many differences in their phonemic inventories, any agreed-upon alphabet would have to accommodate all the attested phonemes in the twenty-one different Mayan languages of Guatemala. For example, since some Mayan languages only have short vowels while others also have long vowels, standardized forms for writing all of them were simultaneously developed. Consonants also show degrees of variation among different Mayan languages,

Table 8.1 *Comparison of IPA and the Academia de Lenguas Mayas de Guatemala (ALMG) orthography.*

Consonants									
ALMG	IPA	ALMG	IPA	ALMG	IPA	ALMG	IPA	ALMG	IPA
b'	[ɓ]	**b**	[b]	**ch**	[tʃ]	**ch'**	[tʃ']	**h**	[h]
j	[χ]	**k**	[k]	**k'**	[k']	**l**	[l]	**m**	[m]
n	[n]	**nh**	[ŋ]	**p**	[p]	**q**	[q]	**q'**	[q']
r	[r]	**s**	[s]	**t**	[t]	**t'**	[t']	**tz**	[ts]
tz'	[ts']	**w**	[w]	**x**	[ʃ]	**y**	[j]	**'**	[ʔ]

but a single overarching system was established that was able to accommodate each of the phonemes in all of the Mayan languages of Guatemala (cf. Hewitt, this volume). A list of these ALMG characters compared to IPA is given in Table 8.1.

In every respect, the alphabet of the ALMG meets the criteria of a proper and accurate orthography. As will be discussed below, however, in the case of the Ch'orti', ideological factors have eroded the use of that orthography to some extent.

The ALMG succeeded in gaining a consensus on a pan-Mayan alphabet that would form the base of all future publications in the various Mayan languages. In 1987, the Guatemalan Ministry of Culture and Sports officially sanctioned a single alphabet for twenty-one of the Mayan languages. Then, in 1988, the ALMG succeeded in establishing its alphabet as 'official' under Guatemalan law. The SIL, however, has continued using its own alphabet in spite of the new law recognizing the official status of the ALMG alphabet.

4 Orthographic Contentions in the Ch'orti' Region

By the 1980s, when the first significant progress was being made for language revitalization groups in Guatemala, there were roughly between 12,000 and 15,000 Ch'orti' speakers. Spanish literacy rates among them were extremely low, and Ch'orti' literacy rates were likely no more than 5 per cent. Thus, for the vast majority of the Ch'orti', nothing could be further from their minds than questions of orthographic conventions. Even in 2000, one of my Ch'orti' consultants responded to my invitation to attend literacy classes with this: *¿Kocha k'ani utakrye'n konde war inpatna tama nichor?* (How is it going to help me when I am working in my cornfield?). The lack of interest on the part of most Ch'orti' was only compounded by the lack of written sources in Ch'orti', outside of several short religious texts produced by the SIL. Readily available

Table 8.2 *Comparison of the various orthographies used to write select Ch'orti' consonant sounds by different authors.*

IPA	tʃ	tʃ'	x	ʔ	ʃ	t͡sʼ	k	k'
Suárez (1892)	ch	ch	j	'	sh	ts	c	c
Membreño (1897)	ch	ch	j	VhV	sh	ts	c, qu	c, qu
Sapper (1897)	ch	ch'	j, h	'	x	tz'	k	k'
Peccorini (1909)/ Becerra (1910)	ch	ch	j, h, g	'	x	tz, s	c	c, k
Wisdom (1940)	tc	tc'	h	'	x	t'c	k, q	k, q'
Girard (1949)	č	č	h	'	š		k, q	k, q'
Oakley (1966)	ch	ch'	x	'	x	tz'	c	c'
Fought (1972)	tx	ʔtx	h	ʔ	x	ʔts	k	ʔk
Lubeck (1989)	ch	ch'	j	'	x	tz'	c, qu	c', q'u
Metz et al. (1992)	ch	ch'	j	'	x	tz'	k	k'
Hull (2005)	ch	ch'	j	'	x	tz'	k	k'
Schumann (2007)	ch	ch'	j	'	x	tz'	k	k'

written literature in Ch'orti' was nearly non-existent, even for those few who could read the language.

Language revitalization efforts eventually began to take hold in the Ch'orti' area. And yet, during the 1980s and up until the mid-1990s, the labours of the PLFM and the ALMG had only marginal effects on the Ch'orti', as the organization of indigenous movements was somewhat slower in taking root among the Ch'orti' than in other Mayan groups. Around the time of the end of the thirty-six-year civil war in Guatemala, however, members of several Ch'orti' Maya language and culture revitalization groups embraced the alphabet of the ALMG along with many of their political and social goals.

The new alphabet differed (understandably) in many respects from orthographies that had been used to write Ch'orti' since the beginning of the nineteenth century (see Table 8.2).

In 1834, Juan Galindo recorded the first known vocabulary, a mere handful of words. There was more significant progress by Alberto Ruano Suárez in 1892 in documenting the language. However, no effort was made by any of the early documenters of Ch'orti' to create a standard orthography. Indeed, at times rampant inconsistencies were prevalent in the work of all these authors.

Important early ethnographers such as Rafael Girard (1949, 1962) and Charles Wisdom (1940, 1950) in the first half of the twentieth century generally followed Spanish-style orthography. In many respects, this mirrored what the SIL would use when they began their evangelization efforts among the Ch'orti'. Since the late 1940s, the American Bible Society, the Friends Mission, the SIL, and other Evangelical groups have been working continuously in the Ch'orti' area. The goals of the missionary-linguist are often at odds with those of indigenous language revitalization groups; the former are eager to change aspects of the culture, whereas the latter are dedicated to preserving it (see Grenoble and Whaley 2006:196). Thus, the SIL uses its own orthography to record the language, to teach literacy, and to train future missionaries in the language, though not as a means of preserving the language per se. Alphabetization and literacy in the hands of religious groups in Mesoamerica have traditionally been used as 'transitory instruments' towards becoming less 'indigenous' rather than tools used to stimulate growth in these languages (Bonfil Batalla 1996:117–118). The role of the Catholic Church in colonial Central America was often to evangelize indigenous groups through education and teaching literacy (Gonzalbo 1994:13–14, 16, 21; cf. Hull 2003:356). Indeed, whereas the goal of the missionary-linguist is one of assimilation through orthography and literacy, the goal of many Maya indigenous groups is one of dissimilation from hegemonic influences.

Missionary efforts, however, do often have highly positive impacts on the expansion of literacy. As is commonly the case, outside religious groups are oftentimes the first to create longer written texts in indigenous languages, specifically biblical texts. For example, Helen Oakely translated the First Epistle of John into Ch'orti' in 1955 and the Gospel of Mark in 1958 (cf. Dahlquis 1995:121). She also went on to write a short grammatical description of the Ch'orti' language (Oakley 1966), and she and others also translated hymns and other religious materials into Ch'orti'. Outside of excerpts that appeared in Wisdom's (1940) work, these were for all intents and purposes the first written, published documents in the Ch'orti' language.

Helen Oakley was also instrumental in developing the first 'official' alphabet of Ch'orti' – one which other Evangelical groups have essentially adhered to since that time. In 1977, McNichols, who was a member of the SIL, published his *Alfabeto chortí* – an effort to formalize the alphabet developed by the SIL in the Ch'orti' area. Larger works by other SIL authors, such as John and Diane Lubeck, also made use of this orthography in their pedagogical grammar of Ch'orti' (1989), as did John Lubeck's full translation of the New Testament in 1996.

Thus, the first material written in Ch'orti' that was readily accessible to the Ch'orti' themselves was written in the SIL alphabet. Previous linguistic work on Ch'orti' had been all but inaccessible to the Ch'orti' people – the vast majority of whom were, in any case, illiterate in the middle of the twentieth century. As missionary efforts increased, so did literacy rates (albeit very slowly) into the 1980s. Again, all available written literature in Ch'orti' was primarily in the SIL alphabet, which probably helped temporarily cement its position of authority in the Ch'orti' area.

During the 1960s and 1970s, the linguist John Fought produced a highly detailed linguistic description of the language and its phonology (1967, 1972).

Fought opted for a phonologically transparent orthography that, while lauded by other linguists, has been generally ignored by everyone else due to its non-reader-friendly presentation for non-specialists (it contains pause marks, hesitations, pitch contours, stresses, and other articulatory components). Although highly nuanced and effective, Fought's orthography was not adopted by any other authors writing Ch'orti' and has had no impact on the debates surrounding Ch'orti' orthography. Fought's was thus a strictly scholarly contribution rather than a practical one.

With the publication of the largest written document in the Ch'orti' language to date – the aforementioned translation of the New Testament by John Lubeck – the SIL alphabet was poised to increase its status among the heavily Christian Ch'orti' population simply by association with this influential religious work. However, Lubeck's translation was pre-empted, in 1994, by the first major PLFM publication in Ch'orti': the *Gramática del idioma ch'orti'* (Pérez Martínez 1994). Then, in 1996, in the same year the New Testament was published and was made available in Ch'orti', the PLFM published their *Diccionario del idioma ch'orti'* (Pérez Martínez 1996) and a book on Ch'orti' legends (Pérez Martínez et al. 1996). Tensions immediately developed between many in Ch'orti' language revitalization groups and Evangelicals as to which alphabet was the 'standard'. In fact, the orthographic systems of the PLFM and the SIL did not vary extensively (see Table 8.3); however, perceived phonetic accuracy was secondary to issues of control, authority, and rights.

I have interviewed many of the key players on both sides of this debate (though more from the Ch'orti' side) among the SIL and Ch'orti' language revitalization groups (principally the PLFM and the ALMG). The divide is wide and the gap seemingly unbreachable. Several of my interviewees in the Friends Mission gave three primary reasons for using their orthographic system: first, time depth – they developed it first; second, it is linguistically sound; and third, most of the literature at that point (mainly in 2002) was written in it, including the Bible, so therefore it should be used by the populace in general.

Table 8.3 *Comparison of IPA, SIL, and ALMG orthographic conventions for representing different velar stops.*

IPA	SIL	ALMG
[k]	c	k
[k']	c	k'
[k]	qu	k
[k']	q'u	k'
[g], [w]	g	w

In interviewing members of the Ch'orti' revitalization groups, numerous reasons were offered as to why their orthographic system should be considered 'standard'. Several among them who have received university degrees in linguistics pointed out that theirs is 'clearly more correct, linguistically speaking'. In order to illustrate this point, the differences in the two orthographies can be compared in the following segment of verse from Mark 1:10 from the New Testament translation into Ch'orti' by John Lubeck (1989). Underlined forms represent variations between the SIL orthography (1) and what the same verse would look like in the ALMG alphabet (2).

(1) Entonces ch'ujya e Jesús, y conda war aloc'oy macuir e ja' uwira que pasc'a ut e q'uin

(2) Entonses ch'ujya e Jesus, yi konda war alok'oy makwir e ja' uwira ke' pask'a ut e k'in
('And straightway coming up out of the water, he saw the heavens opened')

The Spanish loanword *entonces* retains the grapheme <c> in the SIL writing but would be changed to <s> in the ALMG since *c* is the Spanish writing of the phoneme in this environment. The ALMG form is also more accurate in the term *makwir* [*makwi'r*], as the pronunciation is /w/, not /u/ as the SIL would write it. Also note that the standard pattern in Spanish of representing the phoneme /k/ with <c> before /i/ and /e/ but with <qu'> before /o/, /a/, and /u/ is observed meticulously in the SIL orthography. All instances of /k/ are written with the grapheme <k> by the ALMG.

Returning to the reasons given by the ALMG for preferring their orthographic system, one of the leaders of the ALMG further stated, 'It's not their language nor their decision.' A leader with PLFM declared, 'We exercise our rights to be free from any chains of colonialism. Writing Ch'orti' is an act of expression of our rights.' These comments divorce the issue from one of linguistic correctness and orthography and link it instead to one of ideology, power, and identity (cf. Bermel 2007; Johnson 2005; Sebba 2012a:3; cf. Sallabank and Marquis, this volume). In other words, the destiny of the Ch'orti' language is to be realized by the Ch'orti' themselves and not by outsider influence (cf. Valdovinos, and Esteban, this volume).

I first learned about this debate when I was asked by a leader in the Ch'orti' ALMG to review a book on Ch'orti' grammar that the organization had just finished and was preparing for publication. I spent about a month and dozens of hours carefully annotating corrections to the text, offering alternative grammatical interpretations of some aspects of the language with lengthy explanations and pointing out more than a hundred typographical errors. The following year when the book was published, I was more than a little taken back to see that not one of the changes I had suggested had been included – not even the typographical errors. I went to the house of the leader who had asked me to review it and asked him what had happened. He said, somewhat sheepishly, 'When I presented your changes to the group, several stood up and angrily resisted their inclusion saying, "This work must be 100 per cent Ch'orti', not that of a *saksak winik* [foreigner]."' All of the members of this group were good friends whom I had known for years while doing fieldwork in the Ch'orti' area. However, in this case, ideology trumped the need for accuracy.

Despite the political issues surrounding which orthographic system should be used to write Ch'orti', what is certain is that the Ch'orti' are reaping the benefits of having their language accessible in written form. The first area that has been most directly impacted is that of bilingual education. Since the 1990s, various Ch'orti' indigenous groups have promoted bilingual education in areas where only Spanish was being taught. The Escuela Normal Bilingüe Intercultural de Camotán, Chiquimula (2002) played an important part in this process. By 2004, trained bilingual teachers were being sent into Ch'orti' hamlets to teach, among other things, the Ch'orti' language. Prior to the 1990s, most of the teachers in the Ch'orti' area had been monolingual speakers of Spanish.

Although limited in terms of its scope, funding, and materials, bilingual education is advancing and has had a significant impact on strengthening literacy rates among the Ch'orti', which, as Adams has noted, is 'probably the most sought-after outcome which leads to long term language health' (2014:232). Organizations such as the PLFM, ALMG, DIGEBI, and numerous others are now producing, for the first time, literature written in Ch'orti'. One of the first translations to be made available to the Ch'orti' in their language was that of the Popol Vuj (ALMG 2001b), the K'iche' Maya mytho-historical document that has deep roots back even into Classic and Pre-classic Maya societies. Other printed Ch'orti' material now includes work on Ch'orti' literature (ALMG 1999), dictionaries produced by native speakers (ALMG 2001a; Pérez Martínez 1996), oral traditions (ALMG 2001c; Pérez Martínez 1996), pedagogical works (ALMG 2005; López de Rosa y Mucía Patal 1997), and grammars (Pérez Martínez 1994; ALMG 2009). In short, the development of an alphabet (actually several competing ones) has been instrumental in increasing literacy rates and thereby giving Ch'orti' speakers access to written material to interact with beyond the prevalent Spanish options. Thus, expanding the domains of Ch'orti' into the printed realm has bolstered its relevance and has facilitated bilingual education.

5   Internal Orthographic Complexities in Ch'orti'

Apart from the historical development and ideological controversies associated with the formation of a 'standard' Ch'orti' alphabet, the language itself also poses several orthographic challenges. For instance, elderly speakers of Ch'orti' today regularly use /g/ and /w/ allophonically in certain contexts. A ready explanation for this variation escapes me since it is not completely systematic, but it clearly patterns out in this way. This complementary distribution can be seen in terms such as *gororoj* ~ *wororoj* 'round' and *ingojr otot* ~ *inwojr otot* 'one house'. What compounds this difficulty is that numerous Spanish words with /g/ have been incorporated into Ch'orti', blurring the lines as to whether or not it is an actual phoneme of the contemporary language. To muddy the waters even more, an intrusive /g/ is found in numerous Spanish words where it replaces the 'silent' *h* of Spanish – such as [aˈoːɾa] 'now' being pronounced [agoːɾa] when speaking Ch'orti'. The SIL and other religious groups write <g> when a /g/ sound is used, but in many cases, even in transcribed texts, <g>s are changed to <w>s in transcriptions by language revitalization groups. On one occasion, after transcribing a text I recorded with a Ch'orti' man, he asked me to change several <g>s to <w>s. I asked why, and he said, 'I worked with the ALMG several years ago, and they instructed me to speak and write with *w*'s, and I don't want them to see my mistakes.' This is one of the ways in which orthographic concerns are having an impact on linguistic behaviour. Today, those taught by the ALMG are using /w/ instead of /g/ not only when they write, but also when they speak. They are being instructed that /w/ is the 'correct' form and that /g/ should not be used in all cases, even when the most common pronunciation of a term is often with /g/.

Members of Ch'orti' revitalization groups have also struggled with how to account for and represent /g/. Since proto-Mayan does not have a /g/ phoneme, some members of these groups who believe in achieving 'language purity' treat /g/ as an 'aberration' and /w/ as the 'original' phoneme (which is historically correct, incidentally). Yet Ch'orti' speakers cannot deny that the consistent allophonic use of /g/ and /w/ exists. Thus, many language revitalization groups tend to use /w/ primarily or exclusively instead of /g/, especially when they are writing creatively (e.g., modern poetry) rather than simply transcribing texts in Ch'orti'.

5.1 The Conjunction /i/

An interesting case of orthographic representation in Ch'orti' today is presented by the conjunction *i*, meaning 'and'. This conjunction is similar in form and function to that of the Spanish *y* – indeed, some have thought it to be a borrowing into Ch'orti'. Although this is a distinct possibility, I suggest that it could also represent a reflex or an adaptation of the Classic Mayan 'i (T679), a preverbal adverb meaning 'and' or 'then' in hieroglyphic texts.

Early publications by the ALMG in the 1990s often transcribed the conjunction 'and' as *y*, just as it would be written in Spanish. In the mid-1990s, there were, however, disagreements in the ALMG meetings as to the best way to represent this morpheme. While all members agreed that /i/ was the correct sound, it was decided that *i* was not how this morpheme should be recorded orthographically. Somewhat unexpectedly, it was suggested that the conjunction 'and' should be represented as *yi*. It should be noted that there is no phonological justification for writing it as *yi*, as the sound is simply /i/. Why then the change? Ideology. As several members stated, 'We write it [the conjunction] as *yi* in order to distinguish it from the Spanish *y*. It's not Spanish, it's Mayan' (my insertion). Phonetic transparency and linguistic correctness therefore took a back seat to ideological concerns (cf. England 2003). While orthographic conventions can at times be constructed almost unconsciously to distinguish two languages, as Sebba (1998) has argued for English and British Creole, the Ch'orti' are making overt political statements through their conscious and determined orthographic choices.

Remarkably, more recent literature by the ALMG has taken this change even further by adding a glottal stop, in an apparent effort to further distinguish this Spanish-looking form from Spanish. Note the following example: *Ch'ujkunik tuk'a tuk'a uk'ab'a' e b'a **yi'** pejkanik* ('Let's look at the various body parts **and** name them') (ALMG 2002:89; my translation). Thus, the progression in the transcription of this conjunction has been <y> to <yi> to <yi'>, none of which is phonologically correct, as the pronunciation is /i/. This desire to distance themselves from Spanish (a language from which contemporary Ch'orti' takes a large number of lexical and grammatical borrowings) occupies much of their language planning efforts, be they in the creation of neologisms to replace Spanish borrowings or the manipulation of grammatical structures that do not reflect spoken Ch'orti'. In this case, the battle for accuracy in transcription was less important than winning the larger 'war', as it were, against Spanish and residual colonial influences in their language. The orthographic representation of the conjunction 'and' has therefore become an ideological act.

6 Conclusion

Orthographic conventions are often not simple matters to settle, especially in indigenous communities where writing itself can be seen as an expressive act of culture and identity. As this chapter has discussed, while Christian missionaries had a dominant influence on issues regarding Ch'orti' orthography for over forty years, considerable disagreement now exists between the SIL as an organization and Ch'orti' language revitalization groups over which is the 'official' or even most appropriate Ch'orti' orthography. The question is, at its core, who has the right or the authority to make orthographic decisions for the Ch'orti' people.

Even as the importance of writing has begun to take root in the Ch'orti' area, with the formation of the ALMG and other language revitalization groups, and with the burgeoning emphasis on bilingual education, most of the Ch'orti' are utterly unaware (or do not care) about questions of orthography. However, for some, especially those who are members of language revitalization groups, orthography has provided opportunity to 'purge' or 'purify' (cf. Bermell 2007:85) centuries of colonial and outside influences on the Ch'orti' language and to allow the Ch'orti' to choose a system that is, as one leader explained it to me, 'truly our own'. Indeed, language purism is often cited as justification for the creation of a new alphabet (cf. Wertheim 2012:81). This struggle to define a 'standard' orthography among the Ch'orti' aptly demonstrates that notions of linguistic correctness can, and in fact do at times, yield to those of ideology.

9 The Difficult Task of Finding a Standard Writing System for the Sioux Languages[1]

Avelino Corral Esteban

1 Introduction

UNESCO (2003b) argues explicitly that a people's right to use their mother tongue, to receive instruction in it and through it, and to express their cultural identity is a fundamental human right and one that cannot be fully realized without the development of a written form of the language in question. Writing an oral language is therefore undoubtedly a matter of great cultural significance, but any process involving the development of orthography in such a language is always a difficult task. In the case of the Lakota and Dakota varieties of Sioux, this does not necessarily entail the creation of a new writing system, but rather choosing one to serve as a standard spelling system.[2]

Accordingly, this chapter analyses and compares these different writing systems in order to determine which reproduces the pronunciation most faithfully. It does not attempt to be normative, since the choice of a standard writing system for this language cannot be reduced merely to a linguistic issue: attention should also be paid to educational/pedagogical, socio-historical, political, technical and personal factors and, more importantly, should reflect the opinions of Sioux native speakers (for an analogous point, see Casquite and Young, and Schreyer, this volume). Section 2 contains basic information on the Sioux language, its linguistic affiliation and the main differences between its dialects. Section 3 offers a linguistic analysis of all the existing orthographies of Sioux. Section 4 attempts to identify a number of educational, socio-historical, political, and technical factors (Seifart 2006; Cahill and Karan 2008; Lüpke 2011) that might lead to the choice of one orthography over another. Section 5 offers a possible solution to this complicated issue by providing several examples of an effective standard orthography for Sioux, which would certainly contribute to its preservation and revitalization in the long term.

2 The Sioux Language

According to Lewis and Simons (2010), Sioux language is at EGIDS level 6b (Siouan, USA and Canada, 20,000 speakers), meaning that it is under serious threat since, although the language is still used in face-to-face communication, the intergenerational transmission chain is in the process of being broken and its users are gradually becoming more scarce. UNESCO (Moseley 2010) likewise considers this language to be critically endangered because the youngest fluent speakers are adults.

Sioux belongs to the Dakotan branch of the Mississippi Valley Siouan language family and is traditionally considered to have two different but largely mutually intelligible dialects, commonly referred to as Lakota and Dakota. Although an over-simplification, the most striking sound difference[3] between the Lakota and Dakota varieties concerns the realization of the Proto-Siouan */R/, whose reflex in Lakota and Dakota (especially Eastern Dakota) are /l/ and /d/, respectively (e.g., Lakota: *Lakxóta*; Western Dakota: *Dakóta*; Eastern Dakota: *Dakóta*).

Within Lakota, minor dialectal differences exist between the southern and northern reservations, most of them mainly concerning vocabulary. Still fewer differences, mostly lexical, appear to exist among the Eastern Dakota and Western Dakota dialects. Western Dakota, especially Yankton, is phonologically closer to Eastern Dakota than it is to Lakota, but lexically, its mutual intelligibility with Lakota is greater (Lakota Language Consortium [hereafter, LLC] 2012:4–6).

3 A Linguistic Comparison of Sioux Orthographic Systems

Despite the oral nature of their language, the Sioux did have a writing system of their own prior to the arrival of the white man – namely one which consisted of representational pictographs, where a drawing resembled the physical object it represented. Nevertheless, in the early nineteenth century, owing to contact with Christian missionaries, their writing system changed significantly, and from that moment on, a number of orthographies have been developed for their language (see Table 9.1; White Hat 1999:3–6; LLC 2012:8–19).[4]

First, the Christian missionaries formulated a written form of Sioux that was used to translate Biblical texts and to compile grammars and dictionaries. Later, individual native speakers, professional linguists, and educational institutions helped by native consultants took part in the process of designing a standardized orthography system for the Lakota and Dakota varieties.

The adoption of a standardized alphabet has always been believed to be highly desirable since, in addition to helping develop more effective curricula and teacher training, a more economical printing of literature, and an easier transfer of teaching skills, it was also seen as definitely contributing to fostering identity and cultural unity. With this aim, in the early 1980s, after countless meetings and considerable discussion, the Lakota Tribal Government accepted the orthography developed by Albert White Hat Sr. as the official way of

Table 9.1 *Sioux writing systems.*[5]

Year	Orthography	Author(s)	Variety
1834	Dakota Mission	S. Pond, G. Pond, S. R. Riggs, and T. S. Williamson	Dakota
1852	Riggs	S. R. Riggs	Dakota
1868	Williamson	J. P. Williamson and S. R. Riggs	Dakota
1924	Buechel 1	E. Buechel	Lakota
1932	Boas & Deloria	F. Boas and E. C. Deloria	Lakota/Dakota
1939	Buechel 2	E. Buechel	Lakota
1940	Traditional	L. Standing Bear Jr., V. Deloria Sr., Charles Eastman, and M. Crow Dog	Lakota
1941	Clark	A. Clark	Lakota
1954	Buechel 3	E. Buechel	Lakota
1970	Manhart 1	P. Manhart	Lakota
1971	Karol	J. S. Karol	Lakota
1971	War Cloud	P. War Cloud Grant	Dakota
1978	UMN 1	R. Flute, T. Dunnigan, A. Rynda, and C. Schommer	Dakota
1976	CU	D. S. Rood and A. R. Taylor	Lakota
1978	Manhart 2	P. Manhart	Lakota
1982	White Hat	A. White Hat Sr., L. One Star, and J. Kills Small	Lakota
1983	BU	P. H. Voorhis and S. Beardy	Dakota
1990	NetSiouan	J. Koontz	Lakota/Dakota
1991	SICC	Saskatchewan Indian Cultural Centre (SICC)	Lakota/Dakota
1991	Txakini	V. Catches	Lakota
1992	LLC	J. Ulrich-Lakota Language Consortium (LLC)	Lakota/Dakota
1994	Starr	E. Starr and I. Starr	Lakota
2004	UMN 2	H. LaFontaine and N. McKay	Dakota
2006	DEDP	C. Mato Nunpa, A. Wilson, and T. Dunnigan	Dakota
2011	Canku	N. Knudson, J. Snow, and C. Canku	Dakota
2013	DIO	Dakhóta Iápi Okhódakičhiye (DIO)	Dakota

writing the Lakota language. Yet, despite this initial attempt to standardize the Sioux writing system, the political and cultural fragmentation of the Sioux Nation, provoked by the U.S. government deciding to settle its peoples on reservations, have led to a situation that could be referred to as 'hyperfragmentation' (Cahill, 2011:2), whereby different communities still use the system with which they are most familiar or that they themselves have developed. To my knowledge, the most commonly used writing systems are those designed by Riggs, Buechel, University of Colorado at Boulder (hereafter, CU), White Hat, Saskatchewan Indian Cultural Centre (hereafter, SICC),[6] and the Lakota Language Consortium (hereafter, LLC).[7]

Table 9.2[8] sets out the phonemic inventory of the Sioux language. I have classified the phonemes into different groups, and these segments, together

Table 9.2 *The phonemic inventory of Sioux.*

Stress
1. Marking of stress
Vowels
2.
• Oral vowels: /a/, /e/, /i/, /o/, /u/
• Nasal vowels: /ą/, /į/, /ų/
Consonants
3. Oral and nasal continuants: /y/, /w/, /l/, /m/, /n/
4. Stops: /p/, /ph/, /pʔ/, /t/, /th/, /tʔ/, /k/, /kh/, /kʔ/
5. Affricates: /č/, /čh/, /čʔ/
6. Stops + fricatives: [px], [tx], [kx]
7. Voiceless sibilant fricatives: /s/, /sʔ/, /š/, /šʔ/
8. Voiced sibilant fricatives: /z/, /ž/
9. Non-sibilant fricatives: /h/, /x/, /ɣ/, /ʔ/
10. Voiced stops: /b/, /d/, /g/

Table 9.3 *Stress.*

Boas & Deloria, Buechel 2, Clark, Buechel 3, Manhart 1, Karol, CU, LLC NetSiouan, Canku War Cloud	⊢	<á, é, í, ó, ú>
	→	Capitalized syllable
Dakota Mission, Riggs, Williamson, Buechel 1, Traditional, UMN 1, Manhart 2, White Hat, BU, SICC, Txakini, Starr, UMN 2, DEDP	⊢	<a, e, i, o, u>

with the suprasegmental feature of pitch stress, will form the basis of my comparison between the distinct writing systems.

3.1 Stress

The suprasegmental feature of stress allows us to classify the existing writing systems in two groups: those orthographies in which stress is marked and those in which it is not (see Table 9.3).

Except for the War Cloud system, where this feature is marked by capitalizing the stressed syllable, there is a general agreement regarding the way that stress should be represented, since all orthographies that mark this suprasegmental feature do so by using an acute accent diacritic above the vowels.

Table 9.4 *Nasal vowels.*

Dakota Mission, Buechel 1, Traditional, War Cloud, Manhart 2, Txakini, Starr	→	\<an, in, un\>
Riggs, Williamson, Clark, Karol, UMN 1, LLC, UMN 2, DEDP, Canku	→	\<aŋ, iŋ, uŋ\>
Boas & Deloria, CU	→	\<ą, į, ų\>
Buechel 2, Buechel 3, Manhart 1, White Hat, SICC	→	\<aŋ, iŋ, uŋ\>
War Cloud	→	\<a̱, i̱, u̱\>
BU	→	\<añ, iñ, uñ\>
NetSiouan	→	\<aN, iN, uN\>

3.2   Nasal Vowels: /ą/, /į/, /ų/

The vowel inventory consists of five oral vowels and three nasal vowels. Table 9.4 indicates the way in which the latter are represented in the different writing systems.

Wider variation is found regarding the representation of vowel nasalization. The most common method, used in up to nine different orthographies (Riggs, Williamson, Clark, Karol, UMN 1, LLC, UMN 2, DEDP, and Canku) consists of using the engma symbol \<ŋ\>. The second most common way of marking nasality in vowels is through the use of the letter \<n\> (Dakota Mission, Buechel 1, Traditional, War Cloud, Manhart 2, Txakini, and Starr). The other five writing systems (Buechel 2, Buechel 3, Manhart 1, White Hat, and SICC) make use of a long-tailed *n* \<ŋ\>. Finally, Boas and Deloria and CU use an underhook called an 'ogonek', War Cloud makes use of underbars, Brandon University (hereafter, BU) adds a macron \<ñ\>, and NetSiouan uses a capital *n* \<N\>.

3.3   Oral and Nasal Continuants: /y/, /w/, /l/, /m/, /n/

All writing systems use the same letters (\<y\>, \<w\>, \<l\>, \<m\>, and \<n\>) to represent the oral and nasal continuants.

3.4   Voiceless Stops: /p/, /ph/, /pʔ/, /t/, /th/, /tʔ/, /k/, /kh/, /kʔ/

An important phonological feature of Lakota and Dakota is the presence of three different sets of voiceless stops – namely the plain voiceless stops, the aspirated voiceless stops, and the ejective voiceless stops (see Table 9.5).

Voiceless stops allow us to classify the different orthographies in three groups: (a) the systems that mark all three series of voiceless stops differently – 17 out of a total of 25 writing systems; (b) those that only distinguish two (Riggs,

Table 9.5 *Voiceless stops.*

Boas & Deloria, Buechel 2	→	<p, pᶜ, p′; t, tᶜ, t′; k, kᶜ, k′>
Manhart 1	→	<ṗ, p, t′; ṭ, t, t′; k̇, k, k′>
CU	→	<p, ph, pˀ; t, th, tˀ; k, kh, kˀ>
Clark, Karol	→	<p, pᶜ, pˀ; t, tᶜ, tˀ; k, kᶜ, kˀ>
Buechel 3, Txakini, LLC	→	<p, ph, p′; t, th, t′; k, kh, k′>
War Cloud, UMN 1, UMN 2	→	<p, p, p′; t, t̩, t′; k, k̩, k′>
White Hat, SICC	→	<p̄, p, p′; t̄, t, t′; k̄, k, k′>
BU	→	<p, pᶜ, p; t, tᶜ, t̩; k, kᶜ, k̩>
NetSiouan	→	<p, ph, pˀ; t, th, tˀ; k, kh, kˀ>
DEDP	→	<p̣, p, p′; t̩, t, t′; k̩, k, k′>
Riggs, Williamson	→	<p, p, p; t, t, t̩; k, k, k̩>
Buechel 1, Traditional, Manhart 2, Starr	→	<p, p, p′; t, t, t′; k, k, k′>
Canku	→	<p, p, p̣; t, t, t̩; k, k, k̇/ k̇/ q̇>
Dakota Mission	→	<p, p, p; t, t, t; k, k, k>

Williamson, Buechel 1, Traditional, Manhart 2, Starr, and Canku); and (c) one system (Dakota Mission) in which no set is differentiated at all. As seen in Table 9.5, a large variety of options are used by the different systems to mark each of the three sets. The plain set is commonly left unmarked, glottal aspiration is normally represented by <h> or a superscript *c*, and, following a well-established tradition in a large number of languages, the ejective set mostly uses the apostrophe.

3.5   Voiceless Post-Alveolar Affricates: /č/, /čh/, /čʔ/

The voiceless post-alveolar affricate phoneme also comes in three different sets – namely plain, aspirated, and ejective (see Table 9.6).

There are systems in which the distinction between all three sets is marked – again, 17 writing systems, orthographies in which only two sets are distinguished (Riggs, Williamson, Buechel 1, Traditional, Starr, Manhart 2, and Canku), and one system (Dakota Mission) in which no difference is made between the three sets. The plain post-alveolar affricate is often left unmarked, an *h* normally accompanies the letter *c* along with a diacritic in the aspirated set (although it is also common to find orthographies in which this set is marked by using an overdot or underdot), and the ejective set generally makes use of the apostrophe.

3.6   Voiceless Stop + Voiceless Uvular Fricative: [px], [tx], [kx]

In Lakota and Western Dakota, voiceless stops can also occur with velar (guttural) aspiration when followed by a uvular fricative phoneme. Indeed,

Finding a Standard Writing System for the Sioux Languages   161

Table 9.6 *Voiceless post-alveolar affricates.*

Boas & Deloria, Buechel 2	→	<c, cᶜ, c′>
Manhart 1	→	<ċ, c, c′>
Clark, Karol	→	<c, cᶜ, c³>
Buechel 3, Txakini,	→	<c, ch, c′>
CU	→	<č, čh, č'>
War Cloud, UMN 1, UMN 2	→	<c, ç, c′>
White Hat	→	<c̄, ċ, c′>
BU	→	<c, ć, ç>
NetSiouan	→	<c^, c^h, c^?>
SICC	→	<c̄, ċ, c′>
LLC	→	<č, čh, č′>
DEDP	→	<ç, c, c′>
Dakota Mission	→	<c, c, c>
Riggs	→	<ć, ć, ɓ>
Williamson	→	<c, c, ç>
Buechel 1, Traditional, Starr Manhart 2	→	<c, c, c′>
Canku	→	<c, c, ĉ>

Table 9.7 *Voiceless stop + voiceless uvular fricative.*

White Hat, SICC	→	<ṗ, ṫ, k̇>	
NetSiouan	→	<ph^/px, th^/tx, kh^/kx>	
Txakini	→	<px, tx, kx>	
LLC	→	<pȟ, tȟ, kȟ>	
Buechel 1, Traditional, Manhart 2, Starr	→	<p, t, k>	=/p, pʰ/, /t, tʰ/, /k, kʰ/
Boas & Deloria, Clark, Buechel 2	→	<pᶜ, tᶜ, kᶜ>	= /pʰ/, /tʰ/, /kʰ/
Buechel 3, CU	→	<ph, th, kh>	= /pʰ/, /tʰ/, /kʰ/
Manhart 1	→	<p, t, k>	= /pʰ/, /tʰ/, /kʰ/
Karol, War Cloud	→	<p, t, k>	= /p/, /t/, /k/

the two types of aspiration for voiceless stops – namely glottal and guttural – represent allophonic realizations and occur in complementary distribution since the former takes place before /i/, /į/, and /u/ and the latter normally occurs before /a/, /ą/, /o/, and /ų/.

As seen in Table 9.7, only five orthographies distinguish the velarized stops from the other three sets, although this is achieved by a number of different means. By contrast, most orthographies fail to distinguish this sequence. It should also be borne in mind that, in the systems originally created for the representation of the Eastern Dakota dialect (Dakota Mission, Riggs, Williamson, UMN 1, BU, UMN 2, DEDP, and Canku), this phonetic feature is not distinguished because it is absent.

Table 9.8 *Voiceless sibilant fricatives.*

Williamson, Boas & Deloria, UMN 1, White Hat, UMN 2, DEDP	→ <s, š, s´, š´>
Buechel 1, Buechel 2, Buechel 3	→ <s, ś, s´, ś´>
Traditional	→ <s, š/s/sh, s´, š´>
Manhart 1, Manhart 2	→ <s, š, s´, š´>
LLC, Starr	→ <s, š, s´, š´>
Clark, Karol	→ <s, š, s', š'>
CU	→ <s, š, s'?, š'?>
War Cloud, Txakini	→ <s, sh, s´, sh´>
BU	→ <s, ṣ, ṣ́, ṣ́>
NetSiouan	→ <s, s^, s?, s^?>
SICC	→ <s, s, ṡ, ṡ´>
Dakota Mission	→ <s, š/x, s, š/x>
Riggs	→ <s, ś, s, ś>
Canku	→ <s, ŝ, s, ŝ>

Table 9.9 *Voiced sibilant fricatives.*

Dakota Mission, Buechel 1, Buechel 2, Clark, Manhart 1, Karol, Manhart 2, White Hat, SICC, Starr	<z, j>
Riggs, Boas & Deloria, Buechel 3	→ <z, ź>
Williamson, War Cloud, UMN 1, UMN 2, DEDP, Canku	→ <z, ż>
Traditional	→ <z, j/ż>
CU, BU, LLC	→ <z, ž>
NetSiouan	→ <z, z^>
Txakini	→ <z, zh>

3.7 Voiceless Sibilant Fricatives: /s/, /š/, /s?/, /š?/

Voiceless alveolar fricative sounds and voiceless post-alveolar fricative sounds come in two sets, plain and ejective (see Table 9.8).

Except for Dakota Mission, Riggs, and Canku, voiceless sibilant sounds are distinguished in all the writing systems, although in different ways. The plain voiceless fricative is normally left unmarked, and the plain voiceless post-alveolar fricative is usually marked by a caron, an acute accent, or an overdot. An apostrophe is frequently used to mark the corresponding ejective sets.

3.8 Voiced Sibilant Fricatives: /z/, /ž/

The two voiced sibilant fricative sounds differ in their point of articulation: one is alveolar and the other is post-alveolar (see Table 9.9).

Table 9.10 *Non-sibilant fricatives.*

Riggs, Williamson, Buechel 1, Boas & Deloria Buechel 2, Buechel 3, Manhart 1, Karol, White Hat SICC, UMN 2, DEDP, War Cloud	<h, ḣ, ġ>
Traditional →	<h, h/ḣ/r, g/ġ>
CU, LLC →	<h, ȟ, ǧ>
BU →	<h, ħ, g>
NetSiouan →	<h, h^, g^>
Txakini →	<h, x, gx>
Canku →	<h, ȟ, ġ>
Dakota Mission →	<h, r, g> = /g/
Clark →	<h, ȟ, g> = /g/
Manhart 2 →	<h, ḣ, g> = /g/
UMN 1 →	<h, ḣ, g> = /g/
Starr →	<h, ȟ, g> = /g/

These two phonemes are marked distinctively in all the writing systems. Whereas the voiced alveolar fricative is always represented by an unmarked letter <z>, there are many different ways of representing the voiced post-alveolar fricative, the most common being the symbol <j>, the letter *z* with an overdot, and the same letter with a caron.

3.9   Non-Sibilant Fricatives: /h/, /x/, /ɣ/

Sioux has three different non-sibilant fricatives, which differ in both their point of articulation and their voicing: /h/ is a voiceless glottal fricative, and /x/ and /ɣ/ a voiceless and a voiced uvular fricative, respectively (see Table 9.10).

A distinction between the voiceless glottal fricative /h/ and the voiceless uvular fricative /x/ is made in all the orthographies. As far as their representation is concerned, whereas the voiceless glottal fricative is normally left unmarked, the voiceless uvular fricative is most commonly marked by using an overdot. By contrast, five cases of under-representation can be observed when the voiced velar stop /g/ is included in the comparison, as Dakota Mission, Clark, UMN 1, Manhart 2, and Starr do not differentiate between the voiced uvular fricative /ɣ/ and the voiced velar stop /g/. The overdot is the most common means of representing the voiced uvular fricative.

3.10   Voiced Stops

The bilabial and velar voiced stops, namely /b/ and /g/, are phonemes which all the orthographies agree upon, as they are represented by the same

Table 9.11 *Levels of phonemic representation.*

[+ phonemic]						[– phonemic]
NetSiouan	Boas & Deloria	Clark	UMN 1*	Buechel 1	Riggs*	Dakota Mission*
LLC	Buechel 2	UMN 2*	BU*		Williamson*	
	Buechel 3	DEDP*	Canku*		Traditional	
	Manhart 1				Manhart 2	
	Karol				Starr	
	War Cloud					
	CU					
	White Hat					
	SICC					
	Txakini					
	DIO*					

symbols – <b> and <g>. We should note that the orthographies use the corresponding symbol <l> or <d> depending on whether they are intended to represent the Lakota or the Dakota dialect.

The remainder of this section provides a summary of the foregoing comparative analysis and discusses other linguistic features displayed by the different orthographic systems. Taking into account the number of contrastive elements that these systems are able to mark, they can be classified as more-or-less phonemic, with a cline showing their degree of phonemic representation.

Table 9.11 shows that the writing systems used to represent the Lakota and Dakota varieties have become increasingly accurate, owing to the fact that a higher number of phonemes have now been distinguished. Most orthographies are situated to the left half of the cline, indicating that these writing systems are (almost) fully phonemic and are therefore capable of representing the pronunciation of this language faithfully since they exhibit a high degree of linguistic accuracy. While there might be the sense that a practical orthography may systematically under-represent distinctive features for the sake of simplicity, it is generally claimed that under-representation is more serious a flaw than over-representation (Smalley 1964) and that it should therefore be avoided. From a purely linguistic point of view, it is clear that the more fully phonemic systems – such as NetSiouan, LLC, Boas and Deloria, Buechel 2, Buechel 3, Manhart 1, Karol, War Cloud, CU, White Hat, SICC, Txakini, UMN 2, or DEDP – will work more efficiently than the less phonemic ones.

A very important issue concerning under-representation is whether or not to mark stress. Owing to the phonemic character of stress in Lakota and Dakota and the fact that its position is mostly unpredictable, some writing systems (such as Boas and Deloria, Buechel 2, Clark, Buechel 3, Manhart 1, Karol, War Cloud, CU, LLC, and NetSiouan) favour marking stress on every word in order to avoid confusion when pronouncing words that differ only in terms of the position of the stressed syllable (e.g., *héna* 'right there' vs. *hená* 'those'; *maYá* 'duck, goose' vs. *máYa* 'garden'). Canku argues that, as stress in Sioux usually occurs on the second syllable, it is only strictly necessary to mark it elsewhere. In contrast, the other writing systems, including those devised by some native speakers (such as White Hat, SICC, Txakini, Starr, and DEDP), do not distinguish such differences in stress, since many of the exceptions (especially those involving the position of the stress on first syllable) are predictable because they are based on specific phonological rules and native speakers can therefore easily guess the position of stress from context.

Another important question concerns the marking of the sequence 'voiceless stop + fricative'. It is widely assumed that an optimal orthography should be based on phonemic distinctions rather than on phonetic differences, and consequently the marking of [px, tx, kx] may be phonemically superfluous because these are actually allophones. Nevertheless, the fact that this series represents 10 to 12 per cent of all stops (LLC 2012:751) demonstrates a high functional load (Seifart 2006:280) and proves that the representation of this phonetic characteristic can contribute to a more explicit pronunciation. The older writing systems created for Lakota (for example, Buechel 1, Boas and Deloria, Buechel 2, Traditional, Clark, Buechel 3, and Manhart 1) seem not to have taken this into account. More modern systems (such as Karol, CU, Manhart 2, and Starr) may have decided not to represent it because the two types of aspiration mostly occur in complementary distribution (LLC 2012:751) and their presence is therefore obvious to both native speakers and even second-language learners. In contrast, some orthographies (such as White Hat, NetSiouan, SICC, Txakini, and LLC) see this as pertinent and, consequently, choose to mark it.

A further complication lies in the use of diacritics which at times is not very coherent, since the same symbol is used to represent different phonological features, constituting a significant impediment to reading and writing. For example,

(i) Williamson marks the ejective voiceless stops and the ejective post-alveolar affricate with an underdot (<p̣, ṭ, ḳ> and <c̣>) but, in contrast, represents the ejective voiceless alveolar and post-alveolar fricatives with an acute accent (<s´, š´>).

(ii) Clark represents the voiceless uvular fricative with an overdot (<ḣ>) but leaves its voiced counterpart unmarked.

(iii) In Manhart 1, an overdot is used to mark the plain voiceless stops (<ṗ, ṫ, k̇>), the plain voiceless post-alveolar affricate (<ċ>), and the two plain uvular fricatives (<ḣ, ġ>) but does not do so with the plain sibilant fricatives (<s, z>).

(iv) War Cloud uses an underdot to represent different kinds of phonemes: the aspirated voiceless stops (<p̣, ṭ, ḳ>), the plain voiceless affricate (<c̣>), and the voiced uvular fricative (<g̣>). However, the voiceless uvular fricative is marked with a different diacritic – namely an overdot (<ḣ>).

(v) UMN 1 marks the voiceless uvular fricative with an overdot (<ḣ>), but its voiced counterpart remains unmarked.

(vi) Manhart 2 also uses an overdot to mark the voiceless uvular fricative (<ḣ>) and leaves the voiced uvular fricative unmarked.

(vii) White Hat uses an overdot to mark the aspirated voiceless affricate (<ċ>), but not the aspirated voiceless stops (<p, t, k>). This diacritic is also used to represent guttural aspiration in voiceless stops (<ṗ, ṫ, k̇>), the voiceless post-alveolar fricative (<ṡ>), and the two uvular fricatives (<ḣ, ġ>). Likewise, unlike the plain sets of fricatives and affricates, it represents the plain voiceless stops with a macron (<p̄, t̄, k̄>).

(viii) BU represents glottal aspiration in voiceless stops by means of a superscript c (<p^c, t^c, k^c>) but in contrast signals the same kind of aspiration in the voiceless post-alveolar affricate through an acute accent (<ć>). Furthermore, this particular orthography sometimes represents ejective sounds with an underdot (<p̣, ḳ, c̣>) and sometimes with a cedilla (<ţ, ş, ş̌>).

(ix) SICC represents the aspirated voiceless affricate with a grave accent (<c̀>) but leaves the aspirated voiceless stops unmarked. It also marks the plain voiceless stops (<p̄, t̄, k̄>) and the plain voiceless post-alveolar affricate (<c̄>) with a macron, but not the plain alveolar fricatives (<s, z>).

(x) Starr marks the voiceless uvular fricative with a superimposed caron (<ȟ>) but leaves its voiced counterpart unmarked.

(xi) DEDP uses an underdot for the plain voiceless stops (<p̣, ṭ, ḳ>) and the plain voiceless post-alveolar affricate (<c̣>) but leaves the plain sibilant fricatives unmarked (<s, z>).

(xii) Canku also shows variation in the representation of ejective sounds, marking the ejective voiceless bilabial stop with the thorn symbol (<þ>) or with the letter *p*; the ejective voiceless alveolar stop with an apostrophe (<t'>); the ejective voiceless velar stop with a plain *k* with a cedilla (<ḵ>), a *k* with an overdot (<k̇>), or a letter *q* with an overdot (<q̇>); and the ejective voiceless post-alveolar affricate with a circumflex (<ĉ>).

In accordance with these criteria, the most appropriate systems would be Buechel 1, Boas and Deloria, Buechel 2, Buechel 3, Karol, CU, NetSiouan, Txakini, LLC, and UMN 2.

Table 9.12 *Lakota and Dakota language resources.*

Dakota Mission	Collection of words and manuscript of grammar (1834–1839)
	Sioux Spelling Book (1836)
	Translation of biblical texts (1837–1852)
Riggs	*A Grammar and Dictionary of the Dakota Language* (1852)
	The New Testament in the Dakota Language (1871)
	A Dakota-English Dictionary (1892)
Williamson	*An English–Dakota Dictionary* (1868/1871/1886/1902)
Buechel 1	*Bible History in the Language of the Teton Sioux Indians* (1924)
	Sioux Indian Prayer and Hymn Book (1927)
Boas & Deloria	*Dakota Texts* (1932)
	Dakota Grammar (1941)
Buechel 2	*A Grammar of Lakota* (1939), *English Lakota Dictionary* (2001) (Ingham), *Lakota* (2003) (Ingham), *Lakota: A Language Course for Beginners* (1995) (Oglala Lakota College)
Clark	Bilingual readers (1941–1954)
Buechel 3	*Lakota–English Dictionary*' (manuscript) (1954)
Manhart 1	*Lakota–English Dictionary* (1970)
Karol	*Everyday Lakota* (1971)
War Cloud	*Dakota Sioux Indian Dictionary* (1971)
UMN 1	*Dakota wohdakapi: Wowapi inonpa* (1974)*Dakota Iapi* (1978)
CU	*Elementary Bilingual Dictionary* (1976), *Beginning Lakota* (1976), *Lakota Readings* (1976), *Sketch of Lakota* (1996)
Manhart 2	*Lakota Tales and Texts* (1978)
White Hat	*Reading and Writing the Lakota Language* (1999)
BU	*Sioux Phrase Book* (1983)
SICC	Language materials (from 1991 onwards)
Txakini	Collections of stories (2001, 2014, 2015)
Starr	*Dictionary of Modern Lakota* (1994)
	*Lakotiyapi: An Introduction to the Lakota Languag*e (1997)
UMN 2	*500 Dakota Verbs* (2004)
DEDP	*Dakota English Dictionary* (2006–present)
LLC/DIO	*Lakota Language Dictionary* (1992/2008)
	Language materials (2004–present)
Starr	*Dictionary of Modern Lakota* (1994)
	Lakotiyapi: An introduction to the Lakota language (1997)
Canku	*Beginning Dakota* (2011)

Finally, the importance of existing teaching materials in terms of choosing a writing system as the standard should not be underestimated. Owing to the existence of a large number of grammars, dictionaries, collections of texts, and so forth, Sioux is a very well-documented Native American language. Table 9.12 lists a selection of the most representative language resources written in the existing orthographies.

Bearing in mind the number and the relevance of these resources, the Riggs, Buechel 1, Boas and Deloria, Buechel 2, UMN 1, CU, White Hat, SICC, LLC, and Canku orthographies could work very effectively for second-language learners. Although an awareness among learners of all the writing systems would be ideal – so that they could transliterate between them – this is completely utopian and would definitely hinder the learning and teaching processes and, consequently, the preservation and revitalization of Sioux.

4 An Analysis of Non-Linguistic Factors

Although linguistic accuracy seems to be an obvious and essential condition in the selection of any orthography, other factors should also be taken into account (cf. Casquite and Young, Valdovinos, Sackett, Hull, and Schreyer, this volume). This is especially so in the case of Sioux, owing to the fact that the level of phonemic awareness among most native speakers of Lakota and Dakota may be rather low.

4.1 Educational Factors

Smalley (1964) and Malone (2004) highlight the importance of two educational criteria in the choice of a writing system – namely learnability and ease of transfer to other languages (cf. Casquite and Young, Shah and Brenzinger, and Sackett, this volume). Learnability seems to be linked to the cognitive complexity of the spelling system according to the level of phonemic representation shown, and consequently, special attention must be paid to the level of readership to which the standard orthography needs to aim. According to Seifart (2006:282–283), whereas for non-proficient readers and writers the teaching and learning of skills such as reading and writing appear to become more complicated when there is no reliable sound-symbol representation of the language, advanced users seem to prefer a 'sight vocabulary' involving the recognition of written words as entire units. In this respect, although none of the orthographies created for Lakota and Dakota to date represent an example of a fully phonetic orthography – since none of them represents the morphophonological changes taking place in fast, informal speech – any of the more shallow orthographies (such as NetSiouan, LLC/DIO, Boas & Deloria, Buechel 2, Manhart, Karol, War Cloud, CU, White Hat, SICC, Txakini, UMN 2, or DEDP) would probably be very successful for non-proficient learners. This kind of learner would probably feel frustrated and need more learning time if they were to use a non–fully phonemic orthography, where the spoken and written languages are mismatched. By contrast, an advanced learner, whose native-like competence allows him or her to make full use of contextual clues, is believed to benefit more from a 'deep' orthography where the graphic form of morphemes is preserved.

According to Powers (2009:142), Sioux is most likely to survive if children learn it from adults and elders in its spoken and written form through natural immersion provided by daily communication at home and within the community. It would therefore seem that the intended users of an orthography for an endangered language are fluent native speakers. First, they are the only available teachers; second, their help as consultants in the preparation of learning/teaching materials is fundamental; and third, they are the ones able to develop literacy by documenting ancestral knowledge in narrative. However, it is also true that younger speakers, who may be interested in revitalizing the language of their ancestors, may also account for a significant number of potential users of such an orthography. Owing to this situation and to the fact that Sioux does not display 'heavy' morphophonological changes, the decision to choose a 'shallow' orthography would be beneficial for elementary and advanced readers alike.

Owing to the strong dominance of the English-speaking American culture, the existence of monolingual speakers of Sioux seems hard to imagine in Sioux communities in the future, leading us to suppose that conformity to the spelling conventions of the national language (i.e., English) should be expected as well as desirable. Thus, following Cahill and Karan (2008:8) the idea of harmonizing the orthography used for the local language with English orthography would certainly minimize the cognitive effort required for the easy transfer of reading and writing skills from one language to the other (cf. Shah and Brenzinger, Leggio and Matras, Sackett, and Hull, this volume). Table 9.13 shows the number of non-English symbols used in each orthography.

When seen from this perspective, orthographies such as Dakota Mission, Txakini, Starr, Manhart 2, or Buechel 1, whose inventory of symbols are closer to the Roman script used in English, would be highly desirable (for a similar point, see Moseley, and Sackett, this volume). There might be some problems, however, in connection with a foreseeable linguistic transfer when using some of the orthographies. For example, it is important to decide which of the three sets of voiceless stops should be left unmarked. If we take into account the fact that these sets of stops are phonemic, that cross-linguistically the most common stop series is the plain voiceless set,[9] and that their pronunciation very closely resembles that of the English unaspirated voiceless stops, it would seem reasonable that the three sets should be marked distinctively and that the set of plain stops should be marked with the letters <p, t, k> with no diacritical marks at all. This situation is illustrated by NetSiouan, Txakini, and LLC.

Another important issue is the representation of vocalic nasalization. The pronunciation of the nasalized vowels is different from that of an oral

Table 9.13 *Use of non-English symbols.*

Orthography			Non-English symbols and diacritics (characters affected)
Dakota Mission	1	(1)	: acute accent
Riggs	4	(12)	: engma, underdot, acute accent, overdot
Williamson	4	(13)	: engma, underdot, overdot, apostrophe
Buechel 1	3	(9)	: apostrophe, acute accent, overdot
Boas & Deloria	5	(18)	: ogonek, superscript 'c', apostrophe, overdot, acute accent
Buechel 2	5	(17)	: eta, superscript 'c', apostrophe, acute accent, overdot
Traditional	3	(10)	: apostrophe, overdot, acute accent
Clark	4	(16)	: engma, superscript 'c', superscript inverted 'c', caron
Buechel 3	4	(14)	: eta, apostrophe, acute accent, overdot
Manhart 1	4	(17)	: eta, overdot, apostrophe, caron
Karol	5	(17)	: engma, superscript 'c', superscript inverted 'c', caron, overdot
War Cloud	4	(16)	: underbar, apostrophe, underdot, overdot
UMN 1	4	(16)	: engma, underdot, apostrophe, overdot
CU	3	(16)	: ogonek, gelded question mark, caron
Manhart 2	3	(8)	: overdot, apostrophe
White Hat	4	(20)	: eta, macron, apostrophe, overdot
BU	7	(16)	: macron, underdot, superscript 'c', acute accent, overdot, caron, superimposed bar
NetSiouan	2	(16)	: question mark, circumflex
SICC	5	(19)	: eta, macron, apostrophe, overdot, grave accent
Txakini	1	(6)	: apostrophe
LLC	3	(19)	: engma, apostrophe, caron
Starr	3	(8)	: apostrophe, caron, superimposed caron
UMN 2	4	(16)	: engma, underdot, apostrophe, overdot
DEDP	4	(17)	: engma, underdot, apostrophe, overdot
Canku	5	(14)	: engma, superimposed circumflex, overdot, thorn, superimposed bar

vowel followed in the same syllable by the nasal consonant /n/, so the best way to represent this feature is not by means of <n> (nor <N>). Neither does it seem linguistically correct to use the letter engma <ŋ>, since it has traditionally been used to denote a velarized nasal consonant. Thus, the marking of nasal vowels by ogoneks <ą, į, ų>, as in Boas and Deloria or CU; an underbar, as in War Cloud; or the letter eta <η>, as in Buechel 2, Buechel 3, Manhart 1, White Hat, and SICC, are probably the most accurate options linguistically.

We should now turn to the representation of the voiced post-alveolar fricative. This phoneme is very frequently represented by the letter *j*. Although this symbol does not seem to be the most linguistically correct way of representing the phoneme in question, owing to the fact that it could result in confusion with the sound normally represented by the same letter in English (a voiced post-alveolar affricate consonant, /dʒ/), many of the more traditional elderly native speakers prefer it, since it has been in use for about 180 years.

There is also a problem connected with the use of <r> in Dakota Mission and Traditional. These systems use this symbol to represent the voiceless guttural fricative, but because of the influence of English, students would pronounce this letter as an alveolar rhotic consonant.

Finally, other minor problems can occur when learning to pronounce words employing certain letters. These include <x>, which serves to mark the plain and ejective voiceless post-alveolar fricatives in Dakota Mission and the guttural sounds in Txakini; <h>, which is mainly used to represent glottal aspiration in Buechel 3, CU, LLC, NetSiouan and Txakini; and, indeed, the <c> in Dakota Mission, Williamson, Buechel 1, Boas and Deloria, Buechel 2, Traditional, Clark, Buechel 3, Manhart 1, Karol, War Cloud, UMN 1, Manhart 2, BU, UMN 2, Txakini, DEDP, and Canku, as this letter represents the voiceless post-alveolar affricate sound rather than, as in English, a voiceless velar stop or a voiceless alveolar fricative.

4.2   Socio-Historical Factors

The fact that Lakota and Dakota only differ superficially simplifies considerably the task of choosing a standard orthography. Indeed, although the earlier orthographies, such as Dakota Mission and Riggs, were initially devised to represent Dakota, they were also subsequently used to write Lakota.

The influence of the national or official language is also considered relevant to the choice of an orthographic system, since local people's attitudes towards that language may be either negative or positive (Cahill and Karan, 2008:10). The turbulent historical relationship between the Lakota and Dakota people and the white settlers brought with it a feeling of resentment that is still palpable in Sioux country. Any foreign attempt to advise their local communities about relevant linguistic issues regarding language preservation and revitalization, such as the choice of a standard orthography, is regarded as imposition rather than professional counsel (Karan 2013:2). The Sioux people see this as an attack on their sovereignty, since it gives the impression that they cannot deal with the issue of language preservation and revitalization themselves and that outside help is needed (cf. Hull, this volume). Thus, regarding the choice of a spelling system, some native speakers appear to lean towards orthographies devised by indigenous people (Traditional, War Cloud, White Hat, SICC, Txakini, Starr, or Canku), or even those that were created by early missionaries (Riggs, Buechel), who are held in high esteem by many Sioux. Because a community is most likely to use an orthography if it has been actively involved in the decision-making process, it is necessary that the chosen orthography appeal to the whole local community (Powlison 1968:3; cf. Moseley, Casquite and Young, Brenzinger and Shah, and Sackett, this volume). Although this decision could, for some language groups, lead to the choice of an inconsistent orthography from a linguistic or psycholinguistic perspective, this does not seem to be the case for Sioux, owing to the large number of linguistically sound orthographies that have been designed by native speakers.

4.3   Political Factors

It is generally assumed that the local people's attitudes towards the national or official language can result in a desire to ensure that their orthography is distinctive. Despite the fact that an emblematic orthography could certainly help them strengthen values such as self-esteem and cultural identity and that they view the influence of English on their language as an outside political weapon used to exert control over them, the Sioux people do not appear to want a very distinctive orthography (contrast Hull, this volume). This is reflected in the fact that many communities do not appear to have qualms about using missionary orthographies, which, owing to the dearth of diacritics, resemble English orthography more closely than do other more emblematic writing systems created later on. Consequently, emblematic distinctiveness does not appear to play an influential role in this case.[10]

4.4   Technical Factors

Technical production and reproducibility could also be considered major issues in the choice of a standard orthography (cf. Sackett, this volume). Most native speakers undoubtedly prefer orthographies that do not involve the use of special characters or diacritics that depend on the technical capabilities of the different local communities, such as the availability of typewriters or computers and the technical training necessary to type diacritics effectively (cf. Shah and Brenzinger, and Leggio and Matras, this volume). There are areas within the Sioux territory where computers are scarce, and even where they are available, some native speakers, especially elders, do not feel comfortable with an orthography including characters that they cannot easily handle on their typewriters or computers. Hence, following Seifart (2006:286) the safest option to ensure the usability of the orthography is still the use of single characters, digraphs, or combinations of letters with diacritics that can be found on the keyboard of a mechanical typewriter. Consequently, the choice of orthographies such as Dakota Mission (1 character affected including diacritics or symbols not used in English), Txakini (6), Starr (8), or Manhart 2 (8) would seem to be the most appropriate writing systems owing to their technical simplicity (see Table 9.13).

Table 9.14 *Non-Unicode fonts.*

Riggs, Williamson, War Cloud, UMN 1, UMN 2, DEDP	<p>, <ç>
Boas & Deloria, Buechel 2	<pᶜ>, <tᶜ>, <kᶜ>, <cᶜ>
White Hat	<p̄>, <t̄>, <k̄>, <c̄>
SICC	<p̄>, <t̄>, <k̄>, <c̄>; <ċ>, <ṡ>
BU	<p>, <ç>, <pᶜ>, <tᶜ>, <kᶜ>
Clark, Karol	<pᶜ>, <tᶜ>, <kᶜ>, <cᶜ>, <p³>, <t³>, <k³>, <c³>, <s³>

As regards the choice of fonts, working with an internationally standardized system such as Unicode might have immeasurable benefits in terms of the ease with which written materials such as books are produced. Thus, the use of a Unicode-compatible font instead of custom-encoded fonts would seem advisable in order to enable archiving as well as a loss-free transmission of information (Cahill and Karan, 2008:11). Some symbols used by the different orthographies are not available in the Unicode (America) subset font, and although they could be created by combining the corresponding letter plus the specific codepoint for each symbol, they are not to be recommended (see Table 9.14).

The only Sioux orthographies in which all the characters are covered by Unicode are Dakota Mission, Traditional, Buechel 3, CU, Manhart 1, Manhart 2, NetSiouan, LLC, Txakini, Canku, Buechel 1, and Starr.

5 Discussion and Conclusion

As discussed by Casquite and Young, and Sackett (this volume), according to Smalley (1964), Swadesh (1965), Bauernschmidt (1977), and Cahill and Karan (2008), among others, a successful orthography must adhere to five major principles for good orthographic development. These are acceptability to the whole community of native speakers, linguistic soundness, ease of learning, linguistic transfer into the national language, and ease of reproduction. Although linguistic factors are basic, community acceptance appears to be the overriding factor determining whether a specific orthography will be used. However, for an orthography to be effective, it also seems clear that all these factors, which often conflict with each other, must be considered and balanced.

In this respect, a good candidate for a standard orthography could be the Txakini writing system because, except for the criterion of widely available language resources, it meets all the necessary factors, including linguistic soundness, learnability, linguistic transfer, readability, community acceptance, availability of fonts, and ease of reproduction. A similar number of criteria are also fulfilled by other congruent orthographies such as LLC, NetSiouan, White Hat, CU, Buechel 2, Boas and Deloria, Buechel 3, SICC, War Cloud, and DEDP. Choosing White Hat and DEDP would be welcomed by both native speakers and second-language learners alike, as their creators (namely the late Albert White Hat and Chris Mato Nunpa) are nationally respected leaders and linguists, and the orthography is consistent and reliable. The selection of the LLC/DIO orthography, in whose development a great number of native speakers were involved, would also be a wise choice, owing to the excellent quality of the learning and teaching materials currently available in this orthography.

Although such a decision would neither be popular nor easy, it is clear that the benefits of orthographic standardization to the Sioux community would be immeasurable. As has been discussed, since an orthography can represent a people's identity, the involvement of the community when selecting a standard orthography is crucial (Simons, 1977:328; Cahill and Karan, 2008:12). However, although some speakers of Lakota and Dakota wish to be 'unified' under one writing system, others do not appear to be ready to make this decision. My view is that, as the legitimate guardians of their local knowledge, the native speakers of Lakota and Dakota must decide for themselves how their wisdom should be shared, for standardization would certainly provide an opportunity for more speakers to gain literacy skills and would consequently facilitate the preservation and revitalization of the Sioux language.

Notes

1. Financial support for this research has been provided by the Spanish Ministry of Economy and Competitiveness (MINECO), FFI2011-29798-C02-01/FILO. I wish to express my gratitude to William K. Powers for his continued support and his valuable and insightful comments.
2. In this chapter, 'Sioux' is used as a cover term to designate the Lakota and Dakota varieties of the language. I am, however, aware that the Sioux themselves prefer to use their own tribal names (i.e., Lakota/Dakota, meaning 'allied').
3. For Riggs (1852:viii–ix), the main distinction between the dialects is that where Lakota and Yanktonai have /g/, Eastern Dakota (and Stoney) has /h/ and Yankton (and Assiniboine) has /k/, especially when this sound is followed by a sonorant.
4. Despite the fact that the systems designed by the first missionaries were based on the Dakota variety, they were later, and for some time, also used to write Lakota.
5. The term 'Dakota Mission' refers to a generalized writing system arising from the orthographies used by the first Dakota missionaries (Gideon and Samuel Pond, Stephen R. Riggs, and T. S. Williamson) between 1834 and 1839. There are three different spelling systems associated with Buechel's name, so the names Buechel 1, Buechel 2, and Buechel 3 roughly correspond to the *Bible History* (1924), the *Grammar of Lakota* (1939), and Buechel's manuscript for the *Lakota–English Dictionary* (1902–1954), respectively. The denomination 'Traditional' serves to

refer jointly to the orthographies used by native speakers such as Luther Standing Bear Jr., Vine Deloria Sr., Charles Eastman, and Mary Crow Dog in their books from the 1940s on. This chapter uses the names 'Manhart 1' and 'Manhart 2' to refer to the writing system used by Paul Manhart in the posthumously published version of the former *Lakota–English Dictionary* (1970) and the *Lakota Tales and Texts* (1978). The names 'University of Minnesota 1' (hereafter, UMN1) and 'University of Minnesota 2' (hereafter, UMN2) are used to designate the orthographies used by Rebecca A. Flute, Timothy Dunnigan, Ann Rynda, and Wahpetunwin Carolynn Schommer (1974), as well as Harlan LaFontaine and Neil McKay (2005), respectively. The *Dakhóta Iápi Okhódakičhiye* (hereafter, DIO) orthography uses a slightly modified version of the Lakota Language Consortium orthography to adapt itself to the phonological features of Dakota.
6. Another attempt at unifying or standardizing the orthography of this language is illustrated by the three Sioux varieties spoken in the province of Saskatchewan – namely Hunkpapa Lakota, Assiniboine Nakota, and Sisseton Dakota, which opted for the SICC orthography created by the Dakota Nations of Canada in 1985 and further adapted by the SICC in 1991.
7. As this project attracted a large number of native speakers, it might also represent a further effort to standardize orthography across the Sioux country.
8. Throughout the chapter, for the sake of neutrality, the standard Siouanist (APA) orthographic notation is used.
9. Jan Ullrich (personal communication, 2014) claims that the plain stops are the most frequent (about 79%), the velarized stops are second in terms of frequency (about 12%), aspirated stops are third (about 7%), and ejectives are the least frequent (about 2%).
10. Setting aside the preference of traditionalist 'full blood' Sioux for orthographies created by native speakers, it is not possible to observe any links between the different orthographies and distinct political groups. It might perhaps be worth mentioning a very interesting religious affiliation between Catholicism (Jesuits) and Buechel's orthography on the one hand and, on the other, Protestantism (Episcopalians and Presbyterians) and the Dakota Mission, Riggs, and Williamson orthographies. Although these religious affiliations were noticeable in the past, they do not appear to be valid today.

10   Orthography Development in Sardinia: The Case of *Limba Sarda Comuna*

Rosangela Lai

1   Introduction

Sardinian is classified as 'definitely endangered' by UNESCO due to the loss of intergenerational transmission.[1] Children no longer learn Sardinian at home, and most young adults are semi-speakers (Rindler-Schjerve 1998, 2000; Marongiu 2007). It is a historical minority language that has only been officially recognized by the Italian Republic as recently as 1999 (Law 482/1999). Since 2006, Sardinian has had a standard orthography, called the *Limba Sarda Comuna* (hereafter, LSC). This orthography was developed to be used by the Autonomous Region of Sardinia in its official documents, alongside Italian. However, in recent years, the adoption of the LSC has also been encouraged for other purposes. This chapter discusses whether, in the light of the principles of orthography design for endangered languages, the LSC can be regarded as an effective orthography for all the Sardinian dialects.

2   A Sketch of Sardinian

Sardinian is a Romance language spoken on the island of Sardinia, part of the Italian administrative territory. A long tradition of Sardinian linguistic studies dates back to the nineteenth century (see, among others, Tagliavini 1982; Campbell and Poser 2008:84).

2.1   *The Geographic Division of Sardinian*

The traditional and widely accepted classification of Sardinian dialects divides the language into two main groups: Logudorese (also known as Logudorese-Nuorese) and Campidanese (Wagner 1941; Blasco Ferrer 1986; Contini 1987; Loporcaro 2009). There are further subdivisions within the macro-areas Logudorese and Campidanese, but both have a certain degree of internal uniformity. Logudorese is spoken in northern and central Sardinia, while Campidanese is spoken in the southern areas of the island.[2]

Important historical changes distinguish Logudorese and Campidanese. Some concern the vocalic and consonant system, but the most notable affect the syllabic structure of words: different consonant cluster evolutions, various kinds of metatheses, liquid deletion, epenthesis and syncope have all contributed to differentiate Sardinian dialects since the Middle Ages (Wagner 1941; Virdis 1978; Contini 1987; see Section 4). Another interesting difference concerns the ancient loanwords. Logudorese often contains a Spanish loanword, while Campidanese has the corresponding Catalan loanword; as one instance of this, Campidanese has *leggiu* and *leggia* 'ugly' (< Catalan *lleig*), whereas Logudorese has *feu* and *fea* 'ugly' (< Spanish *feo*) (Wagner 1997:184ff).

Thus, some differences stem from the historical evolution from Latin, others come from the acquisition of loanwords from different languages, and still others are due to synchronic processes, which differ in different dialects (Wagner 1941; Virdis 1978; Contini 1987). The different diachronic evolution has also had repercussions for the morphological system of the two macro-areas, especially in verbal and pronominal morphology (Jones 1993; Manzini and Savoia 2005).

2.2   A Brief History of Sardinian

In the Middle Ages, the island of Sardinia was divided into four independent kingdoms, also known as *giudicati*: Kálaris (south-eastern area), Torres (north-western area), Arborea (central-western area) and Gallura (north-eastern area).[3] The official languages of these kingdoms were local Sardinian dialects. This peculiar situation has made Sardinian one of the Romance languages with the largest number of ancient texts (private legal acts and legal codes) (Tagliavini 1982). Once the various kingdoms had lost their independence, Sardinian was replaced in all administrative functions by various dominant languages: Catalan, Spanish, and Italian, in that order.[4] Thus, since at least the thirteenth century, Sardinian has coexisted with the aforementioned languages, which have all left a mark on the Sardinian lexicon. Spanish and Italian loanwords are widespread in all the Sardinian dialects, while those from Catalan are concentrated in Campidanese. As mentioned, in many cases, the same referent is designated by a Catalan loanword in Campidanese and by a Spanish loanword in Logudorese.

Despite its co-existence with a number of dominant languages, Sardinian has a long written tradition whose golden age was in the Middle Ages but which survives to this day, mostly for literary purposes. Two main traditional orthographies can be distinguished: one is based on Logudorese and the other on Campidanese. Within these two main traditions there is some degree of variation in that writers can use some graphemes to indicate sounds that are present in the phonology of their local varieties. Thus, the absence of a standard did not prevent the development, use and diffusion of the traditional orthographies (Tufi 2013:157).

3   Towards the *Limba Sarda Comuna*

In 1997, the Autonomous Region of Sardinia (hereafter, ARS) approved a regional bill for the promotion and safeguard of Sardinian language and culture. Two years later, in 1999, the Italian Republic approved the Historical Minorities Protection Act (Law 482/1999). With this bill, the Italian Republic officially recognized twelve historical minority languages for the first time, and Sardinian was among them (Savoia 2001, 2002; Dell'Aquila and Iannàccaro 2004:51–58). Since the 1990s, a renewed interest can be observed towards endangered and minority languages. One prominent actor on the Sardinian scene is the Movimento Linguistico Sardo (hereafter, MLS), a cultural and political movement which explicitly sets itself the goal of developing a national language for Sardinia (Corongiu 2013; Lőrinczi 2013; Tufi 2013; Porcu 2014). MLS firmly argues against those who emphasize the linguistic and cultural diversity of the island (Corongiu 2013; Tufi 2013:150). In their opinion, the linguistic division of Sardinian dialects into Campidanese and Logudorese is spurious.[5]

In 2006, under the centre-left administration led by Renato Soru, an MLS activist by the name of Giuseppe Corongiu was appointed as director of the Bureau of the Sardinian Language. Corongiu was given a second term in office by the centre-right administration of Ugo Cappellacci until 2014. In 2001, a first attempt at a standard orthography, called the *Limba Sarda Unificada* (hereafter, LSU) had failed. As Tufi (2013:150) reported, 'Its publication caused a public outcry which ultimately made the implementation of such a standard impossible. [Among the alleged shortcomings of the LSU was] the mismatch between the declared intent of the LSU – a proposal – and its *de facto* standardization of Sardinian' (my insertion). Another reason for rejection was that the LSU was clearly modelled on Logudorese, and Campidanese was not at all considered (Calaresu 2002; Lőrinczi 2013; Tufi 2013). According to Lőrinczi (2013), even though the LSU was developed by a regional committee, it was 'fundamentally set up by Diego Corraine', also a member of the MLS. Lőrinczi (2013) also points out that the design of the LSU had been pioneered in Corraine (2000).[6]

In 2006, a new standard orthography, the *Limba Sarda Comuna* (LSC) was proposed and adopted by the ARS. Several scholars note that the LSC is, in a way, a 'milder version' of the LSU, to quote Tufi (2013:150) (cf. also Calaresu 2002, 2008; Mastino et al. 2011; Lőrinczi 2013; Porcu 2014).[7] Aside from the objections of linguists, intellectuals and historians, the speakers themselves were once again far from enthusiastic. A remarkable opposition, especially in the south of the island, culminated in the orthographic counter-proposal by the province of Cagliari (Campidanese area) called *Arrègulas* ('rules'). Interestingly, *Arrègulas* were written both in Campidanese and Italian, while the LSC guidelines were only written in Italian. The reasons put forward by the authors of *Arrègulas* to justify a proposal that stood in open contrast with the official norm was that the LSC reminded them of the LSU because it advocated one norm only for Sardinian – namely a Logudorese norm (Provincia di Cagliari, Provincia de Casteddu [*Arrègulas*] 2009:24). They also emphasized that the LSC would discriminate between Logudorese and Campidanese speakers. Logudorese speakers would be able to use their native language in offices and at school, while the native language of Campidanese speakers would not be represented anywhere. For these reasons, the authors of *Arrègulas* argue that the two macro-dialectal groups *tenint – e depint tenni – sa matessi dinnidadi* ('they have – and must have – the same dignity') (*Arrègulas* 2009:16).

In short, scholars, the southern local authorities and many Campidanese speakers agree that the LSC is very close to Logudorese and thus cannot serve the rest of the island, especially Campidanese. The following sections focus on the orthographic and linguistic features of the LSC in order to determine if it can be considered an effective orthography for all Sardinian dialects.

4   Criteria Adopted in the Development of the LSC

The LSC guidelines are presented in a document entitled *Limba sarda comuna. Norme linguistiche di riferimento a carattere sperimentale per la lingua scritta dell'Amministrazione regionale* ('Experimental reference standard for the written language of the regional Administration'). It is written in Italian and is fifty-six pages long. It contains not only orthographic norms but also conjugation tables, paradigms of pronouns and articles, and lists of adverbs and adjectives. Unlike those of the LSU, the orthography developers of the LSC are unknown.

The LSC guidelines define this orthographic system as the outcome of mediation among the Sardinian dialects (LSC 2006:5, 6, 13, 14). This seems to hint at a multilectal approach (cf. Schreyer, this volume). One would therefore expect an orthography designed to extend to all dialects, building on a comparison of the various phonological systems (cf. Simons 1977; Seifart 2006; Karan 2014). However, an in-depth reading of the guidelines themselves reveals a different state of affairs.

The guidelines claim that the LSC has been developed according to two criteria: first, the etymological criterion and, second, the 'Sardinian distinctiveness

Table 10.1 *Examples of words that feature in the LSC guidelines. Adapted from www.regione.sardegna.it/documenti/1_72_200604181 60308.pdf (last accessed 21 June 2015).*[8]

	Latin	Sardinian dialects	LSC
-t-	ACETU(M)	[aketu]	*Aghedu*
		[akeðu]	
		[aɣeðu]	
		[aʔeðu]	
		[aheðu]	
		[adʒeðu]	
		[adʒeɾu]	
		[aʒeðu]	
-cr-	ACRU(M)	[akɾu]	*Agru*
		[alʔu]	
		[ahɾu]	
		[aɣru]	
		[dɾaɣu]	
		[aɾɣu]	
		[aɾgu]	
		[aɾku]	
		[algu]	
-ngu-	LINGUA(M)	**[limba]**	*Limba*
		[liŋgwa]	

criterion' (LSC 2006:7–8). The etymological criterion means that, among the different Sardinian outcomes, one must choose that which is closest to Latin, the language from which Sardinian evolved. The 'Sardinian distinctiveness' criterion (LSC 2006:6, 7) was adopted in order to safeguard the uniqueness of Sardinian: diachronic developments that are absent or less widespread in the Romance languages must be preferred (for further discussion of 'distinctiveness' in orthography development, see Valdovinos, this volume).

Table 10.1 reproduces a few examples as they appear in the LSC guidelines. The first two exemplify the etymological criterion, and the third illustrates the 'Sardinian distinctiveness' criterion.

Latin graphemes are given in the first column of Table 10.1. The second column has Latin etyma, whose historical outcomes in various dialects are listed in the third column. The corresponding LSC graphical form is given in the fourth column. As one can see from Table 10.1, the orthography developers examine the Latin etyma and then pick the attested diachronic evolution that is closest to Latin (see the first two items) or the most distinctive (see the last item).

The attentive reader will note that even though the orthography developers claim to apply an etymological criterion, this is not always true. For example, in the first two items, the outcomes closest to Latin are ACETU(M)>*aketu* and ACRU(M)>*akru*, respectively. In fact, the systematic application of the etymological criterion selects central Sardinian, a sub-group of Logudorese Sardinian. Central Sardinian dialects (such as Nuorese Sardinian) are well known to Romance linguists because they are the only Sardinian dialects that were exempt from diachronic lenition – for example, FOCU>*foku*. However, the LSC ends up selecting another Logudorese dialect – namely central-western Logudorese.

Logudorese Sardinian does not display many of the diachronic developments that Campidanese Sardinian (southern Sardinian area) underwent. One of these is the palatalization of Latin C + *i,e* sequences (cf. Virdis 1978:46). Logudorese dialects preserved the velar stop; for instance, the Sardinian outcomes of Latin CENA(M) are [ʧɛna] (Campidanese) and [kɛna] (Logudorese).

Logudorese and Campidanese also behave differently with respect to final vowels. Campidanese, unlike Logudorese, shows the result of word-final raising of /ɛ/ and /ɔ/, which became *i* and *u*, respectively. Thus, in final position, Campidanese only has three vowels /i, u, a/, whereas Logudorese has /i, u, ɛ, ɔ, a/; e.g., the Sardinian outcomes of Latin CANEM are [kani] (Campidanese) and [kanɛ] (Logudorese).

Another typical Campidanese phenomenon is the reanalysis of Latin word-initial trills. In the phonological system of Campidanese, initial trills are banned. Since the Middle Ages, every Latin word with an initial *r* was reanalysed, with the insertion of a word-initial vowel, and the subsequent trill appears geminated (Latin ROSA> [ɔrrɔza] (Campidanese)] (cf. Wagner 1941:§74–75; Virdis 1978; Contini 1987).

Besides these changes involving single segments, there were also changes that affected consonant clusters (for example, the reflexes of Latin consonants + /j/). Most importantly, Campidanese dialects were affected by several types of diachronic metatheses and liquid deletion that have completely changed the underlying form of many words (cf. Lai 2013, 2014). These diachronic changes have also had repercussions in the morphosyntactic system of Campidanese (cf. Manzini and Savoia 2005). Thus, it is not surprising that, in the application of the etymological criterion, the choice most often fell on Logudorese forms.

The second criterion adopted is that of 'Sardinian distinctiveness' criterion (LSC 2006:6, 7) – adopted, as previously mentioned, to safeguard the uniqueness of Sardinian. By looking at the examples of Sardinian distinctiveness considered by the LSC authors, it is clear that they refer to those diachronic developments that are absent, or less widespread, in the Romance languages. For example, Latin labialized velars evolved as follows in Logudorese – AQUA> [abba], LINGUA> [limba] – while Campidanese has [akkwa] and [liŋgwa], respectively (Wagner 1941:227–230; Virdis 1978:71; Contini 1987: 68–69, map 33). Here, the etymological criterion suggests the adoption of the Campidanese forms; the authors, though, prefer the Logudorese forms as more 'identity-making' (LSC 2006:6; cf. Lüpke 2011:330ff; Hull, Sackett, and Leggio and Matras, this volume). Thus, the distinctiveness criterion again privileges Logudorese over Campidanese.

Note also that not all the (Logudorese) forms deemed 'distinctively Sardinian' are guaranteed to be so. The prosthetic vowel in words such as SCHOLA>*iscola*, which sets Logudorese apart from Campidanese, cannot be seen as especially distinctive in a Romance context: it is shared by Spanish (*escuela*), French (*école*), Portuguese (*escola*), and Catalan (*escola*). In fact, in this case, 'distinctive' seems to mean 'different from Italian', which has *scuola* (cf. Seifart 2006:287).

In short, central-western Logudorese forms are always preferred. The guidelines do not therefore undertake a comparative treatment and careful mediation among the dialects. In fact, as Table 10.1 demonstrates, the authors do not discuss the different phonologies that correspond to different dialects. They consider the Latin etyma, and then, from among the different attested diachronic developments, they select the one closest to Latin or the most distinctive.

Note also that the items in the third column of Table 10.1 are defined as 'pronunciations in the Sardinian dialects' (my translation). Defining the items listed in the third column as different Sardinian pronunciations is misleading, as is the choice to list the phonetic rather than the phonological forms of the respective varieties. Those items are the result of different diachronic developments that phonologically do not necessarily have the same underlying form, contrary to what the term 'pronunciation' seems to suggest. It is to their different phonological forms (already modified with respect to Latin by several diachronic processes) that synchronic processes apply nowadays, and (again) with geographic variation.

The reiterated claim that Sardinian dialects 'only differ in pronunciation' crucially depends on an assumed notion of 'different pronunciation' that is vague to the point of being meaningless. The fact is that corresponding items in the different Sardinian dialects are the result of complex historical processes that can be, and typically are, entirely opaque to speakers without a formal training in historical linguistics. In choosing graphical forms that closely follow the Logudorese forms, LSC de facto proposes a standardized lexicon, as opposed to a mere orthography, and this lexicon can easily be recognized as Logudorese. One could reasonably surmise, then, that the phonologies of the modern Sardinian dialects would have provided better foundations to what is declared to be a mediation effort.[9]

4.1 The Orthographic Design of LSC: Options and Choices

The strengths and weaknesses of the LSC will now be analysed in order to see if this orthography can be regarded as an adequate writing system for Sardinian. To evaluate the LSC, one should take into account the socio-political situation of the area and the phonologies of the Sardinian dialectal groups to check if LSC can satisfactorily be extended across dialects. Section 5 addresses socio-political issues, and the present section focuses on linguistic ones. Reasons of space prevent a full discussion of the viability of the LSC in every micro-dialectal area. Rather, the two macro-areas of Logudorese and Campidanese are considered. In what follows, some general points about the LSC with regard to variation are discussed. They are not always made explicitly but can be inferred from the guidelines, especially by paying attention to the Latin etyma that the authors use to develop the LSC.

As previously mentioned, the LSC is a unilectal orthography closely modelled on the Logudorese dialect of Sardinian. Broadly speaking, it serves Logudorese well. More precisely, the LSC can be defined as an effective orthography for the Logudorese dialects from the central-western area. As we will see, in some respects, LSC strictly follows Italian orthography; in others, it opts for new solutions. In some cases, the traditional orthographies are taken into account; however, other choices clearly diverge from the Sardinian tradition. Some choices were probably made to reflect contrastive oppositions which are present in the phonological system of Logudorese.

4.1.1 Vowels
Sardinian dialects have seven vowels: /i/, /e/, /ɛ/, /a/, /ɔ/, /o/, /u/. Some dialects have minimal pairs that oppose: /ɛ/ and /e/, /ɔ/ and /o/. However, the functional load of these contrasts is very low: very few minimal pairs of this type can be found in Sardinian dialects, so the authors chose to represent only five vowels in the LSC – namely <i, e, a, o, u>.

As already mentioned, Logudorese and Campidanese behave differently with respect to final vowels: Logudorese has /i/, /u/, /ɛ/, /ɔ/, /a/, whereas Campidanese shows only three vowels – /i/, /u/, /a/ – due to the raising of /ɛ/ and /ɔ/ that became /i/ and /u/, respectively. Nevertheless, the LSC prescribes five vowels like in Logudorese (LSC 2006:13). This is a potential problem for Campidanese speakers. The final vowel raising of Campidanese is traditionally regarded as a diachronic change. However, for some generative scholars, it is a synchronic process and Campidanese still retains five underlying vowels. In any case, Campidanese speakers are not aware of this process, and to quote Snider (2014:40), 'Orthographies should not represent distinctions of which the native speaker is not aware'.

4.1.2   Consonants   The LSC adopts the Italian orthographic conventions to represent the velar stops /k/ and /g/ (LSC 2006:7, 10). Thus, the voiceless stop /k/ is represented by the graphemes <ch> (before *e* and *i*) and <c> (other contexts) and the voiced stop /g/ by <gh> (before *e* and *i*) and <g> (other contexts). On page 7, the authors justify this choice as follows: 'We deemed it necessary not to give up to anti-historical and differentialist temptations, such as the use of graphemes that would hardly be popular, e.g., *ka, ke, ki, ko, ku* in place of *ca, che, chi, co, cu*.'[10] A potential advantage of their choice is that it can facilitate the transfer of literacy skills from Italian to Sardinian (cf. Casquite and Young, Shah and Brenzinger, Hull, and Sackett, this volume): the language of literacy in Sardinia is exclusively Italian. In contrast, for the sake of learnability within Sardinian, it would have been better to avoid the replication in Sardinian of the inconsistencies of the Italian orthography. In fact, as argued by Seifart (2006:285), the 'idiosyncratic spelling conventions [of the dominant language] should in general not be replicated in newly developed orthographies' (my insertion).[11]

One feature of the LSC that does take into account the phonological system is the representation of phonetic geminates. Unlike Italian, Sardinian does not have length contrasts in obstruents word internally. Sardinian obstruents are usually pronounced long, even though phonologically they are simplex obstruents.[12] Presumably, the LSC authors have taken this fact into account. The LSC usually represents phonetic geminates as simplex stops (LSC 2006:9). As an aside, one should note that this choice does not conform to the etymological criterion that the authors claim to adopt. Under the etymological criterion, words with Latin geminate stops should have kept the geminate in the LSC. The only two stops that can be written as doubled consonants are the voiced bilabial stop and the voiced retroflex stop. Therefore, <bb> is used to represent the voiced bilabial stop in words such as [abba] that evolved from the Latin labialized velar consonants (e.g., ACQUA>*abba* 'water').[13] Also, <dd> is adopted to represent the voiced retroflex stop that evolved from the Latin -LL-. In fact, an example selected and exemplified is PELLE >[pɛɖɖɛ] <pedde> (LSC 2006:19). However, even in the guidelines themselves, the authors are not consistent. For example, on page 9, two occurrences are found of the word for 'town' spelt <bida>. Since the word [biɖɖa] is from the Latin VILLA, one would expect <bidda>.

The LSC distinguishes between the voiceless alveolar affricate and the voiced alveolar affricate as follows: /ts/ is represented as <tz> and /dz/ as <z>, even though the functional load of the relevant opposition can be estimated to be zero. To the best of my knowledge, in Sardinian dialects, there are no minimal pairs of voicing involving the alveolar affricate.

The different realizations of word-initial obstruents at word boundaries are not represented (LSC 2006:9).

4.1.3 Morphophonemic Alternations Morphophonemic alternations are not represented (LSC 2006:8–9), so the identity of morphemes is preserved in spite of the various phonological processes that affect Sardinian. The guidelines list some examples on page 9, such as the *is-* prefix, which is represented with the graphical form *is-* even though it can assimilate to the consonant that follows.[14]

4.1.4 Accents In the LSC, the grave accent is used on all vowels (i.e., *à, è, ì, ò, ù*) to mark stress. Words ending with stressed vowels (such as the loanword *tribù*) and words stressed on the antepenultimate syllable (e.g., *fèmina, pìbera*) have the tonic vowel written with a grave accent.

4.1.5 The Apostrophe The apostrophe is used only in cases where certain monosyllables and a few other elements are elided (LSC 2006:11). To illustrate this point, the orthography developers list the following: *su, sa, mi, ti, si, nde, nche, bi, ddi, ddu, dda* and the indefinite articles *unu* and *una*. As can be seen, the elements are either determiners (definite: *su, sa*; indefinite: *unu, una*) or clitic pronouns. In fast speech, Sardinian dialects display other cases of elision, but the authors explicitly state that only the aforementioned cases can be marked graphically – for example, *s'ànima, un'òmine*.

4.1.6 Clitics The LSC uses interpuncts (·) to signal the boundary between members of an enclitic cluster (LSC 2006:9–10). The use of interpuncts in enclitics is justified on pedagogical grounds (LSC 2006:9). Note that the dominant language (Italian) does not have interpuncts and does not separate enclitics. Thus, this choice is likely due to the perceived need of an emblematic orthography (cf. Seifart 2006:284ff; Hull, and Valdovinos, this volume). By contrast, proclitics are written separately.

4.2   A Sample of the LSC

The LSC was always declared to be strictly for the administrative use of the ARS. Below, I reproduce a sample of a bill written in LSC which has been taken from the website of the Autonomous Region of Sardinia and is part of the Article 3 of Sardinia's statutory laws:

Bìndighi mìgia eletores o bator consìgios provintziales chi rapresentent nessi su chimbanta pro chentu de sa populatzione regionale podent rechèdere su referendum pro s'abrogatzione totale o partziale de una lege.[15]

One important accusation levelled at the LSC is that it reads as if it is literally translated from administrative Italian (Calaresu 2008:175ff). In fact, the similarities between the lexicon and the syntactic structure of the corresponding bill in Italian are evident. Compare the LSC version with the Italian version of the same bill:

Quindicimila elettori o quattro consigli provinciali che rappresentino almeno il cinquanta per cento della popolazione regionale possono richiedere il referendum per l'abrogazione totale o parziale di una legge.[16]

As may be seen, the syntactic structure closely follows the Italian structure, and most of the lexicon is Italian with Logudorese morphology. The rest of the lexicon is recognizably Logudorese, and this cannot be written off as a merely orthographic matter.

To sum up, one can say that LSC is to all intents and purposes a Logudorese dialect. This is apparent from its design features. It reflects the historical evolution of Logudorese dialects: lack of syncope, lack or low incidence of metathesis, prosthesis before *s*C- clusters, lack of prosthesis before initial *r*, conservation of liquids, five vowels in final position. The entire verbal and pronominal morphology is distinctly Logudorese.[17] These features in themselves objectively undermine the nominal acceptance of the non-Logudorese lexicon, as the Campidanese lexicon unavoidably involves the phonetic and morphological developments discussed earlier.

5 Non-Linguistic Factors in the Development of the LSC

The orthography developers underestimated the socio-political and pedagogical context when developing the LSC. As mentioned previously, MLS activists have been the main actors in language policy in Sardinia, and the MLS denies the existence of the two linguistic macro-areas of Logudorese and Campidanese. However, the orthography developers adopted (despite claims to the contrary) a unilectal approach for the LSC, modelling it on Logudorese, and this choice has caused considerable discontentment in the south of the island (the Campidanese area). The very existence of the *Arrègulas* testifies that a non-negligible sector of the southern society feels unrepresented by the proposed standard (for the second time – the first being their rejection of the LSU).

In case of dialectal variation, the viability of a unilectal approach depends on several socio-political factors (cf. Seifart 2006:285; Cahill 2014:12). For instance, it can be adopted if people acknowledge the chosen dialect as having higher prestige. The reality of the LSC suggests that its designers implicitly saw Logudorese as the most prestigious among Sardinian dialects. The strong confrontation that the LSC has met in the south of the island makes it clear that many Campidanese speakers do not share this opinion. The fact that the south happens to be the economic and political core of the island has made this outcome all the more predictable. As a side note, it is also worth mentioning that the choice also runs contrary to a current tendency in dialect change: in the Campidanese domain, a number of very southern features (identified with the capital, Cagliari) are advancing northward (cf. Wagner 1941).

As far as external factors go, the most recognizable weakness of the LSC is its 'top-down' nature (cf. Calaresu 2008; Lőrinczi 2013; Casquite and Young, and Schreyer, this volume). No involvement of the local communities was sought, no testing was carried out (cf. Cahill 2014:20), and even the public communication that did take place was at times misleading. The claim that the LSC mediates among the Sardinian dialects (see LSC 2006:5, 6, 13, 14) does not, as should be clear by now, fit the facts. Another critical point is that, while the LSC was always declared to be strictly for the administrative use of the ARS, the three-year plan of Sardinian language and culture[18] promoted it to the status of a standard language. Again, the communication could have been better (cf. Calaresu 2002, 2008; Mastino et al. 2011; Tufi 2013).

To Campidanese speakers, the LSC is obviously not a consistent orthography: no grapheme-to-phoneme mapping can be consistently employed in mapping speech onto the LSC and vice versa; rather, it is necessary to memorize the spelling of every single word. The task is thus burdensome and might conceivably hinder literacy in this densely populated region of the island, which also includes the capital (Cagliari). It is also worth adding that many Campidanese teachers have lamented the fact that the implementation of the LSC in the southern communities has increased the speakers' uncertainty and insecurity about their own language (Lőrinczi 2013). A further difficulty lies in the fact that all Sardinian speakers are currently educated in Italian: Italian orthography contains a good degree of consistency, so Campidanese speakers might find the obstacles represented by LSC discouraging and give up on Sardinian literacy. Preliminary testing on Campidanese speakers might have advised against the adoption of LSC in its current form, but to the best of my knowledge, no such testing has ever been carried out.

Problems with the LSC also arise in the context of central Sardinian dialects. Although these are close to Logudorese dialects, they do not share several features of the latter. Suitable heuristics would have to be devised by the speakers in order to compensate for the Logudorese-like forms of the LSC. This is no trivial task for schoolchildren without formal training in linguistics.

6   Conclusions

The LSC presents both linguistic and socio-political problems for its users. Linguistic variation and the phonologies of modern dialects were not taken into account in its development, and speakers were not involved at any stage. The adoption of a unilectal orthography based on Logudorese has resulted in most of the island feeling that they have not been represented, which has the potential of hindering Sardinian literacy. In such a socio-politically sensitive situation as the Sardinian one, orthography development would have benefitted from more caution and wider debate.

Notes

1. In the *UNESCO Atlas of the World's Languages in Danger*, Sardinian is referred to as Campidanese (southern Sardinian) and Logudorese (central-northern Sardinian). Both varieties are considered 'definitely endangered' (see Moseley 2010).
2. This chapter focuses exclusively on the Sardinian language group and does not consider the other languages spoken in Sardinia – namely two Italo-Romance languages (Sassarese and Gallurese) spoken on the northern coast, a Catalan dialect traditionally spoken in the town of Alghero, and a Ligurian dialect (Tabarchin) spoken in the small towns of Carloforte and Calasetta (south-western coast of Sardinia). These languages were not considered during the development of the official orthography.
3. The content of this section is adapted from Lai (2013:11–23).
4. The most ancient loanwords in Sardinian are from Pisan (Old Tuscan from the city of Pisa). Unlike Catalan, Spanish, and Italian loanwords, Pisan loanwords are usually assimilated into the phonological system of Sardinian (cf. Wagner 1941; Lai 2009).
5. The MLS activists downplay dialectal variation. Corongiu (2013:109, 111), former director of the Bureau of the Sardinian Language and part of the MLS, blames linguists for what he sees as an obsession with hair-splitting, 'unsupported by facts', and for allegedly lending support to prejudices about the linguistic and cultural divisions among the Sardinian people. In Corongiu's view, linguistics has even been instrumental in the decline of Sardinian (cf. Corongiu 2013:47–149).
6. Strong similarities with Corraine (2000) can also be recognized in this second attempt at a standard orthography, the LSC. Some passages of the LSC guidelines seem to have been translated literally from the original Sardinian of Corraine (2000). Compare, for example, Corraine (2000:263, a) with LSC (2006:8, d):

Corraine (2000:263, a)	LSC (2006:8, d)
'favorire sa costántzia morfolozica de sas paraulas (in s'incumintzu, in mesu e in agabu), indipendentemente dae sos cámbios fonosintáticos (numerosos in sardu comente, de su restu, in áteras limbas'	'privilegiare la costanza morfologica delle parole (nella loro parte iniziale, mediana e finale), indipendentemente dalle modificazioni fonosintattiche, numerosissime in sardo come del resto in altre lingue'

Compare also Corraine (2000:263, b) with LSC (2006:8, h), Corraine (2000:264, e) with LSC (2006:8, f), etc.

7. On the other hand, for more charitable assessments of the regional policies, see Dell'Aquila and Iannàccaro (2010) and Loporcaro (2012).

8. The Sardinian outcome chosen for the development of the LSC is in boldface font. For reasons of space, I do not deal here with inconsistencies, typological errors and mistakes reported in the guidelines when these are not essential to the present discussion. For example, in the guidelines, the Sardinian outcomes of Latin ACRU(M) in the phonetic transcriptions are given an alveolar flap instead of the alveolar trill, contrary to fact.
9. On multilectal orthography design, see, for example, Simons (1977), Seifart (2006), Grenoble and Whaley (2006:151), and Karan (2014).
10. Note that the ancient Sardinian documents represent /k/ with the grapheme <k>. The grapheme <k> can also be found in traditional orthographies.
11. Seifart (2006:287) argues that the disadvantages in using orthographic conventions of the dominant language include the fact that the dominant language may contain inconsistencies and that it may be 'less emblematic'.
12. For reasons of space, the exposition has been simplified considerably. The issue of Sardinian geminates is controversial (cf. Wagner 1941; Virdis 1978; Contini 1987; Lőrinczi 1996; Bolognesi 1998). This chapter offers my personal view on Sardinian geminates (cf. Lai 2015).
13. Note that *abba*, 'water', is one of the words that were selected because of their 'Sardinian distinctiveness'.
14. Note that the authors explicitly take into account the *is-* prefix for the elaboration of the LSC. The prefix *is-* is part of Logudorese morphology. The corresponding Campidanese prefix is *s-*. Indeed, all the verbs listed on page 9 of the LSC guidelines that exemplify the absence of morphophonemic alternations are taken from Logudorese dialects.
15. From *Lege istatutària de sa Regione Autònoma de Sardigna*, www.sardegnacultura .it/documenti/7_93_20071002122433.pdf (last accessed 23 June 2015).
16. From *Legge statutaria della Regione Autonoma della Sardegna*, www.regione .sardegna.it/documenti/1_46_20070328190430.pdf (last accessed 23 June 2015).
17. The only concessions to Campidanese are these: (a) the definite article *is* as an acceptable alternative to the Logudorese *sos* and *sas*, and (b) the Campidanese clitics *ddi, ddu, dda* as acceptable alternatives to the corresponding Logudorese forms *li, lu, la* (see LSC 2006:25, 28, 37ff).
18. Cf. *Piano triennale degli interventi di promozione e valorizzazione della cultura e della lingua sarda 2011–2013*.

11 Breton Orthographies: An Increasingly Awkward Fit

Steve Hewitt

1 Introduction

Breton has a venerable, if increasingly skewed, orthographical tradition, so there can be no question of developing a Breton orthography from scratch. Early Modern Breton begins in 1659, when Julien Maunoir introduced the iconic <c'h> against French <ch> to differentiate clearly between /ɦ/~/x/ and /ʃ/, and began to indicate initial consonant mutations systematically. For most of the nineteenth century, one track continues traditional Early Modern habits, the other innovating and systematizing (not always felicitously), leading ultimately to the 1908–1911 KLT (Kerne-Leon-Treger) standardization, which in turn fed into the 1941 *Peurunvan* (ZH; 'fully unified' [with the traditional Gwened (Vannetais in French), G, SE]) orthography. The 1955 *Orthographe universitaire* (OU) ('university orthography'), 'while removing certain inconsistencies, introduces new ones' (Jackson 1967). The 1975 *Orthographe interdialectale* (ID) ('interdialectal orthography'), aimed at including the best of both ZH and OU while ensuring better coverage of regular dialect correspondences, did not go as far as possible in that direction. My own *etymological orthography* (E) builds on ID to demonstrate that several additional powerful and useful supradialectal conventions are possible. At each stage of modern spelling reforms, unfortunate choices have been made, often owing to insufficient comprehension of etymological considerations and the related interdialectal correspondences. At the same time, the implications of the massive shift in users during the second half of the twentieth century from native speakers to learners have not been taken properly into account. Finally, at no point has there been an informed debate on the relative merits of a simple monodialectal standard versus a more complex supradialectal standard (cf. Moseley, this volume).

1.1 Thematic Considerations

Breton is an endangered language because natural intergenerational transmission has completely ceased (the Breton of learner-activists is not really a

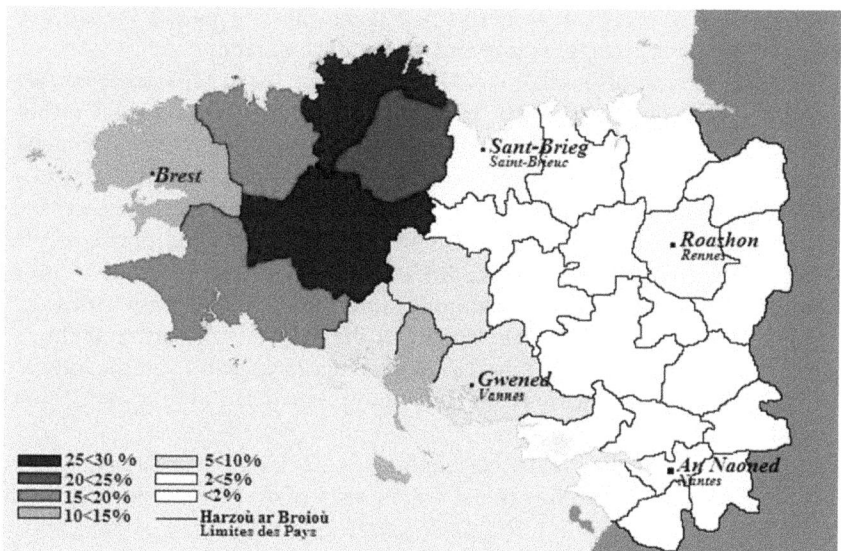

Figure 11.1 Estimates of percentages of Breton-speakers in 2004,[1] http://up load.wikimedia.org/wikipedia/commons/a/ab/Distribution_relative_des_brit tophones_en_2004.png

continuation of the same language; native speakers do not perceive it as such, at any rate). Most of the 200,000-odd traditional, mainly rural, native speakers are today over 60 years old, and there are practically none under 45 (see Figure 11.1). There is no more than 0.2–0.3% functional literacy (such as the ability to write a personal letter) in Breton among such speakers. The activist community consists overwhelmingly of learners, is not very numerous (5,000–10,000 with a reasonable command of the rather artificial literary language and perhaps another 10,000 with some exposure to it), and is almost completely cut off from the traditional speech community, with whom most learners can barely communicate in Breton.

A good orthography for *any* language, whether endangered or not, would have a relatively straightforward grapheme-to-phoneme mapping (cf. Sackett, Lai, this volume). In the case of languages like Breton, with significant dialect variation, there are basically two possible approaches to orthography design: (i) a mononomic (monodialectal) system based on a single, usually prestige, dialect or (ii) a polynomic (supradialectal) system in which orthographic conventions make it possible to derive local reflexes in fairly regular fashion (such a system is usually etymological, going back to a state from which most modern dialect reflexes can be derived). This chapter argues that the latter is preferable for Breton (cf. Casquite and Young, this volume).

The main Breton orthography (ZH, *Peurunvan*, 1941) falls between two stools: it represents an artificial merger of the mainly L-based KLT orthography with the traditional G orthography of the highly aberrant SE dialect (see Section 1.2), without taking into account any of the majority 'innovating' central dialects along a north-east–south-west axis. Decisions on the orthography have been largely out of the hands of the traditional native speech community (cf. Shah and Brenzinger, Valdovinos, and Hull, this volume), which is still overwhelmingly illiterate in Breton, ever since the advent of ZH in 1941. It will be seen that the majority ZH orthography is linguistically particularly ill suited to Breton and contributes significantly to poor pronunciation by learners, thus helping perpetuate the very significant native/learner gap.

Of the three competing modern orthographies, ZH is used by a large majority (85% +). It was chosen as the official orthography of the private, state-assisted Diwan ('sprout, germinate') Breton-language immersion school system in 1980, with the result that nearly all pedagogical materials are now published in it. With traditional native speakers now ageing and overwhelmingly illiterate in Breton, there is little prospect that they are suddenly going to become literate in their mother tongue and begin actively using the written language. Written Breton is thus likely to remain largely confined to the learner-activist community and to remain a minority interest. Breton is thus not about to become a language of public administration – there are nowhere near enough people competent to staff such a service, and public demand for it is insignificant. So even though the learner-activists are still far less numerous than traditional native speakers, they are likely to remain the main users of written Breton. Most of them take the ZH orthographical norm as primary, rather than the living dialects, which they know poorly.

Breton seems to have stumbled into its current orthographical mess. Certainly, at no point has a conscious methodology been used for orthography development, with the partial exception of the two post-ZH orthographies, OU (1955) and ID (1975), neither of which has been particularly successful.

1.2   Speaker Demography

As Table 11.1 demonstrates, all traditional native speakers speak dialect; there is no generally agreed oral standard. Functional literacy (ability to write a personal letter) is well under 1 per cent. Literate native speakers in formal situations speak their own dialect clearly, sometimes moving towards more literary morphology.

Table 11.1 *The speaker demography of Breton.*

Type of speakers	Number of speakers	Percentage of activists	Orthography	Political views
Traditional spontaneous native speakers	200,000, all local dialects, 0.2–0.3% functional literacy in Breton (ability to write a simple personal letter)		? any, if literate, or more likely, spontaneous forms	95% same as French mainstream
Popularizing activists	Optimistic estimate: 10,000–20,000, 95% of whom are learners (i.e., no more than 500–1,000 Breton-literate native speakers)	10–14%	OU (Orthographe universitaire – *Skolveurieg*)	90% same as French mainstream, plus support for Breton language
		1–2%	ID (Interdialectale – *Etrerannyezhel*)	Support for Breton, regional autonomy
Neologizing activists		85–90%	ZH (*Peurunvan* – 'fully unified')	Support for Breton, regional autonomy, independence

Learners for the most part pronounce what they see with basically French phonetic habits. They have little idea of Breton idiom or phraseology. Their syntax is either calqued on French or hypercorrectly different from French (e.g., overuse of fronting with initial focus). Their lexicon is much more purist than spontaneous Breton, most of the neologisms being quite opaque to traditional speakers. While no single one of these factors (with the possible exception of the lexicon) is sufficient to impede mutual comprehension outright, the cumulative effect is to make communication between learners and native speakers laborious at best, and usually unfeasible in practice.

Breton dialects are traditionally divided into Leon/Léon (L), Treger/Trégor (T), Kerne/Cornouaille (K), and Gwened/Vannes (G) (see Figure 11.2). This has some validity, although isoglosses naturally do not necessarily follow the boundaries of these traditional pre-revolutionary bishoprics. L and G are peripheral, linguistically conservative dialects; these were traditionally devout areas, both of which produced numerous priests who used their native dialect with the faithful. There thus arose separate L and G semi-standards; there was much less dialect writing in T or K. K, L, and T on the one hand and G on the other are not really mutually intelligible, especially to traditional speakers not

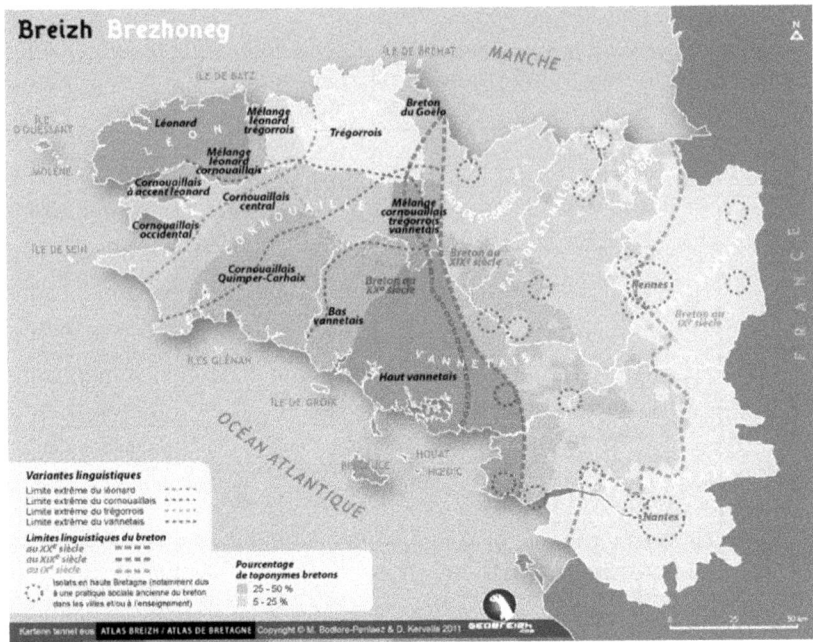

Figure 11.2 Dialects of Breton.[2]

literate in Breton. For such speakers, intercomprehension is also difficult between L and the more distant varieties of K and T; Broudic (1995) notes numerous testimonials to the difficulty T and K speakers, especially those in areas remote from L, had in understanding their L-speaking priests.

There is a T-K, north-east–south-west innovating axis (*aire de Carhaix*, a medieval centre radiating linguistic innovations) along which there is relatively easy intercomprehension, but these dialects have little literary tradition (a weak tradition in T and none at all in K). L was used by the Catholic Church in L, K, and T, and G in G, but contrary to the learner-activists' claim, it is not really true that L was actively accepted as a literary language by speakers from T and K.

1.3   The Phonological Development of Breton

Tables 11.2–11.6 present the development of the phonological system of Breton and how the sounds were most commonly represented in the contemporary orthography, from Old Breton (OB) to Middle Breton (MB) and the Modern Breton (ModB) dialects.

Breton Orthographies: An Increasingly Awkward Fit

Approximants/Fricatives and Graphemes

Table 11.2 *Old Breton (OB).*

	Approximants and fricatives[3]					Most common graphemes				
1	μ	β	δ		γ		m	b	d		g
2	f	θ	s	x	h		f	th, dt	s		ch, h	h
3	(f'h)	(θ'h)	(s'h)	(x'h)			?	?	sh, ss	?

Table 11.3 *Middle Breton (MB).*

	Fricatives and one affricate						Most common graphemes					
1	ṽ	v	ð		(ɣ)		ff, fu	v, u	z			ch, h
2	v̥[4]	ð̥[5]	z	ʒ	ḥ[6]	h	f	z, -tz	s	j, ig	ch, h	h
3	f	θ	s	ʃ	x		ff	zz, zh	ss, sh	ch	ch
4		tθ?[7]/ts						cz, çz, çc, ç			

Underlying Lenis and Fortis Series of Initial Fricatives in Modern Dialects

Table 11.4 *Modern Breton (ModB).*

	Fricatives						'Etymological' orthography					
1	~v	v					ñv	v	ż			
2	v̥[1]		z	ʒ	ḥ[3]	h	f	zh	s	j	x[8]	h
3	f		s	ʃ	x		ff	zzh	ss	ch	xx[9]	

Table 11.5 *Geographical reflexes in Modern Breton of the dental fricatives of Middle Breton.*

ð	z,-h-	—	ð'h	s	—	ð̥	z	z	ð̥'h>θ	s	s
‹ż›	—	—	‹żż›	—	—	‹zh›	z, -	h	‹zzh›	s	h

Table 11.6

	Simplified modern system of fricatives						'Peurunvan (ZH)' orthography					
1	~v	v	z	ʒ	h		ñv	v	z, zh			
2		f	s	ʃ	(x)			f	zh	z, -s	j	c'h	h
								f	sh	s	ch	c'h	

Table 11.7 *Underlying L lenis and F fortis series of Modern Breton initial fricatives and realization according to geographical area and mutation status*[10]: *radical/lenition/provection.*[11]

L	<f> - <s> - <j> - <c'hw> -															
F	<ff> - <ss> - <ch> -															
	Type 1: NW, far W, SW				Type 2: CW				Type 3: NE, C, (CS)				Type 4: SE			
	radical				radical				radical				radical			
L	f	s	ʃ	xw[12]	f	s	ʃ	xw	v̝	z	ʒ	ḥw	f	s	ʒ	hɥ
F	f	s	ʃ		f	s	ʃ		f	s	ʃ		f	s	ʃ	
	lenition[6]				**lenition**[6]				(lenition)				(lenition)			
L	v̝	z	ʒ	ḥw	v̝	z	ʒ	ḥw	v̝	z	ʒ	ḥw	f	s	ʒ	hɥ
F	v̝	z	ʒ		f	s	ʃ		f	s	ʃ		f	s	ʃ	
	(provection)				(provection)				**provection**[6]				**provection**[6]			
L	f	s	ʃ	xw	f	s	ʃ	xw	*f*	*s*	*ʃ*	*xw*	f	s	ʃ	hɥ
F	f	s	ʃ		f	s	ʃ		f	s	ʃ		f	s	ʃ	

As Kergoat (1974:22) states, 'In a single place it is sometimes difficult to establish a straightforward rule. At Plogoneg (Kerne Isel), for instance, people say *chupenn/ar chupenn* "jacket, the jacket" but *chiletenn/ar jiletenn* "vest, the vest" or *saro/ar saro* "smock, the smock" but *sac'h/ar zac'h* "sack, the sack". The language is extremely capricious in that regard. An orthography cannot be' (my translation).[13]

Initial fricatives and neo-lenition and neo-provection (from the MB period on) have been unevenly addressed in the various orthographies. There appear to be two underlying series of initial fricatives in E orthography – a lenis series <f->, <s->, <j->, <xw- (c'hw-)> and a fortis series <ff->, <ss->, <ch-> – with realizations as radical, lenited, and provected as shown in Table 11.7, according to geographical area (see also Figures 11.6, 11.7, and 11.8 for greater detail). KLT showed some neo-lenition, but not very systematically. The authors of ZH decided not to show any neo-lenition at all, as it is mostly inoperative in G and messy over the whole area of KLT. OU systematized neo-lenition, but for both the L and F series mentioned previously, giving for E *kals a ssukr* 'much sugar', an improbable OU *kalz a zukr*, which practically no one says. Thus far, no orthography (apart from E, which is not being actively promoted) indicates neo-provection, an important rule over a significant part of the Breton-speaking area (see Figure 11.8). Learners who try to sound like T are usually unaware of this rule: *selled, me so o sselled* 'look.INF, I am PROG looking' T /zelët, 'me zo 'selët/, and pronounce it wrongly as [me zo 'zelët].

2   Linguistic Issues

This section indicates the principal ways in which the dialects of Breton differ linguistically.

2.1   Sandhi Rules

Neither of the Breton rules of final obstruent devoicing/voicing is natural for French speakers (see Table 11.8). Final obstruent voicing is a less natural rule than devoicing – more difficult for learners. With an increasing proportion of learners among the users of written Breton, it is important to write as many lenis/voiced finals as possible. (For the native speaker, it does not matter so much, since they are incapable of pronouncing wrongly; their sandhi habits carry over into French – for example, *du vin rouche* 'red wine', *n'imporde où* 'anywhere'.) The pernicious effect for learners of writing voiceless finals in ZH may be seen here, and in the recording of learners' speech transcribed towards the end of this chapter:

    (E) *mad* 'good' /maːd/ [maːt]; *mad eo* 'it is good, it's OK' /ˈmaːd 'eː/

    (ZH) *mat* 'good' /maːd/ [maːt]; *mat eo* 'it is good, it's OK' /ˈmaːd 'eː/; learners: /mat/, /ˈmat 'e-o/

    (E) *gweled meus* [seen I.have] 'I have seen' /ˈgwęːlëd 'mœːz/ [ˈgwęːlëd 'mœːs]

    (ZH) *gwelet em eus* [seen I.have] 'I have seen'; learners: [gwelɛt ɛmœs]

2.2   E \<s> / \<ż> / \<zh> (and fortis \<ss> /\<żż> / \<zzh>)

Only ID and E clearly distinguish \<s>, \<ż>, \<zh> from OB /s/, /ð/, /θ/ (modern dialect reflexes are given in Figures 11.3, 11.4, and 11.5).

Table 11.8 *Final <-b, -d, -g / -p, -t, -k> and Breton sandhi rules.*

• Final obstruent devoicing in pause or before voiceless consonants:								
↓	b	d	ɟ	g	v̝	z	ʒ	ɦ
	p	t	c	k	f	s	ʃ	x
• Final obstruent voicing before vowels and voiced consonants:								
↓	p	t	c	k	f	s	ʃ	
	b	d	ɟ	g	v̝	z	ʒ	

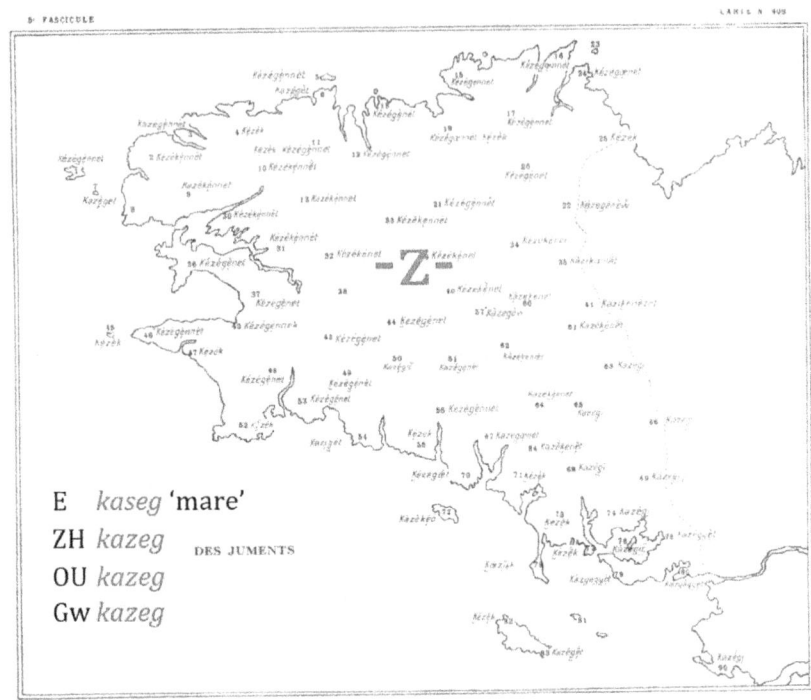

Figure 11.3 <s>: *kaseg, keseg* 'mare(s)' – /z/ everywhere [s/z- -z- -z/s] (Old Breton /s/)
Old Breton *s* is pronounced internally /z/ everywhere; initially, see Figures 11.6, 11.7, and 11.8.

Breton Orthographies: An Increasingly Awkward Fit 199

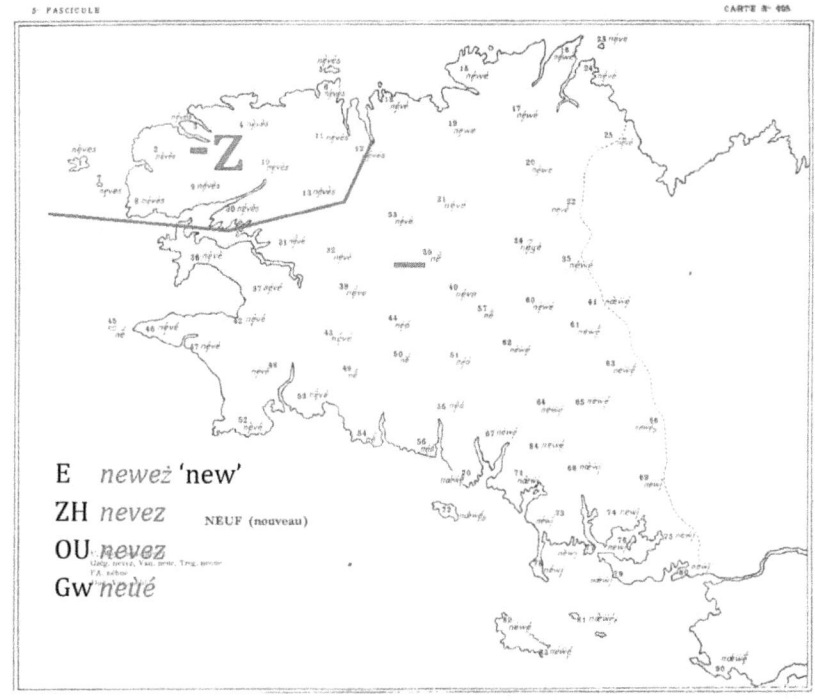

Figure 11.4 <ż>: *neweż* 'new' – L /z/, elsewhere not pronounced (Old Breton /ð/)
The 'z léonard', going back to OB /ð/, is pronounced only in L, NW.

Figure 11.5 <zh>: *kazh* 'cat' – K, L, T /z/; G /h/ (Old Breton /θ/). The <zh> digraph – used in ZH, ID, and E – has modern reflexes K, L, T /z/, G /h/.

2.3 Initial Fricatives – Voiceless/Voiced, Neo-Lenition, Neo-Provection

There is a NE-CS band where the radical of initial fricatives <s->, <f->, <j-> is voiced. Neo-lenition of initial fricatives operates in approximately the western third of the Breton-speaking area. No voicing or neo-lenition occurs in G. (See Figures 11.6, 11.7, and 11.8.)

Initial underlying fortis fricatives <ss-, ff-, ch-> are less prone to neo-lenition than the lenis series <s-, f-, j->, and this operates in a smaller area of the west.

In the NE-CS band of voicing of initial fricatives, the corollary of neo-lenition – namely neo-provection – operates. Words of Celtic origin tend to have <s-> and <f-> for initial fricatives, but for loanwords, the treatment is quite arbitrary and unpredictable (see Table 11.9).

Breton Orthographies: An Increasingly Awkward Fit 201

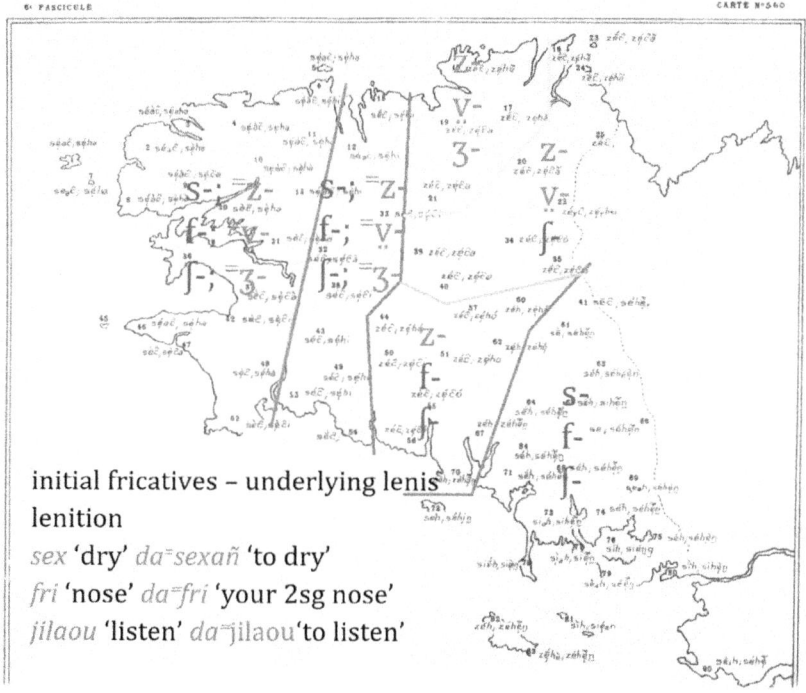

Figure 11.6 Initial fricatives, underlying lenis <s-, f-, j->, and neo-lenition.

202 Steve Hewitt

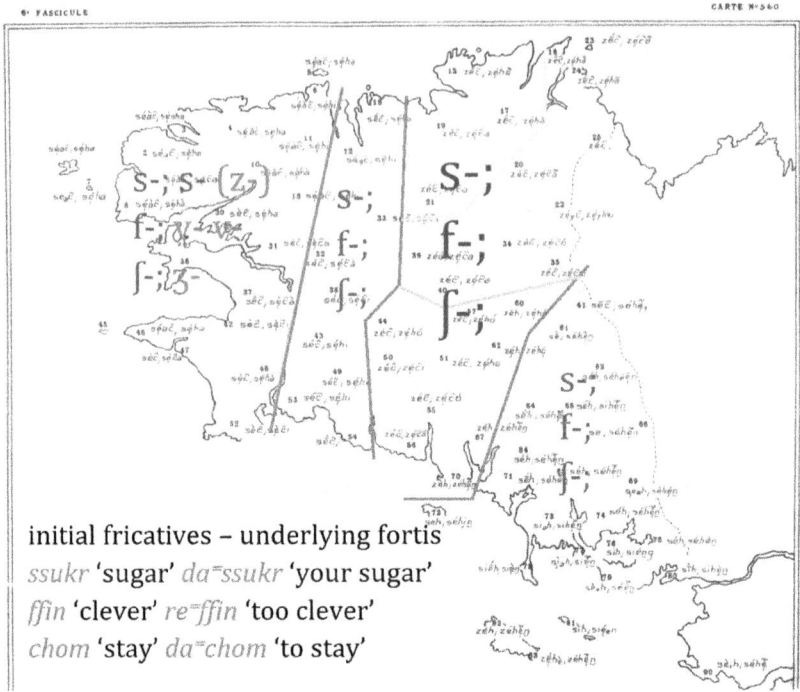

Figure 11.7 Initial fricatives, underlying fortis <ss-, ff-, ch>, and neo-lenition.

Breton Orthographies: An Increasingly Awkward Fit

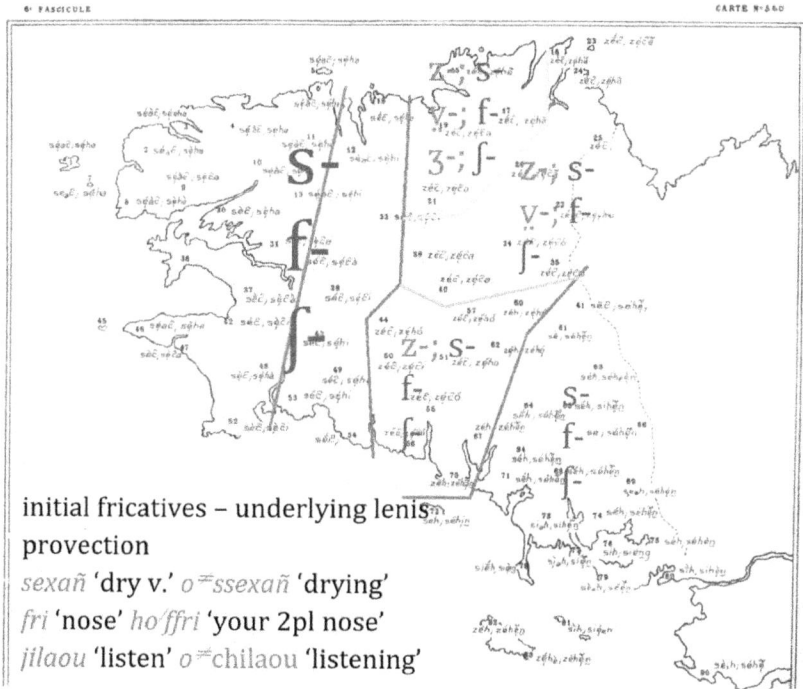

initial fricatives – underlying lenis
provection
sexañ 'dry v.' *o=ssexañ* 'drying'
fri 'nose' *ho ffri* 'your 2pl nose'
jilaou 'listen' *o=chilaou* 'listening'

Figure 11.8 Initial fricatives, underlying lenis <s-, f-, j->, and neo-provection <ss-, ff-, ch->.

Table 11.9 *Voicing or not of initial fricatives in loanwords in Treger.*

/v-/	/f-/
foenn 'hay'	*ffamilh* 'family'
foñss 'bottom'	*ffèbl* 'weak'
fontañ 'melt'	*ffèblessite* 'weakness; blindness'
forest 'forest'	(*ffèiż* 'faith')
forssiñ 'force'	*ffelloud* 'want, need'
fourniss 'furnish, provide'	*ffèriñ* 'iron [clothes]'
ar Frañss 'France'	*ffin* 'end; sly, crafty, clever'
frisañ 'curl; whizz along'	*ffleur* 'flowers'
	ffotañ 'want, need'
	ffourañ 'put, bung'
	ffoutr '[give] a damn'
	ffrikañ 'crush'
/z-/	/s-/
sac'h 'sack, bag'	*ssampar* 'recovered, back in good health'
santoud 'feel'	*ssaro* 'smock'
seblant 'semblance, sign, ghost'	*ssautiñ* 'explode'
serriñ 'close, gather'	(*sseizh* '7' *da seizh* ...)
sigaretenn 'cigarette'	(*sseiteg* '17' *da seiteg* ...)
sinañ 'sign (document)'	*ssèñtier* 'worksite'
siniffioud 'mean, signify'	*sseulamant* 'only, however'
simant 'cement'	*ssîekl* 'century'
soup 'soup'	*ssidr* (S) 'cider'
soubenn 'broth'	*ssort* 'sort, kind'
sourssenn 'source, spring'	*ssukr* 'sugar'
sur 'sure'	*ssystem* 'system, way of doing something'
/ʒ-/	/ʃ-/
jardin 'garden'	*chañss* 'luck'
șervij 'serve, service'	*chapel* 'chapel'
șikour 'help'	*cheiñch* 'change'
jiletenn 'vest'	*chik* 'handsome, nice'
șistr (N) 'cider'	*choas* 'choose, choice'
șoñjal, T *joñsal* 'think'	*chom* 'stay, remain, live'
journal 'newspaper'	*chupenn* 'jacket'

2.4 <Cẘa/Cẘoa, Cw, -w-/-ẘ-, aw/ao>

Another complex problem is the treatment of OB /w/, which rapidly split into /w/ (E <ẘ>) before back vowels and /ɥ/ (E <w>) before front vowels. Traditional graphs were <o> for E <ẘ> and <u> for E <w>, but these were infelicitously merged by Le Pelletier, Le Gonidec, and KLT (in order to make the *gw > w* mutation appear simpler in print) into <(g)w> for both; elsewhere <c'hoa> for E <xẘa>, <c'hwe/i-> for E <xwe/i->, <-v-> for E <-w-> intervocalically, and finally, <-iou, -eo, -ao, -aou> (/-əu/) (G <-iù, -èu, -aù, -eù>).

Breton Orthographies: An Increasingly Awkward Fit 205

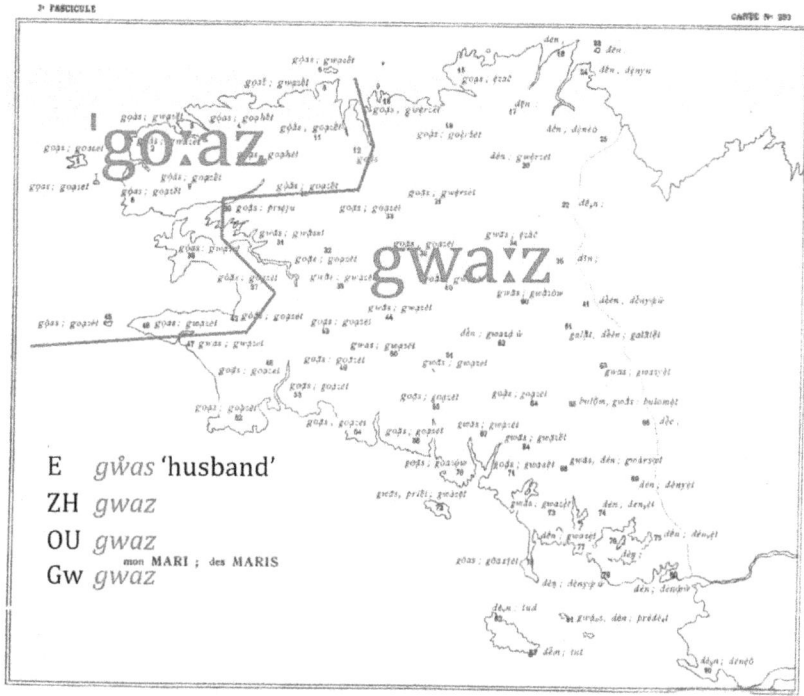

Figure 11.9 ŵa: gŵas 'husband' – everywhere /gwa:z/, L /'go:az/

There are three solutions for E <w>: (1) L, K /Cɥ-, -v-, -w/; (2) T /w/ everywhere; and (3) G /ɥ/ everywhere, as may be gathered from Figures 11.9 to 11.12.

ŵ/w ŵ *diwall* 'be careful', everywhere **-w-**; but *pewar* 'four', *béwañ* 'live', like *w*.

	W, KU	T	G
xw-	Cɥ-	/w/	/ɥ/
gw-			
-w-, *⁼w-*	-v-		
-w	-w		
xŵ-	/w/		
gŵ-			
-ŵ-, *⁼ŵ-*			

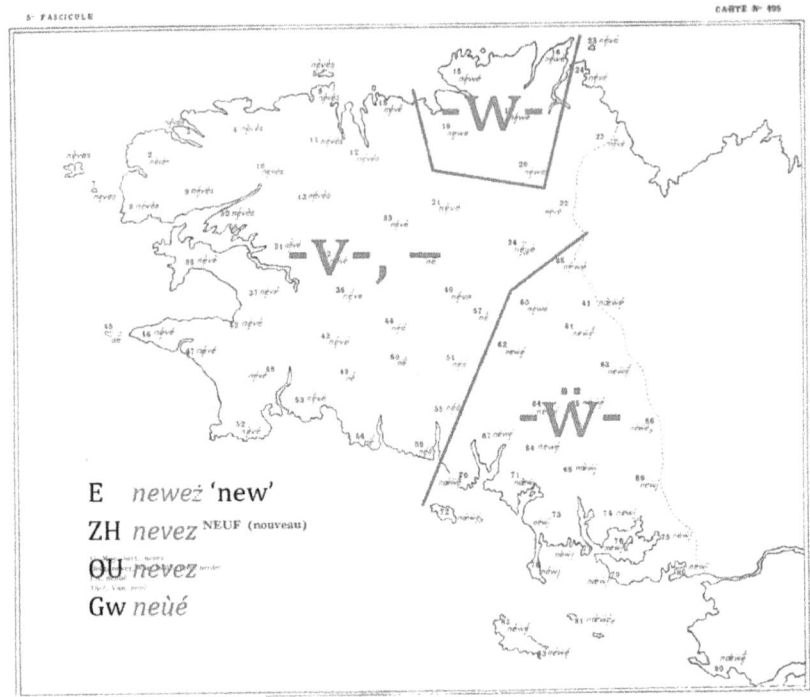

Figure 11.10 <w>: *neweż* 'new' – K, L /v/; T /w/; G /ɥ/

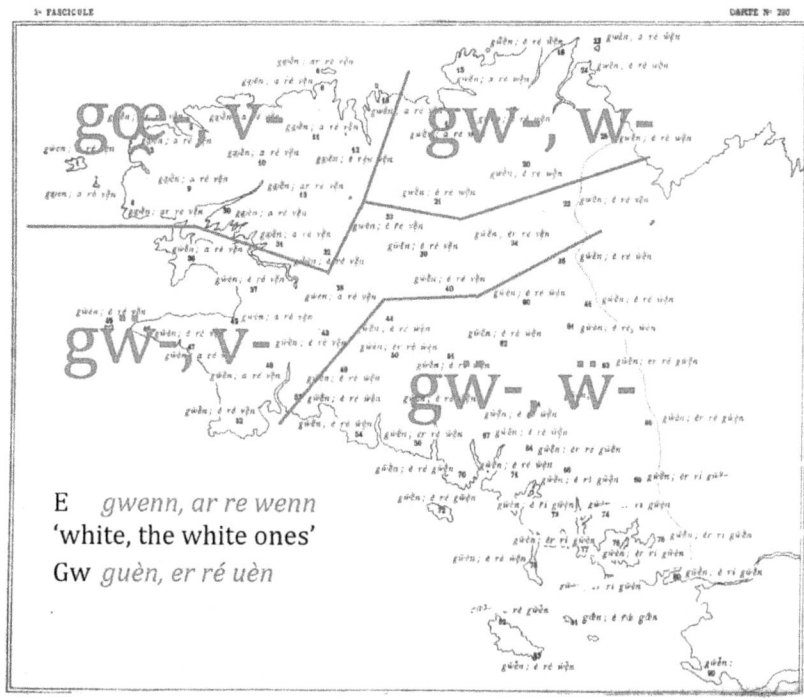

Figure 11.11 <gw-, ⁼w->: *gwenn* 'white', *ar re wenn* 'the white ones' – NW /gœ-, ⁼v-/; C, SW /gɥ- ⁼v-/; NE /gw-, ⁼w/; SE /ɟɥ-, ⁼ɥ-/

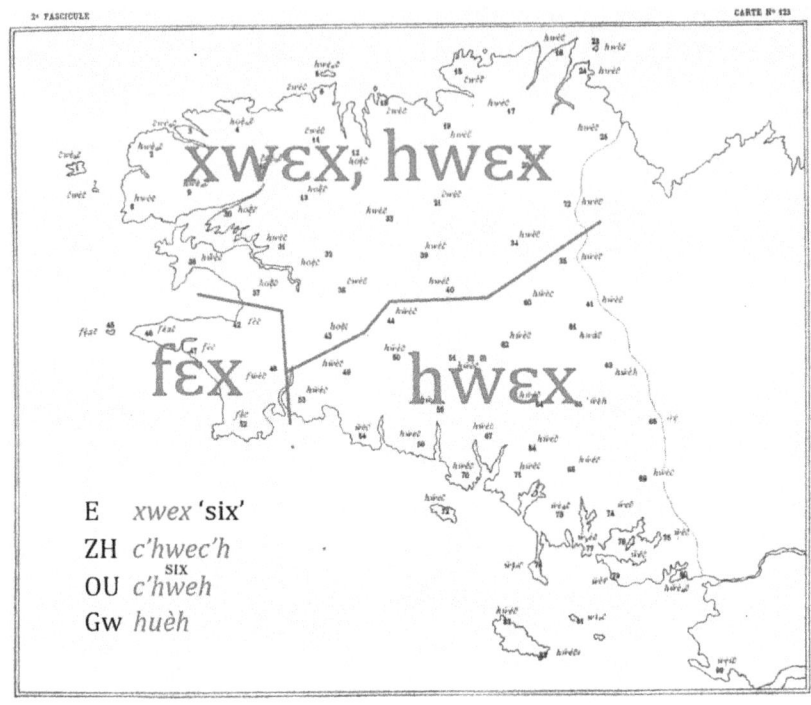

Figure 11.12 <xw>: *xwex* 'six' – N /xw-, hw-/; extreme SW /f-/; SE /hɥ-/

2.5 Distribution of E <oa> (see Figures 11.13–11.14)

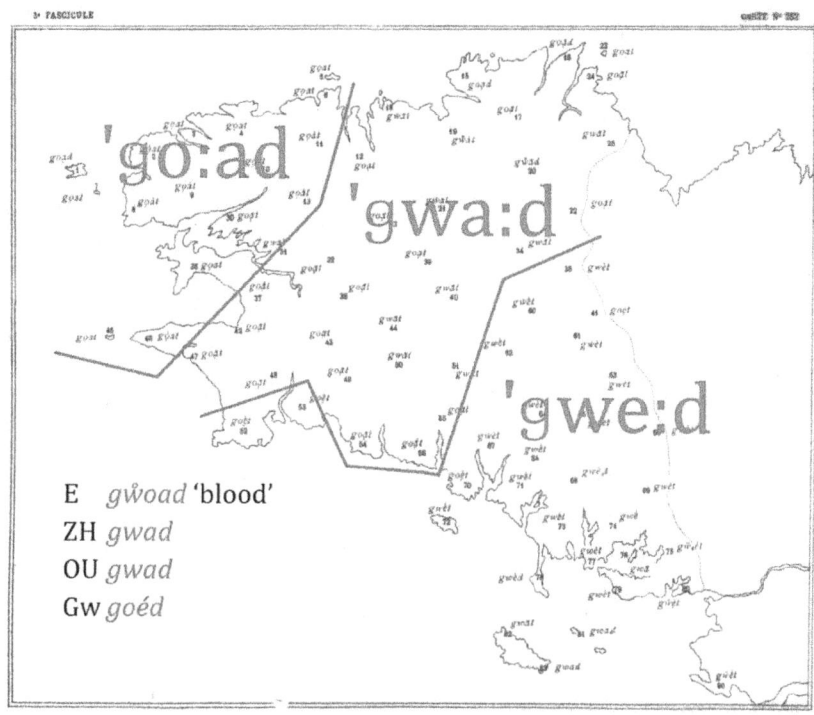

Figure 11.13 *ẘoa: gẘoad* 'blood' – NW /ˈgoːad/; NE-SW /gwaːd/; SE /gweːd/. Only E distinguishes between *gẘas* for /wa/ everywhere, and *gẘoad* for KLT /wa/, G, SE /we/ (/ˈoːa/ is an automatic adjustment in L for /wa/ in stressed monosyllables, whatever the origin).

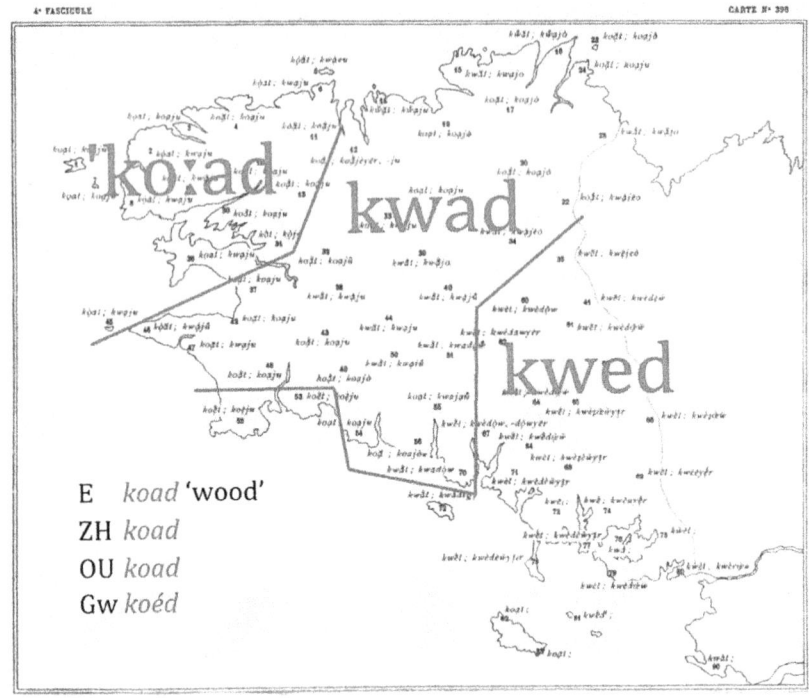

Figure 11.14 <oa>: *koad* 'wood' – NW /ˈoːa/; / NE-SW /wa/; SE /we/

2.6 **<aw/ao>** *braw* KLT /braw/, G /braw̃/paotr L /paot/, KT /poːt/, G /pəut/ (see Figure 11.15)

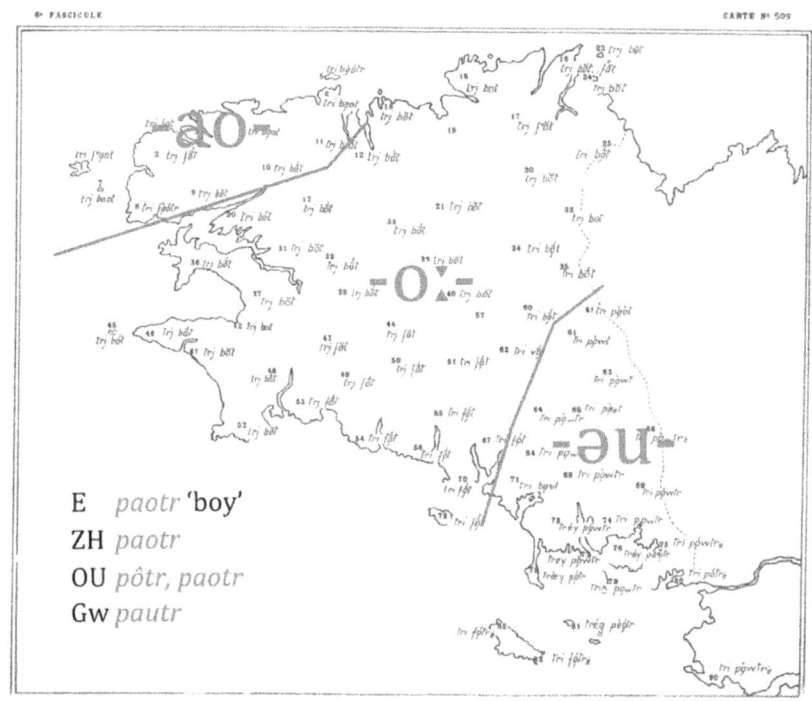

Figure 11.15 <ao>: *paotr* 'boy' – L /aˑo/; K, T /oː/; G /əu/. Only E distinguishes between <ao> (L /ao/, NE-SW /oː/, G /əu/) and <aw> – e.g., *braw* 'fine' (KLT /aˑo/, G /au̯/).

2.7 Initial /h/ (see Figure 11.16)

Initial <h-> is never omitted from L texts even though not pronounced there.

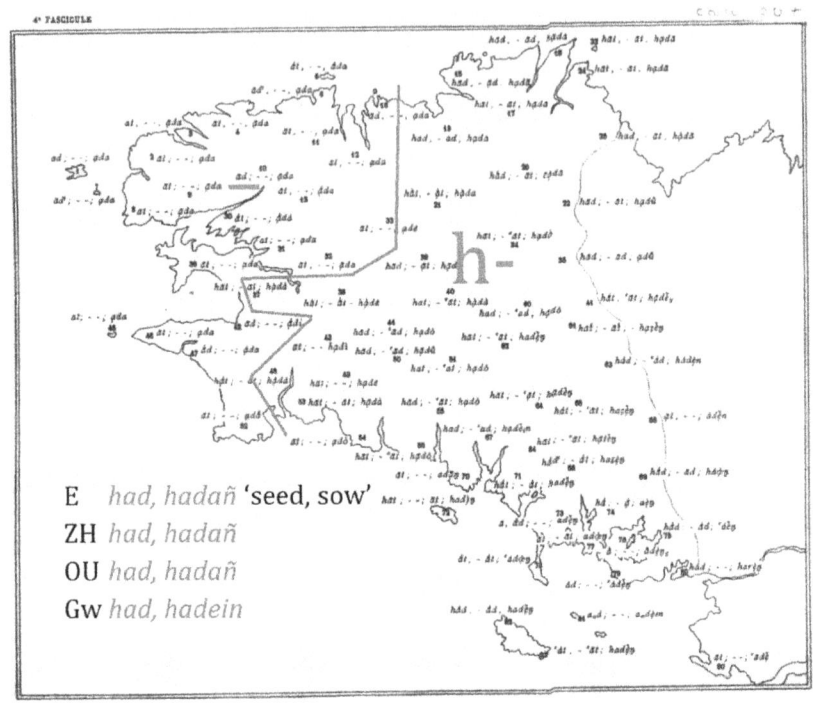

Figure 11.16 Initial <h->: *had, hadañ* 'seed, sow' – W -; E /h?-

2.8 -oN > L ouN (see Figure 11.17)

This was rarely written, except in pure L texts not expected to be used outside L. No present or past orthography has ever systematized *oun* for *on*. It operates in L only when there is contingent nasality on the *o*; where there is no nasality, there is no change of vowel – *tomm* 'hot' /tom/ even in L (*tuem* in G).

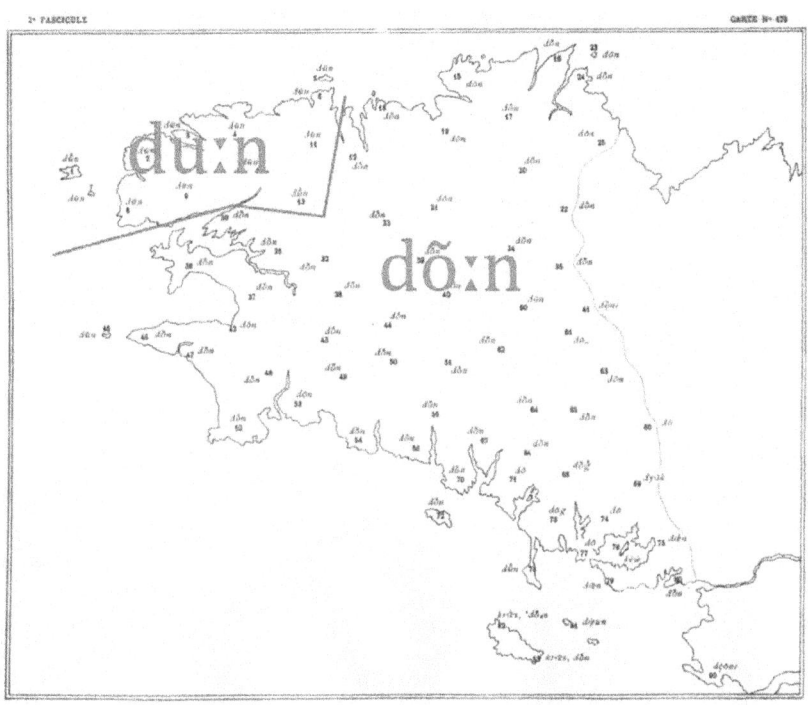

Figure 11.17 <oN>: *don* 'deep' – /õːN/ > L /uːN/

2.9 /ñv/ (see Figure 11.18)

The reflex of OB /μ/ has been written <ñv> ever since KLT; it is written <ñù> in G, but the map shows no final diphthong in /ɥ/.

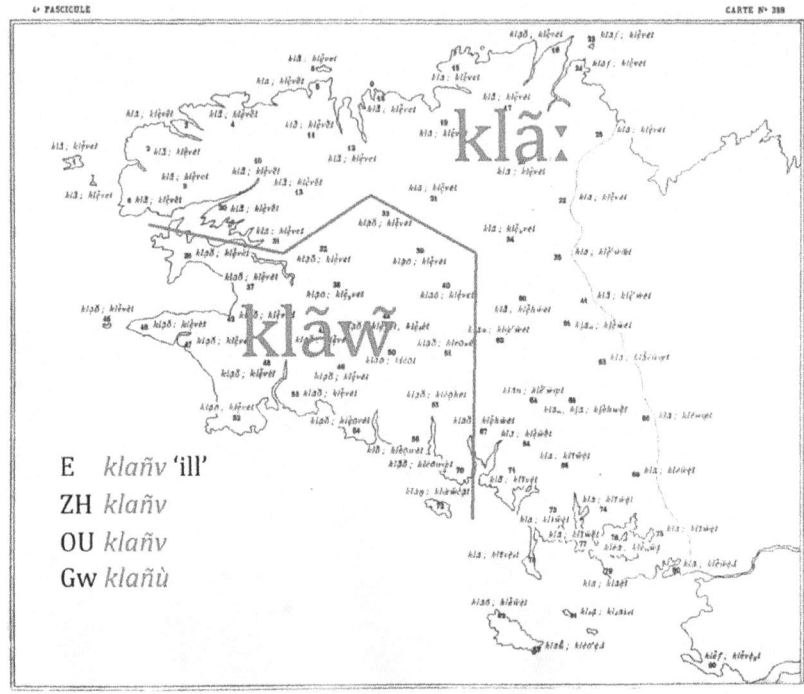

Figure 11.18 <ñv>: *klañv* – /ã:/; SW /ãõ/ (Old Breton /μ/)

Breton Orthographies: An Increasingly Awkward Fit

2.10 Plural <-où> (see Figure 11.19)

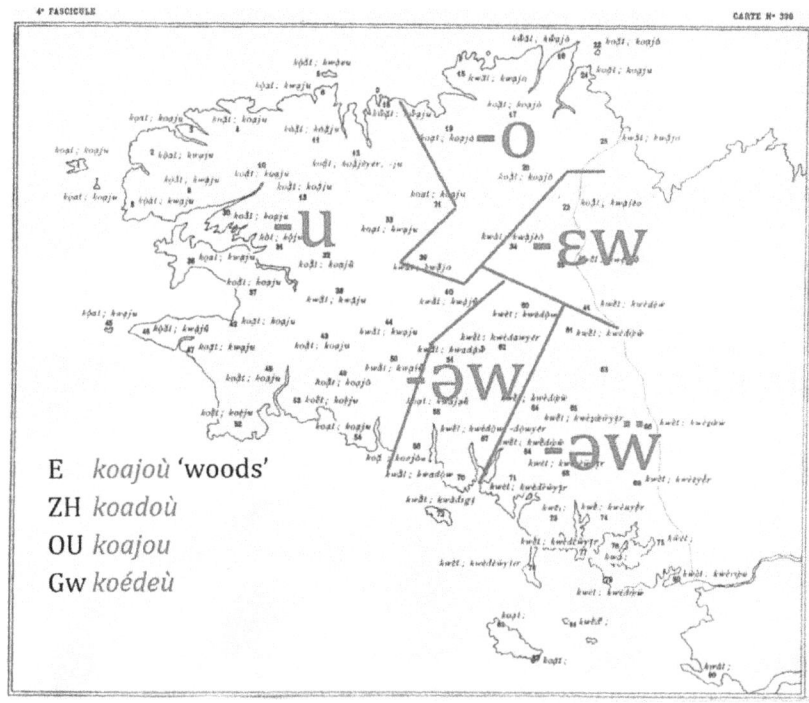

E *koajoù* 'woods'
ZH *koadoù*
OU *koajou*
Gw *koédeù*

Figure 11.19 Plural ending <-où> – W /u/; T /o/, EKU /ɛo/; WG /əu/; G /əɥ/

2.11 Plural <-joù/-doù> (see Figure 11.20)

In ZH, the unpalatalized plural in <-doù> is preferred even though it is found only in G.

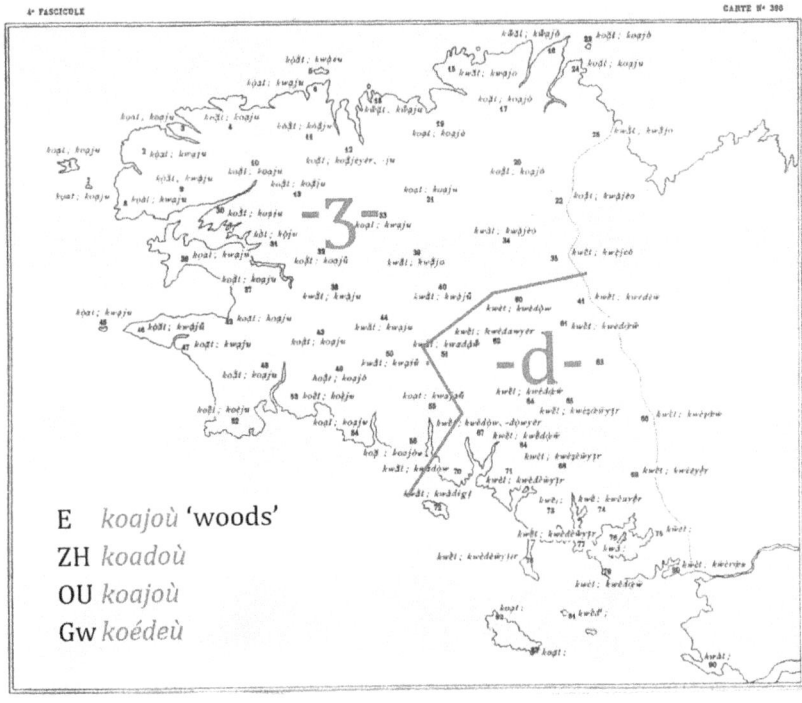

Figure 11.20 Palatalization in plural of words in <-d>: *koajoù* 'woods' – K, L, T /-ʒ-/; G /-d-/

2.12 Plural <-choù/-toù> (see Figure 11.21)

In ZH, the unpalatalized plural in <-toù> is preferred even though it is found only in G.

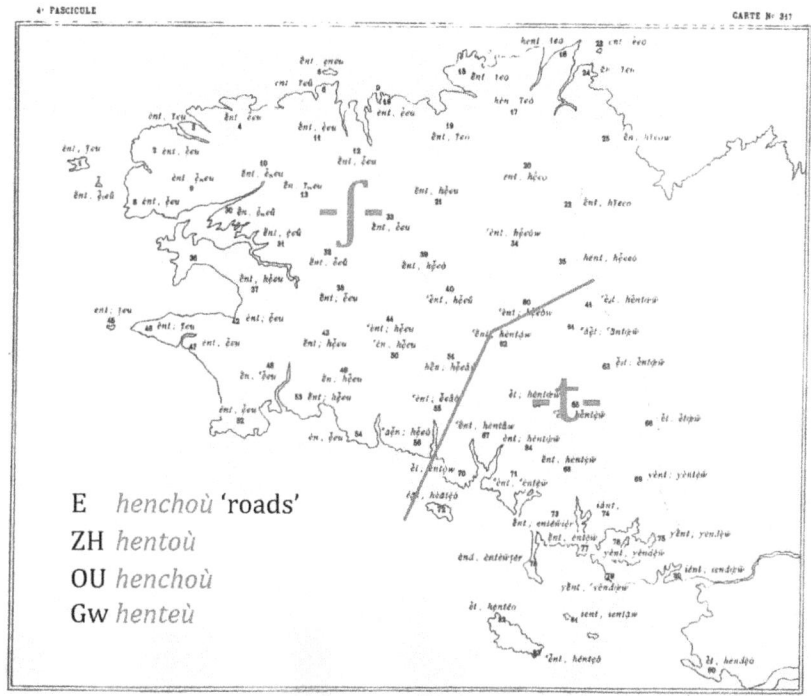

Figure 11.21 Palatalization in plural of words in <-t>: *henchoù* 'roads' – K, L, T /-ʃ-/; G /-t-/

2.13 Infinitive Endings <-iñ> and <-añ> (see Figure 11.22)

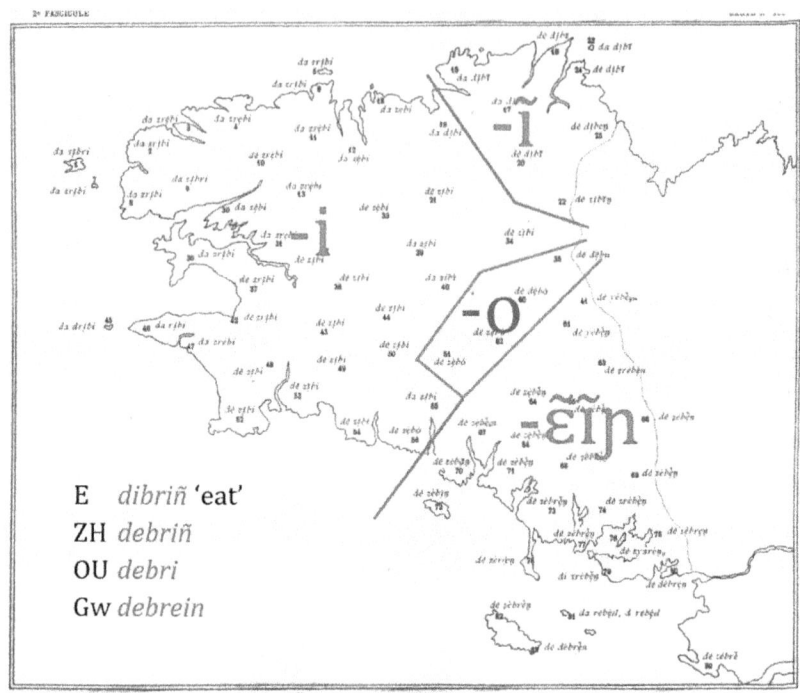

E   *dibriñ* 'eat'
ZH *debriñ*
OU *debri*
Gw *debrein*

Figure 11.22 Infinitive ending <-iñ>: *dibriñ* 'eat' – W /-i/; ET /-ī/; C /-o/; G /-ɛ̃ɲ/ (similar distribution for <-añ>)

2.14   3PL Preposition Ending <-e/-o> (see Figure 11.23)

KLT, ZH, and OU tend to prefer <-o> as the standard 3PL ending for conjugated prepositions, even though <-e> is more widespread. This is a reflection of the dominance of L for the KLT written standard.

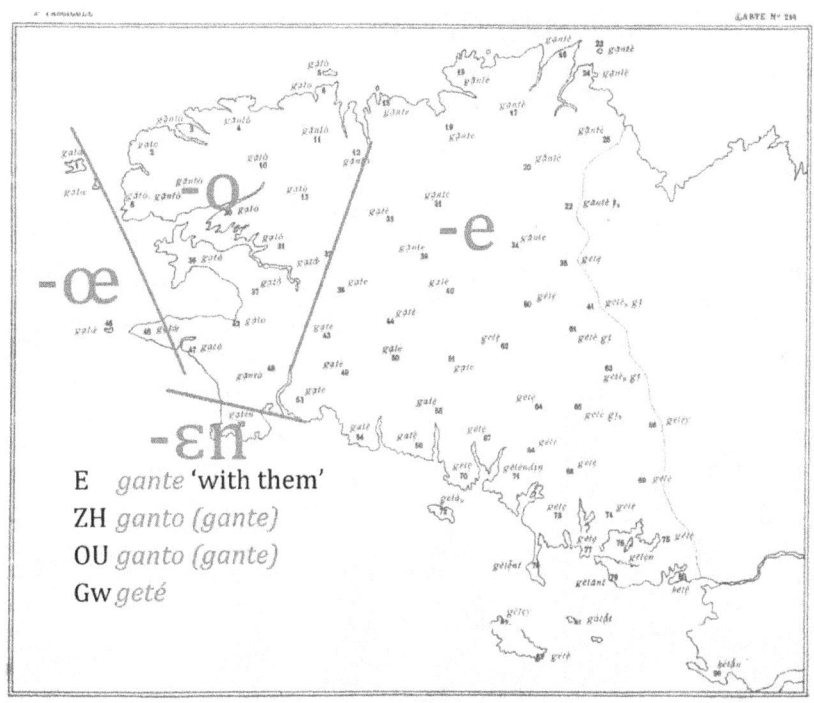

Figure 11.23 <-e/-o> 3PL ending of prepositions: *gante/ganto* 'with them' – L, WK /-o/; T, EK, G /-e/; Cap Caval /-œ/; Pays Bigouden /-ɛn/

2.15 Conditional Infix <-ff-/-eff-/-eh-> (see Figure 11.24)

Figure 11.24 Conditional infix <-ff-, -eff-, -eh-> – K, L, T /f-/; EK, /-εf-/; G /-eh-/

2.16 Object Pronoun: Post-Verbal Independent or Preverbal Clitic (see Figure 11.25)

KLT *ma welffenn aneżi/'nei*; KLT literary, obsolete: *ma he gwelffenn*; G *ha p'he gwelehenn*.

There is a profound difference between the old G and new KLT systems. Literary Breton tends to favour the old system, even though it is no longer well understood in KLT. While this may be attributable to linguistic conservatism, the more likely reason is that the old proclitic system is isomorphic with French – *si je <u>la</u> voyais* – and therefore more natural to French-speaking learners.

2.17 Other Morphological Problems

Space does not make it possible to show maps of all morphological difficulties. It should nevertheless be clear that Breton faces serious problems in

Figure 11.25 Object pronoun construction 'if I saw her': KLT post-verbal *a*-marking; G proclitic pronoun

standardizing some of its most frequent grammatical features. The great variety of forms for a given person of 'have', for instance, has prompted news broadcasters to make excessive use of the passive in order to avoid having to use one form of 'have' rather than another: *Maniffestet so bed gant al labourerien-douar* ... 'It has been demonstrated by the farmers ...' rather than *Al labourerien-douar o deus maniffestet* ... 'Farmers have demonstrated ...' because of the difficulty of choosing a consensus form for 'they have'.

    'you have 2SG': lit. *ac'h eus, az peus*; pop. *peus, teus, ffeus*
    'we have': lit. *hon eus*; pop. *hon deus, hor beus, hom meus > meump, neusomp*
    'they have': lit. *o deus* ; pop. *deus, neus > neusont, deuint, neuint*
    'we': lit. *ni*; pop. *nei, nign, nimp, mimp, mump*
    'they': *i, int-i, int, hint, hê, ġi*
    'my': *va, ma*
    'our': *hon, hon/hor/hol, hom, ho' X domp* ('our X to.us')
    future plural and conditional, KLT: -<*ff*>-, G -<*eh*>-

Future plural:	W	T, K	G
1PL	*-imp*	*-ffomp*	*-eemp*
2PL	*-ot/-ox*	*-ffet/-ſet*	*-eet*
3PL	*-int*	*-ffont*	*-eent*

3   Orthographic Principles

There are three basic possible approaches to dealing with dialects in orthography design:
- Mononomic (monodialectal) system: problem of choice of dialect base – Breton-speakers will not accept imposition of a single dialect; historically, there have been separate norms for KLT and G; OU has parallel systems for L and G (the OU G standard is little used, in part because it is not very different from the well-established traditional G)
- Binomic (bidialectal) system: ZH is a single system based on L; some ZH conventions are meant to include G; L and G are two conservative, peripheral dialects – no account is taken, in this solution, of the majority innovating central dialects
- Polynomic (supradialectal) umbrella system: inherent in this approach is the problem of the amount of variation to be allowed; ID was the first attempt at a true supradialectal system; E goes considerably further in this direction

Breton Orthographies: An Increasingly Awkward Fit   223

3.1   Orthographies of Breton

In the following chronological review of the main orthographies, drawbacks and good points are indicated with reference to E graphemes, which cater to the main modern dialect reflexes (see Figures 11.3–11.22). For greater detail, see Ar Merser (1980, 1996), Wmffre (2007), and the useful summary in http://fr.wikipedia.org/wiki/Orthographe_du_breton (last accessed 21 June 2015).

Old Breton (800–1250) continues the Insular Celtic Brythonic tradition (see Table 11.2).

Middle Breton (1350) 1450–1659) orthography has become French-based with a few extra conventions: <-iff, -aff, -off> /-ĩṽ, -ãṽ, -õṽ/; <ch> /ʃ ~ x, ḥ/; <ç/çz/cz> /ts (tθ?)/; <z> /ð, ọ̆/, <-tz> /-θ/ (see Table 11.3)

Drawbacks
    <ż/zh> confusion: *neuez* 'new'; *brezonec* 'Breton' (E *neweż, brezhoneg*)
    <x/xx> confusion: *sechaff* 'to dry'; *sechaff* 'driest' (E *sexañ, sexxañ* /s~zę:ḥa/, /s~zęxã/)
    <ẘa/oa> confusion: *goas* 'husband'; *goad, goed* 'blood' (E *gẘas, gẘoad*)
    <aw/ao> confusion: *glau, glao* 'rain'; *pautr, paotr* 'boy' (E *glaw, paotr*)

Early Modern Traditional (begins 1659 with Maunoir >1800~1900+) mainly Leon (L, NW)-based; also Gwened (Vannetais – G, SE); initial consonant mutations written for first time; MB <-iff, -aff, -off> /-ĩ(ṽ), -ã(ṽ), -õ(ṽ)/ are replaced by <-in, -an, -on>; and <ch> is now unambiguous for /ʃ/ and, most iconically, <c'h> is introduced for /x, ḥ/

Drawbacks
    <ż/zh> confusion; <x/xx> confusion; <ẘa/oa> confusion; <aw/ao> confusion (as for MB)

Throughout the nineteenth century, spontaneous EMT orthographies continued alongside LG, with orthographies in use split into traditionalist and reformist (activist) camps. EMT orthographies are probably actually dominant in terms of volume.

Le Pelletier (LP, 1753) introduces *gwa, gwe, gwi* instead of traditional *goa* but *gue, gui*, but not systematic: *dioüall* 'take care' instead of *diwall; diveza* 'last' instead of *diweza(ñ)*.

Drawbacks
    <ż/zh> confusion; <x/xx> confusion; <ẘa/oa> confusion; <aw/ao> confusion (as for MB and EMB)
    <ẘ/w> confusion: earlier *goaska, da (v)oaska* '(to) press' and *guelet, da velet* '(to) see' become *gwaska, da waska, gwelet, da welet* (E *gẘaskañ, da ẘaskañ; gweled, da weled*)
    LP (1753) introduces (in E terms) <ẘ/w> confusion, which is also re-introduced by LG, along with <s/ż/zh> confusion (hitherto only <ż/zh> confusion).

224   Steve Hewitt

Pre-Modern Reforming (Le Gonidec, LG, et al. 1807–1900+), mainly L-based, adopts hard <g-, k-> instead of <gu-, qu-> before front vowels. Like LP, uses *gwa, gwe, gwi* instead of *goa-, gue-, gui*; uses <-s-> for earlier intervocalic <-ss->; and uses <-z-> for earlier <-s-> (< OB /s/ and <-z->/θ, ð/; MB /ẓ, ð/) – so it is henceforth impossible to tell which is not pronounced outside Leon (E <ż>), which is pronounced /h/ in Gwened (E <zh>), and which is pronounced /z/ everywhere (E <s>).

Drawbacks

<x/xx> confusion; <ŵ/w> confusion; <ŵa/oa>, <aw/ao> confusion (as previously)
<s, ż, zh> confusion (<z> for E <s, ż, zh>) *braz, nevez, brezonek* (E *bras, neweż, brezhoneg* 'big, new, Breton')

Gwened (*Vannetais*) finally stabilized 1902, Guillevic and Le Goff. G is an excellent fit for Upper Gwened (around the town of Gwened/Vannes).

KLT (*Kerne-Leon-Treger*) 1908–1911, mainly L-based (without L <oN > ouN> *brezouneg, choum* for *brezoneg, chom*), continues Le Gonidec <s/z> confusion; adopts *gwa-/gwe-* confusion (to please T); imposes final <-p, -t, -k> for all categories except nouns, so *mat* 'good', everywhere /ma:d/ – goes against native speaker intuitions and distorts learners' pronunciation (not a major factor at the time).

Drawbacks

<s/ż/zh> confusion; <x/xx> confusion; <ŵ/w> confusion; <ŵa/oa> confusion; <aw/ao> confusion (as before)
***mat/mad* confusion:** earlier *mad* written *mat* because not a noun (possible in L, because all monosyllables lengthened: *pesk* 'fish' /pe:sk/; *lak* 'put' /la:k/ , but not outside L; E always *mad*)
<s/ss> confusion: old *lous* 'dirty' /lu:z/ (Gonidec *louz*) and *douss* 'soft' /dus/ (Gonidec *dous*) fall together as *lous, dous* even though everywhere distinguished by length and lenis/fortis consonant; because <s> is now [-s-] internally, it is often interpreted by learners as [-s] finally, when it is actually phonemically /-z/ (this becomes increasingly pernicious as the proportion of learners among users increases)
<f/ff> confusion: old *difenn* 'defend' /-v̥-/, but *differañs* 'difference' /-f-/ become *difenn, diferañs*
Generalization of voiceless finals (except for nouns): so *brezonek* 'Breton, adj.', but *brezoneg* 'Breton, noun, name of language' (no possible difference in pronunciation anywhere); no problem for native speakers, who apply final obstruent devoicing/voicing automatically; for learners, it is important to use the voiced final as often as possible because final obstruent *devoicing* is a much more natural and easily acquired rule than final obstruent *voicing*, especially for French speakers: *grand oncle* /gʁɑ̃:t ɔ̃:kl/, Bourg-en-Bresse /buʁk ɑ̃ bʁɛs/; failure to apply final obstruent voicing is rampant among learners today

It is only with KLT (1908–1911) that the reformist camp finally wins out. The surprising thing in this blow-by-blow survey of the evolution of Breton orthographies is that it was actually KLT that introduced the greatest number of regrettable conventions, rather than ZH, which is seen as the big culprit by most linguistically aware Breton scholars. Some people today look back fondly to KLT as constituting a kind of prelapsarian ideal before the acrimonious stand-off between ZH and OU. But it was KLT that confirmed the <ŵ/w> confusion of LP and LG and introduced <f/ff> confusion as well as, with disastrous results for learners' pronunciation, both <s/ss> confusion and the generalization of <-p, -t, -k> in finals except for nouns.

ZH – *Peurunvan* (**fully unified**) 1941 – mechanical merger of KLT and Gwened, L-based; <zh> for L <z> and G <h> (a number of common words in E <ż> have <zh> because of hiatus consonant in G: *anezhañ* 'of him', *kouezhañ* 'fall', etc., suggesting /-z-/ pronunciation in K, T); confusing final <-v> for KLT <-o/-ou>, where T has <-w> and G <ù> (e.g., E *marw* 'dead', *merwel* 'die' > *marv, mervel*); continues undifferentiated *gwa-/gwe-* of KLT and imposes final <-p, -t, -k> for all categories except nouns, so *mat*, everywhere /ma:d/ – goes against native speaker intuitions and distorts learners' pronunciation

Drawbacks
    <s/ż> confusion; <x/xx> confusion; <ŵ/w> confusion; <ŵa/oa> confusion; <aw/a>o confusion; *mat/mad* confusion; <s/ss> confusion; <f/ff> confusion (as previously)
    Erroneous <ż/zh> distribution
    Confusing final <-v> for E <-w>: ZH *piv, bev, blev, glav*; E *piw, béw, blew, glaw*
    Somewhat complex to learn

ZH was promulgated in 1941 by Roparz Hemon, a non-native-speaker and cultural activist on the Gestapo payroll in 1941–1945, at the insistence of *Sonderführer* Leo Weisgerber, a German Celticist bilingual in French and German (born in Metz) who was sent to Brittany to act as a kind of Nazi cultural commissar for Breton matters. Weisgerber did not know much Breton but felt that it was time to merge the two literary standards, KLT and G; he therefore put pressure on Roparz Hemon to do so. The dubious political origins of ZH (see Blanchard 2003; Calvez 2000; Ar Merser 1999; Wmffre 2007) are breezily dismissed by most nationalist activists today, who do not always understand that others may not be so indifferent to such considerations. Most of the linguistically undesirable conventions of ZH were already present in KLT. The main innovations were the iconic <zh> – which was also incorrectly assigned to a number of <ż> words, making it useless as a predictor of reflexes in K and T – and the confusing use of final <-v> for E <-w>. There have recently been calls, notably by Le Ruyet (whose personal preference goes to ID) to rectify the three worst aspects of ZH by introducing voiced finals, like OU, applying an etymologically correct <z/zh> distribution, and replacing final <-v> with <-w>, as in ID. However ZH supporters tend to claim that ZH is already perfect and hence not in need of costly and confusing modification.

OU – *Orthographe universitaire/Skolveurieg* 1955 – turns its back on the <zh> and <v> of ZH, introduces parallel standards for KLT and G (G version very little used; most G writers continue to prefer traditional G)

Good points
    Generalizes voiced finals <-b, -d, -g, -z> in many cases – good for learners' pronunciation
    Eliminates *mat/mad* confusion: *mad* 'good'/*da vat* 'good and proper'
    Eliminates <s/ss> confusion: *louz/dous*
    Eliminates <x/xx> confusion: *seha* 'to dry', *an hini sec'ha* 'the driest' – the first orthography to do so
    Eliminates <f/ff> confusion: *divenn* 'defend'; *diferañs* 'difference' (at the price of E <f/v> confusion)

Drawbacks
    Introduces <h/x> confusion: *had* 'seed' /h/ not pronounced in W, *gad* 'hare', *da had* 'your hare' /h~ḥ/ pronounced everywhere
    Imposes, grammaticalizes 'neo-lenition': <f-, s-, ch-, c'hw-> 'f-, z-, j-, hw-> (for both underlying lenis and fortis series) – e.g., *da zukr* 'your sugar', which it seems no one says with /z/ (for fortis series, very minority usage)

After the Second World War began a mass shift away from transmitting Breton to children, a process which became complete by about 1970. OU was launched in 1955 by the anti-nationalist Falc'hun (a native speaker from Ar Vourc'h Wenn/Le Bourg Blanc in WL; Falc'hun 1953, 1981) with the twin aims of enhancing the grapheme-phoneme correspondence for teaching purposes (cf. also Casquite and Young, this volume) and, at the same time, setting up a rival orthography to the nationalists' ZH. The generalization of voiced final obstruents was very welcome, as were the elimination of the <s/ss>, <x/xx> and <f/ff> confusions (E <f> confusingly written as <'f- -v- -v>). But the concomitant new <h/x> confusion was less desirable, as was the imposition in writing of neo-lenition for both the lenis *and* fortis series (Falc'hun was a WL speaker). This reaction against ZH was bound to produce a counter-reaction among the more nationalist-minded ZH supporters, and the resulting stand-off between ZH and OU supporters has lasted until the present day.

ID – *Interdialectale/Etrerannyezhel* 1975 – adopts 3-way <s-z-zh/ss-zz-sh> distinction; generalizes <w> for T /w/, G /ẅ/; adopts the <-b, -d, -g> finals of OU

Good points
    Eliminates <s/ż/zh> confusion
    Eliminates *mat/mad* confusion (like OU)
    Eliminates <s/ss> confusion (with <s/ss> rather than <z/s> of OU)
    Generalizes <w> for T /w/, G /ẅ/

Drawbacks
    Maintains <ẘ/w> confusion; realization rules complex; somewhat complex to learn

ID was the result of talks between ZH and OU supporters in the early 1970s. It was launched prematurely in May 1975 with the publication of Morvannou's *Le Breton sans peine* (Assimil), without consulting the parties to the talks and therefore without their green light. That 'coup' prompted many ZH and OU supporters to claim that they had been 'stabbed in the back', and most reverted to their inflexible pre-talk positions. ID never gained widespread acceptance, and fell off sharply following Diwan's 1980 adoption of ZH as its official orthography. Nevertheless, it is linguistically the best public attempt at a true polynomic system, combining the phonetic advantages of OU with the supradialectal ambitions of ZH, and indeed going much further than ZH in that direction. Deshayes (2003) has elaborated ID further, introducing, independently, some of the innovations of E.

E – *Étymologique* from about 1999 – a personal elaboration of ID, with the addition of regular distinctions <ao/aw, ẘa/oa, ẘ/w>; 3-way distinctions <h/x/xx> and <v/f/ff>; lenis <f, ż, zh, s, j, x> versus fortis <ff, żż, zzh, ss, ch, xx>, etc.

Good points
  Eliminates <s/ż/zh> confusion
  Eliminates *mat/mad* confusion (like OU)
  Eliminates <s/ss> confusion (with <s/ss> rather than <z/s> of OU)
  Eliminates <x/xx> confusion (with <x/xx> or <c'h/c"h> rather than <h/c'h> of OU)
  Eliminates <f/ff> confusion
  Eliminates <ẘ/w> confusion
  Eliminates <ẘa/oa> confusion
  Eliminates <aw/ao> confusion

Drawbacks
  Somewhat complex to learn, but this will always be true of a supradialectal system; that is the price of an orthography which caters successfully to a range of dialects; cf. Faroese.

Following Hewitt (1987), I continued to refine my 'etymological' (E) system, which stabilized in its current form around the late 1990s. In view of the tense atmosphere surrounding any attempt to discuss the orthography in public – including acrimonious ad hominem attacks – I have never sought to promote it actively. Rather, I see it as an intellectual exercise aimed at demonstrating that it is perfectly feasible to have a more truly polynomic and linguistically accurate system without undue complexity, pending the improbable day when a more serene debate becomes possible in Brittany. Unfortunately, by that time, most traditional native speakers will have disappeared and the need for a polynomic system will no longer be so acute.

3.2 A Sample of Learners' Breton, Clearly Influenced by the ZH Orthography

The link in Table 11.10 is to a discussion in French-sounding standard Breton between two young learners – one a radio journalist, the other a staff member of the Quimper Arts Museum – about an exhibition on 'Picasso and Women' (*Radio Kerne, An Divskouarn o nijal: Picasso hag ar maouezed 2* 'Ears flying: Picasso and women'). The examples in Table 11.10, taken from the first few minutes of the interview, show how the ZH orthography (column 1) has influenced the learners' pronunciation (column 2), which should be different (column 3), corresponding to E orthography (column 4). Especially numerous are examples of voiceless pronunciation of final obstruents before initial vowels or sonorants, which native speakers find upsetting. There is also

Table 11.10 *Examples of how the ZH orthography has influenced learners' pronunciation: www.radiobreizh.net/bzh/episode.php?epid=11899 (last accessed 21 June 2015).*

ZH	IPA	Should be IPA	E
ur vaouez 'a woman'	œʁ ˈvawɛs	œʁ ˈvəwɛs	*ur vaoues*
e vez anavezet ur vaouez 'one can recognize a woman'	e ve ãnaˈvezɛt œʁ ˈvawɛs	ə ve ãnˈveːəd œʁ ˈvəwəs	*e veż anveżed ur vaoues*
c'hoazh 'still'	xwas	hwas	*xwazh*
emaomp dirak un dra 'we find ourselves in front of something'	emɔ̃m diˈʁak œn dʁa	mɔ̃m diˈʁag ˈœnː dʁa	*emomp dirag un dra*
mil nav c'hant '1900'	mil nao ˈxãnt	mil ˈnao hãn	*mil naw xant*
gant ar blakenn 'with the plaque'	ˈgãːt aʁ ˈblakɛn	gãn ʁ ˈblakən	*gant ar blakenn*
Kemper (Quimper)	kæ̃ːˈpɛːʁ	ˈkempəʁ, ˈkepʁ	*Kemper*
a c'hell bezañ disheñvel 'may be different'	a ˈxɛl bea di ˈsæ̃ːvɛl	ʁ ˈhel bea di ˈsẽːvəl	*a xell bezañ disheñvel*
pouezus e oa 'it was important'	ˈpweːzys eˈwa	ˈpwęːzyz ə ˈwaː	*pouesus e oa*
chomet e gwenn 'it stayed white'	ˈʃɔmɛt eˈgwen	ˈʃɔ̃məd eˈgwenː	*chomed e gwenn*
ha dedennus eo ivez 'and it's interesting'	a deˈdɛnys eˈiːe	a deˈdenːyz eˈiːe	*ha dedennus eo ive*
lakat al liv 'put the paint/colour'	ˈlakat alˈliːu	ˈlakʁd ʁ ˈliu	*lakad ar liw*
labourat e unan 'work himself'	laˈburat eˈyːnãn	laˈbuːʁed i ˈhỹːn	*labourad e hûn*
den ebet ober an dra-se 'nobody do that'	ˈden eˈbɛt oˈbɛʁ ãn ˈdʁa-ze	ˈdẽːn əbed ˈobəʁ n ˈdʁaː-he	*den ebed ober an dra-se*
eñ 'he'	jɔ̃	(h)ẽ̞õ	*heñv*
ne oa ket ur vignonez 'was not a female friend'	ne wa ˈkɛt œʁ viˈɲɔ̃nɛs	nə ˈwa këd œʁ vĩ ˈɲɔ̃ːnës	*ne oa ked ur vignones*
den ne oar 'nobody knows'	dɛn ne waʁ	ˈdẽːn nə ˈwaːʁ	*den ne ŵoar*
mont a rae 'he went'	mɔ̃n a rae	ˈmɔ̃nː ə ˈʁeː	*mond a rae*
evit ul levr 'for a book'	evit œl lɛɔʁ	vid œ ˈleœʁ	*ewid ur levr*

confusion over whether or not to pronounce the <ż>: second example *e vez anavezet* /e ve ãna'vezɛt/; normal would be either L /e vez ãna'veːzɛd/ or TK /ə ve ãn'vęːëd/, but not the mixture produced. The general impression is of a strong French accent, which is not true of the subsequent audio links of native speakers from T.

    Examples of authentic native speech, in T dialect:

www.ina.fr/video/RN00001367127 Ur valss a garantez

www.wat.tv/audio/maria-prat-ar-melexour-13qu2_2g74z_.html
    Maria Prat "Ar Meleżour"

www.youtube.com/watch?v=zQY44BhTTJY Maria Prat ha Roje Laouenan

www.youtube.com/watch?v=Lm9JeAEk2RU Maria Prat ha Roje Laouenan 2 (all last accessed 21 June 2015)

4 Conclusion

The striking thing about the evolution of Breton orthographies is that, as shown in this chapter, practically each new version, with the notable exception of the recent ID (1975), actually introduces fresh linguistic drawbacks – it is in this sense that they constitute, collectively, 'an increasingly awkward fit'.

All modern orthographies (ZH, OU, ID, E) contain numerous conventions which are not motivated in a given dialect; this is the natural price of supra-dialectal aspirations. Better, then, that non-motivated distinctions should serve that supradialectal purpose as fully as possible. From the point of view of native speakers, there can be no question of imposing one dialect over another; all dialects need to have equal validity (cf. Sackett, and Hull, this volume). For this reason, a mononomic standard is a non-starter in Brittany. A polynomic standard is the only logical alternative, and it is ID or E which best meet that ideal. For learners without family roots in a particular dialect, in contrast, there is a lack of a clear oral standard which actually corresponds to authentic native speech (for discussion of a 'multilectal' approach, see Cahill 2014:13). The current practice of adopting essentially French phonetic habits for what the user sees in ZH is highly unsatisfactory, and constitutes a major obstacle to learner/native-speaker communication. It should be possible to stabilize the oral standard for learners – for instance by adopting CK-like majority solutions across the board. It is much easier to do this with reference to ID or E than to ZH or OU.

There has never been a full public debate on the principles that should underpin Breton orthography, and certainly no clear conclusions on what kind of system is desirable, mononomic or polynomic. If Breton were a language without a written tradition, the most practical solution might be a

Table 11.11 *Summary of Breton Orthographies*

E item	English	E – 1999	OU – 1955	ZH – 1941	KLT – 1908–1911
f	nose, defend, belly	*fri, difenn, kof*	*fri, divenn, kov*	*fri, difenn, kof*	*fri, difenn, kof*
ff	sly/end, spit, coif	*ffin, tuffañ, koeff*	*fin, tufa, koef*	*fin, tufañ, koef*	*fin, tufa, koef*
ż	sit, new	*aseżañ, neweż*	*azeza, nevez*	*azezañ, nevez*	*azeza, nevez*
żż	newer	*neweżżoc'h (-x)*	*nevesoh*	*nevesoc'h*	*nevesoc'h*
zh	old, port	*kozh, porzh*	*koz, porz (G koh, porh)*	*kozh, porzh*	*koz, porz*
zzh	oldest	*kozzhañ*	*kosa (G kohañ)*	*koshañ*	*kosañ, kosa*
s	look, mare, husband big, time, a lot	*selled, kaseg, gẁas, bras, amser, kals*	*selled, kazeg, gwaz braz, amzer, kalz*	*sellou^X, kazeg, gwaz^X, bras^X, amzer, kalz*	*sellou^X, kazeg^N, gwaz^X, bras^X, amzer, kalz*
ss	bigger, sugar, place, sweet, person	*brassoc'h (-x), ssukr, plass, douss, persson*	*brasoh, sukr, plas, dous, person*	*brasoc'h, sukr, plas, dous, person*	*brasoc'h, sukr, plas, dous, person*
c'h (x)	dry *vb*	*sec'hañ (sexañ)*	*seha*	*sec'hañ*	*sec'ha*
c"h (xx)	driest	*sec"hañ (sexxañ)*	*sec'ha*	*sec'hañ*	*sec'hañ, sec'ha*
c'hẁa (x)	play *vb*	*c'hẁari (xẁari)*	*c'hoari*	*c'hoari*	*c'hoari*
c'hẁoa (x)	sister	*c'hẁoar (xẁoar)*	*c'hoar*	*c'hoar*	*c'hoar*
gẁa, ẁa	husband, be careful	*gẁas, diwall*	*gwaz, diwall*	*gwaz^N, diwall*	*gwaz^N, diwall*
gẁoa	blood	*gẁoad*	*gwad*	*gwad^C*	*gwad^C*
c'hwe~i (x)	six, you *pl*	*c'hwec'h, c'hwi (xw-)*	*c'hweh, c'hwi*	*c'hwec'h, c'hwi*	*c'hwec'h, c'hwi*
gwe~i	white, wine	*gwenn, gwin*	*gwenn, gwin*	*gwenn, gwin*	*gwenn, gwin*
w	colour, coloured	*liw, liwed*	*liou, livet*	*liv, livet^X*	*liou, livet^X*
	alive, live *vb*	*béw, béwañ*	*beo, beva*	*bev, bevañ*	*beo, beva*
	hair, strand of hair	*blew, blewenn*	*bleo, blevenn*	*blev, blevenn*	*bleo, blevenn*
	rain, rainy	*glaw, glaweg*	*glao, glaveg*	*glav, glavek^X*	*glao, glavek^X*
	dead, died	*marw, marwed*	*maro, marvet*	*marv, marvet^X*	*maro, marvet^X*
ñv	ill, illness	*klañv, kleñved*	*klañv, kleñved*	*klañv, kleñved^N*	*klañv, kleñved^N*
-b	without	*heb*	*heb*	*hep^X*	*hep^X*
-d	good	*mad*	*mad*	*mat^X, mad^N*	*mat^X, mad^N*
-g	ten, Breton *n~adj*	*deg, brezhoneg*	*deg, brezoneg (G –h–)*	*dek^X brezhoneg^N, -ek^X*	*dek^X, brezhoneg^N, -ek^X*
-s	big, dirty, husband	*bras, lous, gẁas*	*braz, louz*	*bras^X, lous^X, gwaz^N*	*bras^X, lous^X, gwaz^N*
oa	wood, forest	*koad*	*koad*	*koad*	*koad*
ao	table, shore	*taol, aot (pl. aochoù)*	*tôl~taol, ôt~aot*	*taol, aod^C*	*taol~tôl, aod^C, ôd^C*
awC	crotch, hunger	*gawl, nawn*	*gaol, naon*	*gaol, naon*	*gaol, naon*
aou	two, young	*daou, yaouank*	*daou, yaouank*	*daou, yaouank*	*daou, yaouank*
ae	milk	*laezh*	*lêz~laez (G lêh)*	*laezh*	*laez~lêz*
aë	thief	*laër*	*laer*	*laer*	*laer*
-añ, -iñ	pull~shoot, learn *inf.*	*tennañ, deskiñ~diskiñ*	*tenna, deski*	*tennañ, deskiñ*	*tenna, deski~diski*
an ar ul	the	*an, ar, ul*	*an, ar, al*	*an, ar, ul*	*an, ar, al*
un ur ul	a, an	*un, ur, ul*	*eun, eur, eul*	*un, ur, ul*	*eun, eur, eul*
-mp	in 1 pl endings	*-mp*	*-m*	*-mp*	*-mp*

C = consonant; V = vowel; ^{N} = nouns; ^{X} = all other categories (important distinction in ZH, KLT and Guened)

E: etymological, S. Hewitt, 1999; **OU**: orthographe universitaire, 1955; **ZH**: peurunvan/unifiée, 1941; **KLT**: Kerne-Leon-Treger, 1908–11; **Guened**: Guillevic-Le Goff, 1902 – systematization of traditional guened. also **ID**: interdialectale, 1975, precursor of E; introduced *s~ss/z~zz/zh~sh*, *-w-*, *-w*; has OU final *-b, -d, -g* in non-nouns, and ZH *-mp*.

Early Modern (1650–1911), mixture of **Middle Breton** (traditional *s~z* distinction starts slipping mainly in 19th c.) and KLT (*c'h; n* for *ñ*); Le Gonidec (1807) introduced *k* for *c, qu*, hard *g* for *gu*, *w* for *o, u*.

Table 11.11 *Summary of Breton Orthographies* (continued)

E item	English	Guened – 1902	Middle Breton – 1400–1650	Welsh cognate
f	nose, defend, belly	*fri, diùen, kof*	*fri, difen(n), cof~coff*	-, *amddiffyn*, -
ff	sly/end, spit, coif	*fin, tufein, koef*	*fin, tuffaff, coeff*	*ffin*, -, -
ż	sit, new	*azeein, neùé*	*asezaff, neuez~nevez*	*eistedd, newydd*
żż	newer	*neùéoh*	*neuezoch~zzoch~zhoch (-v-)*	*newyddach*
zh	old, port	*koh, porh*	*coz~cozz, porz~portz*	*coth* (Corn.), *porth*
zzh	oldest	*kohan*	*cozzaff, cozhaff*	*cotha* (Corn.)
s	look, mare, husband big, time, a lot	*sellet^x, kazeg^N, gwaz^N, bras^x, amzer, kalz*	*sellet, casec, guas~goas, bras, amser, cals*	*syllu, caseg, gwas bras, amser*, -
ss	bigger, sugar, place, sweet, person	*brasoh, sukr, plas, dous, person*	*brassoch (-sh-), czucr (ç, cz), placz, doucz (ç, çz), pers(s)on*	*brasach, siwgr, plas*, -, *person*
c'h (x)	dry *vb*	*sehein*	*sechaff*	*sychu*
c'h (xx)	driest	*sehan*	*sechaff*	*sychaf*
c'hwa (x)	play *vb*	*hoari*	*(c)huari, (c)hoari*	*chwarae*
c'hwoa (x)	sister	*hoer*	*(c)huoer, (c)hoer, (c)hoar*	*chwaer*
gẁa, ẁa	husband, be careful	*goaz^N, dioal*	*guas, goas, diual(l), dioal(l)*	*gwas, diwallu*
gẁoa	blood	*goed^x*	*guoed~goed~goad*	*gwaed*
c'hwe~i (x)	six, you *pl*	*hueh, hui*	*(c)huech, (c)hui*	*chwech, chwi*
gwe~i	white, wine	*guen, guin*	*guen(n), guin*	*gwyn, gwin*
w	colour, coloured	*liù, liùet^x*	*liu~liou, liuet~livet*	*lliw, lliwiedig*
	alive, live *vb*	*biù, biùein*	*beu~beo, beuaff~bevaff*	*byw, bywio*
	hair, strand of hair	*bleù, bleùenn*	*bleu~bleo, bleuen~bleven*	*blew, blewyn*
	rain, rainy	*glaù, glaùek^x*	*glau~glao, glauec~glavec*	*glaw, glawiog*
	dead, died	*marù, marùet^x*	*maru~maro, maruet~marvet*	*marw, (marwol)*
ñv	ill, illness	*klañù, kleñùed^N*	*claff, cleffet*	*claf, clefyd*
-b	without	*hep^x*	*hep*	*heb*
-d	good	*mat^x, mad^x*	*mat*	*mad*
-g	ten, Breton *n~adj*	*dek^x, brehoneg^N, -ek^x*	*dec, brezonec*	*deg, Brythoneg*
-s	big, dirty, husband	*bras^x, lous^x, goaz^N*	*bras, lous, guas~goas*	*bras*, -, *gwas*
oa	wood, forest	*koed*	*coet, coat*	*coed*
ao	table, shore	*taul, aud*	*taul~taul, aut~aot*	*taflen, allt* (cliff)
awC	crotch, hunger	*gaul, nan*	*gaul~gaol, naun~naon*	*gafl, newyn*
aou	two, young	*deù, iouank~ieùank*	*dou~daou, iouanc~iaouanc (y-)*	*dau, ieuanc*
ae	milk	*leh*	*laez, lez*	*llaeth*
aë	thief	*laer*	*lazr*	*lladr(on)*
-añ, -iñ	pull~shoot, learn *inf.*	*tennein, deskein*	*tennaff, desquiff~disquiff*	*tynnu, dysgu*
an ar ul	the	*en, er*	*an~en*	*y C, yr V, V'r*
un ur ul	a, an	*un, ur*	*un, vn*	- *(un)*
-mp	in 1 *pl* endings	*-mb*	*-mp, -m*	*-m (-n)*

C = consonant; V = vowel; ^{N} = nouns; ^{X} = all other categories (important distinction in ZH, KLT and Guened)
E: etymological, S. Hewitt, 1999; **OU**: orthographe universitaire, 1955; **ZH**: peurunvan/unifiée, 1941; **KLT**: Kerne-Leon-Treger, 1908–11; **Guened**: Guillevic-Le Goff, 1902 – systematization of traditional guened. also **ID**: interdialectale, 1975, precursor of E; introduced *s~ss/z~zz/zh~sh*, *-w-*, *-x*, has OU final *-b*, *-d*, *-g* in non-nouns, and ZH *-mp*.
Early Modern (1650–1911), mixture of **Middle Breton** (traditional *s~z* distinction starts slipping mainly in 19th c.) and KLT (*c'h; n* for *ñ*); Le Gonidec (1807) introduced *k* for *c, qu*, hard *g* for *gu*, *w* for *o, u*.

mononomic standard based on CK; but that would be to ignore the longstanding L and G written traditions and is thus quite out of the question.

ZH supporters dismiss the linguistic shortcomings of ZH by claiming that an orthography need not be phonetically exact and that proper pronunciation can always be taught, regardless of the orthography in use. While that is a defensible position, the fact is that good Breton pronunciation is almost never taught (see Madeg 2010; Ar Merser 1996; Le Ruyet 2009), with the disastrous results that one can hear daily from the great majority of learners.

If the Breton of the future is to be shorn of its native pronunciation and its unique syntax and idiom, arguments in favour of preserving it, with the activists' abnormally purist vocabulary, degenerate into little more than a kind of lexical xenophobia. Everything about the neo-speakers' Breton is French except the (to most native speakers) quite impenetrable stock of neologisms. On the other hand, one is bound to concede that prospects for the survival of traditional native Breton speech are now dim. The only form of Breton that is likely to persist, in small networks of aficionados, is that of learner-activist neo-speaker. Maintenance of ZH without any modification as the dominant orthography is likely to ensure that the Breton of the future in no way resembles the living language of traditional native speakers. It is no pleasant task to have to deliver this gloomy diagnosis and forecast.

Abbreviations

=	lenition (voicing of voiceless stops; spirantization of voiced stops and *m*)
/	provection (devoicing of obstruents)
≠	mixed mutation – lenition/provection
°	spirantization
1,2,3	first, second, and third persons
ALBB	*Atlas linguistique de la Basse-Bretagne* (Le Roux 1924–1963)
C	centre, central
E	East
E	Etymological orthography (Hewitt, stabilized from 1999)
EMT	Early Modern Traditional orthographies (pre-Le Gonidec)
F	feminine
F	fortis consonant
G	Gwened – Vannetais; standardized G orthography (1902)
ID	*Interdialectale/Etrerannyezhel* (1975) orthography
INF	infinitive
K	Kerne – Cornouaille
KI	Kerne Isel – Basse-Cornouaille

Breton Orthographies: An Increasingly Awkward Fit   233

KLT	Kerne-Leon-Treger (1908–1911) orthography
KU	Kerne Uhel – Haute-Cornouaille
L	lenis consonant
L	Leon – Léon
LG	Le Gonidec (1807–1847) orthography
lit.	literary
LP	Le Pelletier (1752) dictionary
M	masculine
MB	Middle Breton
ModB	Modern Breton
NALBB	*Nouvel atlas linguistique de la Basse-Bretagne* (Le Dû 2001)
N	North
OB	Old Breton
OU	*Orthographe universitaire/Skolveurieg* (1955) orthography
PL	plural
pop.	popular, non-literary
PROG	progressive particle
S	South
SG	singular
T	Treger – Trégor
W	West
ZH	*Peurunvan* (fully unified) orthography (1941)

Notes

1. http://upload.wikimedia.org/wikipedia/commons/a/ab/Distribution_relative_des_br ittophones_en_2004.png (last accessed 23 June 2015).
2. www.geobreizh.bzh/geobreizh/fra/carte-langue.asp (last accessed 23 June 2015).
3. OB /µ/, /β/, /δ/, /γ/ are intervocalic approximants, derived from Brythonic /m/, /b/, /d/, /g/. MB has true voiced fricatives: /ṽ/, /v/, /ð/, /ɣ/ (/ḥ/).
4. /v̱/ has more breath and friction than a normal /v/; it is the result of 'neo-lenition' of OB /f/. Neo-lenition = lenition/voicing of voiceless fricatives from Early MB. Thus, OB /f/, /β/ > MB, ModB /v̱/, /v/.
5. /ð̱/ had more breath and friction than a normal /ð/; it was the result of 'neo-lenition' of OB /θ/. Thus OB /θ/, /δ/ > MB /ð̱/, /ð/. ModB dialect reflexes are somewhat complex; see Table 11.5.
6. /ḥ/ is an abstract symbol representing a lenis fricative with various realizations, either with some velar friction [hˣ, ɣ, ɣ̊], etc., or a purely glottal voiceless [h], in which case it is not separate from /h/ (historically initial <h->); it is the result of 'neo-lenition' of OB /x/ *or* the reflex of OB /γ/ (the two fell together). Thus OB /x/, /γ/ > MB, ModB /ḥ/~/h/.

7. The MBr affricate variously written <cz>, <çz>, <çc>, <ç> – e.g., *danczal* 'dance', mainly from Old French <ç>, <z> – may have been dental /tθ/ rather than alveolar /ts/. That would account for the frequent (80–90%) use of <z> (MBr /θ/ /ð̞/, /ð/) in the grapheme, and also for the behaviour of certain Old French loanwords such as *voiz* 'voice' > MB *moez* ModB *mouezh*, where MB <z> ModB <zh> patterns exactly with the reflexes of OB /-θ/.
8. or <c'h>
9. or <c"h>
10. Effective mutation within a given type is in ***bold + italics***.
11. Provection is a phonetic process whereby a voiced consonant becomes unvoiced.
12. Also, variously, /xɥ/, /h̞ɥ/, /hɥ/, and, notoriously, in the far south-west, /f/. The important thing is that both /xw/ and /xɥ/ undergo neo-lenition.
13. Treger radical (unmutated) forms: *ssaro* /s-/, *sac'h* /z-/, *chupenn* /ʃ-/, *jiletenn* /ʒ-/, which means that Plogoneg lenites after the article where Treger has the voiced fricative as radical but does not lenite where Treger has the voiceless fricative as radical.

12 Spelling Trouble: Ideologies and Practices in Giernesiei/Dgernesiais/Guernesiais/ Guernésiais/Djernezié ...

Julia Sallabank and Yan Marquis

1 Introduction

The indigenous language of Guernsey is not standardized and has no official orthography. It is highly endangered, but there is a significant increase in demand for written Giernesiei. Examination of writing practices reveals a wide range of spellings, as well as inconsistencies between rhetoric and practices. Some speakers and learners, influenced by diglossic notions of 'correctness' and prestige, favour French-style spellings for Guernesiais, but most islanders are literate in English only. Language activists may focus on differentiation from dominant or related languages. Learners, meanwhile, may benefit from a systematic, transparent, practical spelling which recognizes the lack of ease involved in typing accents on English-style keyboards. The resolution of such tensions does not depend on impartial assessment of which orthography is the most efficient, but rather on community dynamics, which may be fluid and not immediately obvious. Given that the future of Dgernesiais rests with learners, it is important to develop an orthography that is useful for learners and teachers, yet acceptable to the remaining native speakers.

Guernsey is the second largest of the Channel Islands, in the Gulf of St Malo off Normandy. Each inhabited island formerly had its own variety of Norman, one of the Langue d'Oïl family of northern France. All the Channel Island Norman languages are now severely endangered; the authors estimate that there are currently only a couple of hundred fluent native speakers of Guernsey's indigenous language, mostly aged 80 or over. The authors are currently aware of only six speakers under the age of 60 who are able to hold a sustained, impromptu conversation on a range of topics (as there is no full linguistic description, there are no formal tests of proficiency). All the current speakers are bilingual or dominant in English.[1]

The Channel Islands are not members of the United Kingdom or the European Union. Nevertheless, British cultural influence is strong, and the nineteenth and twentieth centuries saw almost complete language shift from the indigenous Norman languages to English. There is also a history of French as the 'High' language in a diglossic relationship which lasted from the fifteenth to the twentieth century. French was used in religion, courts of law, politics, and schools, and its prestige still influences linguistic ideologies and practices, especially in the areas of writing, teaching, and performance (Marquis and Sallabank 2014). The research in this chapter is based on semi-structured and ethnographic interviews conducted by Sallabank with over fifty speakers, 'semi-speakers', latent/post-latent speakers, and 'new speakers' or learners of Guernesiais, as well as on examples of writing in Giernesiei collected by both authors.

1.1   What's in a Name – and Its Spelling

Despite the establishment of a government language commission in 2013,[2] Guernsey's language has no official recognition, and its continuing low status is reflected by the fact that it does not even have an official name. It is often known as 'Guernsey French', and also as 'the Patois'.[3] In our research, speakers express preference for the name /ˌdʒɛrnɛzjeɪ/, which is often spelt *Guernésiais*, following the De Garis dictionary (re-issued 2012; see Section 1.3), but alternative spellings in use include *Guernesiais, Guernesiaise* (sic.), *Dgernesiais, Giernesiei*, and *Djernezié*. The last three examples are attempts to demonstrate the pronunciation of the name more accurately, as it is generally mispronounced by Anglophones. The following post on the Guernsey Society Facebook page (24 October 2012), discussing the publication of a children's language guide, *Warro!* (Dowding and Marquis 2012), which is supplemented by online videos,[4] illustrates the problem:

Can I ask about the pronunciation of 'Guernesiaise'? The chap in the vid[5] pronounces it 'jern-uh-si-ai'. I'd always thought of it as 'Gern-uh-si-ays'. Is it a matter of opinion or am I definitely wrong? Always happy to learn.

This common mispronunciation is exacerbated by the spelling *Guernésiais*, especially the initial <gu> and the acute accent on the second syllable (the latter seems to be interpreted as a stress marker, as in Spanish), as well as the <–s> on the end, all of which together lead to the pronunciation /gɜːrˌnɛziɛz/ – used so frequently in broadcast media that it has virtually become an unofficial name for the language. Unfortunately, other spellings (e.g., *Dgernesiais*) also lead to problematic pronunciations such as /dgɜːrnɛziɛz/. This chapter will mainly use the spellings *Guernesiais* and *Giernesiei*, reflecting the authors' own preferences and the general inconsistency found in writings.

1.2 Language Variation and Change

There are several types of variation in Guernesiais. First, the traditional regional dialects divide into two main groups: the West, known as the *haut pas* or 'high country', and the North, the *bas pas* or 'low country'. These are distinguished chiefly by vowel diphthongization, more 'advanced' palatalization such as /kj/ > /tʃ/, and some lexical differences. Regional variation within Guernesiais is a core value for many speakers and is seen as a source of richness (Sallabank 2010), but also as a disadvantage when it comes to writing. Iconic regional variants such as /o/ ~ /aʊ/ are frequently cited as reasons why Giernesiei cannot be standardized, or even written. And a perceived lack of written texts is often cited as a reason why Giernesiei cannot be taught – a circular argument which is moreover unsupported by evidence, as there is a considerable corpus of literature in Guernesiais.[6] The second type of variation that is relevant to spelling is age related. Ferguson (2013) conducted an apparent-time study with approximately fifty speakers of Giernesiei (aged 42–100), comparing the grammatical usage of older and younger speakers and their self-reported language practices during their childhood and nowadays. She commented that ongoing change poses a challenge when compiling reference materials: at what stage of development should the language be codified, and whose usage is taken as canonical? And as we point out in Marquis and Sallabank (2014), who decides? Third, there is contact-influenced change. As noted earlier, there has been considerable Anglicization in Guernsey over the past two centuries (Jones 2002; Crossan 2007), and influence from English can be seen even in early nineteenth-century writings.

All languages change, but, as discussed in Marquis and Sallabank (2013 and 2014), this is not always accepted by speakers. Purist reactions are common, especially in language revitalization contexts, where contact influence from majority languages is often perceived as degeneration and/or as pernicious. Moreover, purism in Giernesiei is often influenced by the prestige of French. The result is rejection of innovations or neologisms: 'changing the language' is equated with influence from English, while influence from French (which could be argued as equally pernicious) goes unnoticed, ignored, or even preferred. This has implications for ideologies of 'correctness' in spelling.

1.3 The Role of French

In Guernsey during the nineteenth century, French was the language of administration, education, religion, and culture (Girard 1978; Crossan 2005; Métivier 1866). Given this situation, and the relatedness of

Guernesiais to French, it is understandable that nineteenth-century writers who wrote in Guernesiais adopted French-style spellings. Readers would undoubtedly have been familiar with the spelling conventions of French, so, armed with this and their knowledge of Dgernesiais, they would have been able to read and understand the texts with minimal effort. It is also probable that the adoption of a French-style orthography could have been an attempt to raise the status of Giernesiei by association (Lebarbenchon 1980): this is the likely origin of the ideology which maintains that French spelling conventions should determine how Guernesiais is written. This ideology continued into the twentieth century and on into the twenty-first; however, spelling practices were (and are) not uniform, and texts often display idiosyncratic spellings (see Section 3).

The first dictionary of Guernesiais was compiled by George Métivier (1870), who has been called 'Guernsey's national poet' (Girard 1980). The reference language of this dictionary was French, for the reasons stated in this section. Although Métivier's spelling in this dictionary, and in his poetry, is clearly influenced by French, it is also possible to discern similarities with that used in the eleventh-century Anglo-Norman epic poem *La Chanson de Roland* (Bédier 1968) – such as <k> for /k/ where French would use <qu>, possibly a conscious evocation of past status.

In 1967, the first edition of the *Dictiounnaire Angllais–Guernésiais* [English–Guernésiais Dictionary] (De Garis 1967) was published, marking a milestone in the history of written Guernésiais. The *Dictiounnaire* embodies the ideology of French-style spellings as 'correct'; however, the use of English for word definitions reflected the reality of language shift in Guernsey, where English had become the dominant language.[7] Even some native speakers feel that it includes too much French influence in both spelling and word choice (cf. Hull, this volume). One interviewee commented:

Ya dei paraul la dau ké jé jomei wi – shé reid du fraessei.[8]
[There are words in there that I've never heard – it's very French.] (Native speaker, 80s)

Although French-style spelling of Guernesiais is overtly preferred by linguistic 'purists' (often termed 'traditionalists'), there are a number of problems associated with its use. First, Giernesiei has sounds that French does not, such as diphthongs and affricates /dʒ/ and /tʃ/, and which French spelling is ill equipped to deal with. Second, since 1905, most Guernsey people have been educated through English and are not familiar with French spelling conventions, leading to the kinds of problems noted in Section 1.1. Third, French influence in writing can influence pronunciation and vocabulary. If readers are familiar with French, they may converge towards French pronunciation, as can be heard on the CD *Les Travailleurs De La Mer* (Lawrence-King 2004), which sets some of Métivier's and traditional rhymes to music (cf. Hewitt, this volume). Some critics therefore see the use of French-based spelling as a threat to the autonomy of Giernesiei (e.g., Ainger 1995). Several interviewees commented that Métivier's writing should not be seen as representative of modern Giernesiei as it is 'too Frenchified':

> If you talk to somebody of my mother's age, they'll look at those poems and they'll be a bit double-dutch because they're quite – those people like Corbet and Métivier and so on, they were quite erudite weren't they? [...] In the Eisteddfod in the past, one or two people have recited poems like that, and the reaction very often from people in the audience is 'Oh, we didn't understand a word of that. What was it?' It's not your common or garden patois as they know it, you know – it's the sort of élite almost. (Semi-speaker, 60s)

A further consideration concerns the use of apostrophes – e.g., in *Bian-v'nus à not'e d'meure* ('welcome to our home') – to indicate where French would insert <e> or <r>. Such practices can support the perception/detraction that Giernesiei is a 'corrupted' form of French.

The importance of maintaining access to the nineteenth-century flowering of literature in Guernesiais is sometimes stressed by supporters of French-style orthography. However, although admittedly French influence is strong in this genre, by no means did all earlier writers follow its conventions, as can be seen in *The Toad and the Donkey*, a collection of literature from Jersey and Guernsey (Jennings and Marquis 2011), and examples in Section 3. The majority of materials written and published to date have not been intended for pedagogical use, and therefore little or no attempt has been made to assist potential learners who struggle, like many speakers, when decoding the French-style spellings. This is discussed further in Section 4.

2 Approaches to Literacy and Orthography

Orthodox Western language ideologies hold standardized, written languages in higher esteem than non-written ones; many minority language supporters therefore feel than a standardized written form is essential for raising the status of their language (cf. Hull, and Esteban, this volume). Conversely, because the High language fulfils the functions and domains for which literacy is required, there is no context for which literacy in the local language is absolutely necessary (Grenoble and Whaley 2006:103; Lüpke 2011). Debates about orthography are therefore not only about the merits of different spelling systems, but also about which domains a language should be promoted in. It can also be argued that focusing on orthography (and, by association, standardization) is a consequence of a 'top-down' ideology of language planning that valorizes literacy and formal education (Schieffelin et al. 1998:17;

cf. Lai, this volume) over oral language use in the community, in domains traditionally occupied by minority language varieties as prioritized by Fishman (1991, 2001).

Following the work of Street (1984) and Grenoble and Whaley (2006), we distinguish between two main approaches to literacy and orthography: an 'autonomous' approach which considers writing to be a neutral technology that can be detached from its social context, and an 'ideological' or 'social literacies' approach which takes into account speakers' purposes for reading and writing, and their contexts of use. Linguists creating orthographies for previously unwritten languages tend to follow an autonomous model where graphemes (letters, characters, etc.) are matched to a phonemic inventory of the language. 'Optimal' orthographies are considered to be ones that offer the most 'efficient' technical solutions to 'problems' such as homonyms, homophones, and regional variation. Principles of orthography which take an autonomous approach include:

(i) To represent the phonemic system of the spoken language
(ii) To reflect the structure of the language in a transparent way
(iii) To avoid confusion due to homonyms and homographs
(iv) To cater for allophones (as identified by linguists)
(v) To reflect etymology
(Fishman 1977; Vikør 1993; Ostler and Rudes 2000)

However, Hinton (2014:140) comments that 'code-external' considerations often override the 'code-internal' factors that linguists hold dear, citing Sebba's (2007:14) comment that orthography is not just a systematized set of letters and spelling rules but also something 'fundamentally ideological' (cf. Hull, this volume). Principles of orthography development which take into account social factors might include:

(i) Reflecting the main domains and genres of use and their history
(ii) Widening domains of use and genres if desired
(iii) Taking into account oral practices
(iv) Using a writing system that is not too unfamiliar if speakers already read and write another language
(v) Taking into account available technology and typefaces
(vi) Distinguishing the language from others

Some of these principles are, of course, contradictory, especially in the second list. We will discuss their relevance to Giernesiei below, with reference to recent examples of writing.

2.1   Ideological Factors in Writing in an Endangered Language

Teaching a language is often a key impetus for orthography creation, revision, or standardization. However, Littlebear (2007:xi) warns that 'Teaching our languages as if they had no oral tradition is one factor which contributes to the failures of our Native American language teaching programs'. In addition to ideological concerns, we have observed in lessons that focus on written form can hinder the development of oral fluency. Bearing in mind these points, as well as Schieffelin et al.'s (1994, 1998) caution about 'buying into' a standardizing ideology, we can identify several reasons for writing in an endangered language such as Giernesiei.

As is the case for many low-status vernaculars, the use of Giernesiei remained largely oral until the nineteenth century; it is still written by relatively few people. For promoters of a language with a primarily oral tradition, one debate concerns to what extent its domains can and should be extended. As illustrated by Johnson (2013), promotion of Guernesiais is often through hypertraditionalized genres: enthusiast groups tend to concentrate on folk songs and dance, poetry, 'traditional' tales, and comic plays as tangible ways of expressing their attachment to the language, which may then become stereotypically 'associated with an unsophisticated, nonlearned folk culture' (Watson 1989:49, writing about Scottish and Irish Gaelic). However, debates about domains do not necessarily follow the archetypal patterns of diglossia. Attempts to extend the use of Guernesiais to domains (or genres) such as social media, which have become staples of everyday communication and thus arguably part of Low domains, are not always welcomed by traditionalists and purists, whereas extra-curricular school lessons and church services that include Guernesiais are encouraged. Domain and genre reflect audience and purpose, and therefore orthographic preferences. Traditional(ist) written genres such as plays are more likely to be read by older native speakers, while new domains and genres are more likely to reflect the interests and needs of new speakers.

Recently we have observed a significant increase in demand for written Giernesiei, in a wide variety of genres: e.g., signage, slogans, tattoos, jewellery, social media, song writing, and art, as well as in language-learning contexts. Increasingly, these examples seem to reflect postvernacular language use, in short formats rather than the traditional forms of storytelling and plays. Indeed, few such original pieces are now being written in Guernesiais, which may be a manifestation of changing demographics, both in the loss of fluency and in changing interests. Musical expression in Giernesiei is also being pushed into new genres by the Song Project initiated by the Guernsey Language Commission to produce new songs which include some Giernesiei.[9] Activists and language planners may wish to increase the amount of their language visible in the 'linguistic landscape' or print environment in order to increase or reclaim status for it, or to raise awareness, since some people are unaware that Guernsey has its own language. This is manifested in the inclusion of Giernesiei in the branding of some local products and services – e.g., coffee, bus timetables, notices at an agricultural show. Another ideological factor is the iconic nature of certain elements of orthography (Sebba 2007), some of which are discussed in Section 4. As particular written forms and orthographical conventions can become associated with particular ideologies or groups, spelling 'can be a lightning rod for all the personal, social and political issues that wrack speech communities' (Hinton 2014:140).

A key motivation in orthography development for a minoritized language, especially one frequently seen as a dialect of a more powerful neighbour, is *Ausbau* (Kloss 1967, 1993; Trudgill 1992): establishing or demarcating a linguistic identity by emphasizing features that distinguish it from a *Dachsprache* (literally 'roof language' – a related, neighbouring, dominant language). Orthography can be a key tool in such strategies: for example, supporters of Gallo, a Romance variety of Eastern Brittany which is closely related to Norman, sometimes follow Breton-style spelling (Rey 2010). *Ausbau* can, of course, run counter to pragmatic use of an orthography familiar to community members. In Guernsey, there are two *Dachsprachen* (French and English) and thus two spelling conventions to potentially avoid or converge with.

3   Perceptions and Practices

The De Garis dictionary is currently the only Guernésiais reference work in circulation, and it enjoys high prestige in Guernsey, especially among traditional speakers. It is assumed by some to represent a de facto 'standard' spelling: for example, adjudicators at the annual Eisteddfod language competition exhorted entrants in the 'written short story' class introduced in 2005 to use its spelling. However, the dictionary is by no means fully consistent, especially between the original English–Guernesiais section and the Guernesiais–English wordlist added in the 1982 edition. Table 12.1 shows not only how the phoneme /dʒ/ is spelt in several ways, but also the inconsistency in definitions.

Table 12.1 *Variations in spellings of the phoneme /dʒ/ (De Garis 1982,* Dictiounnaire Angllais–Guernésiais*)*.

Dictiounnaire entry		Pronunciation
p. 74	**group** *n*. djaine, guaine	/dʒeɪn/
p. 242	**dgère, guère** *adj*. few	/dʒɛːr/
p. 242	**dguaine** *n.f.* circle of people, throng	/dʒeɪn/
p. 242	**djère** *adj*. few	/dʒɛːr/
p. 254	**guainnaïe, guaine** (soft g) *n.f.* mob, gang, crowd	/dʒenaɪ/, /dʒeɪn/

The *Dictiounnaire* also gives little guidance on pronunciation (apart from indicating 'soft g' in some instances, which itself is confusing, as it might refer to /ʤ/ or /ʒ/ and is not stated in all cases). Fluent speakers, learners, and latent speakers wishing to re-activate their Giernesiei all find this confusing:

> The funny thing is it's like you look in here [*Dictiounnaire*], and for me it's like, 'How would I say that?' – you know the Guernsey French – and then of course you hear it, and it's like, 'Ah!' that means something [...] [I]n terms of pronunciation, like I say, I actually find it quite hard, but you listen to it and I can understand it. (Latent speaker, 60s)

In Sallabank's PhD research (2007), a questionnaire on language use was distributed through La Société Guernesiaise (a local-interest society) and face-to-face interviews; in total, 120 responses were analysed. Relatively few reported writing in Guernesiais, of whom most claimed to use the *Dictiounnaire* spelling. There is a notion amongst some members of the speech community of unstated boundaries of acceptability based on the spelling conventions of French, as discussed in Section 1.3. Nevertheless, an examination of practices shows that writers (including self-identified 'traditionalists') often deviate from both French conventions and the *Dictiounnaire*. In the following poem, divergences in both spelling and French-style agreement of silent grammatical endings are underlined.

> Nous vait les pus viarr
> Se torchier les yiars
> Dauve les manches d'leux bllu corsets d'loine
> I' pense au passaï
> Et n sont jaumais lassaï
> D'pallaï des Regates de Rocquoine.
>
> [We can see the oldest men
> Wiping their eyes
> With the sleeves of their blue woollen jumpers
> They think of the past
> And never tire
> Of talking about the Rocquaine Regatta.]
>
> (Helier d'Rocquoine: *Les Regates de Rocquoine*)

It transpired from talking to writers, as well from our own experience, that it is very laborious to check every word in the *Dictiounnaire*, especially given its internal inconsistency. One official who was asked to translate a 176-word statement for the British-Irish Council website told Sallabank that it had taken all morning since he was at pains to check each word in the dictionary.[10] So writers tend only to look up words they are not sure of.

More examples of divergence include:
(i) /w/ may be written <w> instead of French <ou> as in *waique* ['where'] (Ozanne in Hill 2000:9)
(ii) Silent 3PL plural markers may be omitted, e.g.,
Par example[11] *nos etats vianne_ d'avai des expaert_ a [...]* [For example, our States (government) have just had some experts to ...] (Girard in the *Island Independent* 1988:11);
Les mouissaons qu'ôime_ iaöue [The birds that love the water] rather than *ôiment* (Jehan 1999, 'Au Réservoir')
(iii) Second and third person markers on verbs may interchange:
Si nous veras des crabbes [if we will see some crabs] rather than *verra*;
Viant vais chique j'ai bâti [Come and see what I have built] instead of *Vians* (Les Ravigotteurs 1999:1,7)
(iv) /tʃ/ may be written using the English digraph <ch> and not the French-influenced <tch> (see previous example as well as the Martin extract later in this section)
(v) /ʃ/ may be written using the English digraph <sh>, not the French <ch>:
Shaiqu'il tait papiste ... [Wasn't he houseproud/meticulous ...] (Ozanne in Hill 2000:47);
shâre /ʃɑːr/ ('share'– 1/2/3SG) (Grut 1927, 'Les Ormars');
Et bian tous lés coue que j'vians ishin v'la shü que j'vait, shés l'viàr assis a la tablle a berre du thée ét fumaïr sa pipe. Eche que vous avaï pas au-tchaöse a faire? [Well, every time I come here what do I see, it's the old man sitting at the table, drinking some tea and smoking his pipe. Don't you have anything else to do?] (Mabel Torode, 'Aen Baté' ['A Boat'], unpublished manuscript)

This last extract was written for reading aloud in a theatrical performance, and the spelling is simple, mostly consistent, following De Garis' spelling in part but departing from it to make certain aspects of pronunciation clearer for non-French-speaking readers (one interviewee went out of her way to praise Mrs Torode's spelling for this). The emphasis is on pronunciation rather than on transparency of grammatical features (e.g., no silent <s> on the end of *coue* ['time'] or <z> on *avaï* [have-2PL], as would be used in French). An umlaut <ü> is used for /y/, as in German, although elsewhere this diacritic is used as a diaeresis similarly to French, to emphasize vowels in a diphthong.

If a text written in French-style spelling is intended to be read by the general public (both speakers and non-speakers), or read aloud for a performance, a 'phonetic' (i.e., English-style) guide is often used; some teaching materials follow this practice, sometimes in addition to *Dictiounnaire*-style orthography. A problem associated with this approach is that English does not have consistent sound–spelling correspondences (although individual words are spelt consistently), so readers have a choice of ways in which to interpret the spellings. The following example is a Christmas carol transcribed for recitation at the Eisteddfod festival. Although relatively systematic, its spelling nevertheless fails to accommodate all of the sounds of Giernesiei (e.g., nasal diphthongs or /y/):

>Trajy la nyay, lay jor de nway
>Lay p'tee Jaysoo foo nye,
>Dons en etarb, parmy lay bate,
>Dong l'kwang Josaf fee son yay.   (From the collection of Doris Heaume)

The largest corpus of written Guernesiais is from the pen of Guernseyman Thomas Martin (1839–1921), who translated the Bible and over a hundred plays from the works of Shakespeare, Pierre and Thomas Corneille, Molière, Voltaire, and Longfellow into Guernesiais. Martin's spellings are idiosyncratic and often diverge widely from French spelling conventions while developing over time (Jones 2008). This large corpus is generally ignored by members of the speech community despite its usefulness as a source of material for festivals. In the following extract, a mixture of Martin's own orthography and French conventions (here silent plural -*s*) can be seen:

>Auve daie douces roses muskies et auve de vertes arbres
>
>[With sweet musk-roses, and with eglantine]
>
>Berchie dans sh'aie fyieurs la auve dans'ries et pyaiezi
>
>[Lulled in these flowers with dances and delight]
>   (Martin, translation of Shakespeare's *A Midsummer's Night Dream*)

In addition to these adaptations of French and English conventions, some 'middle generation' speakers (in their 60s and 70s) have developed their own original ways of writing Giernesiei, for their own purposes (unrelated to performance). For example:

LEH WEET DE JORNVEH DEEZE-NUR SHORE NORNAT WEET JEYETAE SESATT AH

[The eighth of January nineteen hundred ninety-eight I have been[12] sixty years [old] (our insertion)]

This orthography is quite systematic, using conventions such as:
(i) English-style <EE> for /i/
(ii) Lack of indication of nasalization, which is reduced among many speakers: e.g., <OR> for /ɔ̃:/, <AT> for /ɛ̃t/

(iii) <J> is used for /ʒ/, as in French
(iv) <H> for a nasal in 'AH', /ɛ̃/ ('years'); this has also been noticed in other writers.

Another speaker, in his late 60s, uses horizontal brackets over two or three letters to indicate elisions and nasals. This is difficult to reproduce typographically, which contradicts one of the principles of orthographies that take into account social factors listed in Section 2, such as available technology and typefaces (cf. Casquite and Young, and Sackett, this volume).

Reproducibility is relevant given that there is increasing use of written Giernesiei in the print environment: both 'traditional' and 'new' speakers are using Giernesiei in social media; and what might be seen as 'symbolic' Guernesiais is seen in non-traditional contexts such as shop signs, T-shirts, car bumper stickers, tattoos, and jewellery. As with the examples reproduced here, a range of spellings can be seen. There are also sometimes unfortunate errors, some of which are due to copying by non-speakers (or to how they feel Guernesiais 'should' look); others are due to mistranslation. For example, the Guernsey Football Club commissioned T-shirts with a translation of its slogan 'Faster, braver, smarter', which was rendered as *Pus brâve, pus fort, pus malin*. This too was discussed on social media, where, in response to a request for a 'reverse' translation, Yan Marquis pointed out that *brâve* is not a word he has heard people use in Giernesiei. It can be argued that both the orthographic and lexical choices here are influenced by notions of 'correctness' from French.

Such examples seem to illustrate a desire to express emotions through local language – perhaps as an expression of ethnolinguistic identity in a postvernacular setting (Shandler 2006) rather than as a means of communication. As such, they do not need to be accurate, just express the 'the idea of Guernesiais'. They are also effective in raising awareness of the language and its endangerment, thus satisfying another of the principles of 'social' orthographies. In response to the post about the football club slogan, another person commented, 'How cool. We need more signs in Patois. It's a dying language and that's sad.' Marquis replied that efforts were being made to revitalize it, to which the response was 'How can we help?'

As described earlier, the Guernsey Song Project is a recent initiative to write songs at least partly in Guernesiais. The project was also designed to encourage interaction between new/non-speakers (mainly musicians) and older, more proficient speakers – a variation on the master-apprentice mentoring approach to language revitalization. The initiative's name in Guernesiais is *la sharsan* /lɑ ʃæsæ̃ₙ/ ('the song'), while the pairing of musicians and speakers is called *ley bohti* /lei bɔti/ ('the buddies') – both written in non-traditional spellings. During the writing process, lyrics were written down using the writers' own preferred notations, probably to help them remember pronunciation: for example, *remuke teh pournais* /rmuk tei pɔːneɪː/ ('shake your parsnips', i.e., 'hurry up'), which includes a mixture of English- and French-style conventions. Finished versions may be edited for 'correctness' by the Guernesiais-speaking partner, but may nevertheless diverge from the *Dictiounnaire*. For example, one includes:

maïre instead of *maïr* /mɑɪr/ ('sea')

veir instead of *veies* /veɪː/ ('to see'); *veir* may be influenced by French *voir*

In his report on experiments in teaching Guernesiais, Tomlinson (1994) remarks that it is difficult for modern learners in a school situation to learn without taking notes (which is also our experience), so the lack of a consistent and practical spelling system hampers learners. We have gathered examples of the ways in which adult learners write down vocabulary and phrases, as well as annotations made on learning materials. Some learners use a mixture of English- and French-inspired spellings or alternate between the two, for example:

Bailler a haut ('give up, retire'), written according to *Dictiounnaire* and French conventions apart from one missing accent, immediately followed by

Souchorne[13] ('support/hold'-3PL)

Another learner, who does not speak French, rewrote the word *bere* /bɛːr/ ('to drink') on a worksheet as <bear>. This is an example of a mnemonic strategy to aid pronunciation, but also of the tendency of English-dominant learners to prefer English-style orthographies (Hinton 2014; cf. Sackett, Hull, and Leggio and Matras, this volume). A further problem, found through lesson observations, is that learners cannot always decode or remember their own notations, especially when they include unfamiliar sounds (not found in English or French) – e.g., <bahk> for /bɛ̃k/ ('beach') was later read back as /bɑːk/.

It is noticeable that most Dgernesiais writings contain considerable inconsistency, both internally and compared to each other. One 'solution' is the acceptance of variability in spelling (including a certain latitude for error). For example, the *Bulletins* of L'Assembllaie d'Guernesiais include short stories and poems that until the late 1990s were written only in Giernesiei but now include English translations. From the 1970s to the 1990s, the introductory pages carried this statement:

Notaai s'y vous pllait: L'Epellage dans [des] les articles du Bulletin a etaai lesi a la discretion des contri[b]uables.

[Please note: spelling in the articles of the Bulletin has been left to the discretion of the contributors.][14]

However, returning to the notion of acceptability, the back cover of *Histouaires Guernésiaises* – a recent publication using what might be described as a 'traditional' orthography – seems to suggest acceptance of alternative spellings, scope for the development of a system for learners, and a move away from the perceived 'tradition': 'Guernsey-French was an unwritten language and therefore there is no "right" way of spelling words when writing it' (Tomlinson 2009).

Although it is tempting to interpret inconsistent spelling as liberating compared with following the rules that apply when writing in French or English, lack of consistency in spelling Guernesiais is due as much to lack of literacy training as to any rebelliousness against standardization – nobody has ever been taught how to read and write in Giernesiei. However, as discussed in Section 4, readers have to be quite fluent to cope with variation in spelling. 'Free spelling' is unhelpful for language learners, who are likely to constitute an increasingly important readership when a highly endangered language is being revitalized.

4 Discussion and Proposals

4.1 Purposes and Readership(s)

To date, the purposes of writing, and the intended readership, have been missing from discussions of how Giernesiei should be spelt. The readership of traditional genres and texts is small and dwindling, while demand for texts in new domains is growing, as is the number of people who want to learn Giernesiei as a second language. The use of 'phonetic' (i.e., English-style) pronunciation aids seems to support the argument that a revised, simplified orthography could help learners.

The majority of both 'traditional' and 'new' writing in Giernesiei (in all genres, published and unpublished) seems not to be intended for communication, but rather for symbolic purposes: for performance, identity construction, or awareness-raising. In contrast, the authors of this chapter e-mail, text, and post Facebook and Twitter messages in Giernesiei at least once a week – to our knowledge the most frequent use of written Giernesiei at the present time. Unlike most of the examples that have been given, our e-mails have real communicative purpose. Over the last six to eight years, we have been experimenting with spelling systems and discuss the results here.

Given that Dgernesiais is highly endangered, our efforts in the past six years have focused on documenting the speech of the last fluent speakers. Our aim is to use the data to produce learning materials – initially for adults, as we see the most urgent problem as the lack of proficient younger adults, without whom there can be no children learning the language. Both the transcription of recordings (to create a searchable corpus of language in use) and materials development are hampered by the lack of a systematic orthography.

Research into reading indicates that 'deep' orthographies – which prioritize grammatical or etymological information over phonology (e.g., French, English, Chinese) – are not necessarily problematic for fluent speakers and readers of a language. But inconsistency *is* problematic, especially for second-language learners: it makes it difficult to decode pronunciation and meaning and to develop reading fluency. A shallow orthography (i.e., with clear sound–spelling correspondences) is easier for beginning readers to process (Wallace 1992; Grenoble and Whaley 2006:142). As shown in Section 3, neither traditional nor new speakers' spelling practices are clear or consistent. Grenoble and Whaley (2006:142) comment that 'It is therefore important to keep the act of learning to read and write as simple as possible, and so orthographies for communities creating revitalization programs should be designed primarily with beginning readers in mind.' A consistent, transparent, and simplified orthography for Giernesiei is therefore increasingly necessary.

In 2013, two Facebook pages were set up by learners, with the aim of providing a forum for written expression without correction or criticism. Some 'new speakers' also started tweeting in Giernesiei. Some (but by no means all) of these social media writings use French-style spellings, for example:

Cor chapin! I fait caoud durnant[15] *la niet*
[Gosh! It's hot in the night.]

Raide embarrasi chutte serai dans les courtils de St Pierre Very busy this evening in the fields of St. P
[translation provided, with a photo of a combine harvester][16]

It is likely that (despite errors) both of these writers consulted the *Dictiounnaire*, possibly for pragmatic reasons given that it is the only dictionary available, but issues of audience and purpose are also relevant. First, there might be a degree of self-censorship, as a few 'traditionalists' also read the Facebook page. Second, if posts do not include a translation, supporters who do not understand Giernesiei often demand one ('What does it mean?!'). As some of these followers know French, it seems that some writers prioritize clarity of meaning over reflection of pronunciation through their spelling choices.

4.2   Orthography as Process

Learners of Giernesiei frequently struggle with pronunciation and complain about lack of exposure to oral input. Although French-style spelling may be felt to clarify meaning, for Giernesiei to survive as a living, spoken language, writing also needs to clarify pronunciation. As noted by Grenoble and Whaley (2006), learners of endangered languages are more reliant on written materials than learners of languages of wider communication, as they are unlikely to have much exposure to the language outside lessons; this is the case in Guernsey. We have therefore developed what we term 'Progressive Learner Spelling' (hereafter, PLS). As the name implies, this orthography is intended to aid learners, not native-speaker writers. It is flexible and responsive: for example, we have altered our proposed spelling of /ɔ:/ from <aw> to <au> to accommodate learners' observed usage, where French-style spelling uses <en> (sometimes <an>), which frequently has a negative impact on pronunciation.

Other considerations we have taken into account include:
(i) Keeping diacritics to a minimum (cf. Moseley, Shah and Brenzinger, Esteban, and Leggio and Matras, this volume) to accommodate English keyboards
(ii) Systematic phonemic representation
(iii) Avoiding unsounded letters
(iv) Dialect variation (e.g., <iao> to represent /jaw/ or /jo/ 'water') (cf., for example, Hewitt, and Lai, this volume)
(v) Avoiding unnecessary multiple vowels (e.g., <iaoue> 'water', in the *Dictiounnaire*)
(vi) Inclusion of some 'iconic' features of 'traditional' spellings
(vii) *Ausbau*, or distanciation

Distanciation is supported by the Guernsey Language Commission, which stresses the need to refer to 'Guernsey's language', not 'Guernsey French' (personal communication, 2014). This is partly to avoid the need to tackle the pronunciation of the name *Giernesiei*, but also to stress autonomy. The principle of *Ausbau* can, however, mean that the PLS can look 'foreign'; for this reason, we feel that it is also important to retain some spellings which have become iconic features of writing in Guernesiais: e.g., <eu> for /œ/, <aon> for /æ̃ŋ/, and <ll> for palatalized l or /ʎ/ before high vowels after stop consonants (*l mouillé*, 'moistened l' in French). The PLS also includes some of the practices of earlier writers such as Métivier and Ozanne, including <k> and <sh>.

A further issue is source orthographies. One option might be to base a systematic orthography on 'traditional' (French-based) usage with inconsistencies ironed out. Another could be to base it on English phonemic representation. However, as noted earlier, neither fully represents all the phonemes of Dgernesiais. A further option might be to look to the spelling conventions of other Romance languages which have undergone similar phonological development to that of Giernesiei with regard to Latin *bl, cl, fl, gl, pl*: e.g., Italian *bianco, chiave, fiore, ghiaccio*; the use of <ll> for palatalized l (and, by extension, /j/) is a Spanish convention. A fourth possibility might be to start from scratch with a new but systematic sound–spelling correspondence. However, these suggestions need to be tempered by a reminder that the majority of adult learners are (only) familiar with English spelling conventions.

Reactions to our proposals have been mixed. Despite Holton's (2009:252) suggestion that some learner-oriented reform is 'so radically different that it escapes puristic corrections from elders', it is perhaps inevitable that the PLS is rejected without consideration by prominent traditionalists. They are not, however, its target audience; our concern is primarily to increase the number and proficiency of new speakers, and already there are some indications that using this spelling seems to improve learners' pronunciation. Nevertheless, many learners desire access to older writings. Despite common perceptions, by no means all of these follow French conventions, as shown in Section 3; arguably, the main problem in accessing these writings is their inconsistency. The key to this problem is increased fluency. Once a new speaker is familiar with the spoken forms of Guernesiais, it becomes much easier to match a written form with a representation in the mental aural lexicon. We argue that the PLS offers significant advantages in terms of attaining fluency.

Given local language ideologies and sensitivities, it would nevertheless be advantageous to have public support or sanctioning from an official body such as the Guernsey Language Commission, which has embraced the need to increase the number of younger adult speakers. Awareness-raising and *Ausbau* seem to strike a chord with political goals to emphasize local distinctiveness and 'island branding', and so ideological factors in orthography choice may coincide with political agendas (see Sallabank 2013).

4.3   Conclusion: New Speakers – New Orthographies?

The future of highly endangered languages such as Guernesiais lies with 'new' speakers', who are starting to write the language in ways that suit their needs. 'Rememberers' (Grinevald and Bert 2011) and semi- or latent speakers who want to 're-activate' their Dgernesiais are important in language revitalization; but the majority of people under the age of 50 who want to learn Giernesiei are second-language speakers with little or no prior experience of the language. They are mainly monolingual and literate in English, and many have little knowledge of French and its spelling conventions.

Social media and learners' notes can provide 'crowd-sourced' spellings as an alternative to 'top-down standardization', so we encourage learners and 're-activating' latent speakers to 'have a go' at using their own spelling ideas.

Admittedly, lack of language knowledge can lead to odd spellings and grammatical forms; these will either disappear with increasing fluency or will become part of the Giernesiei of the future. A crucial issue is whose voices are heard in the development of a language. Should spelling be a 'link to the past' or a 'bridge to the future', in the words of one of Sallabank's students? 'Hypertraditionalization' and the valorization of 'last speakers' are common themes in endangered language discourses, so until recently little or no allowance has been made for the needs or views of new speakers. We argue that decisions regarding language and orthography development should be taken by learners and future users.

Notes

1. One positive development is that one of the youngest adult speakers has a small child who is being raised in both English and Guernesiais.
2. http://language.gg/ (last accessed 24 September 2016)
3. *Patois* is French for 'dialect' with connotations of inferiority and incorrectness, although Guernsey people are often unaware of these.
4. www.youtube.com/watch?v=0AJWnoMAZH4 (last accessed 22 June 2015)
5. Yan Marquis, co-author of *Warro!* and the present chapter.
6. Examples include poetry (by George Métivier 1831, 1843, 1866; Denys Corbet 1871, 1874, 1884; Lenfestey 1875; Mahy 1922); collections such as Pitts (1883) and Henly (1949); unpublished works by Nico Guilbert, R. H. Tourtel, Hélier d'Rocquoine, and several others; short stories by Marjorie Ozanne (Hill 2000) and Denys Corbet; plays by Marie de Garis, Mabel Torode, and others; Thomas Martin's colossal but little-known translations of the Bible, plays by Shakespeare, and plays by Molière and other French authors (Jones 2008; see also Section 3); in the twenty-first century, stories collected and written by Hazel Tomlinson (2006, 2009); and songs produced by the Guernsey Song Project (see Section 2.1).
7. Revised editions were published in 1967, 1973, 1982, and 2012.
8. Transcriptions of oral Giernesiei quotes in this chapter follow the authors' preferred 'Progressive Learner Spelling' described in Section 4.2. Written quotations are spelt as in the originals.
9. For details see www.guernseysongproject.org.gg/ (last accessed 24 September 2016).
10. www.britishirishcouncil.org/work/guernesiais.asp (last accessed 17 August 2006; page no longer available).
11. This spelling follows French pronunciation with *-le* rather than *-lle* typical of Giernesiei.
12. For past actions before today, fluent speakers use the preterite rather than perfect.
13. This would probably be spelt <soutchiannent> using *Dictiounnaire* precepts, although the specific verb form is not given there. In Tomlinson's (2008) 'Descriptive grammar', the root is given as <tiennent> – a French spelling which does not reflect Guernesiais pronunciation, which is given 'phonetically' as 'tyon'.

14. Since the 1990s, especially since the advent of word processors, this disclaimer has disappeared, and pieces published in the Bulletin seem to have undergone editing to make them converge more towards French conventions.
15. A misspelling of *duràrnt*.
16. The second example also shows French influence – or perhaps a literal translation from English – in the choice of lexis (*chutte serai* instead of *a ceisé* for 'this evening').

13 Orthography Development on the Internet: Romani on YouTube

D. Viktor Leggio and Yaron Matras

1 Orthography Development on the Internet

This chapter investigates the role of new communication technologies as an alternative to the nation-state approach to language standardization. We examine the emergence of written forms of Romani among video networks on YouTube, giving consideration to the choice of dialectal forms and orthographies in users' interactions.

The 'multilingual Internet' has been the subject of growing attention (Danet and Herring 2007; Wright 2004a), prompted not only by the presence of many languages on the Internet but also by multilingual practices such as code-switching in chat room messages and forum posts. The position of online interaction as a blend between spoken and written discourse has allowed languages that have so far lacked a written form to expand into the public domain. Earlier limitations on orthographic choices imposed by the constraints of the American Standard Code for Information Interchange (hereafter, ASCII) character set have in the meantime been removed, by and large, through the availability of Unicode conventions. The Internet has thus transformed the process of domain expansion of smaller and endangered languages (cf. Casquite and Young, this volume). Whereas in the pre-Internet age support for such languages depended on 'top-down' and centralized language planning efforts (Kaplan and Baldauf 1997; Wright 2004b) – with choices of variety, script, and orthography being determined by a small circle of individuals in authority positions (cf. Cahill and Karan 2008; Lüpke 2011) – the Internet offers opportunities for organic, 'bottom-up' processes of domain expansion. In such processes, plurality of forms is often embraced by users, and a unified standard seems redundant (Rajah-Carrim 2009:504). Shared writing norms may even emerge spontaneously and – as reported for Nigerian Pidgin, Jamaican (Deuber and Hinrichs 2007), and Haitian Creoles (Schieffelin and Doucet 1994) – they often differ from the conventions proposed by language planning experts. Moreover, the choice of scripts and orthographies shows innovative solutions. For example, speakers of dialectal Greek (Themistocleous 2010; Tseliga 2007) and Arabic

(Palfreyman and Al Khalil 2007) use the Roman alphabet but avoid phonetic transcriptions. Instead they favour visual patterns in which Roman letters and numbers are employed based on their visual similarity to Greek or Arabic characters (on a similar point, see Moseley, this volume).

While the aforementioned practices are typical for the development of new orthographies on Web 1.0 environments (chats, forums, e-mail, website), little is so far known about the impact that the introduction of social networks (Web 2.0) has had on emerging writing conventions. Compared to Web 1.0, Web 2.0 is open to the contributions of thousands of users, and the networks owners have much less control over the content posted by users. Among the various social networks, YouTube is the most easily accessible to researchers since its entire content is publicly available. First launched in February 2005, YouTube currently counts more than one billion users and offers the possibility to upload and watch videos and to comment on videos and other users' profiles.[1] YouTube can therefore offer insights into the writing practices of a wide and loosely regimented community, and it provides an opportunity to observe bottom-up processes of language codification.

2 The Case of Romani

With upwards of 3.5 million speakers, Romani is one of the largest minority languages in Europe. It is unique in terms of its geographical dispersion in the continent and beyond, in the Americas and Australia, and in its Indo-Aryan origins. Structurally, Romani can be characterized as a combination of late Middle Indo-Aryan and early New Indo-Aryan morphology with Balkan-type syntactic structures. Romani populations migrated from the Balkans into all parts of Europe starting in the late fourteenth century, and it is assumed that at that point they spoke a more or less homogenous language (cf. Elšik and Matras 2006; Matras 2002). Nowadays, Romani dialects form a geographical continuum, with structural differences accumulating with greater distance. A zone in Central Europe, roughly coinciding with the historical frontier that divided the Austrian and Ottoman Empires in the sixteenth and seventeenth centuries, hindered the diffusion of structural innovations following the period of settlement, and it continues to show a dense bundle of isoglosses today. This dialectal 'Great Divide' limits intelligibility between the Romani dialects of Western and those of Central and Eastern Europe. Furthermore, since all adult Roma are bilingual in different languages, code-switching may impede intelligibility. By and large, however, Romani dialects remain mutually intelligible (Elšik and Matras 2006; Matras 2005).

In spite of its relatively high number of speakers, the *UNESCO Atlas of World Languages in Danger* considers Romani as definitely endangered.[2] Halwachs (2009) suggests that the UNESCO criteria are applied in this way to Romani as a whole, while as a dispersed language, its vitality should be assessed in relation to individual dialects. The *Ethnologue* offers a more nuanced picture, as it lists various dialects.[3] However, these all score 5 or higher on *Ethnologue*'s Expanded Graded Intergenerational Disruption Scale (EGIDS), suggesting that they are somewhat limited. The problem with both the UNESCO criteria and EGIDS is that they are characterized by a form of methodological nationalism (Wimmer and Glick Schiller 2002). Both indicators assume that a language must conform to the model of the nation-state and thus function in all possible domains through a standard and serve as an ideological rallying point.

The efforts initiated in the 1970s to increase the status of Romani and expand its use to institutional domains had a clear ideological, rallying function for Roma activists (see Matras 1999). In the early 1990s, such efforts intensified, while at the same time use of the language on the Internet increased. In the absence of a form of political governance and any large-scale resources, however, the 'institutionalization' of Romani remains dependant on outside intervention and support. It also hinges on the prospects of transnational cooperation and on the exploitation of opportunities offered by new communication technologies. The status of Romani is thus being negotiated in a context that might be described as transnational and polycentric. The result of such efforts appears to be a network of initiatives that accept and actively promote linguistic pluralism – the usage and acceptance of various orthographies and varieties (cf. Matras 2015). Romani, therefore, will continue to score high on language endangerment scales as long as the criteria for language vitality are based on the century-old understanding of public and written language as a centralized, unified emblem of identity.

3   Mapping User Networks on YouTube

In order to identify and investigate Romani networks on YouTube, we used NodeXL, an open-source template for Microsoft Excel which provides automated tools that allow users to map, analyse, and visualize social media networks. The template includes a tool to import different kinds of YouTube networks: user and video networks (Hansen et al. 2011). User networks are comprised of individual profiles that are connected through subscription to other user profiles. They represent personal connections but do not guarantee that language interactions are actually taking place among those who are linked. Video networks consist of videos that are connected through a shared topic, identifiable through the tags, titles, descriptions, and categories that users assign to videos. Users commenting on videos further strengthen these networks, which thus represent both shared topicality and subjects of interaction.

Table 13.1 *List of selected video networks.*

Video network	Keyword searched for	Videos	Edges	Comments containing Romani
G1	abiav	10	15	40
G2	lovara	9	9	93
G3+G5+G9	ricardo kwiek+gypsy kubanec+khangeri	18	44	250
G4+G10	sevcet+bijav	12	24	251
G6	prinzo	6	13	183
G7+G12	abiav+francuzo	10	11	62
G8	abijav	5	7	30
G11	bijav	4	4	15

As we were interested in interactions around Roma-specific topics, we investigated video networks. Based on preliminary observations, we established that videos posted by Roma fell into three main categories: weddings, religious (Pentecostal) gatherings, and performances by singers. In order to cover a range of countries of origin and different communities, we searched for videos containing the Romani word for 'wedding' in different dialectal pronunciations and spellings: *abav, abijav, abiav, abjav, bijav, biav, bjav*. To identify music videos, we searched for names of singers: Ševčet (spelled 'sevcet' as is commonly done by Roma from former Yugoslavia; see Leggio 2013) from Macedonia; Francuzo from Poland, Gypsy Kubanec from the Czech Republic; and Prinzo from Germany. For Pentecostal videos, we searched for *khangeri* 'church' and for the name *Ricardo Kwiek*, a Polish Romani pastor based in Germany. Finally, we had noticed a series of videos relating specifically to the Lovara Roma, a group whose origins are in Transylvania but whose extended family networks have spread all across Europe and the Americas since the late nineteenth century, and so we also ran a search for the word *lovara*.

Once the videos are identified, NodeXL maps the relationships between them. There are three available options: shared tag, shared commenter, and shared video reply. Our interest was in the relations among users who comment on videos in Romani, and we therefore chose to map shared commenters. We limited our searches to fifty videos per keyword and then selected the networks of videos for analysis. We selected networks that included between three and ten videos and had received more than thirty comments containing some Romani (Table 13.1). These criteria were established in order to obtain a manageable corpus that could be analysed manually while at the same time containing enough data to allow comparison between networks. The decision to analyse the corpus manually took into account the absence of a standardized spelling for Romani, which makes the use of corpus analysis software impractical.

NodeXL cannot check the language used by commentators. Considering that bilingualism is widespread among the Roma, we expected that some of the connections identified by the software would represent users commenting exclusively in a language other than Romani. Similarly, we expected some connections to be missing, as some users might have employed Romani to comment on videos without common keywords, and therefore NodeXL would not have identified these connections. In order to obtain a more accurate picture of interaction in Romani, we manually deleted connections representing commentators who did not use Romani and added those representing users commenting on pairs of videos without common keywords.

Once these operations were completed, the network structure in Figure 13.1 was obtained. The searches for *abav, abjav, biav*, and *bjav* only returned isolated videos without comments on them.

Network G1 (identified by searching for *abiav*) showed connections with G2, G3, G4, and G10. All videos in G1 contain the English word 'Gypsy' in their titles or descriptions, showing how the users who uploaded them are not targeting just Romani speakers. However, the usage of the English 'Gypsy' also attracted a large number of Romani speakers, thus explaining the number of connections with other networks. Therefore, we expected to find a high degree of variation both in dialectal features and in spelling in the comments.

G2 (identified by searching for *lovara*) is mostly isolated but for G2j, which is connected to G1f, G3f, G6c, G7b, and G12c. Given this network's group-specific theme and the fact that the Lovara constitute a tight social network of diasporic communities that are dispersed across numerous urban centres throughout Europe, we expected to find a dominance of characteristic structural features of the Lovara dialect. Given the considerable geographical dispersion of the Lovara (and therefore the acquisition of literacy in various contact languages), we also expected considerable variation in orthographic representation.

G4 (identified by searching for *sevcet*) merged completely with G10 (based on the search for *bijav*). Various edges were lost or thinned down, as many users only employed German in their comments. The frequent usage of German, coupled with the fact that Ševčet is a Macedonian singer living in Germany, suggests that users within this network might be part of the widespread Balkan Romani diaspora (Silverman 2012). This is partially confirmed by the fact that *bijav* is a spelling commonly employed in Macedonia, representing the pronunciation of the word in Southern Balkan dialects of Romani. On this basis, we expected both dialectal features and spelling conventions in these videos to reflect, broadly at least, the Macedonian model of Romani standardization (Friedman 2005), with influences from German spelling. Due to the connections with G1, we also expected that features of other spelling systems and

Orthography Development on the Internet: Romani on YouTube 259

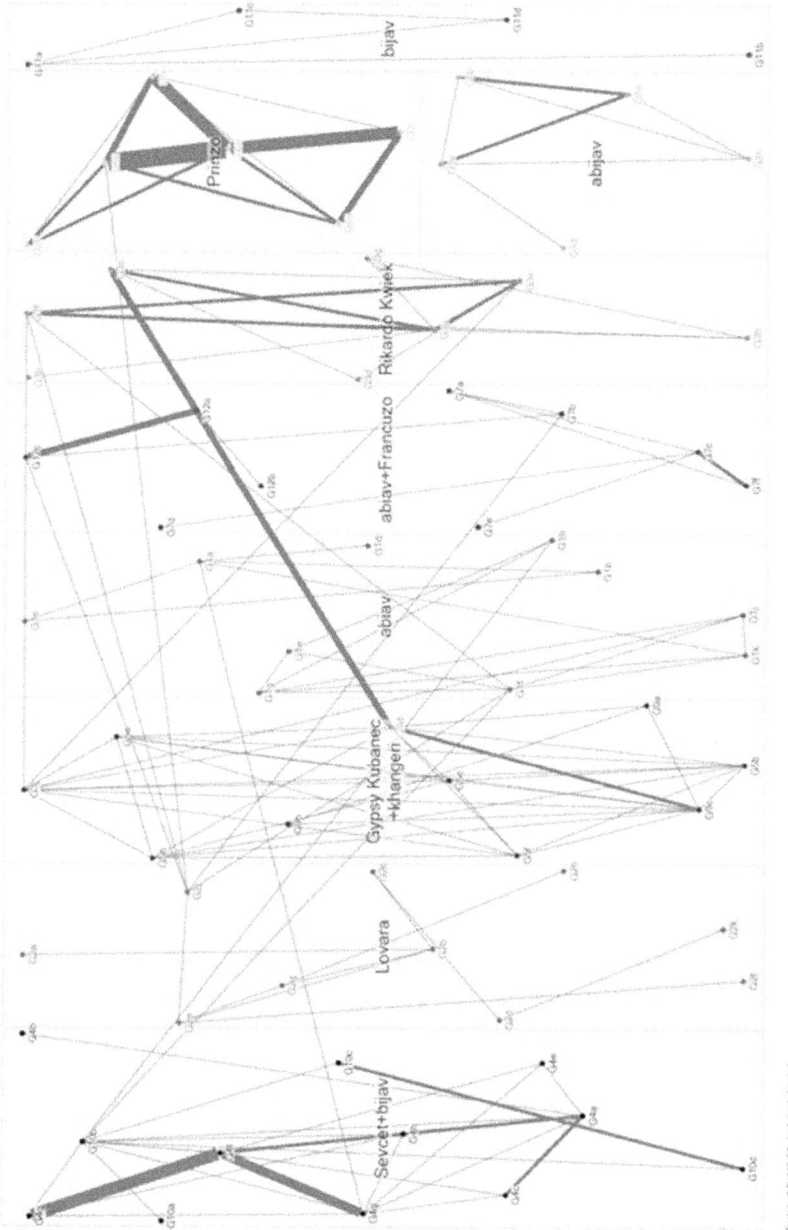

Figure 13.1 Selected video networks. Videos represented as nodes. Shared commenters represented as edges, the lines joining the nodes. The thicker the edge, the more commenters it represents.

dialectal features from outside the Southern Balkan region might occur in this network.

G7 (identified by searching for *abiav*) and G12 (compiled by searching for *Francuzo*) also merged completely. Francuzo is a Polish Romani singer, and some users wrote their comments exclusively in Polish. This suggests that G7 and G12 videos attract a Polish Romani audience. We therefore expected to find dialectal features that are characteristic of 'north-eastern' Romani dialects, such as the varieties of central and northern Poland, the Baltics, and northern Russia; of the 'central' dialects of southern Poland; or of Vlax Romani communities based in Poland (for an overview of dialect groups, see Matras 2002).

A more complex merger between networks occurred between G3, G5, and G9. G3 (compiled by searching for *Ricardo Kwiek*) and G9 (found by searching for *khangeri*) both include videos about Romani Pentecostalism. Some edges were lost or thinned down when excluding non-Romani content, while, in contrast, connections between G3c and G3j with G9d were also found.

In G5 (identified by searching for *gypsy kubanec*), we found that only a single user inserted Romani words into messages in Czech, while all other commenters used Czech exclusively. Thus, a number of videos were excluded from the sample since they contained no Romani comments. Although the remaining videos in G5 did not relate to Pentecostalism, the user who commented on them in Romani also employed some Romani in his comments to videos G9c, G9d, and G3j. The addition of these edges led to the merger between G5 and G9, in which G3j was also grouped. This confirmed the impression that the connection between G3 and G9 is a strong one, and we therefore treated these two networks as a single network. Considering the potential of the religious topic to attract Roma from various backgrounds, we expected to find the highest variation in dialectal features and spelling in these networks.

The remaining three networks – G6 (found searching for *prinzo*), G8 (found searching for *abijav*), and G11 (found searching for *bijav*) – remained mostly isolated except for the connection between G6c and G2j. A few edges in G6 were also thinned down, but this did not alter the network's structure. Given the isolation of G6 and the fact that it includes videos by a Sinti singer, we expected to find the dialectal features of the Sinti-Manouche varieties and predominantly German spelling influences (reflecting the presence of the majority of the speakers of this dialect in Germany). The videos in G8 and G11 did not match our criteria for the number of comments containing some Romani and were therefore excluded from analysis.

All the video networks, with the exception of G6, lost a considerable number of edges once non-Romani comments were filtered out. This shows how the networks attract an audience that includes both users who write in Romani and those who prefer to write in another language. YouTube, like other online environments, offers a space for multilingual, vernacular language practices. In the case of our sample, the other languages used alongside Romani were Serbian/Croatian, Macedonian, Albanian, Polish, Czech, Slovak, Russian, Hungarian, Romanian, German, French, Italian, English, and Spanish.

4   The Variables Analysed

To obtain a picture of dialectal variation in the corpus, we compiled a number of key morphological and phonological variants which represent salient isoglosses in Romani (cf. Matras 2013). The geographical distribution of individual features allows associating variants in our corpus with varieties of Romani spoken in particular regions. The picture is complicated by the fact that some Romani communities constitute 'diasporas': that is, they originate in a particular region but have since dispersed into others, where they continue to maintain a distinct dialect. Some of these diasporas, such as the communities of the Lovara and other related groups referred to as 'Vlax' in association with historical Wallachia, dispersed more than a century ago from Banat, Transylvania, and adjoining regions in western Romania. Others, such as the Romani community of Mitrovica in Kosovo, represent more recent migrations – in this case in connection with the Yugoslav conflict of the mid-1990s (Leggio 2013).

The fact that we can associate particular structural features with known dialectal varieties of Romani allows us to recognize, tentatively at least, the origins of users in certain Romani population groups and sometimes in certain regions. A high degree of consistency of variants within a network can suggest membership in a particular Romani community, whether regional or diasporic, or alternatively a motivation to accommodate to a particular dialectal variety (cf. Pivot and Bert, this volume). Conversely, the noticeable variability of features within a single network can indicate users' diverse dialectal backgrounds and the absence of any motivation to accommodate to a single norm. The mapping of dialect features onto video networks therefore serves as our key indicator for the considerations on variety selection that users entertain in a spontaneous process of language codification.

Attention was given to the following salient structural features (Table 13.2), for which we found sufficient documentation to enable identification of the users' chosen variety of Romani.

(i) The consonantal prothesis in *j-* (*javel* 's/he arrives', *joj* 'she') predominates north of the Great Divide and is absent to the south (*avel* 's/he arrives', *oj/voj* 'she'). Vowel prothesis in *a-* (*abjav* 'wedding', *ašun-* 'to hear') is generally found in the dialects of Romania, Moldova, and Ukraine, as well as in out-migrant Vlax dialects.

(ii) The past-tense 2SG person marker is *-al* (*tu kerdal* 'you did') in the Sinti-Manouche dialects of Western Europe, in Finnish Romani, and in the

Table 13.2 *Dialectal features investigated.*

Feature	Variants	Distribution
Consonant prothesis	j-	North of Great Divide
	None	South of Great Divide
Vowel prothesis	a-	Romania, Moldova, and Ukraine, out-migrant Vlax
	None	other
2SG.PERF marker	-al	Western and Central Europe, Finland
	-an	other
Copula root	h-	Sinti-Manouche, some dialects of Transylvania, Macedonia (all persons); Central Europe, Finland, Balkans (third person)
	s-	other
Subjunctive copula	ov-	Balkans, Romungro
	av-	elsewhere, Vlax
Demonstrative pronouns	kada, kava, kado, aka va, ada, kadava, etc.	Dialect specific

central dialects of Slovakia, southern Poland, the Czech Republic, northern Hungary, and parts of Romanian Transylvania, Slovenia, and south-eastern Austria.

(iii) The copula root *h-* is found for all persons (*hom* 'I am', *hal* 'you are', etc.) in the Sinti-Manouche dialects as well as in some isolated dialects spoken in Macedonia, Hungary, and Romanian Transylvania, while copula forms in *s-* (*som/sem* 'I am', *san/sal* 'you are', etc.) are found elsewhere. For the third person, forms in *h-* also appear in the Central European and Finnish Romani dialects (often matching the distribution of the past-tense 2SG person marker *-al*) and, as optional variants, in some of the out-migrant Vlax dialects of south-eastern Europe.

(iv) Subjunctive forms of the copula verb derive from *ov-* (originally 'to become') in the dialects of south-eastern Europe as well as in the Romungro dialects of Hungary and Slovakia, while forms deriving from *av-* (originally 'to arrive') are common elsewhere, including in the Vlax out-migrant dialects in south-eastern Europe.

(v) The distribution of individual demonstrative forms is complex due to the presence of a four-term system in most Romani dialects and due to the high diversity of individual forms. Demonstratives in the corpus therefore help identify regional and sometimes local varieties of the language. Examples of demonstratives systems are *akava/okova/adava/odova* as well as *adavka/odovka* in the Southern Balkans; *kava/kova/kadava/*

kodova in the out-migrant Vlax dialects of south-eastern Europe; *kado/ kodo/kako/kuko* in the dialects of the Banat and Transylvania region and out-migrant Vlax dialects in Central and Northern Europe; *dava/adava/ dova/odova* in the dialects of Poland, Russia, and the Baltics regions; *ada/ oda/kada/koda* in the central dialects of southern Poland, Slovakia, northern Hungary, Slovenia, and north-western Romania (Transylvania); and *kava/kova* in the Sinti-Manouche varieties.

Since nearly all comments were written in the Roman alphabet, we focused our attention on those sounds for which Roman-based alphabets show variation and for which we can therefore expect to see variation in the choice of spontaneous spelling used in Romani comments. Here, we will look in detail at the post-alveolar affricate /tʃ/, the post-alveolar fricative /ʃ/, and the velar fricative /x/ (see Table 13.3 for solutions adopted for other sounds). We also looked at those sounds that are distinctive of Romani and which have often been the subject of intense discussions among language activists: the aspirates /ph/, /th/, /tʃh/, and /kh/ and the reflexes of the retroflex trill /ʈ/, realized in different dialects as [rr], [ʀ], or [ʈ]. Attention to the graphemic representation of these phonological features allows us to establish the degree to which YouTube commentators tend to follow the norms of their respective contact languages or apply creative solutions.

For each user, we recorded the occurrences of individual structural features and of spelling solutions. The majority of users only posted one or two short comments, in which investigated features and spellings were usually represented by an average of three tokens each. It was thus difficult to assess whether individual users were consistent in their choices, as the impression remained limited to a small sample for each variable. However, the assembly of relevant tokens for each variable across the entire group of users within a given network provided an impression of the degree of coherence within networks and allowed us to carry out comparisons between them.

5 Choice of Variety

The occurrence of prothesis phenomena shows clear distribution patterns (see Figure 13.2). Users in G4+G10 show forms that are typical of Southern Balkan dialects: the absence, by and large, of both *j-* prothesis and *a-* prothesis. In G7+G12, all relevant tokens showed *j-* prothesis, indicating that the users originated from Northern or Central Europe. In G1, all target words found underwent *a-* prothesis, while only one target word underwent *j-* prothesis, pointing to a Vlax background. In the case of G2 and G3+G5+G9, we found all the different variants. However, we also see that in G2, Southern Romani variants (low frequency of *j-* prothesis) dominate, while in G3+G5+G9, Northern Romani variants (high frequency of *j-* prothesis) are dominant. G6 did not include any of the relevant target words.

Table 13.3 *Inventory of common Romani sounds, and common orthographic variants used.*

Romani (a) sounds	Academic/activist orthography	YouTube (b) orthography
/i/	<i>	<i>
/e/	<e>	<e>
/a/	<a>	<a>
/o/	<o>	<o>
/u/	<u>	<u>
/w/	<w>	<u, w>
/j/	<j>	<j, i, ij, y>
/p/	<p>	<p>
/ph/	<ph>	<p>
/b/	<b>	<b>
/t/	<t>	<t>
/th/	<th>	<t>
/d/	<d>	<d>
/k/	<k>	<k>
/kh/	<kh>	<k>
/g/	<g>	<g>
/m/	<m>	<m>
/n/	<n>	<n>
/r/	<r>	<r>
/rr, ʀ ṭ/	/ř, rr/	/r, rr/
/f/	<f>	<f, v>
/v/	<v>	<v, w>
/s/	<s>	<s>
/z/	<z>	<z>
/ʃ/	<š>	<s, sh, sch>
/ʒ/	<ž>	<z, j>
/tʃ/	<č>	<c, ch, tsch>
/tʃh/	<čh>	<c, ch, tsch>
/dʒ/	<dž>	<dz, dj, g, j>
/x/	<x>	<h, ch, g, j>
/l/	<l>	<l>

For the past-tense person markers of the 2SG (Figure 13.3), we found *-al* only in G3+G5+G9 (albeit in a small number of cases compared with the counterpart variant) and in G6, where it is used exclusively. For G6, the results may suggest an origin of most users in the Sinti-Manouche community, though the low token count does not allow a clear conclusion on the basis of this isolated feature. For G3+G5+G9, considering the tendency to pattern with northern dialects, the low frequency of *-al* suggests that 'north-eastern' speakers (originating from communities in central and northern Poland, the Baltics,

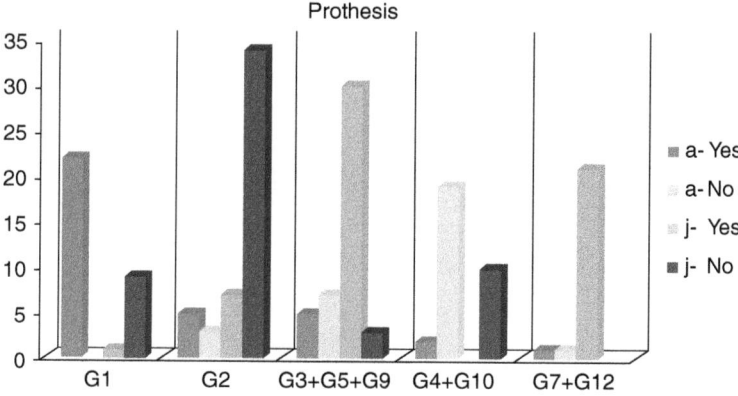

Figure 13.2 Prothesis phenomena.

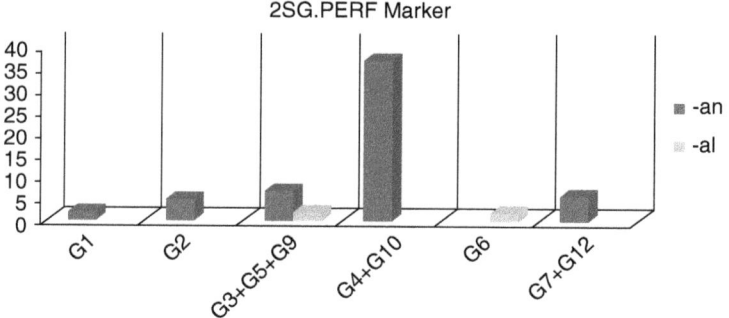

Figure 13.3 Selection of 2SG perfect concord markers.

or Russia) may constitute a majority. For G7+G12, the total absence of -*al*, despite the presence of prothesis phenomena that are shared by the central and northern dialects, similarly suggests an origin in the north-eastern cluster and rules out both the Sinti-Manouche or 'north-western' cluster and the Central European dialects. For the other networks (G1, G2, G4+G10), the complete absence of -*al* tokens is in line with the tendencies observed and recorded here to pattern with southern usages.

In our sample, *h*- copulas were encountered in G3+G5+G9, G4+G10, and G6 (Figure 13.4). In G3+G5+G9 and G4+G10, *h*- copulas constituted a minority of tokens and appeared alongside counterpart forms in *s*-. The variation confirms the impression gained earlier that users in G4+G10 originate from the Southern Balkans and, more specifically, that they are speakers of Arli varieties (spoken

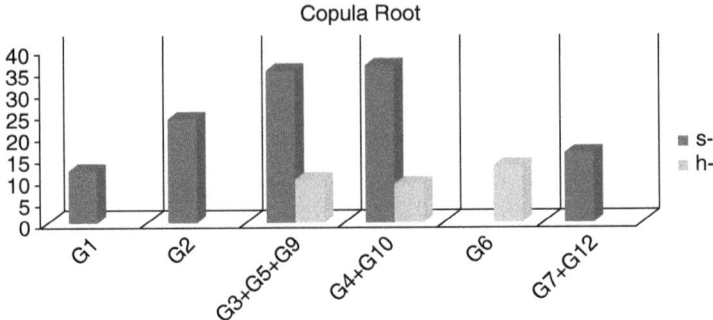

Figure 13.4 Selection of copula root.

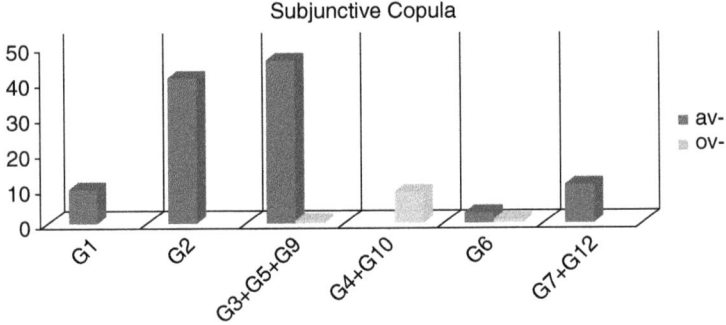

Figure 13.5 Selection of subjunctive copula root.

mainly in Macedonia and Bulgaria), in which both copula stems can be found. In the case of G3+G5+G9, the occurrence of *h-* copulas, coupled with the presence of typically northern forms seen before, indicates a presence of speakers of the Sinti-Manouche (north-western) or central dialects among the users. In G6, *h-* copula forms were used exclusively. Taking into account the distribution of other forms, the exclusive usage of *h-* copulas suggests that the users in this network are Sinti-Manouche speakers. The complete absence of *h-* copulas in G1, G2, and G7+G12 is consistent with the usages so far identified for these networks – namely Vlax (Romanian-Transylvanian-Moldovan-Ukrainian cluster) for G1 and G2 and north-eastern (Polish-Baltic-Russian) for G7+G12.

Also relating to the copula is the selection of *ov-* 'to become' or *av-* 'to come' for the subjunctive (Figure 13.5). Central and Southern Balkan dialects show selection of *ov-*, while in the remaining spaces the subjunctive copula is *av-*. The Central and Southern Balkan form occurs only in G3+G5+G9 and

Orthography Development on the Internet: Romani on YouTube 267

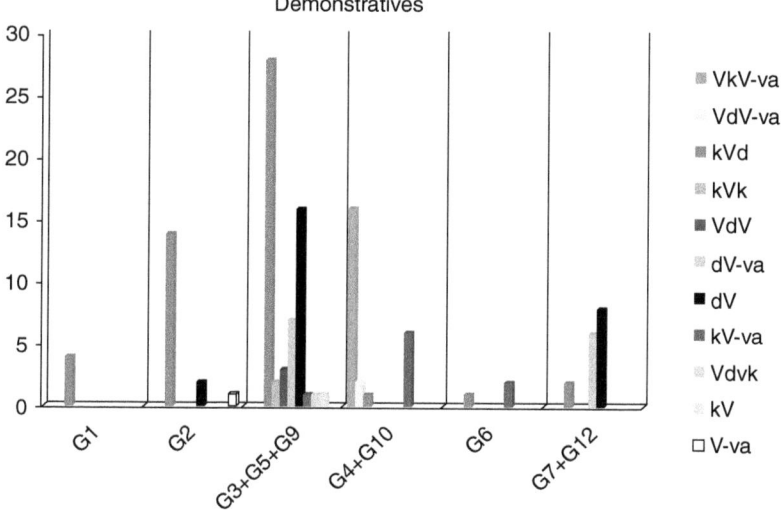

Figure 13.6 Selection of demonstrative forms.

G4+G10. In G3+G5+G9, the occurrence of these forms and their overall low token count suggest the presence in this network of a minority of speakers of central dialects. In G4+G10, the exclusive usage of *ov-* as the subjunctive copula confirms that Southern Balkan speakers constitute the majority of users. G6 does not offer any conclusive indicators, as we find an overall low count of relevant tokens.

For demonstratives (Figure 13.6), G1 shows only forms in *kad-*. In G2, the same forms are dominant, but we also found two tokens of *da-* forms. Since these reduced forms are typical of the north-eastern cluster of dialects (Poland, Baltics, Russia), and considering the occurrence of northern tokens for prothesis phenomena (see earlier), we can conclude that this network is primarily comprised of Vlax speakers but that it also attracts some speakers of north-eastern dialects. In G3+G5+G9, we found that Vlax forms constituted the majority of the tokens. Central and north-eastern forms such as *ada, da*, and *dava* were also frequent.

In G4+G10, the high occurrence of Southern Balkan demonstratives (*akava/ adava*) confirms the dominant presence of Southern Balkan speakers in this network. The occurrence of six *kava* tokens also confirms the presence of speakers from a different background. These forms, besides being characteristic of the north-western cluster, are also present in out-migrant Vlax varieties spoken in the Southern Balkans, such as the Gurbet dialect (Boretzky 1986; Leggio 2011). Since no northern feature was found in this network, the occurrence of *kava* demonstratives is a clear indicator of the presence of Gurbet speakers among G4+G10 users. G7+G12, with high occurrence of *dava* and *da* demonstratives, can be associated once again with north-eastern speakers, although two *kada* tokens indicates the participation of some Vlax speakers. As usual, G6 is the hardest network to evaluate due to a low token count.

6 Choice of Orthography

A point of interest in the analysis of the corpus is the representation of Romani sounds for which the various contact languages employ different graphemic solutions. Diacritics such as <š>, <đ>, <ž>, and <ć> are used in various alphabets of the relevant contact languages, and the symbols <č>, <dž>, <š>, and <ž> have a tradition of being used in the transliteration of Romani in academic and some activist publications. In the comments on YouTube videos, diacritics occur only rarely (for discussion of diacritics, see Moseley, Shah and Brenzinger, and Esteban, this volume). Instead, we find plain counterparts – that is, the relevant characters lacking diacritic symbols. This behaviour of Romani YouTube users mirrors the established norm of majority language speakers to employ plain characters when diacritics are not available or difficult to transmit (Anis 2007 for French; Hentschel 1998 for Serbian/Croatian).

In the case of the unvoiced post-alveolar affricate /tʃ/ (Figure 13.7), we can observe how the favourite choice is <c> in G1 and G4+G10. The main model for imitation is, it appears, <č>, which is used in the majority of Romani printed materials, following the usage of Slavic languages of central and south-eastern Europe (Czech, Slovak, Slovene, Croatian). Another solution adopted to represent /tʃ/ is the English-like <ch> (in some cases modelled on Spanish; see following). This is found in all networks and is the favourite choice in G2, the Lovara network. In G6 (the Prinzo network) German <tch> is used almost exclusively. In G7+G12 (weddings and Francuzo videos), Polish combinations <ci> and <cz> are dominant, suggesting that the <c> found in this network is modelled on Polish <ć>. The occurrence of <ci> in G2 and G3+G5+G9 is in all likelihood also based on Polish norms. For G2, we know that there is a strong Lovara community based in or originating from Poland. For G3+G5+G9, most users show north-eastern dialect features, which are in line with the dialect of the Polska Roma of central and northern Poland. On this basis, we can once again interpret the grapheme <c> in these two networks as modelled on the Polish <ć>. Network G4+G10 showed no north-eastern dialect features, and its content suggests that it attracts users who belong to diasporic Romani communities originating from former Yugoslavia. We can therefore assume that the single token of <ci> found here is modelled on Italian orthography, since various members of these communities have settled in Italy. As <c> also represents /tʃ/ before front vowels in G4+G10, this reinforces the impression of an Italian influence.

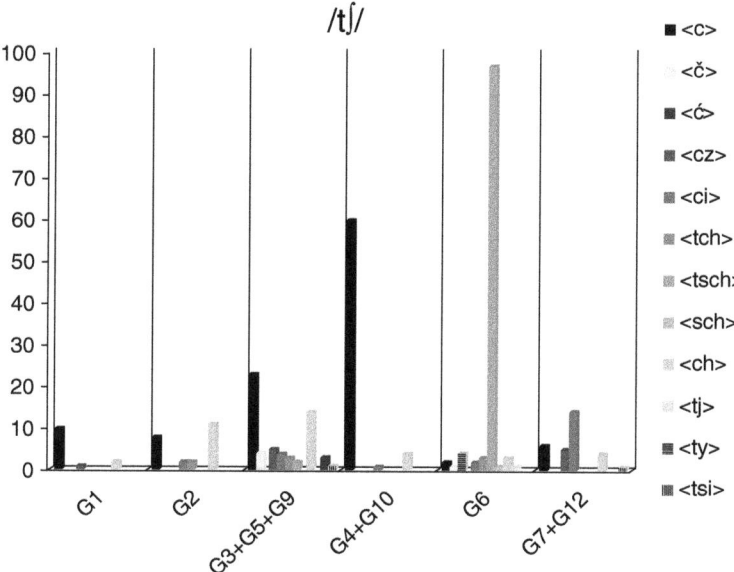

Figure 13.7 Representation of the unvoiced post-alveolar affricate.

The spellings used for the voiceless post-alveolar sibilant /ʃ/ (Figure 13.8) show a similar distribution across networks to that observed for /tʃ/. Most networks show predominantly <s>. Once again, we find different solutions in G7+G12 and G6. In G7+G12, we find the Polish combinations <sz> and <si> and only two tokens of <s>, presumably replicating the Polish <ś>. G6 once again shows almost exclusive usage of a German-based combination – <sch>. English-like <sh> is found as the second preferred choice in all networks except for G7+G12. In G3+G5+G9, we find diverse representations. In this network, the usage of <s> is likely modelled on multiple sources. Some users in this network employed <s> for /ʃ/, modelled on Hungarian, while at the same time using the Hungarian combination <sz> for the dental sibilant /s/. In the remaining networks, <s> is always the favourite choice. In G1 and G4+G10, it is in all likelihood modelled on central and south-eastern European Slavic <š>. In G2, considering the Polish influences found in this network, it might replicate either <š> or <ś>. It is interesting to note that in G2, we found a single token of <Ш> from the Cyrillic alphabet.

Two main solutions are employed across the networks for the velar fricative /x/: <h> and <ch> (Figure 13.9). By contrast, the spelling employed in most academic and activist literature is <x>. Although this symbol is easily

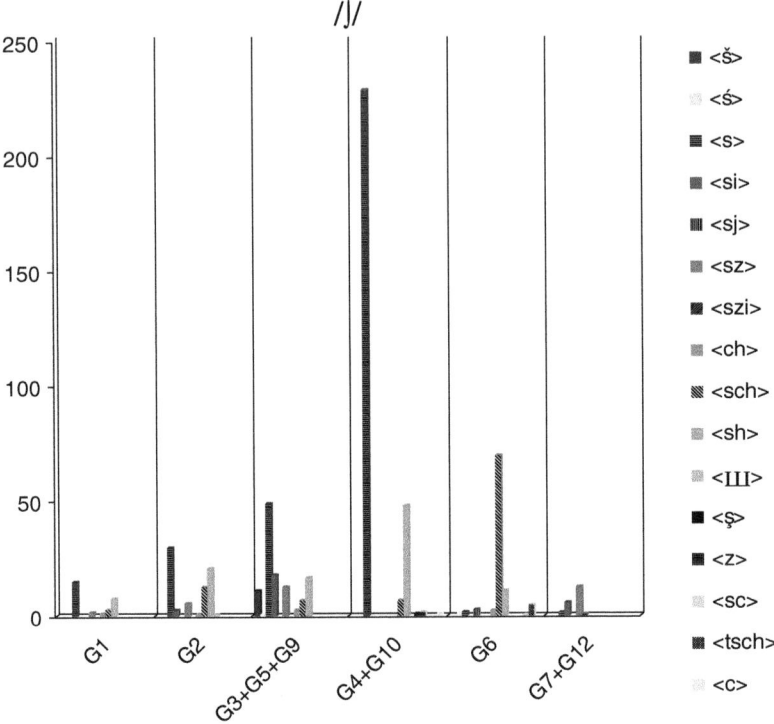

Figure 13.8 Representation of the voiceless post-alveolar sibilant.

accessible on any keyboard, it is employed only occasionally in the corpus, suggesting that the vast majority of YouTube users have little exposure to published academic and activist literature in or on Romani and therefore are not influenced by it. Both <h> and <ch> are available in Polish and Czech/Slovak. The fact that they show similar frequency in G3+G5+G9 and G7+G12 demonstrates once again how users in these two networks draw from these languages. In G6, the almost exclusive usage of <ch> points instead to a stronger German influence, while the exclusive usage of <h> in G4+G10 is based on Serbian/Croatian. The tokens of <j> and <g>, the latter always preceding front vowels, found in G1, G2, and G3+G5+G9 instead show influences of Spanish. Since many Kalderaš and Lovara Roma are settled in Latin America and many of them are Pentecostal, it is not surprising to find them commenting on these networks. Furthermore, their presence implies that some of the tokens of <ch> for /tʃ/ may be based not on English, but on Spanish. Finally, in G2, we find a single token of Cyrillic <X>.

Orthography Development on the Internet: Romani on YouTube 271

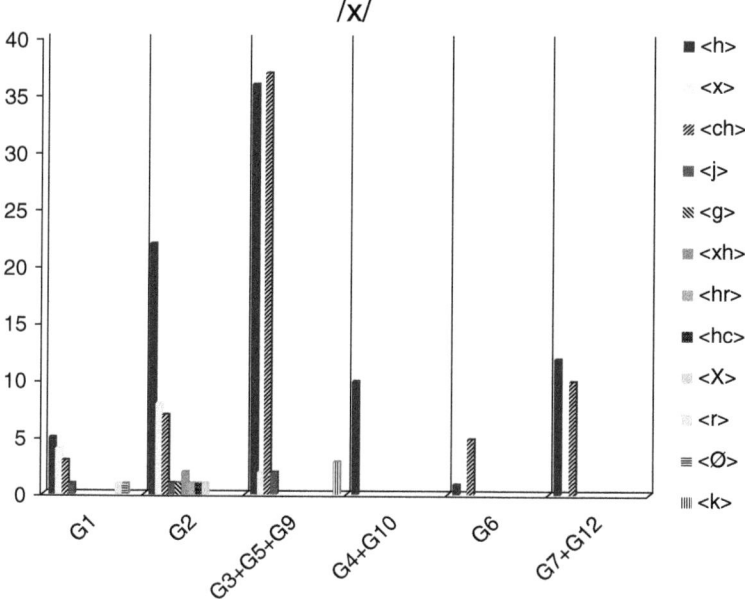

Figure 13.9 Representation of the unvoiced velar fricative.

While the sounds discussed so far are shared between Romani and the major European languages, the aspirated consonants /ph/, /th/, /tʃh/, and /kh/ and the reflexes of the retroflex trill /ṛ/ (realized as [rr], [ʀ], or [ɽ]), are specific to Romani. Conscious of the symbolic value of these sounds as representing the distinctiveness of Romani and its Indic origin, activists have insisted on their distinctive spelling (cf. Moseley, this volume). They follow the academic conventions, where aspirated consonants are indicated by combining the stop grapheme with <h>, while /ṛ/ is usually rendered as <ř> or <rr>. As in the case of /x/, we found that academic and activist conventions are seldom followed in the YouTube corpus.

Only in G2 was <rr> the preferred choice, most likely, again, under Spanish influence, while all other networks showed almost exclusive usage of <r> (Figure 13.10).

With the exception of /ph/ in G2 and G7+G12, aspirated consonants are dominantly represented by graphemes for the simple consonants <p>, <t>, <k>, and <č> (Figure 13.11). This trend among YouTube users shows that they are not using Romani as a symbol of unity among the Roma and of their shared Indian origin, as activists often do, but strictly as a communicative tool.

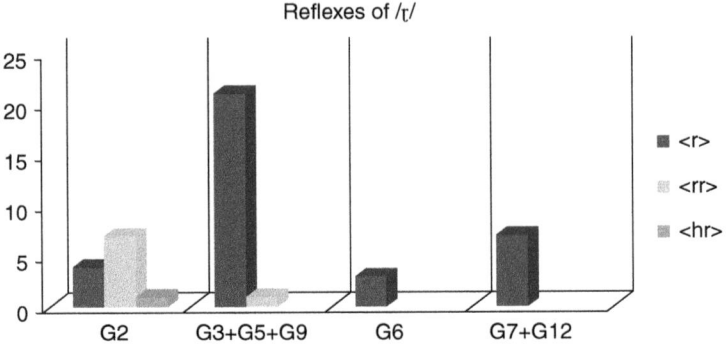

Figure 13.10 Representation of the reflexes of the retroflex trill.

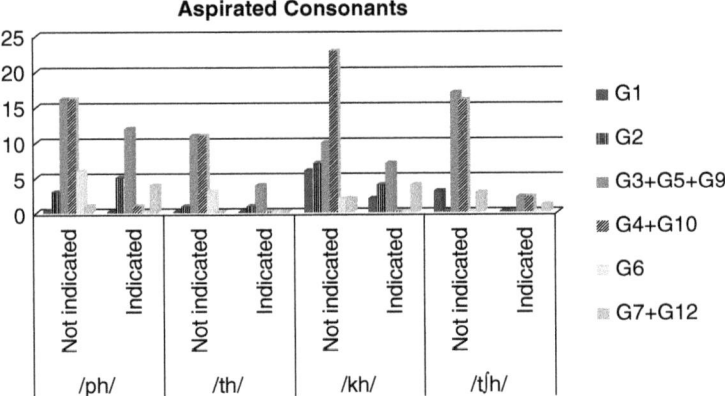

Figure 13.11 Representation of aspirated consonants.

7 Conclusions

The video networks discussed generally represent Romani communities that shared a tradition of face-to-face oral communication in their locations of origin. However, with the exception of the Sinti community of Western Europe, these communities are now dispersed as a result of migrations from Central and Eastern Europe to the west. In G1, users employ Vlax dialectal features. The orthography used is based mostly on Serbian/Croatian and Italian conventions, with occasional English and Spanish influences. We can conclude that the majority of G1 users are Vlax speakers who settled in the Balkans and have more recently moved to Italy. In G2, users employ a variety of Romani closely related to that used in G1. Here, however, Czech/Slovak and Polish spelling dominates, but instances of Romanian, Hungarian, German, and Spanish conventions can also be found, suggesting an origin in Central Europe and a wider dispersal than among G1 users. In G4+G10, the prevalence of Southern Balkan features, the occurrence of some Vlax features, and use of Macedonian and Serbian/Croatian indicates that users are from former Yugoslavia. Here, the orthography is modelled on Serbian/Croatian and thus reminiscent of that employed in Macedonia (Friedman 2005) but showing influences from Italian and German, confirming that users are members of the Balkan Romani diaspora. In G7+G12, where the dialect of the Polska Roma is used, we observe a stronger tendency towards uniformity in orthography. Here, Polish conventions are followed systematically. Users in this network are clearly Polish Roma, but mentions of countries like the United Kingdom suggest that some of them are emigrants. In G6, we recognized Sinti users. The prominent use of German and occasionally of French and Dutch alongside Romani confirms that they still reside in their historical locations. Since they have not emigrated, they have not come into contact with multiple writing norms. The few users employing non-German spellings also show dialectal features that do not belong to the Sinti-Manouche dialects. We can see how, despite spelling differences, using Romani allows people to communicate in writing even if they do not share a single contact language or a standardized variety of Romani.

This opportunity is clearly taken up by users in G3+G5+G9. These users are not brought together by a shared regional origin, but rather by their common belonging to Pentecostalism. Although Romungro, Slovak (central), and Polska Romani (north-eastern) forms are prevalent, many other dialects are employed. Spelling conventions confirm a multiplicity of origins and current locations, as all influences identified in the other networks can be found here as well. However, matching the predominance of central and north-eastern Romani speakers, Czech/Slovak, Polish, and Hungarian spellings occur more frequently.

We thus witness the emergence of a new domain of communication, made possible by YouTube and most likely also by other social networks. Romani speakers use technology to remain in contact or to establish new relationships with fellow Roma across distances. This expansion into a new domain requires the use of a written language. This leads to unstructured literacy and to the emergence of new practices. The most obvious change is the use of Romani – so far the language of private communication within the family – in a public environment. The availability of new communication technologies would not have enabled this language development on its own. Crucial here is the need that Romani speakers feel to communicate across transnational networks. Moreover, users display flexibility and creativity in accepting and using all the resources available in their own and other users' linguistic repertoires. The lack of prescriptive attitudes about Romani orthography, visible in the absence of comments criticizing other users' choices, encourages a plurality of contributions. The development of Romani literacy can therefore be described as an organic process rather than an engineered change implemented in the form of traditional language planning and policy procedures. This change is a 'bottom-up' process, emerging spontaneously rather than at the initiative of an elite with an ideological agenda. It is unstructured, and none of the actors involved appears to take on any institutional roles.

The development is polycentric: each YouTube network acts as an innovation centre for the selection of variety and orthography. Dialectal features usually derive from the spoken variety of the users, while orthographies are modelled on the primary contact languages in which literacy has been acquired (cf. Moseley, Casquite and Young, Shah and Brenzinger, and Sackett this volume). What happens on YouTube is not significantly different from the picture of printed media in Romani. Here too the overwhelming tendency is for a polycentric codification process, with centres consisting of individuals or small organizations supported by national or European authorities (Friedman 2005; Halwachs 2012; Matras 2015). The difference on the Internet is the density of links between centres and the fact that they all operate under the same constraint on the availability of particular characters. This results in more reciprocal influences between the centres and in more homogeneous, although still varying, orthographies emanating from each centre (see Table 13.3).

The connection between territory and language, characteristic of traditional language standardization efforts, is still not entirely dismantled. However, the territory experienced by Romani speakers has never been a bounded space, but rather a diasporic space. In this diasporic space, spatial locations are points of contact with different languages and scripts. As all these languages and scripts are employed flexibly, pluralism in linguistic practice arises. Nonetheless, the choice of Romani has a clear identity construction function (cf. Sackett, and Lai, this volume). This can be seen in particular in the case of the Pentecostal Roma, where the choice of Romani facilitates the development of non-territorial networks by including Romani speakers even if they lack a commonly shared contact language that can be used in written communication. Domain expansion via social networking sites is thus based on well-established offline social groupings. Ideology – religious ideology, in our case – can bring together people from different groupings based on a shared perception of their common identity. New media can thus support the expansion of language use into new domains without the need for uniformity or standardization.

Notes

1. www.youtube.com/yt/press/en-GB/statistics.html (last accessed 2 February 2015).
2. www.unesco.org/culture/languages-atlas/en/atlasmap/language-id-405.html (last accessed 26 March 2015).
3. www.ethnologue.com/language/rom (last accessed 26 March 2015).

14 Orthography Creation for Postvernacular Languages: Case Studies of Rama and Francoprovençal Revitalization

Bénédicte Pivot and Michel Bert

1 Introduction

This chapter considers the place of orthographic creations in the process of revitalization of languages that we consider to be 'postvernacular' and questions the role that writing fulfils and its usefulness in such context, according to the actual practices of writing of its different users. Our study is based on the analysis of two glotto-political situations of revitalization. The first one is that of the Rama language in Nicaragua, and the second that of Francoprovençal (hereafter, FP) in France. The two languages are both considered highly endangered according to the vitality criteria of UNESCO (Moseley 2010). In both cases, the last native speakers are elderly, there is no more family transmission or public use of the language (except for some rare, official events), and spontaneous uses in the private sphere are infrequent. These two principally oral languages were first written down by linguists. Even though the populations involved are obviously very different – one is Amerindian and at the bottom of the social ladder of the poorest area of Central America, and the other is neither ethnically nor socially distinguishable and blends into French society – both are characterized by socio-political authorities as 'linguistic communities' and often considered as still forming 'communities of practice'. They are also both the object of linguistic projects in favour of language revitalization, which aim to maintain a certain level of knowledge of the language within the community involved and even to foster language transmission.

These situations have been described in recent research as being 'postvernacular' (Pivot 2014), a notion coined by Shandler (2006). This chapter begins by introducing this notion, since it highlights some disagreements between the various actors of revitalization. The chapter then goes on to describe the vitality of both languages and the reasons why they should be considered as postvernacular. Finally, it introduces the writing practices of different actors and their choice of orthography, while situating them in their respective contexts – contexts which clearly differ in each case in terms of the social constructs linked to the notion of written form and norm. The chapter demonstrates that both contexts fit into ideological and pragmatic approaches which influence orthography creation strategies (Milroy 2001).

2   Postvernacular Languages

The term 'postvernacular language' was coined by Shandler to refer to the social and linguistic practice of Yiddish in New York. It will be used in this chapter to describe the sociolinguistic status of both FP in France and Rama in Nicaragua. Our choice of this term is based on the observation and analysis of speech and linguistic habits in both countries, where it was found that social praxis surrounding the linguistic issues of Rama and FP fell under functions that did not belong to those expected of everyday communication. Claims made about their revitalization by local actors did not correspond to the demands of the re-vernacularization of those languages either. The notion of postvernacularity does not define the state of a language that would appear once it is no longer vernacular, but rather refers to dynamics of social practices when the semiotic symbolic function of language prevails over its semiotic-communication function, as Shandler (2006:4) explains:

In semiotic terms, the language's primary level of signification – that is, its instrumental value as a vehicle for communicating information, opinions, feelings, ideas – is narrowing in scope. At the same time its secondary, or meta-level of signification – the symbolic value invested in the language apart from the semantic value of any given utterance in it – is expanding. This privileging of the secondary level of signification of Yiddish over its primary level constitutes a distinctive mode of engagement with the language that I term postvernacular Yiddish. In the postvernacular mode, familiar cultural practices – reading, performing, studying, and even speaking – are profoundly altered. Though it often appears to be the same as vernacular use, postvernacularity is in fact something fundamentally different in its nature and intent.

Postvernacular languages are thus characterized primarily by social dynamics in a context of decline of language practice in the language for communication functions in public, educational, and private spheres. The social praxis that develops around a language in a context of decline is what Shandler (2006:4) calls a 'mode of engagement' – in other words, a voluntary act with varying degrees of consciousness, realized through an 'elective act' and a 'performing act' (Shandler 2006:24) that does not aim at the re-vernacularization of the language. Traditionally, in the literature on endangered languages, revitalization is understood as actions that aim to reverse language shift (cf. Costa 2010; Costa and Gasquet-Cyrus 2013; Costa 2013 for a critical analysis of such ideas), but it should be noted here that postvernacular dynamics do not aim at reversing language shift, nor to a return to the everyday use of the language in public and private spheres. They correspond to a functional shift, a change of social status for the language through actions aiming to keep the language alive[1] rather than actions perceived as a re-establishment of those language practices that are considered as missing: 'we don't speak any more'.[2]

3 Rama and Francoprovençal: Two Postvernacular Languages

3.1 Rama in Nicaragua

The description of the sociolinguistic status of the Rama language, its vitality, and its revitalization began in 1986 (for detailed information, see Grinevald and Pivot 2013; Pivot 2014). Rama is the 'ethnic language' of an Amerindian population of the Atlantic coast of Nicaragua and a 'very endangered' language according to the UNESCO Atlas. Indeed, this primarily oral language has not been transmitted to children for three generations. Language shift started at the beginning of the twentieth century, with the dominant language now an English Creole that is linguistically close to Miskitu Coast Creole (hereafter, MCC)[3] (Grinevald 2005).

As a consequence, the language of first socialization of the members of the Rama ethnic community is MCC, and the Rama language has lost its everyday communication function. Out of a native population of about three thousand, there was only one Rama monolingual couple left by 2013, and they lived quite isolated, in the tropical forest. Less than 1 per cent of the population can be considered as fluent in Rama. Stigmatized and denigrated by Moravian missionaries from the end of the nineteenth century onwards, the language had become, for most of the community, a 'tiger language' (a language spoken by savages). Indeed, many young Rama adults only discovered the Rama language during workshops organized by the Rama Language Project (hereafter, RLP), as part of a revitalization plan.

RLP was initiated as a response to an official request made by the community chief to the Sandinista government for aid in rescuing the Rama language in the context of peace negotiations during the war between the Sandinistas and the Contra (Pivot 2014). At the beginning of the project, the members of the community were quite hostile and sceptical and did not support the revitalization of Rama. Speakers denied the fact that they spoke the language or that they knew any words of it. In contrast, today children going to the community school and young adults are proud to say that they can speak Rama because they know 'some words'. They have learned these words in Rama classes first taught by an illiterate (female) semi-speaker for ten years (1987–1997), then by a native speaker up to 2012, and finally by a few teachers who are not speakers of Rama but were involved in the revitalization project and use resources produced by it. This knowledge does not make the young learners linguistically competent in terms of conversational skills, but they do know lists of words such as the names of animals and colours, and they can count up to ten. The attitudes of the members of the community have also evolved positively towards Rama. They do not call it a 'tiger language' any more, but rather their 'treasure language' (Grinevald and Pivot 2013). Even though they do not have highly developed conversational skills and their linguistic competence is not the same as that of fluent speakers, for most of them the language has a symbolic value. It is linked to their identity, making them 'one people', and 'one nation'.[4] The recognition of Rama by official authorities as an ethnic language enables them to wave their language as a flag, legitimizing their ethnicity, their territoriality, and their social difference.

Functionally and socially, being able to say a few words in Rama (especially in public) and being able to identify Rama as 'our language' has become evident since the first decade of the twenty-first century. This 'staging' of the language is a specific characteristic of postvernacular languages.

3.2 Francoprovençal in France

FP is a Gallo-Romance language spoken in France, Switzerland, and Italy. Its status and vitality vary in each of these three countries. This chapter focuses on the case of FP in France, and especially in the Rhône-Alpes region.

3.2.1 An Evaluation of the Vitality of Francoprovençal[5] The *UNESCO Atlas of the World's Languages in Danger* estimates the number of speakers of FP as some ten thousand and describes it as 'definitely endangered'. However, this estimate must be considered in the context of its level of vitality in France, where it has not been transmitted as a mother tongue for several generations. Such lack of transmission could already be noted several centuries ago in a few cities such as Lyon, and by the end of the Second World War, the use of the vernacular among children had almost totally ceased. In the Valle d'Aosta in Italy, however, some children are still raised speaking FP today. The number of native speakers in France is very low nowadays. According to the results of a survey conducted in 2007–2009 in the Rhône-Alpes region (Bert and Costa 2009), the number of native speakers of FP can be estimated at forty thousand – that is to say, much less than 1 per cent of the population. People with some knowledge of FP are generally older than 60 and are mainly semi-speakers or rememberers.

The use of the language in the private sphere is very limited today, and in public it is restricted to the staging of language events such as festivals organized by groups promoting FP. The language is almost non-existent in 'new media' such as radio, television, and the Internet. Teaching FP is not officially possible, unlike the situation with most regional languages. Therefore, few children have any knowledge of it. To date, there exists no educational material published specifically for teaching it, and no common practical orthography has been chosen. An older literature in FP does exist, but it is not very comprehensible to the general public, and speakers are generally unaware of its existence.

The speakers themselves are often ambivalent towards their language. Some of them reject it, having subscribed to the dominant French ideology that denies regional varieties the status of 'language' and still being affected by memories of punishment when speaking the language was forbidden in school. Even speakers who are emotionally attached to their language and are involved in local groups promoting FP often doubt the benefits of teaching the language. Indeed, those who are most in favour of teaching FP are often non-native speakers, or people who do not speak the language at all. The case of FP in France thus appears as more fragile than the UNESCO estimate.

3.2.2 The Actors of Revitalization Unlike other regional languages of France – like Breton or Occitan – FP does not have a long-established and organized activist tradition. The language was only identified quite late (Ascoli 1873) as that of a distinctive linguistic area, situated between Occitan in the south and the Oïl languages of the north of France. Its name, which was chosen by linguists, is still unknown by the majority of its speakers and the general public. A feeling of shared belonging to the same linguistic community has never existed.

The first significant action in favour of FP goes back only forty years (Pivot 2014), and the social movement that followed has gathered momentum only in the past ten years. Today, it is led by two main types of actors: local groups and the regional government. In the Rhône-Alpes region, about fifty *patois* groups meet regularly (*patois* being the term they use for their regional languages). Some of these groups have already existed for thirty years, but most are more recent. These local groups almost always cover small areas composed of just a few villages. Territorial anchoring is thus important to the members of these groups, who are almost exclusively retired people and generally semi-speakers whose feeling of linguistic insecurity is relatively high. Native speakers tend not to join these groups, and conversely, some of the most active members do not have much contact at all with FP. The groups generally meet once or twice a month, though activities are suspended during the summer. During the meetings, those participants most comfortable with FP recite stories they have written or read translations. They all sing traditional or more recent songs together and exchange anecdotes and memories. Most do it to honour their elders and to maintain the emotional bond that links them to the language of their childhood. In some cases, meetings are also spent preparing publications: monographs, dictionaries, and life stories/ethnographic texts, or rehearsing plays, sketches, or songs which they then perform in public. The groups also sometimes organize 'awareness campaigns' for adults or children. Volunteers teach children lists of words and conjugations, expressions, and songs. They also talk about times past and the value of local heritage.

Several characteristics show that the social practices of these groups typically correspond to postvernacular dynamics:

(i) The language of activities during the meetings is almost always French, and the name of the language which is used by those attending is almost exclusively *patois*. The term *Francoprovençal* is only really used in exchanges with 'outsiders' such as journalists, the general public, scholars, or politicians. This scholarly term is then used to legitimize the cause promoted by these groups, who insist that FP be given the status of a 'language'. It is worth noting here, however, that some members remain convinced that their 'patois' cannot be considered a 'true' language, at least not in the same way as French. They associations do not aim to teach children the language. Sometimes the creation of 'language classes' is suggested, but such suggestions often meet with indifference on the part of most of members – and sometimes even actual hostility. And yet a certain type of linguistic transmission does appear to be happening, by 'immersion', during the shared activities, especially in the case of those who have been exposed to the language in the past. This kind of transmission is not identified as such by the groups. However, public awareness of FP is clearly something they aim at during their public actions, such as when language is introduced in a class or a library or 'staged' at village fairs.

(ii) The groups often say that they want to 'make the language live'; in other words, they are trying to give value to the language and to perpetuate its memory, since otherwise it is bound to disappear.

(iii) Local groups do not hold onto the hope that FP will again become the language of their region. They do not even wish to see it used as an everyday language between the members of the group. For them, the 'patois' has a very important symbolic function – namely to link them with the past and with their respective territories. Their desire is not to pass it on, but rather to keep its memory alive. This vision of the language does not match that of the regional Rhône-Alpes government, which has recently become involved in the promotion of regional languages spoken in its territory – FP and Occitan.

Unlike other French regions, such as Brittany and Aquitaine,[6] Rhône-Alpes has only recently established a linguistic policy (in 2009; for details, see Grinevald and Bert 2014). However, the region is promoting a 'unified' FP language rather than a set of local languages; it even condemns the use of the term 'patois' by local groups. The instructions sent to the local groups, such as 'Speak your language!' and 'Pass it on!' also reveal a deep misreading of the local situation, to the extent that these recommendations are addressed to people who, for the most part, do not feel fluent in FP and who suffer from clear linguistic insecurity. Moreover, the regional linguistic policy, promoted by the department of cultural services, does not really promote the daily activities of the local language groups. It tells them to 'make the language look pretty' (according to their own criteria based on the conception of a relatively élitist culture) and to be innovative and not old-fashioned. This is the department's reaction to plays that portray times past, plays in which the hierarchy between languages appears (with dignitaries speaking French and the common people speaking *patois*). Such plays tend to be seen as stigmatizing by officials, whereas the local groups and their audiences enjoy them for their self-deriding humour.

The regional linguistic policy therefore reveals how the non-written nature of FP and its dialectal diversity are negated. The decline of the language is not taken into account, and FP is considered a language that could still be transmitted naturally and could continue to enjoy some everyday communicative functions. The Rhône-Alpes region, influenced by the models applied to 'big' regional languages, is therefore in favour of teaching FP in school, whereas the local groups do not prioritize this for the reasons explained earlier.

The dynamics of the local groups are typically postvernacular and, as such, are not understood by policy makers; this misunderstanding has an impact on the role of writing, and hence the choice of orthographic forms

4 On Writing These Languages

4.1 The Written Form of Rama

4.1.1 Creating an Orthography for Rama Rama is an oral language documented by the linguist Colette Grinevald (then Craig) during the first phase of the RLP in the late 1980s. At that time, the issue of creating an orthography was not considered in the context of the standardization of the Rama language, but rather as a technical process that would enable Craig to describe and transcribe the language. There were no written texts in Rama then, except for a few lexicons or linguistic sketches written at the turn of the twentieth century by a few researchers, none of them with linguistic training (Lehman 1920; Conzemius 1927). The Rama people had never had access to the first writings, and when Craig showed Lehman's text to the few Rama who were literate, it was agreed by all that the orthographic choices he had made were too complicated. It should be noted that if the Rama could not be literate in Rama because of the absence of a literacy tradition in Rama, the fact of the matter is that in 1986 most were in fact completely illiterate. Indeed, the kind of English-based Creole that is their language of first socialization (a variant of the MCC) was not a written language either, and the Rama people who benefited from an education – which was in the official language, Spanish – were very few. From the Sandinista revolution onwards, Rama children were schooled in Spanish, a language they master only partially since their teachers are not fluent in it themselves, and people over 40 were, and still are, more or less literate.

The task of creating an orthography for Rama was thus initiated by a professional field linguist working with three main informants, only one of whom was literate. Craig followed the tradition she had established for transcribing the Mayan languages of Guatemala (cf. Grinevald 2002). The choice made was that of 'practical alphabets' – namely, alphabets that can be produced easily on the keyboards of Spanish typewriters, as opposed to transcriptions produced in the International Phonetic Alphabet (hereafter, IPA), which uses symbols and complex diacritics not found on a typewriter.

The graphic choice for writing Rama – one such 'practical alphabet' used to transcribe the language at a phonological rather than phonetic level – was also coordinated with the graphic choices made for the other languages of the Atlantic coast of Nicaragua by a group who called themselves 'Linguists for Nicaragua' that had been working together since the early 1980s. Of those languages, only the dominant indigenous Misquito/Miskitu[7] language has enjoyed a literacy tradition, established by Moravian missionaries in the nineteenth century. Today, a significant literature in Miskitu is available, as well as material in the other smaller languages, such as the various Sumu languages, Mayangna, and Ulwa. It is clear that by standardizing the orthographic principles used for all the indigenous languages of the region, the linguists helped provide a new social status (that of 'true' language) to the smaller ones, by proving that they too could be written and read in the same way that Miskitu was.

The creation of an orthography for Rama has not caused any problems within or outside the community. 'How it was written' did not matter; what mattered was the fact that the language could be written and be made visible through writing. Comments were sometimes made, however, about the lexical or phonological choices made, with an illiterate speaker judging them to be 'korek' or 'no korek'.[8] The issues raised in this context were more to do with the acceptability of the extensive variation found in Rama, rather a judgement on the way in which the orthography was being created.

Members of the Rama community do not generally write in Rama, because they do not need to. However, the fact that Rama is not a language in use also limits the potential uses of writing it down. For example, why does it need to be written down? And for whom?

The answer is that writing in Rama fulfils various functions within language revitalization.

4.1.2 Writings in Rama When writing is used to describe and document a language, the written form has a scientific function. It is a tool used by the RLP team, and it makes it possible to produce linguistic, pedagogical, and ethnolinguistic materials such as, for example, the encyclopaedic dictionary available on the Turkulka website.⁹ Such a function does not require any adjustment to be made to the existing orthographic system, because users are linguists and the examples provided in Rama are taken from Craig's work rather than new data. The members of the Rama community do not consult this website.

However, the documents produced can sometimes be used to teach Rama – for example, by young teachers trying to pass on the knowledge they have acquired to the children of the community. Little books of ethnographic texts and a few pedagogical books are often the only linguistic sources easily available to teachers. But such resources are few in number, and teachers who are not trained to use them may find them difficult to use. As a consequence, literacy in Rama does not develop within the school context. However, for the Rama community, the fact that such books exist represents proof that Rama is a language like any other – because not only is it written, but it can also be taught in school. Here, the visibility of the language prevails over the use of the object produced: a textbook in Rama is needed, but its content and the teaching methods used are secondary matters.

4.1.3   The Functions of Written Rama   In recent years, Rama has appeared on road signs, postcards, and promotional flyers for cultural events, all of which are mainly produced in order to promote the language for outsiders. What is written does not matter – indeed, as has been discussed, hardly any Rama can read and understand what is written. What matters is that outsiders can see that such material is written in Rama (Avanza and Laferté 2005; Pivot 2013; see Figure 14.1).

4.2   Writing in Francoprovençal

4.2.1   The Different Orthographic Systems Created for FP   From the Middle Ages onwards, FP has been used to write literary texts, but this literature – less abundant and prestigious than that of Occitan – remains unknown to most of its speakers. Scientific analysis of this literary corpus has shown that the orthography of FP has never been standardized; ancient authors generally tried to reproduce local phonetic characteristics using via the orthographic rules of French. For the linguistic analysis of FP, the only orthography that has ever been used is the phonetic alphabet – initially the 'French' version used in the *Atlas linguistique de France* (Linguistic Atlas of France), but more recently the IPA. Both of these clearly remain impenetrable for non-linguists.

When FP started to be of interest to non-linguists, a proposal relating to orthography was proposed by the Savoy region, following the model of

Orthography Creation for Postvernacular Languages 285

Figure 14.1 Rama features alongside Creole and Spanish in Bluefields' calendar (2010).

the orthographies developed in French-speaking Switzerland and in Italy. This so-called 'Conflans' orthography is phonetically based and aims to reproduce local pronunciation. However, writings in Conflans are not very accessible to people who are not speakers of the local language that has been transcribed. More recently, Stich recommended the creation of a unified, supradialectal orthography for FP (Stich 2003; cf. Martin 2005).

4.2.2 Issues Surrounding Writing in Francoprovençal The use of a written form of FP is quite rare today. Very few members of local focus groups can write in the language, and for most, even reading FP is difficult. The way in which local groups write in FP depends very much on why they are writing it. Private writings, such as notes on which to base stories or anecdotes to be told during meetings, are usually written in a member's idiosyncratic spelling system; indeed, the authors themselves sometimes struggle to decipher what they have written. Collective writing (such as song lyrics and plays) are generally more standardized, with the group agreeing on a few general principles but also allowing geographic variation to be reflected in the spelling used.

This means, of course, that one word may be written in many different ways, even within the same text. As these writings are principally a prompt for speech, such variation does not generally cause any problems of comprehension (see Figure 14.2).

This kind of orthography is also used in activities that aim to increase awareness of FP among the general public. The members of one focus group reported how, when they tell children that 'patois has no orthography', the children respond that they love that. In the French context, where the pressures exerted by the orthographic norm are very heavy and, consequently, orthographic insecurity very evident, writing in FP seems to represent a 'liberation' from the normative constraints that weigh on the French language. The FP texts that appear on the Internet often exhibit orthographic variation, a sign that the Internet is also considered as a space which is less subjected to the norms of a standard written form. However, standardization is deemed necessary for texts that are intended for publication – such as monographs, dictionaries, or ethnographic texts, whose main function is to make the language visible rather than understood (this is demonstrated by the fact that publications of this kind always include a translation in French). These texts are endowed with the prestige of 'published writing', in which orthographic variation does not seem permissible. Indeed, the very existence of an FP supradialectal orthography project contributes to the feeling of linguistic insecurity, as speakers generally feel that if FP were to have an orthography, that orthography should then be respected by all.

The establishment of a regional policy to promote the creation of a unified orthography could possibly encompass a certain degree of orthographic variation (although the principles that would then allow such an orthography to be used for teaching have yet to be established). The implementation of such a project, however, would inevitably meet with several hurdles in Switzerland and Italy, where orthographic models already exist, and particularly since the Rhône-Alpes region has taken the first steps towards creating an international FP charter that it would like both of these countries to sign. This charter would, among other things, call for a committee to be established which could monitory the 'quality' of the language, an institution that typifies the French vision of what a written language should be – namely, with an academy in charge of promulgating an established and accepted norm. Such a charter could therefore, paradoxically, weaken the position of local focus groups when searching for financial support for their publications. It is easy to imagine how tensions could arise if the manuscripts of these groups were deemed to contain too many traces of borrowing and obsolescent features which might be seen to fall beneath the standard normally expected of a 'language'.[10]

Jusé : - Ouah ! Ouah ! Peuye po allo pli vite que la musique, é peu mon piti orté me fa mo, je peuye à peine supporto mu z'équieu !

Mile : - Oh ! A te passero avin quà me reprenne !

Tatave arrive avec un fé d'herbes, il se prend les pieds et étale tout parterre

Mile : Ah ! Bonjou de bonjou é po poussible d'étre si maladré, te n'a foutu plein la quisine. Allez bougue de branquignol ramassa mé qué baza

Il s'active dans un joyeux désordre et repart coiffé de brindille en cahotant de ci de là

Mile : - Qu'ina bande de bras casso ! ! !

Le lever du Granpa

Mile : - Bonjou, vous z'alove bian, vous ove bian deurmi?

Granpa: -Woua, coume de coutime, tré mô ; jé mo de pretou ; fa po bon deveni vié, leu chambre veule pli me pourto.

M : - Oh vous z'o bian fa votre timps !

Gp· : - Di, to qu'a nou méttre dian la bouite yeure, a sara fini !

Mile (en aparté au public) - Inqueu loi, va po mo, mé la viéille quota groube !

Le lever de la Granma

Fanny : - Bonjou la ma, te sio coume lou pa, to mâ deurmi,

Gm : - Oh woua ! Ton pa a viro toute la na, iqueu ayé penible, é pé u l'a carcavelo la méta d'o timps, coume té feu fore pre dormi ?

Mile (en aparté au public) - T'o qu'a po te coucha, t'évitera bian de te levo, sala bétieu

Gm : - Di Fanny, te vo alto eu marché aujourda ?

F : - Woua, woua

Gm : - A feudra acheto 4 ou 5 poules, a n'ya que sian po jouénes !

Gp : - Lou chantâ eussé, u l'é vié, feudra n'adure in'eutre !

M : - Sé a feu changeo tout iqueu qué vié, n'ya queuque z'in que serian plu itié depé po mo de timps !

Le lever des enfants

Le Mile : - Bon a feudri beyeu levo lu matrus !

La Fanny : - Wouah ! y van étre en retâ après !

Figure 14.2 The different ways of writing 'yes' by the Francoprovençal association of Anneyron.

5 Conclusions

The different positions taken by different actors with respect to the role of writing, and therefore to the selection of an orthographic form, can be explained by analysing the different meanings that those actors give to the concept of 'revitalization'. For example, Huss (2008:12) claims that

> revitalization is commonly understood as giving new life and vigor to a language which has been steadily decreasing in use. It can be seen as a reversal of an ongoing language shift (cf. Fishman 1991), or it can be regarded as 'positive language shift', denoting the process of reclaiming an endangered language by its speakers.

This process of revitalization, with the aim of recovering all the prior communicative functions of a language, is based on the linguistic ideologies that the 'institutional actors' – the elite or the decision makers – of both the Rama and the FP speech communities share. As they negotiate the recognition of the endangered language as a 'true' language, they assert its need to acquire the same functions and characteristics as the dominant languages.

Within this ideology, the written form is one of the elements that legitimizes a linguistic variety as a 'true' language, since writing fulfils the prestigious function of providing a literary and cultural basis for the elites. For these elites, therefore, it is important that the endangered language be written and that this is facilitated and supported via the development and transmission of a standardized orthography, cleansed of the variation typical of oral languages. The need for a standardized orthography is also seen as essential before an endangered language can be taught effectively – and of course many 'big' world languages are essentially taught via their written form. Moreover, standardized orthographies are seen by many contemporary Western societies as essential for the creation of a literature. Finally, a postvernacular language needs an orthography because of its function as a marker of identity for its speakers.

And yet another meaning of *revitalization* exists, one in which the linguistic practices and actions that aim to keep an endangered language alive do not aim at re-vernacularization and do not claim to re-establish a language's prior communicative functions in the public and private spheres: this we term 'postvernacularity'. In such a situation, the language has a mainly symbolic function, and the written form does not fulfil all the expected functions. The social project organized to promote such a language is based on other linguistic ideologies – namely identification and belonging. Writing becomes an identity marker (cf. Sackett, Hull, and Valdovinos, this volume), and it goes without saying that standardizing the orthography would in some cases deny the expression of such local identity. Writing a postvernacular language is not necessarily linked to its traditional practice, which remains the preserve of those who keep it alive as an essentially oral language (and therefore not necessarily endowed with prestige). However, making such a variety 'concrete' via writing gives it a symbolic and valuable status as a 'real' language. Apart from the case of a few actors who find the existence of a standardized orthography useful to support their claims of distinct linguistic identity, creating such an orthography is not generally considered to be one of the main concerns of postvernacular linguistic situations. Indeed, what counts most for local actors is that the orthographic system used to write their language be as phonetically and lexically representative as possible of their local speech (as seen with FP in France) or be capable of endowing it with the status of a 'true' language (as seen with Rama in Nicaragua).

The issues that surround the creation of an orthography for an endangered language are often political. When they are associated with justifying the revitalization of such languages, they may even create situations of social discrimination, where those who master the 'standard' can create conditions for the legitimization or de-legitimization of the practices and action of other actors. Even when there is an apparent consensus about an orthographic system, the writing practices of 'non-official' local actors may be relegated to the margins of 'legitimate' practices. And even where the use of idiosyncratic orthographic systems may seem to be encouraged ('Don't worry about how you write, just write!'), writings produced by local actors may nonetheless be considered 'unsuitable' for literature and teaching, and it is often deemed necessary for them to be re-written in standardized orthography for them to be understood 'by everyone'. In this way, under the guise of making such writings intelligible to a greater number of people, a gap is created between those who master the standardized orthographic system and those who do not. In the case of languages such as FP in France and Rama in Nicaragua, the great majority of speakers happen to belong to the latter category, and such a course of action could well have an impact on their actions in favour of the language and on their attitudes towards its transmission. It also has the potential to create power struggles in the context of teaching the language, as the fact that teaching is usually associated with (and based on) a standardized writing system can result in illiterate speakers and semi-speakers being de facto excluded – even if they are fully literate in their native language (the dominant language). Contemplating a type of teaching that would be based on orality would require the re-negotiation of dominant models and a re-definition of what a language is and what its functions are.

Notes

1. This expression is used by members of local groups working to promote Francoprovençal to explain their actions on behalf of the language.

2. Words uttered by the members of activist associations when they talk about their context in relation to FP language practice.
3. MCC is an English-based Creole spoken by the majority Creole population in the southern region of the Atlantic coast (Holm 1978).
4. Words taken from interviews with members of the community during fieldwork conducted by Pivot in 2010.
5. This paper was written before the retracing of regional boundaries. Since 2016 the Rhône-Alpes Region is now called Auvergne Rhône-Alpes Region as these two were joined in one territorial unit.
6. This paper was written before the retracing of regional boundaries. Since 2016 the Region Aquitaine is now named Nouvelle-Aquitaine and is the merge of old Aquitiane and old Limousin.
7. Ideological choice of using the grapheme <k> for the phoneme /k/ rather that <c> or <qu>, which were considered too close to Spanish or to English orthography (cf. Hull, this volume), from which the indigenous communities of Latin America wanted to distance themselves in the 1980s.
8. MCC for 'correct' and 'incorrect'
9. www.turkulka.net/diccionario/ (last accessed 2 July 2015)
10. The writings of local groups show a loss of some traits considered characteristic of FP, such as paroxytonic stressing (which distinguishes FP from Oïl languages) or the double treatment of the Latin A (which distinguishes FP from Occitan).

15 Changing Script in a Threatened Language: Reactions to Romanization at Bantia in the First Century BC

Katherine McDonald and Nicholas Zair[1]

1 Introduction

The ancient Mediterranean was highly linguistically diverse: there is extant written evidence for dozens of languages and dialects, and there were certainly many more which were never written down or for which no direct evidence survives. Other than Latin, Greek, and a few others whose daughters survive to the present day, we know that these ancient languages underwent language death. We also know, therefore, that there was a stage at which they were endangered languages, and we assume that our latest written evidence often corresponds to the period when these languages and their writing systems were under threat. In many cases, this gives us an opportunity to try to understand how these ancient languages and their orthographies responded to external pressure from the languages which replaced them.

Of course, we can only use written, and not spoken, evidence in this kind of investigation, and this leads to some difficulties. We rarely know how long ancient languages were spoken after they ceased to be written, though it is usually assumed to be only a handful of generations (Adams 2003:112, 146–147; Clackson and Horrocks 2007:83; Wallace 2004:812). To put this another way, ancient linguists tend to assume that the cessation of writing corresponds to a language's transition from EGIDS level 1 or 2 (widespread official and governmental use at a national or regional level) down to 6b or 7 (use in face-to-face situations only, probably losing users to another language and/or not being passed on to the next generation), with a relatively swift progression towards extinction. How well these twentieth- and twenty-first-century criteria correspond to historical situations before the creation of nation-states is a matter for debate. But in the ancient world, particularly in the western Mediterranean, where Latin became the dominant spoken and written language around the first century BC, we tend to see languages swiftly declining from being the primary language of 'high' domains such as law, officialdom, and religion in politically independent communities across a widespread area to

Table 15.1 *The Roman alphabet used to write Oscan at Bantia.*

Letters/digraphs	a	b	c	e	f	g	h	i	l
Phonemes	/a/	/b/	/k/	/ɛ/	/f/	/g/	/h/	/e/, /i/, /j/	/l/
Letters/digraphs	m	n	o	p	q	r	s	t	u
Phonemes	/m/	/n/	/o/	/p/	/kw/	/r/	/s/	/t/	/u/, /w/
Letters/digraphs	x	z							
Phonemes	/ks/	/z/							

being used only for personal or casual writing such as graffiti or even, quite abruptly, no longer being written at all.

The other limitation of our written sources is that it is often difficult for us to know which, if any, of the languages of the ancient world were salient to their communities' identities and whether any of them held onto any symbolic value for their communities after they ceased to be written or spoken (Lomas 2013: 71–73; cf. also Sackett, and Leggio and Matras, this volume). In general, we have little evidence of this kind of symbolic value continuing for long after the languages ceased to be written, if they ever held this kind of significance at all, though some scholars have argued for these languages gaining a kind of symbolic or even 'nationalistic' value at the stage when they were threatened (Adams 2003:114–116; Lomas 2008:124; Lomas 2013).

We can, however, make a number of observations about how ancient languages and their orthographies seem to respond to being threatened. In the generation or two before they cease to be written, there are a number of changes in the written forms of a number of ancient languages. As with the languages spoken today, there may, for example, be extensive borrowing from the language which is becoming dominant (cf. Hull, this volume); sometimes there are 'mistakes' in the texts, or an apparent lack of familiarity with the language on the part of the composer or inscriber, which may reflect a wider loss of competence in the community.[2] In several cases, including Umbrian and Oscan in Italy and Gaulish in southern France, there is a change away from the community's traditional script towards the script used by the politically or economically dominant language – in these examples, a switch to using the Roman alphabet (e.g., in Umbrian: Wallace-Hadrill 2008:87–88).

This chapter deals with a change of orthography in the town of Bantia in southern Italy, one of the most discussed locations in our histories of ancient language obsolescence. The use of the Roman alphabet for writing Oscan (the town's traditional language) in Bantia, particularly in the *Lex Osca Tabula Bantina*, has been seen as an example of script change as part of an attempt at language revitalization in the face of severe pressure from Latin and loss of knowledge of Oscan (see Table 15.1). We would like to question this assessment based on the epigraphic evidence of how different scripts were used in Bantia and how the Roman alphabet was adapted to the needs of the Oscan language. We will explore more closely alternative possible motivations for the change of script, and what it might tell us about the stages of language endangerment at Bantia.

2 Language and Script at Bantia

Bantia lies in the north-east of the ancient region of Lucania, southern Italy (modern Banzi, in Basilicata).[3] From the fourth century to the first century BC, the written language of most communities in Lucania (along with the neighbouring regions of Campania to the north and Bruttium to the south) was Oscan.[4] We assume that Oscan would have been the language spoken by much of the population, although other languages such as Greek, Latin, Messapic, and Etruscan would also have been present in the area, and multilingualism would have been common. Greek/Oscan and Latin/Oscan bilingualism may have been particularly widespread (McDonald 2015). Some cities of the region, particularly along the coast, had Greek as their main written language for at least part of this period. The Latin colony of Venusia was founded about 30 km from Bantia in 291 BC and probably had a considerable Latin-speaking population of soldiers and other settlers throughout the third and second centuries.

Oscan was the written language of many independent communities across central and southern Italy. We do not know whether Oscan speakers felt any particular unity with each other, and these communities were all politically independent of one another, though Graeco-Roman sources imply that there were wider 'tribal' affiliations (Lomas 2013:71–74). The Oscan language was written in several different scripts. In Campania and Samnium, it was written in what is known as the Central or Native or National Oscan alphabet (see Figure 15.1). This script was ultimately based on the Etruscan alphabet and was written right to left. In Lucania and Bruttium, probably because of greater contact with neighbouring Greek cities, Oscan was written using the Greek alphabet, written left to right. This script was very slightly adapted, mainly to add a sign for /f/, which Greek lacked. These scripts influenced and interacted

·ᛌӖᛁИНІM·ᗡITᗺՈ·ᛌᐊᗺ8ՈV

upfals. patir. miínieis. 'Opfals father of Minis' (Capua 38)

Figure 15.1 An inscription in the National Oscan alphabet.

with each other (Zair 2013; McDonald 2015:63–93; Zair 2016:136–166), but both had stable orthographies in the regions where they were used.

For most of the period from the fourth to the first century BC, Oscan was used in these regions in 'high' domains such as administration, law, religion, and so on, and we have no reason to think that it was not a prestigious and well-used language. In the first century BC, there was a considerable change in the political situation in ancient Italy, marked in particular by the Social War (approximately 91–88 BC, though fighting continued long after this in some areas), in which Rome fought many of its Italian neighbours.[5] The aftermath of the Social War saw considerable resettling of Oscan-speaking areas by Latin-speaking Roman veterans and colonists, as well as the replacement of Oscan with Latin as the official language in 'high' domains. This combination of population movement and a loss of domains seems to have forced Oscan to become a threatened language very quickly. After the Social War, we have little to no evidence of Oscan being written, beyond a few isolated graffiti (Clackson and Horrocks 2007:83; McDonald 2012). It seems likely that the political and economic situation in Italy after the Social War, in which the whole peninsula was now administered directly by Rome in Latin, discouraged speakers from passing the Oscan language on to their children, and ancient linguists usually hypothesize that there were no more speakers of Oscan by the end of the first century AD (e.g., Wallace 2004:812, and, on preservation of Oscan in first-century Pompeii, Cooley 2002 and McDonald 2012).

What we do not know, and what this chapter seeks to address, is whether Oscan was already threatened before or during the Social War, and in particular whether the language and orthography of the *Lex Osca Tabula Bantina* can be used in evidence in answering this question. Latin/Oscan bilingualism was probably already common in most of the Oscan-speaking areas of Italy by the outbreak of war,[6] but was Oscan already losing speakers to Latin, or was the bilingualism relatively stable? Was the ethnolinguistic vitality of Oscan still strong before the war? Previous scholars have argued both sides, and the inscriptions produced at Bantia have been a key part of this debate.

Only two or three Oscan inscriptions have been found at Bantia, but among them is the longest and perhaps most important extant Oscan inscription: the *Lex Osca Tabula Bantina* (Bantia 1[7]; hereafter, Tabula Bantina; see Figure 15.2). The Tabula Bantina consists of seven fragments of a large bronze tablet, six of which once formed a single large piece of about 0.28 m high by 0.37 m wide. On one side of the tablet, there is a legal text in Latin; on the other, a legal text in Oscan. The text on both sides is written in the Roman alphabet, left to right. The fragment preserves around five hundred words of each text. It is now widely agreed that the Latin text predates the Oscan one, judging by the position of the nail holes in the tablet in relation to the text (Crawford 1996:195–196). The Oscan text is not a translation of the

Figure 15.2 Detail of the Tabula Bantina.

Latin – rather, the writers seem to have made use of the blank side of a bronze tablet with a redundant Latin law on the other side. The Latin text is dated, based on the comparative evidence of other known Roman laws, to the last decades of the second century BC or the beginning of the first century BC (Crawford 1996:199). The date of the Oscan text (100–91 BC) is based on the fact that it appears to have been inscribed at some point after the Latin text. There is no archaeological reason why the text could not be later than normally supposed, but in general it is agreed that a text which refers to the concept of a 'citizen of Bantia' (Oscan: *ceus Bantins*) was probably produced while the community was still politically independent and not after the Social War. This does not necessarily rule out a date during the Social War, but scholars have assumed, with Crawford, that they would have been busy with other concerns at that time.

There have been many different interpretations of the Tabula Bantina, which is an exceptional text in the Oscan corpus. Most discussions have dwelt on two key features: the use of the Roman alphabet for a text in the Oscan language and the apparent reliance on Roman legal language, phraseology, and content, much of which appears to date to the third century BC, in an Oscan text. Most interpretations have assumed that the script, the use of Roman legal language, and a number of apparent 'mistakes' in the text suggest that Oscan was already threatened, or even moribund, at Bantia by around 100 BC. It has therefore been suggested that the use of Oscan does not represent the use of the élite's usual written and spoken language, but rather that the use of Oscan represents a 'revival' of the language which reflects 'anti-Roman' sentiments.[8] Recently, Bispham (2007) has given a slightly more nuanced view, suggesting that the text 'almost gives the impression of the use of what had ceased to be a living, evolving language (for legal purposes at least)' (2007:143), but asking as well

> whether we may not see the lex Osca Bantina less as an attempt to revive a dying language, than as one to find a local idiom and make it the community's own, despite its obvious Latinity, and in the process make a political statement (as well as producing a political document) about Bantian distinctiveness in the face of an increasingly exclusive and intransigent Rome. ... I think we should see in the lex Osca Bantina ... an élite trying to lead a community towards a comfortable identity within changes which could not be resisted. Bantia was becoming more Roman, but, I would argue, was also appropriating the expression of those changes to adopt a distinctive and non- (as opposed to anti-) Roman position. (Bispham 2007:145–147)

This view, which rightly acknowledges that legal language is not necessarily representative of the state of the language generally, seems to us a better starting position than that of assuming a full-scale language revitalization – a rare event for which there are no ancient comparanda. But others have denied that the Tabula Bantina proves that Oscan was under threat at all, and have instead seen Bantia as a site of stable societal bilingualism until the Social War (Wallace-Hadrill 2008:89–90). In this view, a change of script shows widespread bilingualism, not language shift (cf. Umbrian, further north: Wallace-Hadrill 2008:87–88), and it would be teleological to see Oscan as threatened before the Social War just because we, with the benefit of hindsight, know that Oscan would cease to be written within the next one hundred years.

Faced with these two opposing views, how should we read the Tabula Bantina and its use of the Roman alphabet? Was Oscan an endangered language when this text was written? Since the Tabula Bantina is the longest and most detailed inscription from the period just before Oscan ceased to be written, it has the potential to tell us a great deal about the timing and nature of the shift from Oscan to Latin – if we can agree what it is telling us and not just what we would like to see. The rest of this chapter will undertake a detailed examination of the language, script, and orthography of the text, with a view to understanding the evidence for language shift at Bantia provided by this text. On the basis of this close reading, we will then attempt a reinterpretation of the motivations behind the orthography of the Tabula Bantina.

3 The Tabula Bantina: Language

Some scholars have suggested that the orthography and language of the Tabula Bantina itself demonstrates that Bantia had already shifted away from Oscan and that the diminishing knowledge of Oscan manifests in spelling and punctuation mistakes in the inscription. Thus, Vetter (1953:21) observed that word dividers were often found erroneously within words. He suggested that this was because the inscriber did not know Oscan; furthermore, he argued that many of the mistakes were due to knowledge of Latin. Thus, in *ex.eic* (line 11, 33) 'this' and *ex.aiscen* (l. 25) 'in these', *ex* was marked off because it was misanalysed as Latin *ex* 'out of'. Similarly in *com.parascuster* (l. 4) 'will have been raised (of a matter)', the first part was taken to be Latin *cum* 'with', and the first parts of *medicat.inom* (l. 16) 'magistracy' and *anget.uzet* (l. 20) 'will have pronounced' were taken as 3SG verbs ending in -*t*, as in Latin. The frequency of misplaced word dividers is certainly unusual, but mistakes in their placement are not unknown in ancient texts of this type (cf. the Umbrian Iguvine Tables [Um 1]), and it may be due to carelessness rather than lack of knowledge of Oscan. *Ex* is also an Oscan word, meaning 'thus', *com* is simply the preverbal version of the Oscan preposition *con*, and Oscan also has verbs ending in -*t*. And confusion with Latin can hardly explain mistakes such as *pocapi.t* (l. 8) 'whoever', where *capit* would give a good Latin word ('[s]he takes'). In general, the idiosyncratic use of word dividers, along with the rather frequent spelling mistakes, suggests lack of concentration on the part of the inscriber but not necessarily lack of competence in Oscan. Even if the inscriber were not a native speaker of Oscan, this does not unavoidably mean that this characteristic also applied to the composer of the law or to the community as a whole, as observed by Adams (2003:115).

In fact, the Tabula Bantina does contain evidence that the composer or inscriber was a native speaker of Oscan. Final /-om/ in the accusative singular of some nouns, and as the ending of infinitives, is written both -*um* and -*om* (e.g., *deicum* [l. 10] 'to say'; *dolom* [l. 5], *dolum* [l. 21] 'trick'). This is apparently due to a more rounded allophone of /o/ before /m/; exactly the same variation is found in Oscan inscriptions in the National alphabet elsewhere, where Oscan is clearly being spoken as a native language. Similarly, the Tabula Bantina shares devoicing of final /-d/ with other inscriptions from Lucania (Zair 2016:133–135), as shown by, e.g., *pocapit* 'whatever' /pokkapid/. These sub-phonemic features imply a native-speaker phonology in the composer/inscriber.

It has also commonly been stated that Oscan was already in decline at Bantia because of the considerable Latin influence on the language of this text. But, while the language of the Tabula Bantina and of Latin legal texts are indeed similar in many ways, this may not provide meaningful evidence for the status of Oscan more generally. In the first place, legal texts in Latin, Oscan, and other languages of ancient Italy demonstrate the existence of a legal register with similar features stretching back to the first half of the first millennium BC, as a result of shared inheritance, influence from Greek legal language, and long-standing cultural and linguistic contact (Poccetti 2009; McDonald and Zair 2012; McDonald 2015). Unfortunately, we do not have enough evidence of Oscan legal language to be able to date the development of many of these similarities with any degree of certainty, and some of the features of the Tabula Bantina may have had a long history in Oscan legal idiom.

However, Oscan legal and official language had also been coming under more profound Latin influence for at least a century prior to the composing of the Tabula Bantina. For example, the magistrates *kvaísstur* and *aídíl*, both loanwords from Latin, are attested in inscriptions from the early second (Potentia 9) and late third centuries (Pompeii 16), respectively. Similarly, the formulaic language of Pompeii 24, dated to the last quarter of the second century, reflects Latin legal language, but we have good evidence that Oscan was still a language used for official purposes and in 'high' domains in Pompeii until the establishment of a Roman colony there after the Social War.[9] If the Tabula Bantina is a translation of, or closely based on, an earlier Latin charter from the colony of Venusia as is often argued (Crawford 1996:276, 281; Bispham 2007:147–152), it is hardly surprising that it should seem Latinate. But it would not be prudent to use the relationship between Latin and the language of the Tabula Bantina as a proxy for the relationship between Latin and Oscan at Bantia as a whole. At most, one could see the Tabula Bantina as reflecting a stage in the loss of Oscan in one domain – legal language.

As already mentioned, it is sometimes assumed that the use of Oscan in the Tabula Bantina is itself a sign of attempted revitalization – the 're-adoption of Oscan' posited by Lomas (2008:125). But such a switch from Oscan to Latin and back to Oscan again is not supported by the evidence. It may be based on the mistaken assumption that the older Latin side of the Tabula Bantina was written at Bantia, but in fact this text was probably inscribed at Venusia (Del Tutto Palma 1995:166; Crawford 1996:199). Otherwise, there is no Latin text from Bantia which is necessarily earlier than the Tabula Bantina (see the discussion of other inscriptions in Section 5).

4   The Tabula Bantina: Script and Orthography

The language of the Tabula Bantina provides very little support for the idea that Oscan was already endangered at the time it was written. However, it is also often assumed that the writing of the inscription in the Roman alphabet is evidence for the endangerment of Oscan at Bantia, due to the loss of literacy in the National alphabet (Crawford 1996:274; Bispham 2007:143). In fact, this view is based on very little data. In the first place, there is no evidence that the National alphabet was ever used at Bantia, although it was used in the nearby region of Campania. Second, as this chapter shall demonstrate, the orthography of the text itself suggests that the composer or inscriber of the text may have been familiar with the Greek alphabet, which was used to write Oscan in Lucania and Bruttium into the first century BC.

We do not know who was responsible for the adaptation of the Roman alphabet, but internal evidence suggests that the orthography was designed, rather than being used haphazardly. There is consistency in the use of vowel symbols (with some exceptions discussed below): Oscan had three front vowels, /i/, /e/, and /ɛ/; and two back vowels, /u/ and /o/. Both /i/ (always) and /e/ (almost always) are spelt with <i>, while /ɛ/ is always spelt with <e>, /o/ with <o>, and /u/ generally with <u>. Clearly, such a system is not ideal from the point of view of a one-to-one phoneme–grapheme match (cf. Sackett, this volume), but it reflects the need to deal with a vowel system with one more front vowel than Latin. Long consonants are written with a single letter, with the exception of /dd/ and /ll/, which are sometimes written double. Non-writing of long consonants would have been an old-fashioned convention in the Roman alphabet by this time, suggesting that this feature was intentional on the part of the composer/inscriber.

Another feature suggesting deliberate thought about how to develop an orthography for Oscan in the Roman alphabet is the use of the letter <z> (also found in Bantia 2). As Crawford stresses, this letter was borrowed into the Roman from the Greek alphabet, at a relatively late stage: the earliest instance of <z> is as a control mark on a coin of 112 or 111 BC (Crawford 2001:311, no. 297).[10] This may be – but need not be – earlier than the Tabula Bantina. Even if it is earlier, it is striking that there is no certainly datable instance of <z> in a Latin inscription prior to the first century BC. Since there is no phoneme /z/ in Latin, <z> was only used in the names of Greeks or other foreigners in the first century. A plausible place for the earliest usage of <z> is on the island of Delos, where traders from Italy were in contact with Greek speakers, and where <z> is attested in an inscription from the second or early first century BC in the Greek name *Zephurus* (CIL 1² 2232). Since the Tabula Bantina is one of the earliest, if not the earliest, Roman-alphabet inscriptions to use <z>, it seems likely that – just as in Delos – the impetus for its presence in the inscription is due to the inscriber being aware of the use of <z> in the Greek alphabet, used in the south of Italy. In fact, the use of <z> in the Tabula Bantina closely matches that of Oscan inscriptions written in the Greek alphabet. Thus, we find spellings such as ειζιδομ (Potentia 1) 'the same' /esedom/, in which <ζ> is used to write the intervocalic allophone [z] of the phoneme /s/ (cf. the spelling εισειδομ Potentia 5).[11] This precisely matches the spelling of forms like *izic* (e.g., l. 7) 'this' /esek/ in the Tabula Bantina. Since Latin had no voiced intervocalic allophone of /s/, there is no precedent for this spelling in Latin orthography, so it was presumably taken over from the practice used when writing Oscan in the Greek alphabet, as was normal in Lucania.

The spelling of vowels and diphthongs also shows some peculiarities which may point to knowledge of the Greek alphabet. In general, the mistakes on the tablet clearly reflect copying errors. Thus, *ex.elg* for *exeic* (l. 11) is a mistake of reading, while many other errors are due to eye-skip to a letter a little later in the line – e.g., *sansae tautam* for *Bansae toutam* (l. 19) 'the people at Bantia' and *phim pruhipid* for *pim pruhipid* (l. 25) 'he may not prevent anyone'. But this is not an obvious explanation for *ceus* (l. 19) 'citizen' /keus/ or *angetuzet* (l. 20) 'they will have pronounced' /angetusent/, which have <e> rather than <i> for /e/ (cf. *angitu*[*st*] l. 2). *Hafieist* (l. 8) 'he will have' is usually taken to be a mistake for *hafie*{*i*}*st*, but there is no obvious reason for such an error. A reading *hafie*{*i*}*st*, implying a verb stem /hafjɛ-/, is contradicted by the evidence of hαfειτουδ in Buxentum 1, which implies a stem /hafe-/.[12] It seems much more plausible to understand *hafieist* as representing /hafest/, either with vacillation in the spelling of /e/ between <i>, consistent with the spelling elsewhere in the Tabula Bantina, and <ei>, leading to both spellings being used at once, or with eye-skip for intended *hafeist*.

For both the spellings <e> and <ei> there is a parallel in Oscan inscriptions written in the Greek alphabet, in which both <ε> and <ει> (as well as <ι>) are used for /e/ (Zair 2016:45–50). Not only are all these letters/digraphs used for these vowels, but they are frequently used inconsistently, with the same sound being written in different ways in the same inscription (for example, all three spellings of /e/ are used in the second century inscription Potentia 1). Consequently, it is possible that the apparent slips in the spelling of these vowels compared with the normal <i> are due to the influence on the composer or inscriber of knowledge of the Greek alphabet and experience of writing Oscan in it. The same possibility arises for the spelling of the complementizer *pous* (l. 9) for /pus/, which parallels the use of <ου> (as well as <o>) for /u/ in the Greek-alphabet inscriptions. In this case, however, the following word is *touto*, so this may be another case of eye-skip.

At the time of the Tabula Bantina, <ou> was also available, in addition to the usual <u>, in Latin inscriptions as a spelling of /u:/. However, *pous* in the Tabula Bantina contains the short /u/, not the long, and in this regard matches the Greek-alphabet digraph <ου>, which is used to write both the short and the long /u(:)/ in Oscan. Similarly, both <e> and <ei> could be used in Latin inscriptions to write /e:/ until the mid second century, but after around 150 BC, this sound had developed to /i:/. If the variation in the Tabula Bantina were due to Roman orthographical habits, it is Oscan /i(:)/ which we would expect to show spellings with <e> and <ei>, not /e(:)/, especially since in *hafieist* it is a short, not a long, /e/ which is represented. By comparison, the

Greek-alphabet equivalents <ε> and <ει> are used to write /e(:)/, both long and short, in Oscan. Consequently, we can rule out the idea that these spellings are Roman-alphabet variants rather than influence from the Greek alphabet.

A similar case of variation is found in the diphthong /ai/, which is usually spelt <ae> in the Tabula Bantina, but sometimes <ai> – for example, in *maimas* (l. 3, 7), *mais* (l. 5, 15), *exaiscen* (l. 25).[13] This variation could be Roman, since both older <ai> and newer <ae> for /ai/ are found as spellings in the second and first centuries, although <ae> is much more common by the start of the first. But given the other evidence for Greek influence on the spelling, the instances of <ai> may be at least partly driven by the consistent spelling of the diphthong as <αι> in Greek-alphabet Oscan inscriptions.[14]

As observed earlier, it has often been assumed that the use of the Roman alphabet was the result of a loss of literacy in the National alphabet, which accompanied a decline in the writing and speaking of Oscan, at least among the upper echelons of society. If, however, the composer and/or inscriber of the Tabula Bantina were aware of the Greek alphabet, which was used to write Oscan not far from Bantia, this changes how we see the adoption of the Roman alphabet at Bantia. The use of the Roman alphabet can then be seen as a positive choice rather than the result of illiteracy in the National alphabet.

There are various possible ways of reading the switch of script from the Greek to the Roman alphabet. One is that the adoption of one script over another should not be seen as ideologically driven, since both may have been primarily associated with a language other than Oscan. Although scripts can and often do involve concepts of identity (Lüpke 2011:322–323; cf. also Sackett, and Leggio and Matras, this volume), we cannot necessarily assume that they must have in this case. In Lucania, it may be that Oscan speakers were set apart from other groups by their language rather than their alphabet, which was shared with their Greek-speaking neighbours and also Messapic speakers to their east and south. Alternatively, given evidence that in the previous century Oscan-speaking communities such as Cumae actively used the idea of Latin as the language of public administration as a way of gaining favour with Rome, it is not unreasonable to suggest that the adoption of the Roman alphabet, at least for 'official' legal and religious texts, may reflect a somewhat positive attitude towards the Roman state.[15]

5   Conclusions

Scholars of ancient languages and societies, working in the light of knowledge of subsequent historical events, have perhaps tended to see language shift and loss of competence in every instance of borrowing and in every change of script, and to put undue weight on individual inscriptions. We believe that evidence from the twentieth and twenty-first centuries should act as a warning against this type of approach. Speakers of endangered languages can have many different needs and opinions on how best to write their language, even within one community (Seifart 2006:281–287). When our evidence is all but limited to one inscription in one community, we cannot make sweeping statements about the state of a language, since whatever was happening may be limited to a single domain or a single part of a community. In addition, while it is tempting to see cases like the Tabula Bantina in the light of modern language revitalization movements, we must be careful not to let our models of language endangerment and obsolescence run ahead of the data.

In the case of the Tabula Bantina, scholars have seen the inscription as symptomatic of a language heavily endangered by Latin suddenly acquiring a new sense of identity in the pressure of a changed political situation: 'the preparation and engraving of the text was intended to symbolize independence from Rome. Would an élite which wished to demonstrate its loyalty have put up a charter in Oscan?' (Crawford 1996:276). Perhaps not, but there are attitudes between 'loyalty' and 'independence'. The use of the Roman alphabet could show a friendly attitude towards Rome without a rejection of autonomy and local traditions, suggesting something closer to Bispham's 'non- but not anti-Roman'.

There is little evidence that either the language of the inscription itself or the change of script is part of a wider loss of competence in Oscan. While Oscan does seem to have disappeared rather swiftly after the Social War, certainly as a written and probably also as a spoken language, comparisons with the official inscriptions of Pompeii show that Oscan was not necessarily endangered prior to the war. The Tabula Bantina is an exceptional text in its date, length, and (probably) in its use of Roman legal language alongside existing Oscan models, and its very exceptionality may not make it a particularly useful tool in assessing the status of Oscan at Bantia or elsewhere.

For the sake of argument, if one were to accept that it demonstrates a stage in the shift from the use of Oscan to the use of Latin, this could fit into a narrative of domain restriction as part of a process of language endangerment (cf. Crystal 2000:82–84). Of our other Oscan inscriptions from Bantia, Bantia 2 is a dedication to the god Jupiter by a magistrate whose title is given as *tr.pl.*, probably standing for *tribuf plífríks*, a title attested in the Oscan National alphabet in several inscriptions, and almost certainly calqued on the Latin magistracy *tribunus plebis* 'tribune of the people' (Poccetti 2002–2003). Bantia 3 (= CIL 1^2 3181) consists of a number of inscriptions from an *auguraculum*, a place from which the flight of birds was observed; at least some of the inscriptions seem to be in Latin. So we could imagine that these inscriptions reflect a stage at which Latin is beginning to take over as the 'public' language of Bantia.[16] However, *tríbuf plífríks* is attested in inscriptions from around 200 BC (Histonium 4) and between 250 and 175 BC (Teanum

Sidicinum 2), so its use in Bantia 2 does not provide proof of endangerment of Oscan c. 100 BC; the use of Latin in Bantia 3 at around the same time could be evidence of stable societal bilingualism rather than shift.

In other words, the claim that Oscan was already endangered at the time of the Tabula Bantina rests largely on seeing the evidence through the lens of post hoc knowledge about the subsequent disappearance of Oscan over the following century. Examination of the evidence provided by the orthography shows that, even with the change of script, there is maintenance of some orthographic habits already in use in the region and some creative adaptation of the Roman alphabet, such as the use of <z> in the same way as in Greek-alphabet Oscan-language inscriptions. What has been seen as a revitalization of writing in Oscan by a Latin-speaking élite is in fact a change, or perhaps an experiment, in the use of the Roman alphabet on one unusually Latin-influenced text. We should be careful of seeing it in the light of an overarching narrative of language endangerment, death, and revitalization.

Notes

1. We would like to thank the Arts and Humanities Research Council for their generous support of the 'Greek in Italy' Project. Katherine McDonald's research has also been funded by Gonville and Caius College, Cambridge, and the British School at Rome. We would also like to thank Mari C. Jones for inviting us to contribute to this volume.
2. For methods of interpreting evidence of language contact in written texts, see in general Adams (2003:1–110) and Mullen (2013:74–83).
3. Bantia has sometimes been described as being in Daunia, i.e., northern Puglia. Del Tutto Palma (1995:165–168) has argued that linguistically the community has closer ties to Oscan-speaking Lucania, though the town's material culture may qualify as 'Daunian'. It may be preferable to see Bantia as a town which was at the crossroads of many different cultural and linguistic influences, including Greek, Lucanian (Oscan-speaking), Daunian (Messapic-speaking?), and Roman.
4. Oscan is a Sabellian language, of the Italic branch of Indo-European. It therefore falls within the same branch of Indo-European as Latin without being closely related enough for the two languages to be mutually intelligible (Wallace 2004:812–813).
5. The motivations of the Italians are much debated; for a recent summary, see Dart (2014:9–22); see also Mouritsen (1998:129–151). The debate centres on whether this was a war to defeat Rome, an attempt to found an independent state, or a fight to gain the rights and privileges of Roman citizenship, which they eventually received some decades later. There is no particular reason, of course, why every community or every soldier would have identical motives. We have no evidence for the Bantian view, except to say that the 'Lucanians' of Roman sources continued fighting long after citizenship had already been offered to the Italians (Appian, *B. Civ.* 1.53; Livy, *Per.* Book 80; McDonald 2015:28–33).
6. There are various literary and epigraphic sources which suggest that Latin was already spoken in Oscan-speaking areas, at least by élite men, during the second and first centuries BC, although we have very little direct evidence of the situation in

Lucania, let alone Bantia itself. Famously, the Oscan-speaking town of Cumae in Campania petitioned Rome to be able to use Latin for their official business in 180 BC (Livy 40.43.1). We also know that the coinage produced by the Italian side in the Social War (a newly created state called 'Italia', with its capital at Corfinium) was Latin/Oscan bilingual, perhaps reflecting a bilingual population which still valued Oscan (Adams 2003:116). There are a few Latin inscriptions in Lucania from the second century BC onwards, including in Oscan-speaking towns such as Tegianum (CIL I^2 1685).

7. All Oscan texts are referred to by the names used in Crawford (2011). Umbrian texts are quoted from Rix (2002).
8. For example, Lomas (2008:125): 'At one level, the re-adoption of Oscan as the official language of record at Bantia in the years before the Social War suggests that the Oscan language – but not necessarily the Oscan scripts – was a powerful symbol of local identity and anti-Roman feeling.' Cf. Crawford (1996:276): 'We also suspect that our text is the work of an élite which normally spoke and wrote Latin and which in any case used the Latin script and wrote from left to right, which became desperate to assert an Oscan identity.' Mouritsen (1998:78) characterized the language of the text as 'barely Oscanised Latin'.
9. The same picture is also found in other Oscan-speaking communities (Mouritsen 1998:79–81).
10. We are grateful to Michael Crawford for this information.
11. The symbol used for both the Greek <ζ> and the Latin <z> was Z; i.e., the actual letter form was identical in the two alphabets.
12. This is also backed up by the comparative evidence of the related languages Umbrian (*habitu* 'let him have', e.g., Um 1 VIa 19) and Latin (*habeō* 'I have').
13. The apparent use of both in *paei* (l. 22) is probably due to eye-skip to the following word beginning with *ei-*.
14. Nishimura's (2005) claim that <ai> in these forms represents something other than a diphthong /ai/ is implausible.
15. This would fit with the fact that the Tabula Bantina seems to be heavily based on a Roman civic law, of which Mouritsen (1998:79) observes: 'No parallels exist for such a full-scale adoption of a Roman constitution: generally the Italians showed considerable independence and originality in their use of Roman models.'
16. Religion is described by Crystal (2000:83) as 'usually the last domain to be affected'. But in ancient Italy, where religion was 'public' as well as 'private', one might expect that public religious inscriptions, such as those by magistrates, could in some circumstances show the same loss of language as other public domains.

Bibliography

Adams, J. N. 2003. *Bilingualism and the Latin language*. Cambridge: Cambridge University Press.
Adams, L. 2014. Case studies of orthography decision making in Mainland Southeast Asia. In M. Cahill and K. Rice (eds.), *Developing orthographies for unwritten languages*. (Publications in language use and education 6). Dallas, TX: SIL International, pp. 231–249.
Ainger, L. M. 1995. *My case unpacked: Memories of evacuation from Guernsey in World War II*. Dunstable: Author.
Alidou, H., A. Boly, B. Brock-Utne, Y. Diallo, K. Heugh, and H. Wolff. 2006. Optimizing learning and education in Africa – the language factor: A stock-taking research on mother tongue and bilingual education in sub-Saharan Africa. Working document presented at the Association for the Development of Education in Africa biennial meeting, Libreville, Gabon, 27–31 March 2006.
Allerton, D. J. 1982. Orthography and dialect: How can different regional pronunciations be accommodated in a single orthography? In W. Haas (ed.), *Standard languages spoken and written*. Manchester: Manchester University Press, pp. 57–69.
ALMG. 1996. *La normalización lingüística de los idiomas mayas*. Guatemala: K'ulb'il Yol Twitz Paxil (Academia de Lenguas Mayas de Guatemala).
ALMG. 1999. *Concurso literario idioma ch'orti'*. Guatemala: K'ulb'il Yol Twitz Paxil (Academia de Lenguas Mayas de Guatemala).
ALMG. 2001a. *Ojronerob' ch'orti': Vocabulario ch'orti'*. Guatemala: K'ulb'il Yol Twitz Paxil (Academia de Lenguas Mayas de Guatemala).
ALMG. 2001b. *Pojp jun*. Guatemala: K'ulb'il Yol Twitz Paxil (Academia de Lenguas Mayas de Guatemala).
ALMG. 2001c. *Utwa'chir e ojroner ch'orti': Tradición oral ch'orti'*. Guatemala. K'ulb'il Yol Twitz Paxil (Academia de Lenguas Mayas de Guatemala).
ALMG. 2005. *Na'tanyaj xe' ayan taka e pak'ab'ob', tzijb'arb'ir tama ojronerob' ch'orti' yi e castellano – tradición oral bilingüe de la cultura ch'orti', ch'orti'– castellano*. Guatemala. K'ulb'il Yol Twitz Paxil (Academia de Lenguas Mayas de Guatemala).
ALMG. 2009. *Ustayaj tz'ijb' te ojroner ch'orti': Gramática normativa ch'orti'*. Guatemala. K'ulb'il Yol Twitz Paxil (Academia de Lenguas Mayas de Guatemala).
Anis, J. 2007. Neography: Unconventional spelling in French SMS text messages. In B. Danet and S. Herring (eds.), *The multilingual internet*. Oxford: Oxford University Press, pp. 87–115.
Ar Merser, A. 1980. *Les graphies du breton (étude succincte)*. Brest: Ar Helenner.

Ar Merser, A. 1996. *Précis de prononciation du breton*, 3rd ed. Brest: Emgleo Breiz/Ar Skol Vrezoneg.
Ar Merser, A. 1999. *Les orthographes du breton*, 4e édition revue et corrigée. Brest: Brud Nevez.
Ascoli, G. 1873. Schizzi franco-provenzali. *Archivio glottologico italiano* 3: 60–120.
Avanza, M. and G. Laferté. 2005. Dépasser la 'construction des identités'? Identification, image sociale, appartenance. *Genèses* 61(4): 134–152.
Baker, C. 2011. *Foundations of bilingual education and bilingualism*, 5th ed. Clevedon: Multilingual Matters.
Baker, P. 1997. Developing ways of writing vernaculars: Problems and solutions in historical perspective. In A. Tabouret-Keller, R. B. Le Page, P. Gardner-Chloros, and G. Varro (eds.), *Vernacular literacy: A re-evaluation*. Oxford: Clarendon Press, pp. 93–14.
Barton, D. 1994. *Literacy: An introduction to the ecology of written language*. Oxford: Blackwell.
Bauernschmidt, A. 1977. The ideal orthography. *Nova lit* 5(3): 1–8.
Becerra, M. E. 1910. Estudio lexicológico. *Bol. soc. mex. geog. estad.*, 30: 97–112.
Bédier, J. (ed.). 1968. *La chanson de Roland*. Paris: Piazza.
Benson, C. 2004. *The importance of mother tongue-based schooling for educational quality*. Commissioned study for EFA Global Monitoring Report 2005. Paris: UNESCO.
Benson, C. and K. Kosonen (eds.). 2013. *Language issues in comparative education: Inclusive teaching and learning in non-dominant languages and cultures*. Rotterdam: Sense Publishers.
Bermel, L. 2007. *Linguistic authority, language ideology, and metaphor: The Czech spelling wars*. (Language power and social process 17). Berlin: Mouton de Gruyter.
Berry, J. 1968. The making of alphabets. In J. A. Fishman (ed.), *Readings in the sociology of language*. The Hague: Mouton, pp. 737–753.
Bert, M. and J. Costa. 2009. Etude FORA: Francoprovençal et occitan en Rhône-Alpes. Etude scientifique. Lyon. Available online at www.rhonealpes.fr/uploads/Document/b3/WEB_CHEMIN_5067_1255705111.pdf (last accessed 21 June 2015).
Billerey-Mosier, R. 2002. JPlotFormants v1.4 Formant-plotting software. Available at www.linguistics.ucla.edu/people/grads/billerey/PlotFrog.htm (last accessed 31 March 2015).
Bird, S. 2001. Orthography and identity in Cameroon. *Written language and literacy* 4(2): 131–162.
Bispham, E. 2007. *From Asculum to Actium: The municipalization of Italy from the Social War to Augustus*. Oxford: Oxford University Press.
Blanchard, N. 2003. *Un agent du Reich à la rencontre des militants bretons: Leo Weisgerber*. Leoriou bihan Brud Nevez 11. Brest: Emgleo Breiz.
Blasco Ferrer, E. 1986. *La lingua sarda contemporanea*. Cagliari: Ed. Della Torre.
Bleek, D. F. 1929a. Bushman folklore. *Africa* 2: 302–313.
Bleek, D. F. 1929b. *Comparative vocabularies of Bushman languages*. Cambridge: Cambridge University Press.
Bleek, D. F. 1956. *A Bushman dictionary*. New Haven, CT: American Oriental Society.
Bleek, D. F. (edited and introduced by T. Güldemann). 2000. *The ǁŋ!ke or Bushmen of Griqualand West: Notes on the language of the ǁŋ!ke or Bushmen of Griqualand West*. (Khoisan forum 15). Cologne: University of Cologne.

Bleek, W. H. I. 1858. *The library of His Excellency, Sir George Grey, K. C. B., Philology.* Volume 1, Part 1: South Africa. London: Trübner and Co.

Blommaert, J. 2004. Writing as a problem: African grassroots writing, economies of literacy, and globalization. *Language in society* 33: 643–671.

Blythe, J. and F. Kofod. 2002. Literature for the semi-literate: Issues for emerging literacies in the Kimberley region of north-western Australia. In R. McKenna Brown (ed.), *Proceedings of the Sixth Foundation for Endangered Languages Conference.* Bath: FEL, pp. 66–76.

Bolognesi, R. 1998. The phonology of Campidanian Sardinian: A unitary account of a self-organizing structure. Unpublished PhD dissertation, University of Amsterdam.

Bonfil Batalla, G. 1996. *México profundo: Reclaiming a civilization.* Austin: University of Texas Press.

Boretzky, N. 1986. Zur Sprache der Gurbet von Priština (Jugoslawien). *Giessener Hefte für Tsiganologie* 3: 195–216.

Bow, C. 2012. Community-based orthography development in four western Zambian languages. *Writing systems research* 5(1): 73–87.

Boynton, J. 2014. Don't paint us white. Unpublished PhD dissertation, University of Virginia.

Bradley, D. 2005. Issues in orthography development and reform. In D. Bradley (ed.), *Heritage maintenance for endangered languages in Yunnan, China.* Melbourne: La Trobe, pp. 1–10.

Brenzinger, M. 2003. Review of 'A Khoekhoegowab dictionary with an English–Khoekhoegowab index' (Wilfrid Haacke and Eliphas Eiseb). *Lexikos* 13: 330–333.

Brenzinger, M. 2013. The twelve modern Khoisan languages. In A. Witzlack-Makarevich and M. Ernszt (eds.), *Khoisan languages and linguistics.* (Research in Khoisan studies 29). Cologne: Rüdiger Köppe, pp. 1–31.

Brenzinger, M. 2014. Classifying the non-Bantu click languages. In L. Ntsebeza and C. Sanders (eds.), *Papers from the pre-colonial catalytic project.* Volume 1. Cape Town: University of Cape Town, pp. 80–102.

Brenzinger, M. forthcoming. Case study: N‖ng. In D. Bradley and M. Bradley (eds.), *Language endangerment.* Cambridge: Cambridge University Press.

Broudic, F. 1995. *La pratique du breton de l'Ancien Régime à nos jours.* Rennes: Presses Universitaires de Rennes.

Brown, R. M. 1998. Mayan language revitalization in Guatemala. In S. Garzon, R. M. Brown, J. B. Richards, and W. Ajpub' (eds.), *The life of our language: Kaqchikel Maya maintenance, shift and revitalization.* Austin: University of Texas Press, pp. 155–170.

Budd, P. and M. Raymond. 2007. Community-oriented outcomes of language documentation in Melanesia. In P. K. Austin, O. Bond, and D. Nathan (eds.), *Language documentation and linguistic theory.* London: SOAS, pp. 51–57.

Cahill, M. 2011. Non-linguistic factors in orthography development. Paper presented at the Linguistic Society of America Annual Meeting. Pittsburgh, PA: 6–9 January 2011.

Cahill, M. 2014. Non-linguistic factors in orthographies. In M. Cahill and K. Rice (eds.), *Developing orthographies for unwritten languages.* (Publications in language use and education 6). Dallas TX: SIL International, pp. 9–25.

Cahill, M. and E. Karan 2008. Factors in designing effective orthographies for unwritten languages. (SIL International electronic working papers 2008–001). Available online at www-01.sil.org/silewp/2008/silewp2008-001.pdf (last accessed 19 April 2017).
Cahill, M. and K. Rice (eds.). 2014. *Developing orthographies for unwritten languages*. Dallas, TX: SIL International.
Calaresu, E. 2002. Alcune riflessioni sulla LSU (Limba Sarda Unificada), *Plurilinguismo* 9: 247–266.
Calaresu, E. 2008. Funzioni del linguaggio e sperimentazioni linguistiche in Sardegna. *Ianua. Revista philologica romanica* 8: 1–17.
Calvez, R. 2000. *La radio en langue bretonne – Roparz Hemon et Pierre-Jakez Hélias: deux rêves de la Bretagne*. Rennes: Presses Universitaires de Rennes/Brest: CRBC.
Campbell, L. and W. J. Poser. 2008. *Language classification: History and method*. Cambridge: Cambridge University Press.
Casad, E. 1984. Cora. In R. W. Langacker (ed.), *Studies in Uto-Aztecan grammar Volume 4: Southern Uto-Aztecan grammatical sketches*. San Diego, CA: SIL – University of Texas at Arlington, pp. 151–459.
Castillo, E. S. 2000. Language related recommendations of the presidential commission on educational reform. *Philippine journal of linguistics* 31(2): 39–47.
Chamberlin, J. E. and L. Namaseb. 2001. Stories and songs across cultures: Perspectives from Africa and the Americas. In P. Franklin (ed.), *Modern Languages Association of America: Profession 2001*. New York: Modern Languages Association of America, pp. 24–38.
Chomsky, N. and M. Halle. 1968. *The sound pattern of English*. New York: Harper and Row.
CIL (Corpus inscriptionum latinarum). Berolini: apud Georgium Reimerum.
Clackson, J. and G. Horrocks. 2007. *The Blackwell history of the Latin language*. Malden, MA; Oxford: Blackwell.
Cojti Cuxil, D. 1992. *Idiomas y culturas de Guatemala*. Guatemala: Instituto de lingüística URLPRODIPMA, Universidad Rafael Landívar.
Collier, K. and M. Collier. 1975. A tentative phonemic statement of the Apoze dialect, Kela language. *Workpapers in Papua New Guinea languages* 13: 129–161.
Collins, C. and L. Namaseb. 2011. *A grammatical sketch of N|uuki with stories*. (Research in Khoisan studies 25). Cologne: Rüdiger Köppe.
Colom, A. 2013. How to … avoid pitfalls in participatory development. *The Guardian*, 4 April 2013. Available online at www.theguardian.com/global-development-professionals-network/2013/apr/04/how-to-design-participatory-projects (last accessed 31 March 2015).
Comisión Nacional de los Derechos Indígenas en México. 2012. *Derechos humanos de los pueblos indígenas de México*. México: Comisión Nacional de los Derechos Indígenas.
Constitución Política de los Estados Unidos Mexicanos (CPEUM). 2011. México: Comisión Nacional para los Derechos Humanos.
Contini, M. 1987. *Etude de géographie phonétique et de phonétique instrumentale du Sarde*. Alexandria: Edizioni Dell'Orso.
Conzemius, E. 1927. Die Rama-Indianer von Nicaragua. *Zeitschrift für ethnologie* 59 3(6): 291–362.

Cooley, A. E. 2002. The survival of Oscan in Roman Pompeii. In A. E. Cooley (ed.), *Becoming Roman, writing Latin? Literacy and epigraphy in the Roman west.* Portsmouth, RI: Journal of Roman Archaeology, pp. 77–86.
Corbet, D. 1871. *Les fleurs de la forêt.* Guernsey: F. Clarke.
Corbet, D. 1874. *Le jour de l'an.* Guernsey: Thomas-Mauger Bichard.
Corbet, D. 1884. *Le chant du draïn rimeux.* St Peter Port, Guernsey: Guérin.
Corongiu, G. 2013. *Il sardo una lingua normale.* Cagliari: Condaghes.
Corraine, D. 2000. Normativizatzione ortogràfica de sa limba sarda. *Revista de filología románica* 17: 257–282.
Costa, J. 2010. Revitalization linguistique : discours, mythes et idéologies; approche critique de mouvements de revitalization en Provence et en Ecosse. Unpublished PhD dissertation, Université Grenoble 3. Available online at http://tel.archives-ouvertes.fr/tel-00625691/ (last accessed 2 July 2015).
Costa, J. 2013. Language endangerment and revitalization as elements of regimes of truth: Shifting terminology to shift perspective. *Journal of multilingual and multicultural development* 34(4): 317–331.
Costa, J. and M. Gasquet-Cyrus. 2013. What is language revitalization really about? Competing language revitalization movements in Provence. In M. C. Jones and S. Ogilvie (eds.), *Keeping languages alive: Documentation, pedagogy and revitalization.* Cambridge: Cambridge University Press, pp. 212–224.
Coulmas, F. 2003. *Writing systems: An introduction to their linguistic analysis.* Cambridge: Cambridge University Press.
Crawford, M. H. 1996. *Roman statutes.* London: Institute of Classical Studies, School of Advanced Study, University of London.
Crawford, M. H. 2001. *Roman republican coinage.* (Reprinted, with corrections). London and New York: Cambridge University Press.
Crawford, M. H. 2011. *Imagines italicae.* London: Institute of Classical Studies, School of Advanced Study, University of London.
Crawhall, N. 1999. San and Khoe rights, identity and language survival in South Africa. In G. Maharaj (ed.), *Between unity and diversity: Essays on nation building in post-apartheid South Africa.* Cape Town: IDASA, pp. 33–57.
Crawhall, N. 2004. !Ui-Taa language shift in Gordonia and Postmasburg districts, South Africa. Unpublished PhD dissertation, University of Cape Town.
Crossan, R.-M. 2005. The retreat of French from Guernsey's public primary schools, 1800–1939. *Transactions of la Société Guernésiaise* 25: 851–888.
Crossan, R.-M. 2007. *Guernsey, 1814–1914: Migration and modernization.* Martlesham, Suffolk: Boydell and Brewer.
Crystal, D. 2000. *Language death.* Cambridge: Cambridge University Press.
Dahlquis, A. M. 1995. *Trailblazers for translators: The Chichicastenango twelve.* Pasadena, CA: William Carey Library.
Danet, B. and S. Herring (eds.). 2007. *The multilingual internet.* Oxford: Oxford University Press.
Dart, C. J. 2014. *The social war, 91–88 BC: A history of the Italian insurgency against the Roman republic.* Farnham, Surrey; Burlington, VT: Ashgate.
Dary, C., S. Elías, and V. Reyna. 1998. *Estrategias de sobrevivencia campesina en ecosistemas frágiles.* Guatemala: FLASCO.
Dawson, B. J. 1989. Orthography decisions. *Notes on literacy* 57: 1–13.

De Châlons P. 1723. *Dictionnaire breton-françois du diocèse de Vannes*. Vannes: F. Bertho.
DeChicchis, J. n.d. Current trends in Mayan literacy. Unpublished document, Kwansei Gakuin University, Sanda, Japan.
De Garis, M. (ed.). 1967. *Dictiounnaire Angllais–Guernésiais*. Guernsey: La Société Guernésiaise.
De Garis, M. (ed.). 1982. *Dictiounnaire Angllais–Guernésiais*, 3rd ed. Chichester: Phillimore.
De Garis, M. (ed.). 2012. *Dictiounnaire Angllais–Guernésiais*, 4th ed. Chichester: Phillimore.
Dekker, D. E. 2003. A case study of the first language component bridging programme in rural Philippines. *Philippine journal of linguistics* 34(1): 143–149.
De Prada-Samper, J. M. 2012. The forgotten killing fields: 'San' genocide and Louis Anthing's mission to Bushmanland, 1862–1863. *Historia* 57(1): 172–187.
De Rostrenen, G. 1732. *Dictionnaire françois-celtique ou françois-breton*. Rennes: Julien Vatar.
Del Tutto Palma, L. 1995. Forme della romanizzazione nell'epigrafia lucana. *Eutopia* 4(1): 151–198.
Dell'Aquila, V. and G. Iannàccaro. 2004. *La pianificazione linguistica. Lingue, società e istituzioni*. Rome: Carocci.
Dell'Aquila, V. and G. Iannàccaro. 2010. Alcune riflessioni sociolinguistiche sulle grafie spontanee dei dialetti sardi e sulla Limba Sarda Comuna. In G. Corongiu and C. Romagnino (eds.), *Sa diversidade de sas limbas in Europa, Itàlia e Sardigna*. Cagliari: Regione Autònoma de Sardigna, pp. 79–89.
Departamento de Educación Indígena. n.d. *Nayerijsïmua'ira'*. Nayarit.
Department of Education, ARMM. 2012. Partners develop Iranun language primer. Available online at http://deped.armm.gov.ph/2012/12/partners-develop-iranun-language-primer.html (last accessed 31 March 2015).
Department of Education, Philippines. 2009. Order No. 74, s. 2009. Institutionalizing mother tongue-based multilingual education (MLE). Manila: DepEd. Available online at www.deped.gov.ph/orders/do-74-s-2009 (last accessed 31 March 2015).
Department of Education, Philippines. 2013. Order No. 28, s. 2013. Additional Guidelines to DepEd Order No. 16, s. 2012. Guidelines on the implementation of the mother tongue based-multilingual education (MTB-MLE). Manila: DepEd. Available online at www.deped.gov.ph/orders/do-28-s-2013 (last accessed 31 March 2015).
Deshayes, A. 2003. *Dictionnaire étymologique du breton*. Chasse-Marée, Douarnenez and Brest: CRBC.
Deuber, D. and L. Hinrichs. 2007. Dynamics of orthographic standardization in Jamaican creole and Nigerian pidgin. *World Englishes* 26: 22–47.
DeVolder, C., C. Schreyer, and J. Wagner (eds.). 2012. *Kala kaŋa bi ŋa kapia – Diksineri bilong tok ples Kala*. Kelowna: Centre for Social, Spatial and Economic Justice.
Dickens, P. 1991. Jul'hoan orthography in practice. *South African journal of African languages* 11(1): 99–104.
DIGEIBIR. 2013. *Documento nacional de lenguas originarias de Perú*. Peru: Dirección general de educación intercultural, bilingüe y rural.

Djité, P. 2009. Multilingualism: The case for a new research focus. *International journal of the sociology of language* 199: 1–8.
Dobrin, L. 2008. From linguistic elicitation to eliciting the linguist: Lessons in community empowerment from Melanesia. *Language* 84(2): 300–324.
Doke, C. 1936. An outline of ǂKhomani Bushman phonetics. *Bantu studies* 10: 433–461.
Dowding, J. and Y. Marquis. 2012. *Warro! Learn Guernsey's language*. Guernsey: Guernsey Museums.
Easton, C. 2003. Alphabet design workshops in Papua New Guinea: A community-based approach to orthography development. Paper presented at the First International Conference on Language Development, Language Revitalization and Multilingual Education in Minority Communities in Asia, Bangkok, Thailand, 6–8 November 2003. Available online at www-01.sil.org/asia/ldc/parallel_papers/catheri ne_easton.pdf (last accessed 31 March 2015).
Easton, C. and D. Wroge. 2002. *Manual for alphabet design through community interaction*. Ukarumpa: Summer Institute of Linguistics. Available online at www .sil.org/resources/archives/51482 (last accessed 31 March 2015).
Ellis, W. 2012. Genealogies and narratives of San authenticities: The ǂKhomani San land claim in the Southern Kalahari. Unpublished PhD thesis, University of Western Cape.
Elšik, V. and Y. Matras. 2006. *Markedness and language change*. Berlin: Mouton de Gruyter.
England, N. C. 1996. The role of language standardization in revitalization. In E. F. Fischer and R. McKenna Brown (eds.), *Maya cultural activism in Guatemala*. Austin: University of Texas Press, pp. 178–194.
England, N. C. 1998. Mayan efforts toward language preservation. In L. A. Grenoble and L. J. Whaley (eds.), *Endangered languages: Current issues and future prospects*. Cambridge and New York: Cambridge University Press, pp. 99–116.
England, N. C. 2003. Mayan language revival and revitalization politics: Linguists and linguistic ideologies. *American anthropologist* 105(4): 733–743.
Exter, M. 2008. Properties of the anterior and posterior click closures in Nǀuu. Unpublished PhD dissertation, University of Cologne.
Exter, M. 2013. Nǀuu Lexikon. Unpublished manuscript, University of Cologne.
Exter, M. 2015. Lexical tones in Nǀuu: A first descriptive approach. Unpublished manuscript.
Falc'hun, F. 1953. Autour de l'orthographe bretonne. *Annales de Bretagne* 60(1): 48–77. Also available online at www.persee.fr/web/revues/home/prescript/article/a bpo_0003-391x_1953_num_60_1_1905 (last accessed 2 July 2015).
Falc'hun, F. 1981. *Perspectives nouvelles sur l'histoire de la langue bretonne*. Paris: Union générale d'éditions. (Revised and expanded version of the author's doctoral dissertation, Rennes, 1951, first published as *Histoire de la langue bretonne d'après la géographie linguistique*. Paris: PUF, 1963).
Fehn, A.-M., T. Güldemann, H. Nakagawa, and C. Naumann. 2014. Proposal for a unified alphabetical treatment of IPA click symbols in orthographies, dictionaries, etc. Paper presented at the Fifth International Symposium on Khoisan Languages and Linguistics, Riezlern/Kleinwalsertal, Austria, 13–17 July 2014.
Ferguson, C. 2013. The subjunctive in Guernsey French: Implications for gauging authenticity in an endangered language. Unpublished PhD dissertation, University of the West of England, Bristol.

Fischer, E. F. 2010. *Cultural logics and global economies: Maya identity in thought and practice.* Austin: University of Texas Press.

Fishman, J. A. (ed.). 1977. *Advances in the creation and revision of writing systems.* The Hague: Mouton.

Fishman, J. A. 1991. *Reversing language shift: Theoretical and empirical foundations of assistance to threatened languages.* Clevedon: Multilingual Matters.

Fishman, J. A. 2001. *Can threatened languages be saved? Reversing language shift, revisited: A 21st century perspective.* Clevedon: Multilingual Matters.

Fleuriot, L. 1964. *Le vieux-breton: éléments d'une grammaire.* Paris: Klincksieck.

Fleuriot, L. 1964, 1985. *Dictionnaire des gloses en vieux-breton.* Paris: Klincksieck. (English edition: C. Evans and L. Fleuriot 1985. *A dictionary of Old Breton/ Dictionnaire du vieux breton: Historical and comparative.* 2 volumes. Toronto: Prepcorp).

Foley, W. A. 2004. Language endangerment, language documentation and capacity building: Challenges from New Guinea. In P. K. Austin (ed.), *Language documentation and description.* Volume 2. London: SOAS, pp. 28–38.

Fought, J. G. 1967. Chorti (Mayan): Phonology, morphophonemics, and morphology. Unpublished PhD dissertation, Yale University.

Fought, J. G. 1972. *Chortí (Mayan) texts.* Philadelphia: University of Pennsylvania Press.

Francis, N. and J. Reyhner. 2002. *Language and literacy teaching for indigenous education: A bilingual approach.* Clevedon: Multilingual Matters.

Friedman, V. A. 2005. The Romani language in Macedonia in the third Millenium: Progress and problems. In B. Schrammel, D. W. Halwachs, and G. Ambrosch (eds.), *General and applied Romani linguistics.* Munich: Lincom Europa, pp. 163–173.

Gamboa Montejano, M. 2008. *Derechos indígenas. Estudio teórico conceptual, de antecedentes e iniciativas, presentes en la LIX legislatura y en los dos primeros años de ejercicio de la LX legislatura (primera parte).* México: Dirección de Servicios de Investigación y Análisis de la Cámara de Diputados de la LX Legislatura – Centro de Documentación y Análisis.

Giffen, R. 2015. We begin to write: Creating and using the first Nabit orthography. Unpublished master's dissertation, University of British Columbia.

Girard, P. 1978. Education in Guernsey – Part II. *Report and transactions of la Société Guernésiaise* 20: 343–365.

Girard, P. 1980. George Métivier, Guernsey's national poet. *Report and transactions of la Société Guernésiaise* 20: 617–633.

Girard, R. 1949. *Los chortís ante el problema maya; historia de las culturas indígenas de America, desde su origen hasta hoy.* 5 volumes. Mexico: Antigua Librería Robredo.

Girard, R. 1962. *Los Maya eternos.* Mexico: Antigua Librería Robredo.

González Galván, J. A. 1994. Reforma al artículo 4 constitucional: Pluralidad cultural y derecho de los pueblos indígenas. *Boletín Mexicano de derecho comparado* 79: 105–111.

Goody, J. 1987. *The interface between the written and the oral.* Cambridge: Cambridge University Press.

Goody, J. and I. P. Watt. 1963. The consequences of literacy. *Comparative studies in history and society* 5: 304–345.

Goody, J. and I. P. Watt. 1968. The consequences of literacy. In J. Goody (ed.), *Literacy in traditional societies*. Cambridge: Cambridge University Press, pp. 27–68.

Grenoble, L. A. and L. J. Whaley. 2006. *Saving languages: An introduction to language revitalization*. Cambridge: Cambridge University Press.

Grinevald, C. 1998. Language endangerment in South America: A programmatic approach. In L. A Grenoble and L. J. Whaley (eds.), *Endangered languages: Current issues and future prospects*. Cambridge: Cambridge University Press, pp. 124–159.

Grinevald, C. 2002. Linguistique et langues mayas du Guatemala. *Faits de langues (Méso-Amérique, Caraibes, Amazonie)* 20: 17–25.

Grinevald, C. 2005. Why the Tiger language and not Rama Cay Creole? Language revitalization made harder. In P. K. Austin (ed.), *Language documentation and description*. Volume 3. London: SOAS, pp. 196–224.

Grinevald, C. and M. Bert. 2011. Speakers and communities. In P. K. Austin and J. Sallabank (eds.), *The Cambridge handbook of endangered languages*. Cambridge: Cambridge University Press, pp. 45–65.

Grinevald, C. and M. Bert. 2014. Whose ideology, where and when? Rama (Nicaragua) and Francoprovençal (France) experiences. In P. K. Austin and J. Sallabank (eds.), *Endangered languages: Beliefs and ideologies in language documentation and revitalization*. Oxford: Oxford University Press, pp. 355–383.

Grinevald, C. and B. Pivot. 2013. On the revitalization of a 'treasure language', the Rama Language Project of Nicaragua. In M. C. Jones and S. Ogilvie (eds.), *Keeping languages alive: Documentation, pedagogy and revitalization*. Cambridge: Cambridge University Press, pp. 181–197.

Gudschinsky, S. C. 1972. Notes on neutralization and orthography. *Notes on literacy* 14: 21–22.

Guillevic, A. and P. Le Goff. 1902, *Grammaire bretonne du dialecte de Vannes*. Vannes: Galles.

Güldemann, T. 2006. The San languages of southern Namibia: Linguistic appraisal with special reference to J. G. Krönlein's N|uusaa data. *Anthropological linguistics* 48(4): 369–395.

Güldemann, T. 2014a. 'Khoisan' language classification today. In T. Güldemann and A.-M. Fehn (eds.), *Beyond 'Khoisan': Historical relations in the Kalahari Basin*. Amsterdam/Philadelphia: John Benjamins, pp. 1–41.

Güldemann, T. 2014b. Towards casting a wider net over N|ng: Chances and challenges of archival Khoisan resources. Paper presented at the N|ng (N|uu) Conference: Past and Present of the Language and Its Speakers, University of Cape Town, South Africa, 17 March 2014.

Güldemann, T., M. Ernszt, S. Siegmund, and A. Witzlack-Makarevich. forthcoming. *A text documentation of N|uu*. Electronic corpus (unpublished, extracted wordlist only).

Güldemann, T. and R. Vossen. 2000. Khoisan. In B. Heine and D. Nurse (eds.), *African languages: An introduction*. Cambridge: Cambridge University Press, pp. 99–122.

Haarmann, H. 1990. Language planning in the light of a general theory of language: A methodological framework. *International journal of the sociology of language* 86: 103–126.

Halwachs, D. 2009. Romani: An endangered language? Paper presented at the Annual Conference of the Gypsy Lore Society, Helsinki, 29 August 2009.

Halwachs, D. 2012. Functional expansion and language change: The case of Burgenland Romani. *Romani studies* 22: 49–66.
Hansen, D., B. Shneiderman, and M. A. Smith. 2011. *Analysing social media networks with NodeXL: Insights from a connected world.* Amsterdam: Morgan Kaufman.
Hatcher, L. 2008. Script change in Azerbaijan: Acts of identity. *International journal of the sociology of language* 192: 105–116.
Heine, B. and H. Honken. 2010. The Kx'a family: A new Khoisan genealogy. *Journal of Asian and African studies* 79: 5–36.
Hemon, R. 1955. La spirante dentale en breton. *Zeitschrift für celtische philologie* 25(1–2): 59–87.
Hemon, R. 1975. *A historical morphology and syntax of Breton.* Dublin: Institute for Advanced Studies.
Henly, A. T. 1949. *Ichin nou pâle l'patouais. Patois spoken here: A selection of poems.* Guernsey: House of Books.
Hentschel, E. 1998. Communication on IRC. *Linguistik online* 1(1). Available online at www.linguistik-online.com/irc.htm (last accessed 27 March 2015).
Heugh, K. 2002. Recovering multilingualism: Language policy developments in South Africa. In R. Mesthrie (ed.), *Language in South Africa.* Cambridge: Cambridge University Press, pp. 449–475.
Heugh, K. 2005a. Language education policies in Africa. In K. Brown (ed.), *Encyclopedia of language and linguistics.* Volume 6. 2nd ed. Amsterdam: Elsevier Science, pp. 414–423.
Heugh, K. 2005b. Teacher education issues: Implementation of a new curriculum and language in education policy. In N. Alexander (ed.), *Mother tongue-based bilingual education in South Africa: The dynamics of implementation.* (Multilingualism, subalternity and hegemony of English 4). Frankfurt am Main: Multilingualism Network and Cape Town PRAESA, pp. 137–158.
Heugh, K. and T. Skutnabb-Kangas (eds.). 2010. *Multilingual education works: From the periphery to the centre.* Hyderabad: Orient Blackswan.
Hewitt, S. 1987. Réflexions et propositions sur l'orthographe du breton. *La Bretagne linguistique* 3: 41–54.
Hill, K. (ed.). 2000. *The collected works of Marjorie Ozanne 1897–1973 in Guernsey-French with English translations.* Volume 1. Guernsey: La Société Guernésiaise.
Hinton, L. 2001. New writing systems. In L. Hinton and K. Hale (eds.), *The green book of language revitalization in practice.* San Diego, CA: Academic Press, pp. 239–250.
Hinton, L. 2014. Orthography wars. In M. Cahill and K. Rice. (eds.), *Developing orthographies for unwritten languages.* (Publications in language use and education 6). Dallas TX: SIL International, pp. 139–168.
Hipfner-Boucher, K., K. Lam, and X. Chen. 2014. The effects of bilingual education on the English language and literacy outcomes of Chinese-speaking children. *Written language and literacy* 17(1): 116–138.
Hockett, C. F. 1955. *A manual of phonology.* Bloomington: Indiana University Publications in Anthropology and Linguistics.
Holm, J. A. 1978. The Creole English of Nicaragua's Miskito Coast: Its sociolinguistic history and a comparative study of its syntax and lexicon. Bibliographical record. London: University of London.

Holton, G. 2009. Creating sustainable language communities through creolization. In A. M. Goodfellow (ed.), *Speaking of endangered languages: Issues in revitalization*. Newcastle upon Tyne: Cambridge Scholars Publishing, pp. 238–265.
Hull, K. 2003. Verbal art and performance in Ch'orti' and Maya hieroglyphic writing. Unpublished PhD dissertation, University of Texas at Austin.
Hull, K. 2005. An abbreviated dictionary of Ch'orti' Maya. A final report for the Foundation for the Advancement of Mesoamerican Studies, Inc. (FAMSI). www.famsi.org/reports/03031/index.html
Huss, L. 2008. Researching language loss and revitalization. *Encyclopedia of language and education*. New York: Springer, pp. 3274–3286.
Ibragimov, G. X. 1990. *Цахурский язык (Tsakhur language)*. Moscow: Academy of Sciences USSR.
Ibragimov, G. X. 1992. Language situation in Dagestan and minority ethnic groups. In V. M. Soltsev and V. Y. Milchalchenko (eds.), *The language situation in the Russian Federation*. Moscow: Russian Academy of Sciences.
Instituto Nacional de Estadística y Geografía (INEGI). 2010. *Censo nacional de población y vivienda*. Mexico City: Instituto Nacional de Estadística y Geografía.
Instituto Nacional de Lenguas Indígenas. 2008. *Catálogo de las lenguas indígenas nacionales: Variedades lingüísticas de México con sus autodenominaciones y referencias geoestadísticas*. Mexico: Diario Oficial de la Federación (14 January).
Jackson, K. H. 1967. *A historical phonology of Breton*. Dublin: Institute for Advanced Studies.
Jaffe, A. 2000. Introduction: Non-standard orthography and non-standard speech. *Journal of sociolinguistics* 4(4): 497–513.
Jehan, R. 1999. *Des poêmes en Guernésiais*. Guernsey: The Author.
Jennings, G. and Y. Marquis (eds.). 2011. *The toad and the donkey: An anthology of Norman literature from the Channel Islands*. London: Frances Boutle.
Johnson, H. 2013. 'The group from the west': Song, endangered language and sonic activism on Guernsey. *Journal of marine and island cultures* 1: 99–112.
Johnson, M. 1994. *Organized phonology data of Kela*. Unpublished manuscript. Ukarumpa: SIL International.
Johnson, S. 2005. *Spelling trouble? Language, ideology and the reform of German orthography*. Clevedon: Multilingual Matters.
Jones, D. 1950. *The phoneme*. Cambridge: Heffer and Sons.
Jones, M. A. 1993. *Sardinian syntax*. London: Routledge.
Jones, M. C. 2002. 'Mette a haut dauve la grippe des angllais': Convergence on the island of Guernsey. In M. C. Jones and Edith Esch (eds.), *Language change: The interplay of internal, external and non-linguistic factors*. Berlin: Mouton de Gruyter, pp. 143–168.
Jones, M. C. 2008. *The Guernsey Norman French translations of Thomas Martin: A linguistic study of an unpublished archive*. Leuven: Peeters.
Kaplan, R. B. and R. B. Baldauf. 1997. *Language planning from practice to theory*. Clevedon: Multilingual Matters.
Karan, E. 2013. The ABD of orthography testing: Integrating formal or informal testing into the orthography development process. *Work papers of the Summer Institute of Linguistics*, University of North Dakota Session (53): 1–19.

Karan, E. 2014. Standardization: What's the hurry? In M. Cahill and K. Rice (eds.), *Developing orthographies for unwritten languages*. (Publications in language use and education 6). Dallas, TX: SIL International, pp. 107–138.

Kaufman, T. 1970. *Proyecto de alfabetos y ortografías para escribir las lenguas mayances*, 5th ed. Guatemala City: Ministerio de Educacíon; Editorial José de Pineda Ibarra, August 1975

Keene, E. O. 2007. The essence of understanding. In K. Beers, R. E. Probst, and L. Rief (eds.), *Adolescent literacy: Turning practice into promise*. Portsmouth, NH: Heinemann, pp. 311–314.

Kergoat, L. 1974. *Reolennoù an doare-skrivañ nevez*. Rennes: Skol an Emsav.

Kibrik, A. and J. Testelec (eds.). 1999. Элементы цахурского языка в типологическом освещении ('Studies in Tsakhur: A typological perspective'). Moscow: Naslediye.

Kilian-Hatz, C. 2003. *Khwe dictionary with a supplement on Khwe place-names of West Caprivi by Matthias Brenzinger*. (Namibian African studies 7). Cologne: Rüdiger Köppe.

Kiparsky, P. 1998. Paradigm effects and opacity. Unpublished manuscript. Stanford University.

Kiparsky, P. 2000. Opacity and cyclicity. *The linguistic review* 17: 351–367.

Kloss, H. 1967. 'Abstand languages' and 'ausbau languages'. *Anthropological linguistics* 9: 29–41.

Kloss, H. 1978. *Die Entwicklung neuer germanischer Kultursprachen seit 1800*. Düsseldorf: Pädagogischer Verlag Schwann.

Kloss, H. 1993. Abstand languages and ausbau languages. *Anthropological linguistics* 35: 158–170.

Krönlein, J. G. 1861. *Vokabular der lNusan-Sprache*. Unpublished manuscript. Grey Collection of the National Library of South Africa, Cape Town.

Kulick, D. 1992. *Language shift and cultural reproduction: Socialization, self, and syncretism in a Papua New Guinean village*. Cambridge: Cambridge University Press.

Kutsch Lojenga, C. 1996. Participatory research in linguistics. *Notes on linguistics* 73 (2): 13–27.

Kutsch Lojenga, C. 2014a. Orthography and tone: A tone-system typology with implications for orthography development. In M. Cahill and K. Rice (eds.), *Developing orthographies for unwritten languages*. (Publications in language use and education 6). Dallas TX: SIL International, pp. 49–72.

Kutsch Lojenga, C. 2014b. Basic principles for establishing word boundaries. In M. Cahill and K. Rice (eds.), *Developing orthographies for unwritten languages*. (Publications in language use and education 6). Dallas TX: SIL International, pp. 73–106.

Lagadeuc, J. 1499. *Le Catholicon: dictionnaire breton-latin-français*. Tréguier: Jehan Calvez.

Lai, R. 2009. Gradi di forza nelle occlusive di una sotto-varietà campidanese dell'Ogliastra. *Rivista Italiana di dialettologia* 33: 85–100.

Lai, R. 2013. *Positional effects in Sardinian muta cum liquida: Lenition, metathesis, and liquid deletion*. Alexandria: Edizioni Dell'Orso.

Lai, R. 2014. Positional factors in the evolution of Sardinian muta cum liquida: A case study. *L'Italia dialettale* 75: 149–160.

Lai, R. 2015. Word-initial geminates in Sardinian. *Quaderni di linguistica e studi orientali* 1: 37–60. doi: 10.13128/QULSO-2421-7220-16515

Lakota Language Consortium. 2012. *New Lakota dictionary*, 2nd ed. Bloomington, IN: Lakota Language Consortium.

Lawrence-King, A. and Harp Consort. 2004. *Les travailleurs de la mer*. Harmonia Mundi – HMU 907330. (CD).

Le Dû, J. 2001. *Nouvel atlas linguistique de la Basse-Bretagne*. 2 volumes. Brest: CRBC.

Le Gonidec, J.-F. 1807. *Grammaire celto-bretonne*. Paris: Rougeron.

Le Gonidec, J.-F. 1821. *Dictionnaire celto-breton ou breton-français*. Angoulême: Trémeau.

Le Gonidec, J.-F. 1838. *Grammaire celto-bretonne*, 2nd ed. Paris: H. Delloye.

Le Gonidec, J.-F. and T. Hersant de la Villemarqué. 1847. *Dictionnaire français-breton*. Saint-Brieuc: Prud'homme.

Le Pelletier, D. L. 1752. *Dictionnaire étymologique de la langue bretonne*, Paris: François Delaguette.

Le Pipec, E. 2015. La palatalisation en vannetais. *La Bretagne linguistique* 20.

Le Roux, P. 1924–1963. *Atlas linguistique de la Basse-Bretagne*. 6 volumes. Rennes-Paris (reprint 1977: Brest: Éditions Armoricaines). Available online at http://sba huaud.free.fr/ALBB/ and http://projetbabel.org/atlas_linguistique_bretagne/ (last accessed 4 July 2015).

Le Ruyet, J.-C. 2009. Enseignement du breton: parole, liaison et norme: étude présentée dans le cadre d'un corpus de qutre règles de pronunciation pour le breton des écoles. Unpublished PhD dissertation, Université Rennes 2. Available online at http://tel.archives-ouvertes.fr/docs/00/45/82/17/ANNEX/thes; http://tel.archives-ouvertes.fr/docs/00/45/82/17/PDF/theseLeRuyet.pdfeLeRuyetResume.pdf; and http://breizh.blogs.ouest-france.fr/archive/2011/01/26/faut-il-reformer-l-orthographe-du-breton.html (last accessed 4 July 2015).

Lebarbenchon, R. J. 1980. *Des filles, une sorcière, Dame Toumasse et quelques autres*. Montebourg: Azeville.

Legge regionale 15 ottobre 1997, n. 26. *Promozione e valorizzazione della cultura e della lingua della Sardegna*. Available online at www.regione.sardegna.it/j/v/86?v=9&c=72&s=1&file=1997026 (last accessed 20 February 2015).

Legge 15 dicembre 1999, n. 482. *Norme in materia di tutela delle minoranze linguistiche storiche*. Available online at www.parlamento.it/parlam/leggi/994821.htm (last accessed 20 February 2015).

Leggio, D. V. 2011. The dialect of the Mitrovica Roma. *Romani studies* 21: 57–113.

Leggio, D. V. 2013. *Lace avilen ko radio*. Romani language and identity on the internet. Manchester: University of Manchester.

Lehman, W. 1920. Die Rama Sprache. *Zentral Amerikas (Beziehungen Zueinander so wie zu Sudamerika and Mexico)*: 416–461.

Lenfestey, T. 1875. *Le Chant des fontaines*. Guernsey: Thomas-Mauger Bichard.

Les Ravigotteurs. 1999. *Jimmain va à la bànque*. Guernsey: Les Ravigotteurs.

Lewis, M. P. 1993. *Real men don't speak Quiché: Quiché ethnicity, Ki-che ethnic movement, K'iche' nationalism*. Guatemala: SIL International.

Lewis, M. P. and G. F. Simons. 2010. Assessing endangerment: Expanding Fisherman's GIDS. *Revue roumaine de linguistique* 55(2): 103–120. Available online at www.lingv.ro/RRL%202%202010%20art01Lewis.pdf (last accessed 3 November 2015).

Lewis, M. P., G. F. Simons, and C. D. Fennig (eds.). 2015. *Ethnologue: Languages of the world*, 18th ed. Dallas, TX: SIL International. Available online at www.ethnologue.com (last accessed 3 July 2015).

Littlebear, R. 2007. Preface. In G. Cantoni (ed.), *Stabilizing indigenous languages*, rev. ed. Flagstaff: Northern Arizona University Center for Excellence in Education, pp. xiii–xv.

Lomas, K. 2008. Script obsolescence, writing and power in pre-Roman and early Roman Italy. In J. Baines, J. Bennet, and S. Houston (eds.), *The disappearance of writing systems: Perspectives on literacy and communication*. London: Equinox, pp. 109–138.

Lomas, K. 2013. Language, identity, and culture in Ancient Italy. In A. Gardner, E. Herring, and K. Lomas (eds.), *Creating ethnicities and identities in the Roman world*. London: Institute of Classical Studies, 70–91.

Longenecker, K., D. Abel, R. Boruru, T. Nandang, G. Reuben, C. Schreyer, and J. Wagner. 2012. *Monitoring village fish resources (Lukautim ples pis na risos bilong en; Koto kana i ŋe ambola ma gele golotome): A school-based fishery project*. s.l.: Pacific biological survey contribution 2012–006.

Longenecker, K., C. Schreyer, and J. Wagner. 2015. Conservation: The relationship between Kala language conservation and marine conservation in coastal Papua New Guinea. Paper presented at the Fourth Annual International Conference on Language Documentation and Conservation, University of Hawai'i at Manoa, Honolulu, Hawai'i Cambridge, USA, 1 March 2015.

López de Rosa, L. and F. Mucía Patal. 1997. *Kanatalwa'r Ch'orti: texto integrado para la primera etapa de post-alfabetización bilingüe idioma Ch'orti'*. Guatemala: CONALFA/Instituto de Lingüística de la Universidad de Rafael Landívar.

Loporcaro, M. 2009. *Profilo linguistico dei dialetti italiani*. Bari: Laterza.

Loporcaro, M. 2012. Non sappiamo come scriverlo, perciò non lo parliamo: mille e una scusa per un suicidio linguistico. *Rhesis: International journal of linguistics, philology, and literature. Linguistics and philology* 3(1): 36–58.

Lőrinczi, M. 1996. Sociolinguistica della ricerca linguistica: punti di vista divergenti sulle consonanti scempie e geminate nell'italiano di Sardegna. *Actas do XIX congreso internacional de lingüística e filoloxía románicas* 8: 311–334.

Lőrinczi, M. 2013. *Linguistica e politica. L'indagine sociolinguistica sulle 'lingue dei sardi' del 2007 e il suo contesto politico-culturale, Actes du XXVIe congrès international de linguistique et de philologie romanes*. Berlin/New York: Walter de Gruyter.

Lubeck, J. E. 1996. *Translation of the New Testament in Ch'orti'*. Electronic version. s.i.: Wycliffe Bible Translators.

Lubeck, J. and D. L. Cowie. 1989. *Método moderno para aprender el idioma Chorti'*. Guatemala: SIL International.

Luelsdorff, P. A. 1987. *Orthography and phonology*. Amsterdam: John Benjamins.

Lüpke, F. 2011. Orthography development. In P. K. Austin and J. Sallabank (eds.), *The Cambridge handbook of endangered languages*. Cambridge: Cambridge University Press, pp. 312–336.

Madeg, M. 2010. *Traité de pronunciation du breton du nord-ouest*. Brest: Emgleo Breiz.
Mahy, T. H. 1922. *Les dires et pensées du 'Courtil Poussin'*. Guernsey: s.n.
Maingard, L. F. 1937. The ǂKhomani dialect of Bushman. In J. R. Jones and C. Doke (eds.), *Bushmen of the southern Kalahari*. Johannesburg: Witswatersrand University Press, pp. 237–275.
Malone, S. 2004. *Manual for developing literacy and adult education programmes in minority language communities*. Bangkok: UNESCO.
Malone, S. and P. Paraide. 2011. Mother tongue-based bilingual education in Papua New Guinea. *International review of education* 57: 705–720.
Manning, P. 1988. *Francophone sub-Saharan Africa*. Cambridge: Cambridge University Press.
Manzini, M. R. and L. M. Savoia. 2005. *I dialetti italiani e romanci. Morfosintassi generativa*. Alexandria: Edizioni Dell'Orso.
Marcellesi, J.-B. 1983. Identité linguistique, exclamatives et subordonnées: un modèle syntaxique spécifique en Corse. *Études corses* 20–21: 399–424. (Reprinted in Marcellesi, J.-B., T. Bulot, and P. Blanchet. 2003. *Sociolinguistique: épistémologie, langues régionales, polynomie*. Paris: L'Harmattan, pp. 209–234).
Marongiu, M. A. 2007. Language maintenance and shift in Sardinia: A case study of Sardinian and Italian in Cagliari. Unpublished PhD dissertation, University of Illinois at Urbana-Champaign.
Marquis, Y. and J. Sallabank. 2013. Speakers and language revitalization: A case study of Guernesiais (Guernsey). In M. C. Jones and S. Ogilvie (eds.), *Keeping languages alive*. Cambridge: Cambridge University Press, pp. 169–180.
Marquis, Y. and J. Sallabank. 2014. Ideologies, beliefs and revitalization of Guernesiais (Guernsey). In P. K. Austin and J. Sallabank (eds.), *Endangered languages: Beliefs and ideologies in documentation and revitalization*. Oxford: Oxford University Press, pp. 151–166.
Martin, J.-B. and J.-L. Goussé. 2005. *Le francoprovençal de poche*. Chennevières-sur-Marne: Assimil.
Mastino, A., A. M. Morace, G. Lupinu, D. Manca, C. Schirru, and F. Toso. 2011. *Osservazioni sul piano triennale degli interventi di promozione e valorizzazione della cultura e della lingua sarda 2011–2013*. Available online at www.sardegnaeliberta.it/docs/uniss.doc (last accessed 4 July 2015).
Matras, Y. 1999. Writing Romani: The pragmatics of codification in a stateless language. *Applied linguistics* 20(4): 481–502.
Matras, Y. 2002. *Romani: A linguistic introduction*. Cambridge: Cambridge University Press.
Matras, Y. 2005. The classification of Romani dialects: A geographic-historical perspective. In B. Schrammel, D. W. Halwachs, and G. Ambrosch (eds.), *General and applied Romani linguistics*. Munich: Lincom Europa, pp. 7–26.
Matras, Y. 2013. Mapping the Romani dialects of Romania. *Romani studies* 23: 199–243.
Matras, Y. 2015. Language and the rise of a transnational Romani identity. *Language in society* 44: 3.
Maunoir, J. 1659. *Le Sacré-Collège de Jésus*. Quimper: J. Hardouin.
May, S. 2001. *Language and minority rights: Ethnicity, nationalism and the politics of language*. London: Longman.

McDonald, K. 2012. The testament of Vibius Adiranus. *Journal of Roman studies* 102: 40–55.
McDonald, K. 2015. *Oscan in southern Italy and Sicily: Evaluating language contact in a fragmentary corpus*. Cambridge: Cambridge University Press.
McDonald, K. and N. Zair. 2012. Oscan φουρουστ and the Roccagloriosa bronze law tablet. *Incontri linguistici* 35: 31–45.
McNichols, J. L. 1977. *Alfabeto chortí*. Guatemala: SIL International.
Melchers, G. 1987. Spelling and dialect. In P. A. Luelsdorff (ed.), *Orthography and phonology*. Amsterdam: John Benjamins, pp. 187–214.
Membreño, A. 1897. *Honduñerismos: Vocabulario de los provincialismos de Honduras*. Tegucigalpa: Tipografía Nacional.
Métivier, G. 1831. *Rimes guernesiaises par un Câtelain*. Guernsey: Barbet.
Métivier, G. 1843. *Rimes guernesiaises*. London: s.n.
Métivier, G. 1866. *Fantaisies guernesiaises: dans le langage du pays, la langue de la civilisation, et celle du commerce*. Guernsey: Thomas-Mauger Bichard.
Metz, B. 2001. Investigación y colaboración en el movimiento Maya-Ch'orti'. In P. Pitarch and J. López (eds.), *Los derechos humanos en el área Maya: Política, representaciones y moralidad*. Madrid: Sociedad Española de Estudios Mayas, pp. 311–340.
Metz, B., T. Ramírez, F. García, and M. García. 1992. Español–Chorti–English – Dictionario [sic]. Unpublished manuscript, 28 September 1992.
Miller, A. 2011. The representation of clicks. In M. van Oostendorp, C. Ewen, E. Hume, and K. Rice (eds.), *The Blackwell companion to phonology*. Volume 1. Malden, MA: Wiley-Blackwell, pp. 416–439.
Milroy, J. 2001. Language ideologies and the consequences of standardization. *Journal of sociolinguistics* 5(4): 530–555.
Mohanan, K. P. 1982. Lexical phonology. Unpublished PhD dissertation, Massachusetts Institute of Technology.
Mohanan, K. P. 1986. *The theory of lexical phonology*. Dordrecht, the Netherlands: Reidel.
Mooney, D. 2015. Confrontation and language policy: Non-militant perspectives on conflicting revitalization strategies in Béarn, France. In M. C. Jones (ed.), *Policy and planning for endangered languages*. Cambridge: Cambridge University Press, pp. 153–170.
Morgan, M. and D. Gurung. 2002. Languages worth writing: Endangered languages of Nepal. In R. McKenna Brown (ed.), *Endangered languages and their literatures*. Bath: FEL, pp. 99–103.
Morvannou, F. 1975. *Le Breton sans peine*. Chennevières-sur-Marne: Assimil.
Moseley, C. (ed.). 2010. *UNESCO atlas of the world's languages in danger*, 3rd ed. Paris: UNESCO. Also available online at www.unesco.org/culture/en/endangeredlanguages/atlas (last accessed 4 July 2015).
Mouritsen, H. 1998. *Italian unification: A study in ancient and modern historiography*. London: Institute of Classical Studies, School of Advanced Study, University of London.
Mullen, A. 2013. *Southern Gaul and the Mediterranean: Multilingualism and multiple identities in the Iron Age and Roman periods*. Cambridge: Cambridge University Press.

Munro, P. 2014. Breaking rules for orthography development. In M. Cahill and K. Rice (eds.), *Developing orthographies for unwritten languages*. Dallas, TX: SIL International, pp. 169–189.

Namaseb, L. 2003. Die alfabet van die ǂKhomani taal of N|u. Unpublished manuscript, University of Namibia.

Namaseb, L. (n.d.). ǂKhomani still alive in South Africa. Unpublished manuscript.

Namaseb, L., B. Sands, A. Miller, and J. Brugman. 2005. *Let's learn to spell N|u!/Laat ons N|u leer spel! Iiisi ǁxaǁxa N|u i kaqleke*. Upington: Communal Property Association (CPA) of the ǂKhomani community.

Nishimura, K. 2005. Superlative suffixes *-ismo- and *-ismmo- in Sabellian languages. *Glotta* 81: 160–183.

Nolasco, R. M. 2008. The prospects of multilingual education and literacy in the Philippines. Paper presented at the Second International Conference on Language Development, Language Revitalization and Multilingual Education, Bangkok, Thailand, 1–3 July 2008.

Oakley, H. 1966. Chorti. In M. K. Mayers (ed.), *Languages of Guatemala*. The Hague: Mouton, pp. 235–250.

O'Connor, M. 1996. Epigraphic Semitic scripts. In P. T. Daniels and W. Bright (eds.), *The world's writing systems*. New York: Oxford University Press, pp. 88–107.

Orpen, J. M. 1874. A glimpse into the mythology of the Maluti Bushmen. *Cape monthly magazine* 9: 1–13.

Ostler, N. and B. Rudes. 2000. *Endangered languages and literacy: Papers from the Fourth Foundation for Endangered Languages Conference*. Bath: FEL.

Ottenheimer, H. J. 2001. Spelling Shinzwani: Dictionary construction and orthographic choice in the Comoro Islands. *Written language and literacy* 4(1): 15–29.

Pabst, H. 1895. Die Kalahariwüste und ihre Bewohner. *Mitteilungen der geographischen Gesellschaft Jena* 14: 48–54.

Page, C. J. 2013. A new orthography in an unfamiliar script: A case study in participatory engagement strategies. *Journal of multilingual and multicultural development* 34(5): 459–474.

Paksoy, H. B. 1989. *Alpamysh: Central Asian identity under Russian rule*. Hartford, CT: Association for the Advancement of Central Asian Research Monograph Series.

Palfreyman, D. and M. Al Khalil. 2007. 'A funky language for teenzz to use': Representing Gulf Arabic in instant messaging. In B. Danet and S. Herring (eds.), *The multilingual internet*. Oxford: Oxford University Press, pp. 43–63.

Paris, H. 2012. Sociolinguistic effects of church languages in Morobe Province, Papua New Guinea. *International journal for the sociology of language* 214: 39–66.

Peccorini, A. 1909. Ligeros apuntes sobre el dialecto Camotán. *Revista Centro América intelectual*, San Salvador: pp. 79–83.

Penn, N. 2005. *The forgotten frontier: Colonist and Khoisan on the Cape's northern frontier in the 18th century*. Cape Town: Double Storey; Athens, OH: Ohio University Press and Swallow Press.

Pérez Martínez, V. 1994. *Gramática del idioma ch'orti'*. Guatemala: Proyecto Lingüístico Francisco Marroquín.

Pérez Martínez, V. 1996. *Leyenda maya ch'orti'*. Antigua, Guatemala: Proyecto Lingüístico Francisco Marroquín.
Pérez Martínez, V., F. M. Federico García, and J. López. 1996. *Diccionario del idioma ch'orti'*. Antigua, Guatemala: Proyecto Lingüístico Francisco Marroquín.
Philippines, Republic of, Congress. 2013. 15th Congress. Republic Act. An Act enhancing the Philippine Basic Education system by strengthening its curriculum and increasing the number of years for basic education, appropriating funds thereof and for other purposes. Available online at www.gov.ph/2013/05/15/republic-act-no-10533/ (last accessed 31 March 2015).
Phillipson, R. 1992. *Linguistic imperialism*. Oxford: Oxford University Press.
Piano triennale degli interventi di promozione e valorizzazione della cultura e della lingua sarda 2011–2013. Available online at www.regione.sardegna.it/documenti/1_106_20110601093442.pdf (last accessed 20 February 2015).
Pike, K. 1947. *Phonemics: A technique for reducing languages to writing*. Ann Arbor: University of Michigan.
Pinnock, H. 2009a. *Language and education: The missing link*. London: CfBT and Save the Children.
Pinnock, H. 2009b. *Steps towards learning: A guide to overcoming language barriers in children's education*. London: Save the Children.
Pinnock, H., P. Mackenzie, E. Pearce, and C. Young. 2011. *Closer to home: How to help schools in low- and middle-income countries respond to children's language needs*. London: CfBT and Save the Children.
Pitts, J. L. 1883. *The patois poems of the Channel Islands*. Guernsey: Guille-Alles Library.
Pivot, B. 2013. Revitalisation d'une langue post-vernaculaire en pays rama (Nicaragua). *Langage et société* 145: 55–79.
Pivot, B. 2014. Revitalisation de langues postvernaculaires : le francoprovençal en Rhône-Alpes et le rama au Nicaragua. Unpublished PhD dissertation, Université Lyon 2.
Poccetti, P. 2002–2003. Una nuova carica pubblica osca (tríbuf plífríks) tra problemi linguistici ed istituzionali. *Studi e saggi linguistici* 40–41: 297–315.
Poccetti, P. 2009. Lineamenti di tradizioni 'non romane' di testi normativi. In A. Ancillotti and A. Calderini (eds.), *L'umbro e le altre lingue dell'Italia mediana antica. Atti del I convegno internazionale sugli antichi umbri, Gubbio, 20–22 settembre 2001*. Perugia: Jama, pp. 165–248.
Pöch, R. 1910. Reisen im Innern Südafrikas zum Studium der Buschmänner in den Jahren 1907 bis 1909. *Zeitschrift für ethnologie* 42(3): 357–362.
Porcu, A. 2014. *Una breve introduzione alla questione della lingua sarda*. Available online at www.rivistaetnie.com/questione-lingua-sarda/ (last accessed 4 July 2015).
Powers, W. K. 2009. Saving Lakota: Commentary on language revitalization. *American Indian culture and research journal* 33–34: 139–149.
Powlison, P. S. 1968. Bases for formulating an efficient orthography. *The Bible translator* 19(2): 74–91.
Prins, F. E. 1999. Dissecting diviners: On positivism, trance-formations, and the unreliable informant. *Southern African humanities* 20(1): 43–62.

Provincia di Cagliari, Provincia de Casteddu. 2009. *Arrègulas po ortografia, fonetica, morfologia e fueddariu de sa norma campidanesa de sa lingua sarda.* Available online at www.provincia.cagliari.it/ProvinciaCa/resources/cms/documents/arregulas .pdf (last accessed 20 February 2015).

Prussin, L. 1995. *African nomadic architecture: Space, place and gender.* Washington, DC: Smithsonian Institution.

Rajah-Carrim, A. 2009. Use and standardization of Mauritian Creole in electronically mediated communication. *Journal of computer mediated communication* 14: 484–508.

Ramírez, D., S. Yuen, D. Ramey, D. Pasta, and D. Billings. 1991. *Final report: Longitudinal study of structured English immersion strategy, early-exit and late-exit transitional bilingual education programmes for language-minority children.* San Mateo, CA: Aguirre International.

Rappa, A. L. and L. Wee. 2006. *Language policy and modernity in south-east Asia: Malaysia, the Philippines, Singapore, and Thailand.* New York: Springer.

Raymond, M. 2007. Literacy work in Papua New Guinea: The accidental and the planned. In P. K. Austin (ed.), *Language documentation and description.* Volume 4. London: SOAS, pp. 174–194.

Regione Autònoma de Sardigna. 2007. *Lege istatutària de sa Regione Autònoma de Sardigna.* Available online at www.sardegnacultura.it/documenti/7_93_20071002122433.pdf (last accessed 23 June 2015).

Regione Autònoma della Sardegna. 2006. *Limba Sarda Comuna. Norme linguistiche di riferimento a carattere sperimentale per la lingua scritta dell'Amministrazione regionale.* Available online at www.regione.sardegna.it/documenti/1_72_20060418160308.pdf (last accessed 20 February 2015).

Regione Autònoma della Sardegna. 2007. *Legge statutaria della Regione Autonoma della Sardegna.* Available online at www.regione.sardegna.it/documenti/1_46_20070328190430.pdf (last accessed 23 June 2015).

Rey, C. 2010. Planning language practices and representations of identity within the Gallo community in Brittany: A case of language maintenance. Unpublished PhD dissertation, University of Texas at Austin.

Rice, K. et al. 2012. Orthography development: The 'midwife' approach. CoLang and InField workshop presentation slides. Available online at www.rnld.org/sites/default/files/Orthography%20Development.pdf (last accessed 31 March 2015).

Rice, K. and M. Cahill. 2014. Introduction. In M. Cahill and K. Rice (eds.), *Developing orthographies for unwritten languages.* Dallas, TX: SIL International, pp. 1–6.

Riggs, S. R. 1852. *Grammar and dictionary of the Dakota language.* (Smithsonian contributions to knowledge). Washington, DC: Smithsonian Institution.

Rindler Schjerve, R. 1998. Codeswitching as an indicator for language shift? Evidence from Sardinian- Italian bilingualism. In R. Jacobson (ed.), *Code switching worldwide.* Volume 1. Berlin and New York: Mouton de Gruyter, pp. 221–247.

Rindler Schjerve, R. 2000. Inventario analitico delle attuali trasformazioni del sardo. *Revista de filología románica* 17: 229–246.

Rix, H. 2002. *Sabellische Texte. Die Texte des Oskischen, Umbrischen und Südpikenischen.* Heidelberg: Universitätsverlag C. Winter.

Roberge, P. 2002. Afrikaans: Considering origins. In R. Mesthrie (ed.), *Language in South Africa*. Cambridge: Cambridge University Press, pp. 79–103.

Ross, M. 1996. Mission and church languages in Papua New Guinea. In S. A. Wurm, P. Mühlausler, and D. T. Tryon (eds.), *Atlas of languages of intercultural communication in the Pacific, Asia and the Americas*. Berlin: Mouton de Gruyter, pp. 595–617.

Roth, D. 2008. *El alfabeto del cora de Santa Teresa, Nayarit*. México: SIL International.

Rudes, B. 2000. When you choose, must you lose? Standard orthography versus dialect diversity. In N. Ostler and B. Rudes (eds.), *Endangered languages and literacy: Papers from the Fourth Foundation for Endangered Languages Conference*. Bath: FEL, pp. 63–70.

Sackett, K. 2013. Developing a linguistically-informed community-based orthography with the Tsakhur in Azerbaijan. Unpublished MA dissertation, Graduate Institute of Applied Linguistics.

Sallabank, J. 2007. Attitude shift: Identity and language maintenance in Guernsey Norman French. Unpublished PhD dissertation, Lancaster University.

Sallabank, J. 2010. Standardization, prescription and polynomie: Can Guernsey follow the Corsican model? *Current issues in language planning* 11(4): 311–330.

Sallabank, J. 2013. *Attitudes to endangered languages: Identities and policies*. Cambridge: Cambridge University Press.

Sands, B., A. Miller, and J. Brugman. 2007. The lexicon in language attrition: The case of N|uu. In D. Payne and J. Peña (eds.), *Selected Proceedings of the 37th Annual Conference on African Linguistics*. Somerville, MA: Cascadilla Proceedings Project, pp. 55–65.

Sands, B., A. Miller, J. Brugman, L. Namaseb, C. Collins, and M. Exter. 2006. *1400 item N|uu dictionary*. Unpublished manuscript, Northern Arizona University and Cornell University.

Santos, S., R. Parra, P. Muñiz, and M. I. Zeferino. 2014. *Wá'mwatye náayeri nyúuka. Curso de cora como segunda lengua*. Tepic: Universidad Autónoma de Nayarit.

Sapper, K. 1897. *Das nördliche Mittel-Amerika nebst einem Ausflug nach dem Hochland von Anahuac*. Braunschweig: Friedrich Vieweg und Sohn.

SASI (South African San Institute). 2012. *Ek is Spesiaal/Na ng Spesiaal. Afrikaans/N|u*. Kimberley: South African San Institute.

Savage, A. 2008. Writing Tuareg. *International journal for the sociology of language* 192: 5–13.

Savoia, L. M. 2001. La legge 482 sulle minoranze linguistiche storiche. Le lingue di minoranza e le varietà non standard in Italia. *Rivista italiana di dialettologia* 25: 7–50.

Savoia, L. M. 2002. Componenti ideologiche nel dibattito sulle leggi di tutela linguistica. *Plurilinguismo* 9: 85–114.

Schieffelin, B. B. and R. C. Doucet. 1994. The 'real' Haitian Creole: Ideology, metalinguistics, and orthographic choice. *American ethnologist* 21: 176–200.

Schieffelin, B. B, K. Woolard, and P. Kroskrity. 1998. *Language ideologies: Practice and theory*. Oxford: Oxford University Press

Schreyer, C. 2015a. Community consensus and social identity in alphabet development: The relationship between Kala and Jabêm. *Written language and literacy* 18(1): 175–199.

Schreyer, C. 2015b. Reading dictionaries in the dark: The significance of evolving language materials. Paper presented at the Fourth Annual International Conference

Bibliography

on Language Documentation and Conservation, University of Hawai'i at Manoa, Honolulu, Hawai'i Cambridge, USA, 28 February 2015.

Schulze, W. 1997. *Tsakhur*. Munich: Lincom Europa.

Schumann, O. G. 2007. *Introducción a la morfología verbal del Chortí*. Mexico: Academic Publishers.

Scribner, S. and M. Cole. 1981. *The psychology of literacy*. Cambridge, MA: Harvard University Press.

Sebba, M. 1998. Phonology meets ideology: The meaning of orthographic practices in British Creole. *Language problems and language planning* 22(1): 19–47.

Sebba, M. 2007. *Spelling and society: The culture and politics of orthography around the world*. Cambridge: Cambridge University Press.

Sebba, M. 2011. Sociolinguistic approaches to writing systems research. *Writing systems research* 1(1): 35–49.

Sebba, M. 2012a. Orthography as social action: Scripts, spelling, identity, and power. In A. Jaffe, J. Androutsopoulos, M. Sebba, and S. Johnson (eds.), *Orthography as social action: Scripts, spelling, identity, and power*. (Language and social processes 3). Berlin and New York: Walter de Gruyter, pp. 1–20.

Sebba, M. 2012b. *Spelling and society: The culture and politics of orthography around the world*. Cambridge and New York: Cambridge University Press.

Seifart, F. 2006. Orthography development. In J. Gippert, N. P. Himmelmann, and U. Mosel (eds.), *Essentials of language documentation*. (Trends in linguistics. Studies and monographs 178). Berlin, New York: Mouton de Gruyter, 275–299.

Sgall, P. 1987. Towards a theory of phonemic orthography. In P. A. Luelsdorff (ed.), *Orthography and phonology*. Amsterdam: John Benjamins, pp. 1–30.

Shah, S. and M. Brenzinger. 2016. *Ouma Geelmeid ke kx'u ǁxaǁxa Nǀuu. Ouma Geelmeid gee Nǀuu. Ouma Geelmeid teaches Nǀuu*. Cape Town: CALDi, UCT. Available online at https://open.uct.ac.za/handle/11427/17432

Shah, S., M. Brenzinger, K. Esau, C. du Plessis, and M.-A. Prins. 2014a. *Illustrated Nǀuu alphabet charts (clicks, consonants and vowels), with English and Afrikaans translations*. Cape Town: CALDi UCT.

Shah, S., M. Brenzinger, K. Esau, C. du Plessis, and M.-A. Prins. 2014b. *Illustrated Nǀuu animal poster, with English, Afrikaans and ǂKhomani Nama names*. Cape Town: CALDi, UCT.

Shandler, J. 2006. *Adventures in Yiddishland: Postvernacular language and culture*. Berkeley/Los Angeles: University of California Press.

Siegmund, S., M. Ernszt, and A. Witzlack-Makarewich. 2008. *Nǀuu text collection*. Unpublished manuscript.

SIL International. 2012. Speech Analyzer – a computer programme for acoustic analysis of speech sounds. Available online at www-01.sil.org/computing/sa/index.htm?_ga=GA1.2.583231857.1425300332 (last accessed 31 March 2015).

Silverman, C. 2012. *Romani routes: Cultural politics and Balkan music in diaspora*. Oxford: Oxford University Press.

Simons, G. F. 1977. Principles of multidialectal orthography design. In R. Loving and G. F. Simons (eds.), *Language variation and survey techniques*. (Workpapers in Papua New Guinea languages 21). Ukarumpa: SIL International, pp. 325–342.

Simons, G. F. 1994. Principles of multidialectal orthography design. *Notes on literacy* 20(2): 13–34.

Sjoberg, A. F. 1966. Sociocultural and linguistic factors in the development of writing systems for pre-literate people. In W. Bright (ed.), *Sociolinguistics*. The Hague: Mouton, pp. 260–276.

Skutnabb-Kangas, T. and K. Heugh. 2010. Introduction – Why this book? In K. Heugh and T. Skutnabb-Kangas (eds.), *Multilingual education works: From the periphery to the centre*. Delhi: Orient Blackswan, pp. 3–39.

Smalley, W. 1964. How shall I write this language? In W. A. Smalley (ed.), *Orthography studies: Articles on new writing systems*. (Helps for translators 6). London: United Bible Societies, pp. 31–52.

Smith, P. 2010. The Bunong culture of silence: Exploring Bunong perspectives on participation at the interface between Bunong culture and development organizations. Unpublished MSc dissertation, University of Lund.

Smith, P. and M. Wisbey. 2013. Signposts to identity-based community development. LEAD Asia. Available online at www.leadimpact.org/identity/ (last accessed 31 March 2015).

Snider, K. 2014. Orthography and phonological depth. In M. Cahill and K. Rice (eds.), *Developing orthographies for unwritten languages*. (Publications in language use and education 6). Dallas TX: SIL International, pp. 27–48.

Stebbins, T. 2001. Emergent spelling patterns in Sm'algyax (Tsimshian, British Columbia). *Written language and literacy* 4(2): 163–193.

Stich, D., X. Gouvert, and A. Favre. 2003. *Dictionnaire des mots de base du francoprovençal : orthographe ORB supradialectale standardisée*. Paris: Bibliothèque des langues de France.

Stoll, D. 1982. *Fishers of men or founders of empire? The Wycliffe Bible translators in Latin America*. London: Zed Press.

Street, B. V. 1984. *Literacy in theory and practice*. Cambridge: Cambridge University Press.

Suárez, R. A. 1892. Vocabularios pocoman y chorti de Honduras. Box 42, Folder 7, in the William E. Gates Collection, Lee Library, Brigham Young University, Provo, UT.

Suleiman, Y. 2003. *The Arabic language and national identity*. Georgetown: Georgetown University Press.

Suret-Canale, J. 1971. *French colonialism in tropical Africa 1900–1945*. New York: Pica Press.

Swadesh, M. 1965. Language universals and research efficiency in descriptive linguistics. *Canadian journal of linguistics* 10(2–3): 147–155.

Tacelosky, K. 2000. Literacy ability and practice in Peru: An indigenous account. In N. Ostler and B. Rudes (eds.), *Endangered languages and literacy: Proceedings of the Fourth Foundation for Endangered Languages Conference*. Bath: FEL.

Tagliavini, C. 1982. *Le origini delle lingue neolatine*. Padua: Patron editore.

Terrill, A. and M. Dunn. 2003. Orthographic design in the Solomon Islands: The social, historical, and linguistic situation of Touo (Baniata). *Written language and literacy* 6(2): 177–192.

Themistocleous, C. 2010. Writing in a non-standard Greek variety: Romanized Cypriot Greek in online chat. *Writing systems research* 2: 155–168.

Thomas, W. and V. Collier. 2002. *A national study of school effectiveness for language minority students' long-term academic achievement*. Santa Cruz: Center for Research on Education, Diversity, and Excellence, University of California-Santa Cruz.

Thomson, R. L. 1969. The study of Manx Gaelic. Sir John Rhys memorial lecture. Reprinted from the Proceedings of the British Academy. London: Oxford University Press.
Tomlinson, Harry. 1994. The teaching of Guernsey French. Unpublished MEd dissertation, University of Wales.
Tomlinson, Harry. 2008. *A descriptive grammar of Guernsey French: With phonetic pronunciation guide and verb tables*. Guernsey: The Author.
Tomlinson, Hazel (ed.). 2006. *P'tites lures Guernaisiaises: A collection of short stories in Guernsey-French and English*. Guernsey: The Author.
Tomlinson, Hazel. 2009. *Histouaires Guernesiaises: Factual articles and fictional stories in Guernsey-French with English translations*. Guernsey: Author.
Traill, A. 1974. *The complete guide to the Koon: A research report on linguistic fieldwork undertaken in Botswana and south west Africa*. Johannesburg: African Studies Institute, University of the Witwatersrand.
Traill, A. 1996. !Khwa-Ka Hhouiten Hhouiten, 'The rush of the storm': The linguistic death of ǀXam. In P. Skotnes (ed.), *Miscast: Negotiating the presence of the Bushmen*. Cape Town: University of Cape Town Press, pp. 161–183.
Traill, A. 1999. *Extinct: South African Khoisan languages*. (CD and booklet). Johannesburg: Department of Linguistics, University of the Witwatersrand.
Trépos, P. 1968. *Grammaire bretonne*. Rennes: Simon (reprinted 1980, Rennes: Ouest France; new edition 1994 Brest: Brud Nevez).
Trudgill, P. 1992. Ausbau sociolinguistics and the perception of language status in contemporary Europe. *International journal of applied linguistics* 2: 167–177.
Tseliga, T. 2007. 'It's all Greeklish to me!' Linguistic and sociocultural perspectives on Roman-alphabeted Greek in asynchronous computer-mediated communication. In B. Danet and S. Herring (eds.), *The multilingual internet*. Oxford: Oxford University Press, pp. 116–141
Tufi, S. 2013. Language ideology and language maintenance: The case of Sardinia. *International journal of the sociology of language* 219: 145–160.
UNESCO. 2000. *Dakar framework for action, education for all: Meeting our collective commitments*. Paris: UNESCO.
UNESCO. 2003a. Language vitality and endangerment. Document adopted by the International Expert Meeting on UNESCO Programme Safeguarding of Endangered Languages, Paris, 10–12 March 2003. Available online at www.unesco.org/new/fileadmin/MULTIMEDIA/HQ/CLT/pdf/Language_vitality_and_endangerment_EN.pdf (last accessed 31 March 2015).
UNESCO. 2003b. *Intangible heritage*. Available online at www.unesco.org/culture/heritage/intangible/meetings/paris_march2003.shtml (last accessed 4 July 2015).
UNESCO. 2006. *Literacy for life. Education for all global monitoring report*. Paris: UNESCO.
UNESCO. 2007a. *Improving the quality of mother tongue-based literacy and learning Case studies from Asia, Africa and South America*. Bangkok: UNESCO. Available online at http://unesdoc.unesco.org/images/0017/001777/177738e.pdf (last accessed 31 March 2015).
UNESCO. 2007b. *Advocacy kit for promoting multilingual education: Including the excluded*. Bangkok: UNESCO. Available online at http://unesdoc.unesco.org/images/0015/001521/152198e.pdf and www.unescobkk.org/education/multilingual-education/resources/mle-advocacy-kit/ (last accessed 31 March 2015).

UNESCO. 2007c. *Promoting mother tongue-based multilingual education.* (DVD). Bangkok: UNESCO. Available online at www.unescobkk.org/education/multilingual-education/resources/mle-advocacy-kit/ and www.youtube.com/playlist?list=PLBEF42A5FE8BE02B1 (last accessed 31 March 2015).
United Nations. 2016. *Sustainable development knowledge platform.* United Nations Department of Economic and Social Affairs. Available online at https://sustainabledevelopment.un.org/ (last accessed on 26 September 2016).
Unseth, P. 2008. The sociolinguistics of script choice. *International journal for the sociology of language* 192: 1–4.
Valdovinos, M. 2015. From policies to practice: The complexity of mediating interactions in Náayeri public education (Nayarit, México). In M. C. Jones (ed.), *Policy and planning for endangered languages.* Cambridge: Cambridge University Press, pp. 80–92.
Valdovinos, M. and Y. Kim. 2014. The interaction of laryngealized vowels, stress, and falling pitch in Mariteco Cora. In R. Bennett, R. Dockum, E. Gasser, D. Goldberg, R. Kasak, and P. Patterson (eds.), *Proceedings of the Workshop on the Sound Systems of Mexico and Central America.* Available online at http://ling.yale.edu/ssmca-proceedings (last accessed 4 July 2015).
Vamarasi, M. 2008. The critical role of language in the construction of Rotuman diasporic identity. *International journal for the sociology of language* 192: 69–73.
Van Dyken, J. and C. Kutsch Lojenga. 1993. Word boundaries: Key factors in orthography development/Les frontières du mot: facteurs-clés dans le développement d'une orthographe. In R. Hartell (ed.), *Alphabets of Africa/ Alphabets de langues africaines.* Dakar, Senegal: UNESCO and SIL.
Vázquez, V. 2002. El conejo. Un cuento de la región cora (Nayarit). Versión bilingüe. *Revista de literaturas populares* 2(1): 5–33.
Venezky, R. L. 1970. Principles for the design of practical writing systems. *Anthropological linguistics* 12(7): 256–270.
Vetter, E. 1953. *Handbuch der italischen Dialekte.* Heidelberg: C. Winter Universtitätsverlag.
Vikør, L. S. 1993. Principles of corpus planning as applied to the spelling reforms of Indonesia and Malaysia. In E. H. Jahr (ed.), *Language conflict and language planning.* Berlin: Mouton de Gruyter, pp. 279–298.
Virdis, M. 1978. *Fonetica del dialetto sardo campidanese.* Cagliari: Edizioni della Torre.
Visser, H. 2001. *Naro dictionary: Naro–English, English–Naro.* D'Kar, Botswana: Naro Language Project.
Wagner, J. 2002. Commons in transition: An analysis of social and ecological change in a coastal rainforest environment in Papua New Guinea. Unpublished PhD dissertation, McGill University, Montreal.
Wagner, M. L. 1941. *Historische Lautlehre des Sardischen.* Tübingen: Niemeyer.
Wagner, M. L. 1997 [1950]. *La lingua sarda, storia spirito e forma.* Nuoro: Ilisso.
Wallace, C. 1992. *Reading.* Oxford: Oxford University Press.
Wallace, R. E. 2004. Sabellian languages. In R. D. Woodard (ed.), *The Cambridge encyclopedia of the world's ancient languages.* Cambridge: Cambridge University Press, pp. 812–839.
Wallace-Hadrill, A. 2008. *Rome's cultural revolution.* Cambridge: Cambridge University Press.

Walter, S. and K. Chuo. 2012. The Kom experimental mother tongue education pilot project report for 2012. Unpublished research report. SIL Cameroon.
Walter, S. and D. Dekker. 2008. The Lubuagan mother tongue education experiment (FLC): A Report of comparative results. Available online at www.sil.org/asia/philippines/lit/2008%2D02-27_Report_to_Congress-Lubuagan_FLC_Paper.pdf (last accessed 31 March 2015).
Walter, S., D. Dekker, N. Duguiang, and R. Dumatog Camacam. 2008. Improving student competence in Filipino and English: The crucial role of the first language in education. Unpublished manuscript.
Warren, K. B. 1998. *Indigenous movements and their critics: Pan-Maya activism in Guatemala.* Princeton: Princeton University Press.
Watson, S. 1989. Scottish and Irish Gaelic: The giant's bed-fellows. In N. C. Dorian (ed.), *Investigating obsolescence: Studies in language contraction and death.* Cambridge: Cambridge University Press, pp. 41–59.
Wertheim, S. 2012. Reclamation, revalorization, and re-Tartarization via changing Tatar orthographies. In A. Jaffe, J. Androutsopoulos, M. Sebba, and S. Johnson (eds.), *Orthography as social action: Scripts, spelling, identity, and power.* Berlin: Walter de Gruyter, pp. 65–102.
Westphal, E. O. J. 1953–1971. ŋǀfiuki/Nǀhuki (BC 1143 C12). Unpublished manuscripts. Cape Town: Westphal Holdings, UCT Special Collections, UCT Archives and Libraries, University of Cape Town.
Westphal, E. O. J. 1971. The click languages of southern and eastern Africa. In J. Berry and J. H. Greenberg (eds.), *Linguistics in sub-Saharan Africa.* (Current trends in linguistics 7). The Hague and Paris: Mouton, pp. 367–420.
White Hat Sr., A. 1999. *Reading and writing the Lakota language.* Salt Lake City: University of Utah Press.
Wimmer, A. and N. Glick Schiller. 2002. Methodological nationalism and beyond: Nation-state building, migration and the social sciences. *Global networks* 2: 301–334.
Wisdom, C. 1940. *The Chorti Indians of Guatemala.* Guatemala: Editorial José de Pineda Ibarra.
Wisdom, C. 1950. *Material on the Chorti language.* (Microfilm collection of manuscripts on Meso-American cultural anthropology 28). Chicago: University of Chicago.
Wise, M. R. 2014. A Yanesha' alphabet for the electronic age. In M. Cahill and K. Rice (eds.), *Developing orthographies for unwritten languages.* Dallas, TX: SIL International, pp. 191–209.
Wmffre, I. 2007. *Breton orthographies and dialects: The twentieth-century orthography war in Brittany.* 2 volumes. Bern: Peter Lang.
Woolard, K. A. 1998. Introduction: Language ideology as a field of inquiry. In B. B. Schieffelin, K. A. Woolard, and P. V. Kroskrity (eds.), *Language ideologies: Practice and theory.* New York and Oxford: Oxford University Press, pp. 3–47.
Woolard, K. A. and B. B. Schieffelin. 1994. Language ideology. *Annual review of anthropology* 23: 55–82.
Wright, S. (ed.). 2004a. Multilingualism on the internet. *International journal of multicultural societies* 6(1). Available online at www.unesco.org/shs/ijms/vol6/issue1 (last accessed 27 March 2015).

Wright, S. 2004b. *Language policy and language planning: From nationalism to globalization*. Houndmills: Palgrave Macmillan.
Zair, N. 2013. Individualism in 'Osco-Greek' orthography. In E.-M. Wagner, B. Outhwaite, and B. Beinhoff (eds.), *Scribes as agents of language change*. Berlin: De Gruyter, pp. 217–26.
Zair, N. 2016. *Oscan in the Greek alphabet*. Cambridge: Cambridge University Press.
Zaretsky, E. and Schwartz, M. 2014. Cross-linguistic transfer in reading in multilingual contexts – recent research trends. *Written language and literacy*, 17(1): vii–ix.
Ziervogel, D. 1955. Notes on the language of the Eastern Transvaal Bushmen. In E. F. Potgieter (ed.), *The disappearing Bushmen of Lake Chrissie*. Pretoria: Van Schaik, 35–63.

Index

Abstand, 26, 28
adult education, 5
Afrikaans, 26, 33, 110, 111, 115, 116, 118, 119, 123, 124
Algeria, 51–52
Ausbau, 26, 32, 33, 34, 242, 250, 251; see also distanciation
Australia, 44, 45, 47, 48, 60, 128, 255
Arabic, 13, 51, 52
Arabic script, 12, 51, 89
Azerbaijan, 33, 88–108
Azerbaijani, 33, 89, 92, 93, 94, 95, 97, 98, 99, 100, 101, 102, 103, 105, 106, 108nn.3, 12, 13, 15, 16, 17

Bible, 41–43, 51, 149, 245
bidialectalism, 7, 10
'bottom-up' policies, 5, 35, 69, 254, 255, 274
Breton, 34, 190–232, 280
Brittany, 225, 227, 229, 242, 281

Chinese, 13, 249
Ch'orti', 33, 142–154
click languages, 33, 109–125
clitics, 20, 21, 185, 189n.17
cognitive factors, 5, 23, 28, 29, 68, 168, 169
colonialism, effects and results of, 22, 25, 32, 39, 43, 48, 49, 50, 51, 52, 70, 71, 144, 150, 153, 154
conjunctive writing, 20, 21, 123
common core approach, 7, 9
computer keyboards, 31, 44, 94, 95, 97, 98, 99, 100, 102, 107, 172, 235, 250, 270, 283
computer-mediated environments, 35
corpus planning, 2, 6, 24, 26, 57
correctness, 10, 142, 150, 153, 154, 235, 237, 246, 247
Croatian, 12, 261, 268, 270, 272, 273
Cyrillic script, 12, 13, 33, 89, 94–98, 102, 105, 106, 269, 270

Cyrillic alphabet, 12, 13, 33, 89, 94, 95, 96, 97, 98, 102, 105, 106, 269, 270
Czech, 26, 260, 261, 268, 270, 272, 273

Danish, 26
de-dialectalization, 10
Devangari script, 12
diacritics, 13, 14, 22, 25, 28, 29, 32, 40, 95, 97, 102, 103, 116, 141n.1, 158, 160, 165, 166, 169, 170, 172, 244, 250, 268, 283
  acute accent, 22, 158, 162, 165, 166, 170, 236
  circumflex accent, 22, 117, 125n.8, 166, 170
  grave accent, 22, 166, 170, 185
dialect, 6–11, 13, 15, 24, 39, 47, 51, 58, 60, 72–74, 77–78, 81, 86, 90, 92, 104, 111, 126, 127, 130–135, 137, 139–140, 155–156, 176–188, 190–194, 229, 237, 242, 250, 245–258, 260, 261–268, 272–273, 282, 291
dialectal approach, 7–8, 130, 132, 134, 139
diatopic variation, 7
digraphs, 28, 29, 97, 103, 172, 200, 244, 292, 300
digraphia, 12, 30
disjunctive writing, 20, 21, 123
distanciation, 23, 25–6, 31, 32, 33, 34, 35, 250
domains of use, 3, 4, 6, 7, 9, 26, 92, 240
Dutch, 25, 26, 273

expanded graded intergenerational disruption scale (EGIDS), 38, 44, 61–62, 89, 127, 155, 256, 291
endographia, 3
English, 11, 18, 20, 25, 27, 28, 34, 39, 41, 42, 45, 46, 49, 50, 61, 93, 94, 97, 98, 116, 127, 137, 138, 139, 153, 169, 171, 172, 235–238, 242, 244, 245, 247–251
Ethnologue, 36, 55, 61, 72, 87, 127, 141, 143, 256
etymology, 17, 240
exographia, 3

331

332   Index

Fiji, 50
France, 33, 235, 276–289, 292
Francoprovençal, 276–289
French, 22, 23, 25, 26, 34, 42, 49, 50, 51, 52, 182, 190, 193, 197, 221, 223, 224, 225, 228, 229, 232, 234n.7, 235, 236, 237–239, 242, 243, 244, 245, 246, 247, 248, 249, 250, 251, 252nn.3, 11, 13, 253nn.14, 16, 261, 268, 273, 281, 282, 283, 285, 286
functional load, 15–17, 21, 22, 34, 131, 165, 183, 184

Galician, 26
graded intergenerational disruption scale (GIDS), 11, 54, 55
graphic system, 12–14, 17
  alphabetic, 12, 13–14, 119
  consonantal, 13
  semi-syllabic, 12, 13
  logographic, 12–14
  phonographic, 13–18
  morphographic, 13–18
graphization, 1, 2
Guatemala, 33, 142–154, 283
Guernsey Norman French, 34, 235–252

Haitian Creole, 25, 26, 254
homograms, 17, 20
homographs, 16, 240
homonyms, 14, 240

ideology, 2, 10, 49, 142, 150, 151, 153, 154, 238, 239, 241, 274, 280, 288
identity, 1, 6, 7, 8, 17, 23, 25, 30, 32, 52, 55–57, 59, 86, 88, 91, 93, 131, 134, 145, 150, 153, 155, 156, 172, 174, 182, 185, 242, 246, 248, 256, 274, 279, 288, 289, 296, 301, 302
India, 45, 46
interdialectal communication, 35, 190
intergenerational transmission, 11, 36, 44, 55, 61, 127, 128, 129, 156, 176, 190
international phonetic alphabet, 13, 112, 113, 114, 117, 119, 121, 144, 146, 149, 283, 284
invariance, 11
Irish, 26, 27, 241
isomorphic considerations, 7, 15, 17, 28, 29, 221
Italian, 176–189, 250, 261, 268, 272, 273
Italy, 33, 52, 176–189, 268, 272, 279, 285, 286, 291–304

Japanese, 13

Kala, 33, 126–141
Kenya, 45, 46

language revitalisation, 1, 2,3, 4, 5, 6, 7, 8, 9, 10, 11, 14, 17, 19, 29, 30, 34, 35, 55, 56, 57, 62, 88, 126, 134, 142, 143, 144–6, 147, 148, 149, 150, 152, 153, 154, 155, 168, 171, 174, 237, 246, 249, 251, 276–90, 292, 296, 298, 302, 303, see also reversing
language shift, 1, 2, 3, 6, 8, 10, 11, 12, 14, 17, 25, 28, 34, 35, 55, 127–128, 138, 139, 236, 238, 277, 278, 288, 296, 301
Latin script, 12, 304
learnability, 18, 28, 29, 32, 33, 142, 168, 173, 184
legacy orthography, 1, 30
Lexical Orthographical Hypothesis, 19–20
literacy, 2–6, 8, 17, 23, 26–28, 30, 32, 33, 34, 35, 36–53, 55, 56–9, 65, 67, 69, 70–4, 74–9, 84, 86, 91, 92, 93, 97, 99, 101, 104, 107, 128, 129, 130, 138, 141n.2, 144, 146, 148, 151, 169, 174, 184, 187, 188, 191, 192, 193, 239–42, 258, 273, 274, 282, 283, 284, 298, 301
literacy programmes, 1, 2–6, 12, 14, 24, 31, 49, 56
  local literacy, 2, 3, 6
  autonomous literacy, 4
  Vai literacy, 4
  new literacy studies, 5
  functional literacy, 5, 191–193

Mali, 51
Manx, 25, 27, 28
maximums, Smalley, 15, 23, 24, 27, 28, 31, 58, 90, 164, 168
Mexico, 33, 47, 52, 53, 69–87
mother-tongue-based, multilingual education (MTB-MLE), 32, 60, 61
morpheme shape, 17
morphophonemic spelling, 17, 18, 19, 20, 30
multilectal approach, 7–10, 133, 134, 179, 229
mutual comprehension, 8, 193

Náayeri, 33, 69–87
nazalisation, 40, 81, 117, 119, 122, 136–140, 159, 169, 245
native speakers
  participation in orthography development, 1, 5, 19, 23, 24, 25, 31, 32, 34, 39, 80, 151, 155, 156, 165, 172, 174, 175nn.7, 10, 225, 226
  as orthography users, 8, 22, 40, 109, 165, 169, 171, 172, 173, 174, 175n.5, 183, 197, 224, 225, 228, 239, 235, 238
  and language use, 10, 19, 20, 168
Nepal, 48

Index 333

new speakers, 30, 34, 232, 236, 241, 246, 249, 251–2; see also neo-speakers
Nigeria, 45, 46, 254
Norwegian, 11
N|uu, 33, 109–125

Occitan, 22, 280, 281, 284, 290n.10
optionality, 11
orthographic depth, 18, 131
Oscan, 35, 292–303
over-representation, 16, 164
ownership, 5, 32, 33, 44, 48, 58, 127, 140

participatory approach, 23, 54, 59, 60–68
Pakistan, 45, 46
Papua New Guinea, 33, 49, 52, 53, 60, 126–141
pedagogy, 28, 30, 57, 59, 88, 116, 124, 131, 151, 155, 186, 192, 284
   materials, 57, 192, 284
Peru, 50, 53
Philippines, 32, 53, 58, 60–5, 66
phonemic principle, 14–18, 21, 33, 34
Polish, 19, 257, 260, 261, 266, 268, 269, 270, 272, 273
polynomia, 8, 191, 222, 227, 229
Portuguese, 26, 48, 182
postvernacular language, 35, 241, 246, 276–289
prestige, 1, 3, 7, 9, 10, 11, 25, 41, 51, 56, 133, 136, 186, 191, 235, 236, 237, 242, 286, 289
primer, 2, 42, 43, 47, 89, 104, 114–115
printing, 31, 43, 44, 156
punctuation, 14, 22, 23, 297

Rama, 276–289
reversing language shift (RLS), 2, 6, 17, 30, 35, 277
Roman alphabet, 12, 32, 33, 35, 36, 40, 51, 77, 88, 89, 92, 94, 95, 96, 97, 99, 100, 101, 102, 103, 104, 105, 106, 112–114, 117, 125n.5, 139, 169, 255, 263, 292, 293, 294, 295, 296, 298, 299, 300, 301, 302, 303
Romani, 35, 254–274
Russian, 92, 93, 94, 108n.3, 261, 266
Russia, Russian Federation, 33, 89, 92, 108n.3, 260, 263, 264, 267

Serbian, 12, 261, 268, 270, 272, 273
Sardinia, 176–189
Sardinian, 34, 176–189
Scottish Gaelic, 26, 27, 241
schools, 2, 42, 43, 50, 60, 63, 68, 72, 74, 76, 91, 93, 129, 130, 138, 192, 236, 247, 284
second-language learner, 17, 29, 30, 165, 168, 174, 249

semi-speakers, 14, 48, 109, 176, 236, 239, 251, 278, 279, 280, 289
sight vocabulary, 30, 168
SIL International, 37, 60, 62, 63, 72, 77, 78, 132, 142–152, 153
Sioux, 34, 155–174
Slovak, 26, 261, 268, 270, 272, 273
sound-spelling correspondence, 13, 14, 17, 18, 245, 249, 251
South Africa, 33, 109–125
Spanish, 26, 27, 50, 70, 72, 73, 74, 76, 77, 78, 79, 82, 83, 85, 86, 86–7n.1, 99, 142, 143, 144, 146, 147, 150, 151, 152, 153, 177, 182, 188n.4, 236, 251, 261, 268, 270, 271, 272, 273, 282, 283, 285, 290n.7
standardization, 2, 6–8, 10, 11, 24, 35, 57, 70, 126, 127, 135, 139, 174, 178, 190, 239, 240, 251, 254, 258, 274, 282, 286
status planning, 4, 9, 24, 26, 32, 57
Sranan, 25
stigmatization, 4, 46, 134, 278, 282
suprasegmental features, 1, 22, 40, 79, 158
   stress, 22, 78, 79, 81, 149, 158, 164, 165, 185, 236, 290n.10
   tone, 14, 21–23, 40, 78, 79, 81, 85, 117–8
Swedish, 26

technology, 23, 36, 48, 91–93, 107, 240, 246, 273
text-messaging, 31, 32, 45, 46
'top-down' policies, 34, 87, 187, 239, 251, 254
transfer of literacy, 23, 26, 32–34, 58, 184
transliteration, 31, 94, 268
Tsakhur, 33, 88–108

under-differentiation, 16, 21
under-representation, 9, 34, 163, 164
UNESCO, 5, 45, 128, 141, 143
   UNESCO Atlas of the World's Languages in Danger, 32, 36, 37, 156, 176, 188n.1, 255–6, 275n.2, 276, 278, 279, 280
Unicode characters and fonts, 31, 173, 254
unilectal approach, 7, 9, 10, 34, 133, 183, 186, 187
United States, 33, 34, 155–175
univocality, 29

vowel length, 14, 22, 79, 117, 122

Welsh, 231
word boundaries, 1, 14, 19, 20–21, 184

Zimbabwe, 45, 46, 49

Lightning Source UK Ltd.
Milton Keynes UK
UKHW021831010720
365839UK00009B/106